Changing
the Narrative

A volume in
Contemporary Perspectives on Leadership Learning
Kathy L. Guthrie, *Series Editor*

Changing
the Narrative
Socially Just
Leadership Education

edited by

Kathy L. Guthrie
Florida State University

Vivechkanand S. Chunoo
Florida State University

INFORMATION AGE PUBLISHING, INC.
Charlotte, NC • www.infoagepub.com

Library of Congress Cataloging-in-Publication Data

A CIP record for this book is available from the Library of Congress
http://www.loc.gov

ISBN: 978-1-64113-335-7 (Paperback)
      978-1-64113-336-4 (Hardcover)
      978-1-64113-337-1 (ebook)

For all the voices we could represent, and even more for those we could not

CONTENTS

PART I

SOCIAL IDENTITY AND SOCIALLY JUST LEADERSHIP EDUCATION

PART II

SOCIALLY JUST LEADERSHIP EDUCATION PROCESSES AND ENVIRONMENTS

FOREWORD

"It's time to plant Hope."
—Dr. Wangari Maathai

I have worked at large predominantly White institutions for most of my higher education career. At one institution, I was the staff person who coordinated all campus student leadership programs. I inherited a leadership series for first-year students that was very popular and I was told I should not tinker with "a great product." As I reviewed this popular leadership series, I noticed two specific things. First, there really wasn't any theoretical base connected to the sessions we offered. Decisions on what was offered were solely connected to "satisfaction" surveys. Second, the only time issues on diversity and inclusion were discussed was during the one session when someone from multicultural affairs on campus dropped by to have a conversation with students.

During my first year at the institution, I was lucky to have a fantastic graduate student who worked with me to develop a solid curriculum connected to a relatively new (at the time) leadership model called the social change model of leadership development (SCM; Higher Education Research Institute, 1996). After grounding our program in SCM, our next step was to weave diversity and social justice themes throughout the curriculum. One addition was we added what we called the "10 Minute Mentor" to the beginning of each session. Faculty, staff, coaches, and community members were asked to drop by and give their personal thoughts on leadership before each session began. This allowed for us to diversify the voices students heard from. We ended each session with a short conversation on how their identities informed their understanding of the topic for that week. We wanted to do more but decided to assess the impact after the first year. At the end of the first year, we received excellent evaluations from the students. Several mentioned they felt valued; others shared that they "found their voice" in the leadership conversation. However, I was surprised when several colleagues on campus mentioned to me how they were confused by the change of the leadership series. Comments included: "Is this a diversity leadership series or a leadership series?" "Shouldn't multicultural affairs coordinate this?" "Stay in your lane, Vernon."

I get it at some level. Historically, the face of leadership education in higher education had been "White, male, heterosexual, and Christian." Leadership programs on campus were initially developed to assist students in established leadership positions, not to develop leadership skills for a changing world. Sadly, even today, there is still a struggle to see the connection between social justice, equity, and leadership. This is so odd to me. Over the last 20 years or so, research on college student leadership has been evolving in which time and time again these connections emerge as critical to leadership and leadership education.

What is exciting about this book is the common thread throughout the chapters that is something I have always believed: *You cannot talk about leadership without talking about social justice and you can't talk about social justice without talking about leadership.* This book invites you on a journey. A journey that asks you to critically assess your current leadership offerings to students. Can all students learn and grow in your programs regardless of what identity groups they are members of? What dominant cultural narratives might be present in your programs that may be silencing students from marginalized identity groups? How do identity and social justice inform the ways we view leadership? How does our lived experiences contribute to differing understandings of relationships and community?

Today's student must be prepared to be leaders, not only in a global community, but also in a community that is committed to justice for all. We want our students to be about change, vision, and relationships. As you dive into this great resource, ask yourself one question: Do my student leadership programs have them wanting to leave the world better for the next generation? My hope is that your answer to this question is yes.

—**Vernon A. Wall**

REFERENCES

Higher Education Research Institute. (1996). *A social change model of leadership development guidebook* (Version III). Los Angeles, CA: University of California, Los Angeles.

AUTHOR NOTE

Vernon A. Wall is director of business development at LeaderShape, and is one of the founding faculty members of the Social Justice Training Institute.

CHAPTER 1

OPENING UP THE CONVERSATION

An Introduction to Socially Just Leadership Education

Kathy L. Guthrie and Vivechkanand S. Chunoo

Preparing students as leaders has been a long-standing goal of American higher education; however, it is time to reclaim higher education's purpose in leadership development (Guthrie & Osteen, 2016) with focused attention on socially just leadership education. Tracing its beginnings to the opening of Harvard College in 1636, dramatic changes have affected how educational experiences are constructed, the demographics of those attending college, and the intended outcomes of higher education, including the conceptualizations of leader and leadership. What it meant to be a leader in the early 17th century is very different from what it means to engage in 21st century leadership processes. More recently, higher education has been situated in postindustrial models of leadership and recognize how leaders are molded and shaped by environments and experiences; not simply as those born into socially advantageous conditions. Appropriately leveraging this notion, campus-based programs in curricular and

Changing the Narrative, pages 1–8
Copyright © 2018 by Information Age Publishing
1

co-curricular contexts focused on leadership learning continually increase. However, one area in which higher education needs to sharpen its focus is socially just leadership education.

SOCIALLY JUST LEADERSHIP EDUCATION

Socially just leadership education is the intersection of leadership education and social justice work. Often, leadership programs and social justice initiatives operate in silos instead of being united; whereas socially just leadership education unifies the narratives of leadership education and social justice work. Socially just leadership education situates itself in the intersection of these two complex topics, using multifaceted pedagogical strategies and assessments of learning. To us, socially just leadership education begins with the acknowledgement that we cannot have relevant leadership education without social justice nor can meaningful social justice efforts exist without leadership knowledge, skills, and values.

As leadership educators and scholars, we believe relevant leadership development programs without social justice lenses do not work. As our dynamic global society requires institutions to train diverse leaders, we must lean into and disrupt the perpetuation of inequalities. One way to accomplish this is by assisting future global leaders in developing tools to use their identity, capacity, and efficacy in leadership processes. Empowering diverse students to develop voice and agency across leadership environments is critical to socially just leadership education.

Conversely, we cannot have optimally impactful social justice work without considering leadership development. When leadership is not considered central to social justice work, it becomes more focused on diversity and inclusion, not true social justice. Leadership education provides knowledge, skills, and tools to act toward positive change, especially in creating a more fair and just world. In our work across both leadership and social justice spaces, we have heard of and directly experienced situations where social justice educators felt marginalized in traditional leadership education spaces and vice versa. This book challenges us all to engage in conversation and efforts around how leadership education and social justice work together in unified spaces to change the narrative. Next, we briefly discuss both leadership education and social justice work to highlight how these intersections emerge organically.

Leadership Education

As Chunoo and Osteen (2016) discussed, leadership is an important outcome of higher education. Postsecondary institutions are charged with developing effective leaders who demonstrate strong character (Nohria & Khurana, 2010). However, important questions remain as educators consider how to best accomplish this in complex college environments. To confront these questions, we expand on Brungardt's (1996) definition of leadership education as learning activities occurring in educational environments, intended to enhance and foster leadership abilities. Leadership education occurs in multiple contexts, including curricular, co-curricular, undergraduate, graduate, discipline-specific, integrative, and interdisciplinary contexts (Guthrie & Jenkins, 2018). Whether operating in one or several of these contexts, leadership instructional techniques can be distinguished from those found in most traditional academic disciplines. In a theoretical analysis of leadership education, Billsberry (2009) suggested leadership is socially constructed and there are myriad ways of viewing it. Similarly, Burns (1978) described leadership as one of the most observed and least understood phenomena. These ideas, among others, add to the complexity of understanding and teaching leadership effectively.

Social Justice Work

Social justice, as defined by Adams et al. (2000), is both a goal and a process. This orientation mirrors descriptions of education broadly (Guthrie & Hampton, 2017). Teaching for social justice adds beautiful complexity which stimulates students and engages them to recognize inequality and work towards changing societal wrongs (Ayers, 1998). However, as Applebaum (2009) points out, social justice education critics allege this topic area is ideological and counter to education. Those who resist such educational lenses argue silencing students whose beliefs are misaligned with those of social justice educators counteract meaningful progress toward educational objectives. This critique can be understood from the concept of ideology and its connection with educational settings. Ideology is the collection of arguments for making certain claims explicit (Applebaum, 2009). When ideology is used in this sense, a person or belief is said to be ideological because it is one-sided or partisan. Ideologies are then argued fallaciously, truth is distorted, and facts are ignored to protect the belief or person (Rakow, 1992). The "real" deepening of understanding cannot be accessed except through discourse in communication (Applebaum, 2009).

Educators' Role in Socially Just Leadership Education

The complexity of an educator's role reaches far beyond knowing a topic well enough to teach it. Instead, teaching is about relationships;

relationships with students, especially in moments of dissonance and clarity, become the heart of teaching and learning. Learning requires choice and action from a student; whereas, teaching requires a relationship, and invitation to take a journey of development and exploration of new information and frameworks. Socially just leadership education is more than informing students of injustices and leadership knowledge and skills, but providing them with tools toward empowerment and change in the world.

Educators for social justice create environments with multiple entry points for learning and varied pathways for success (Ayers, 1998). Dialogue, as a method of communication, moves awareness forward through both content exchange and seating arrangement allowing for *true* understanding of self and others (Zúñiga, 2003; Bohm, 1996; Banathy & Jenlink, 2005). These processes allow us to make sense of the world we live in and ourselves. Social justice pedagogy that includes dialogue, focuses on critical thinking and reflection on personal experiences and experiences of others. Teaching *for* social justice is not only based in moral and ethical development, but rather arousing critical thinking, student reflection, and experiential responses to a better understanding of what social justice actually means (Greene, 1998).

CHANGING THE NARRATIVE

This book aims to change the current narrative of leadership education, which is still dominated by theories overwhelmingly created by White, male, heterosexual, Christian voices. The organization of this book offers an introductory section, which sets the stage for socially just leadership education. Two distinct parts follow the introduction that look at socially just leadership education through the lens of social identity and through processes and environments. In addition to this chapter, which opens the conversation to socially just leadership education, Trisha S. Teig discusses integrating social justice with leadership education in Chapter 2. Trisha explores social justice topics in leadership education, tracing its roots to K–12 education, as well as to who is teaching social justice education. She provides examples of three postsecondary institutions who integrate social justice into leadership education and provides recommendations of structural integration through theoretical frameworks and suggested readings.

Miguel Angel Hernandez, in Chapter 3, provides clarity around concepts of nationalism, equity, diversity, multiculturalism, and social justice. Often these terms are misunderstood and interchanged inappropriately, Miguel not only clarifies each of these, but discusses how we can have transformation towards inclusion in socially just leadership education contexts. Finally, Chapter 4 written by Marshall Anthony Jr. explores the intersections between activism, social justice, and leadership. He builds an argument for culturally relevant leadership learning as the foundation to activism appreciation, activism heterogeneity, activism psychology, and activism behavior. Bringing these concepts together creates powerful tools for socially just leadership education.

Social Identity and Socially Just Leadership Education

Chapters 2 through 4 provide a foundation of socially just leadership education from which Part I of this book builds upon. The first part of this book focuses on social identity connections to socially just leadership education. Although we aspired to include as many diverse voices in this book as possible, many voices are missing. We honor the voices of Asian, Native American, multiracial, LGBTQ, and individuals with disabilities and hope this is a starting point to our conversation, as we need all voices in changing the narrative in socially just leadership education. We view this as merely a starting point to the conversation and the first small step in changing the narrative. We look forward to all individuals to engage in this movement towards socially just leadership education in all postsecondary institutions.

For the voices we were able to include, Part I explores how various social identities influence socially just leadership education. In Chapter 5, Sonja Ardoin discusses social class and socially just leadership education through the constructs of capital. She provides suggestions for practice from utilizing asset-based frameworks to showcasing leaders from all walks of life. Paige Haber-Curran and Dan Tillapaugh, in Chapter 6, help us understand the historical and current context of gender and leadership. The practical tools they impart to advance socially just leadership education through the lens of gender are useful across contexts.

In Chapters 6 and 7, LaFarin R. Meriwether and Dorsey Spencer Jr. dig into Black female and Black male leadership development. Honoring the intersectionality of race and gender, while considering culturally relevant leadership learning in order to create socially just leadership education programs is critical. Maritza Torres in Chapter 9 and Juan R. Guardia and Cristobal Salinas Jr. in Chapter 10 continue the conversation of intersectionality of race and gender by exploring Latina leader identity development and Latino male leadership.

Vivechkanand S. Chunoo and Gabrielle Garrard continue the conversation of social identity and socially just leadership education by focusing on faith and philosophical communities in Chapter 11. By using interfaith as a blueprint for social justice and drawing on various faith leaders' knowledge base and skill set, the authors provide suggestions of practice to be implemented in curricular and co-curricular contexts, such as case studies, service-learning projects, site visits, and guest speakers. In Chapter 12, Erin Sylvester discusses the implications of assumed leadership self-efficacy in first generation students. Erin focuses on building leader capacity and its social justice implications. The last chapter in Part I, Chapter 13 by Jennifer Farinella, focuses on nontraditional family structures, specifically foster care youth, and the impact on leadership development. It is acknowledged that nontraditional family structures can vary widely and each family has their own unique circumstances. There is much to learn about socially just leadership education from digging into culturally relevant leadership learning of diverse individuals. Part I helps us explore how social identity influences socially just leadership education. Part II furthers this conversation and moves us further into how we can act by putting systems into place to ensure socially just leadership education is occurring.

Socially Just Leadership Education Processes and Environments

Rose Rezaei begins Part II in Chapter 14 by discussing brave spaces. She argues the need for brave spaces within leadership education and provides guidance on how to create brave spaces through the leader identity development model (Komives, Owen, Longerbeam, Mainella, & Osteen, 2005). Chapter 15 discusses the role of liberatory pedagogy in socially just leadership education. Cameron C. Beatty and Amber Manning-Ouellette examine leadership studies through a critical lens and provide strategies for teaching through resistance using liberatory pedagogy. Moving from curricular to co-curricular contexts, Chapter 16 by Kathy L. Guthrie and Jane Rodriguez, discusses socially just leadership program development in co-curricular spaces. They provide strategies for educators and advisors to craft such experiences.

Including leadership education in advising identity-based student organization is the focus of Danielle Morgan Acosta's Chapter 17. She deconstructs the professional competency of advising student organizations and how postsecondary institutions cultivate leaders in identity-based organizations. Robyn O. Brock moves us forward in bringing forth emotional intelligence as a tool for socially just leadership educators to consider when developing programs.

Although service-learning is often used as a pedagogy in leadership education, there are significant criticisms when considering social justice initiatives. Jillian Volpe White, in Chapter 19, addresses the major criticism of service-learning and strategies for socially just service-learning in leadership education. Erica Wiborg in Chapter 20 continues to move the conversation forward by discussing critical theories and pedagogies. She explores how to create and sustain a coalescing community, with practical implications for culturally relevant leadership learning. Finally in Part II, Vivechkanand S. Chunoo and Kathy L. Guthrie strongly state the imperative for action, that the call for action is no longer acceptable. They provide critical considerations for socially just leadership education as we collectively work together to change the narrative.

Collectively Changing the Narrative

The process of education is a constant struggle. As educators, we struggle over how to convey realistic hope for a better life to our students. We wrestle to understand and figure out ways to achieve a better life ourselves and then pass that learning on to hopeful students. This struggle is seen in institutions of higher education every day. Creating a space where people with all types of backgrounds and experiences feel welcome to discuss topics such as racism, oppression, and inequality is a daunting task. Providing supportive, yet challenging environments across campus can shift an entire institutional culture where having these dialogues are natural.

As we have outlined, this book focuses on how we can collectively change the narrative of this important work. We need to move from leadership education and social justice initiatives operating separately to socially just leadership education. Now, more than ever, our collective voices need to be heard to train future leaders in creating positive, sustainable change towards a more equitable and just world. Changing the narrative is not simply a call to action, but a demand for tangible action. Talking about how socially just leadership education needs to occur is not good enough, we, as educators need to take action in how we develop, deliver, and assess socially just leadership education programs. We hope you engage in this material and critically think about your responsibility and place in changing this narrative.

REFERENCES

Adams, M., Blumenfeld, W., Castañeda, R., Hackman, H., Peters, M., & Zúñiga, X. (2000). *Readings for diversity and social justice: An anthology on racism, antisemitism, sexism, heterosexism, ableism, and classism.* New York, NY: Routledge.

Applebaum, B. (2009). Is teaching for social justice a "liberal bias"? *Teachers College Record, 11*(2), 376–408.

Ayers, W. (1998). Popular education: Teaching for social justice. In W. Ayers, J. A. Hunt, & T. Quinn (Eds.), *Teaching for social justice* (pp. xvii–xxv). New York, NY: New Press.

Banathy, B. H., & Jenlink, P. M. (Eds.). (2005). *Dialogue as a means of collective communication.* New York, NY: Kluwer.

Billsberry, J. (2009). The social construction of leadership education. *Journal of Leadership Education, 8*(2), 1–9.

Bohm, D. (1996). *On dialogue.* New York, NY: Routledge.

Brungardt, C. L. (1996). The making of leaders: A review of the research in leadership development and education. *The Journal of Leadership Studies, 3*(3), 81–95.

Burns, J. M. (1978). *Leadership.* New York, NY: Harper & Row.

Chunoo, V., & Osteen, L. (2016). Purpose, mission, and context: The call for educating future leaders. In K. L. Guthrie & L. Osteen (Eds.), *New directions for higher education, No. 174, Reclaiming higher education's purpose in leadership development* (pp. 9–20). San Francisco, CA: Jossey-Bass.

Greene, M. (1998). Teaching for social justice. In W. Ayers, J. A. Hunt, & T. Quinn (Eds.), *Teaching for social justice* (pp. xxvii–xlvi). New York, NY: New Press.

Guthrie, K. L., & Hampton, A. (2017). So just make a difference: A unique approach to leadership and social justice education. *eJournal of Public Affairs, 6*(1), 65–86.

Guthrie, K. L., & Jenkins, D. M. (2018). *The role of leadership educators: Transforming learning.* Charlotte, NC: Information Age.

Guthrie, K. L., & Osteen, L. (Eds.). (2016). New directions for higher education: No. 174. Reclaiming higher education's purpose in leadership development. San Francisco, CA: Jossey-Bass.

Komives, S. R., Owen, J. E., Longerbeam, S. D., Mainella, F. C., & Osteen, L. (2005). Developing a leadership identity: A grounded theory. *Journal of College Student Development, 46*, 593–611.

Nohria, N., & Khurana, R. (2010). Advancing leadership theory and practice. In N. Nohria & R. Khurana (Eds.), *Handbook of leadership theory and practice: A Harvard Business School centennial colloquium* (pp. 3–26). Boston, MA: Harvard Business Press.

Rakow, L. F. (1992). Gender and race in the classroom. *Feminist Teacher, 6*(1), 10–13.

Zúñiga, X. (2003). Bridging differences through dialogue. *About Campus, 7*(6), 8–13.

CHAPTER 2

INTEGRATING SOCIAL JUSTICE IN LEADERSHIP EDUCATION

Trisha S. Teig

Social justice involves an idealized concept of a society where all persons have access and opportunity in an equitable manner (Noble, 2015). Unfortunately, the history and current iteration of leadership in multiple examples around the world does not represent these lofty ideals. Where can leadership educators move to disrupt and deconstruct the narrative of leadership for some but not all? American higher education claims to educate leaders for the future of our country and world (Astin & Astin, 2000). As a result of this assertion, leadership education programs have proliferated at colleges and universities across the nation (International Leadership Association, 2016). As leadership educators seek to identify the most relevant, important, and influential ways to encourage the growth and development of students, crucial social justice consciousness and competency must be considered and included (Noble, 2015).

> It is critical that leaders expand their focus to encompass a broader accountability and embrace leadership that is centered on social justice—the fair and impartial distribution of resources, opportunities, and benefits of society to

Changing the Narrative, pages 9–25
Copyright © 2018 by Information Age Publishing

all of its members, regardless of position, place, or other exclusionary criteria. (Noble, 2015, p. 44)

For the future of leadership learning to have lasting impact, we, as leadership educators, must become familiar with social justice education. This chapter focuses on the history and some basic concepts of social justice education, including how these ideas have, and have not, been integrated into leadership education. Leadership programs listed in the International Leadership Association (ILA) Directory (2016) are reviewed for inclusion of social justice-focused courses. Additionally, I highlight three undergraduate leadership studies programs in their efforts to incorporate social justice concepts and action in the curriculum. I conclude with recommendations about how social justice can be incorporated into leadership learning through theory and resources.

WHAT IS SOCIAL JUSTICE EDUCATION?

The racial integration of the nation's institutions of higher education following the civil rights movement of the 1960s elicited many needs previously unrecognized on college campuses. By admitting increasingly larger amounts of White women and people of color, universities became more demographically diverse, but still functioned within the historic frameworks upon which they had been built (Brunsma, Brown, & Placier, 2012). These foundations acted as barriers to success for students who did not represent White, upper- or middle- class, and male identities (Landreman & MacDonald-Dennis, 2013).

The field of social justice education arose to address these issues. Initially implemented with the moniker of "multiculturalism," this work focused on highlighting the culture of "others" who were historically underrepresented on college campuses (Landreman & MacDonald-Dennis, 2013). "Multiculturalism rests upon ideals and principles of equity that challenge monocultural assumptions" (Landreman & MacDonald-Dennis, 2013, p. 6). However, the focus of multiculturalism failed to meet the challenge of overcoming historic systemic oppression within higher education systems. Therefore, in the 1990s, multiculturalism educators shifted focus to concepts of social justice to further address these challenges in a more holistic fashion (Landreman & MacDonald-Dennis, 2013). *The Art of Effective Facilitation: Reflections from Social Justice Educators* (Landreman, 2013) highlights the key purpose of connecting social justice tenants within the learning environment: "Educators committed to justice are searching for a pedagogical strategy and movement that challenges the assumptions, practices, and norms embedded in the notion that we live in a homogeneous society" (Landreman & MacDonald-Dennis, 2013, p. 7). To further connect these ideas to our role as leadership educators, we must be prepared to recognize and critique oppressive structures and processes on our campuses, "reflect on our own socialization" (Landreman, 2013, p. xiv), and work to integrate social justice education into the leadership learning process.

EXAMINING SOCIAL JUSTICE CONCEPTS IN LEADERSHIP EDUCATION

Leadership education, as the pedagogically-oriented building of human capacity through leadership learning (Andenoro et al., 2013), encompasses elements of training and development (Allen & Roberts, 2011; Brungart, 1997). Leadership education resides within leadership studies; a unique yet multifaceted discipline in higher education (Andenoro et al., 2013; Inter-Association Leadership Education Collaborative [ILEC], 2016). Leadership education has been a swiftly growing field with scholarly and academic focus in its own area since the early 1990s (Komives, 2011). Curricular focused undergraduate leadership education programs have haphazardly proliferated within the growth of the discipline, often taking hold in spaces close to the department (academic, student affairs, or a combination of both) from which they originated (Andenoro et al., 2013). Due to this diversity of development, there is a varied and unique nature to each credit-bearing leadership program. Within this wealth of variation, some programs may weave social justice education into the curriculum. This takes the form of dedicated courses or integrated conversations and readings throughout the classes offered.

While a degree of social justice focus may be present in current programs, leadership studies, and leadership education as a whole, it is framed from and influenced by a challenging past focused on privileged voices (Dugan, 2011; Guthrie, Bertrand Jones, & Osteen, 2016). In a discipline where the foundational cannon includes "Great Man" and masculinity based trait theories (Northouse, 2015), there is a need to engage in the theory and practice of leadership that acknowledges this discriminatory history and advances a just and equitable future; one which is representative of broader voices and understandings of leadership (Bordas, 2012; Haber-Curran & Tillapaugh, 2017).

Socially just leadership education requires intensive exploration of social justice tenants. Specifically, it must include examination of social identities both in the context of individual identities (i.e., race, gender, ethnicity, social class) and identities from an intersectional lens (i.e., race + gender, social class + ethnicity; Haber-Curran & Tillapaugh, 2017; Mitchell, Simmons, & Greyerbiehl, 2014). "Increased attention to dimensions of social identity (e.g., gender, socioeconomic status, ethnic identity) and societal systems of oppression are necessary to unpack contextual influences in leadership development" (Dugan, 2011, p. 82). Leadership education should be a space for establishing the connection between complex social issues which need leadership (Heifetz & Linsky, 2001) and the building of understanding, capacities, and efficacy for considering the complexities of power, privilege, and oppression in our society.

Social Justice Leadership in K–12 Education

While the pairing of leadership and social justice is a fairly recent phenomenon (Noble, 2015), scholars in educational leadership have been advocating a pedagogy of leadership for social justice in the K–12 environment for decades (Oplatka & Arar, 2016; Dentith & Peterlin, 2011). Stemming from seminal works such as Freire's (1979) *Pedagogy of the Oppressed,* the field of education has been significantly impacted by considering how social justice issues must be addressed through leadership action (Brown, 2004). "Leadership for social justice is ground[ed] in critical theories and situated within a deep moral commitment to...communities, replete with reflective habits of mind that lead to more humane and equity-focused leadership" (Dentith & Peterlin, 2011, p. 36). While the professional programs in K–12 education have been discussing this route for some time, the shift to a social justice focus has not pervasively infused the undergraduate leadership education curriculum. "Historically, many leadership education and preparation programs have been underprepared to address the elements of social justice, and...were not necessarily focused on understanding the inequalities in society or tackling the challenges of equity work" (Noble, 2015, p. 50). However, an emergent movement within leadership studies is focused on critical leadership pedagogy (see this volume, Chapter 20), influenced by Black feminist and critical pedagogy (hooks, 1994; Hill Collins, 2000), can engender a paradigm shift in how leadership is taught and learned in higher education (Dugan, 2011; Guthrie et al., 2016).

The (Social Justice) State of Leadership Studies

In a 2012 review of the "state of leadership studies" Perruci and McManus considered the history of the leadership studies discipline and its future directions. This review included six recommendations for the field. Three connected to the concepts of integrating social justice into the leadership studies curriculum. These include an exploration of the history of leadership as a subject, the imperative need to understand the "role that context, complexity, and culture play" in leadership, and the use of various methodologies to further comprehend the leadership process (Perruci & McManus, 2012,

p. 52). Stemming from Perruci and McManus's (2012) recommendations, engaging the history of leadership from a methodologically critical lens allows for consideration and critique of the lack of diverse voices and emphasis placed on privileged groups which currently sustains the field's historical foundations and theoretical texts (i.e., Northouse, 2015). Curricula must contain information about systems of structural inequality and examination of social identities as contextual representations of the complexities of culture in the process of leadership (Dugan, 2011). Critical leadership pedagogy, influenced by critical and feminist theories, can be implemented as a framework for enacting leadership education which addresses these complex issues in authentic, developmental ways (Pendakur & Furr, 2016).

Leadership Education's Agenda and Call to Action

Recent meetings of leadership educators across disciplines have led to the establishment of an agenda and subsequent calls to action (Andenoro, 2013; ILEC, 2016). The National Leadership Educator's Research Agenda: 2013–2018 identifies two focal areas: pedagogical priorities and content-based considerations, which clarify seven research priorities (Andenoro et al., 2013). Within these, "influences of social identities," directly targets concerns of social identities in leadership education: "Leadership scholars and educators should more effectively center considerations of social identity in leadership research, education, and practice" (Andenoro et al., 2013, p. 19).

In a more recent collaborative venture, higher education, student affairs, and leadership education association representatives constructed a call to action and future direction document. Direction from this piece identifies building inclusive leadership learning communities as a key priority (ILEC, 2016). This includes a focus on: "Intentionally examin[ing] the intersections of multiple identities within formal and informal learning experiences and contexts and invit[ing] and include[ing] multiple perspectives on leadership concepts, theories, and models" (ILEC, 2016, p. 6).

All of these recommendations center a need for leadership education to be incorporating tenants of social justice in our everyday practice. If these are the recommendations for the future of our field from experts and colleagues, it is necessary to consider where leadership education has been incorporating social justice to this point.

WHO TEACHES SOCIAL JUSTICE EDUCATION?

The ILA provides members an opportunity to submit descriptions and basic information regarding academic leadership programs from U.S. and international institutions of higher education. This directory houses data from 1,570 programs from within the United States who self-selected to be listed in the ILA database as a curricular "leadership program" (ILA, 2016). In a further examination of these programs through data collected from each institution's website, information regarding program's course offerings and sequencing was gathered. These data were further examined to find references to the terms "social justice," "diverse/diversity," "multicultural/cultural," and specific social identity ("gender" and "race") related courses. These data were specifically considered from undergraduate major or minor leadership programs, which have a disproportionately smaller representation ($n = 325$) in the directory as compared to graduate programs ($n = 983$). Certificate programs represented in the research are from both undergraduate and graduate programs ($n = 250$; Guthrie, Teig, & Hu, 2018). From this research, 74 undergraduate programs, representing majors, minors, and certificates, contained courses with explicit connection, based on the course title, to teaching social justice in the leadership classroom. Of these 74 programs, just under half ($n = 35$) of the courses listed were as a part of the elective requirements for the student to complete. Furthermore, within these electives, there were other courses, not focused on social justice, which a student could opt for in lieu of the social justice course option. The data revealed 39 programs which include a core, required course or courses integrating social justice concepts. Of these 39 programs, nine contain more than one course which, by course title, is inclusive of social justice focus. Table 2.1 provides a list of these nine programs, with the course titles.

A clear limitation of this study is recognizing that not all courses which do integrate social justice components into their curriculum have visibly identifiable social justice titles, as determined by the research criterion. Furthermore, the ILA directory, or any other resource, cannot contain a fully comprehensive list of all leadership related programs. However, these data represent a considerable number of majors, minors, and certificates across the United States. With this in mind, why do so few undergraduate programs clearly designate an integration of social justice education as a key component of their course offerings? And, if these courses are present, why are many of them elective classes as compared to required coursework? Leadership programs must restructure from this smaller representation of social justice in some courses to encompass a more holistic, inclusive integration of social justice education in the study of the leadership phenomenon. Examining examples of the programs found in this research can help us explore ways social justice education is present in the leadership curricula.

TABLE 2.1 Leadership Programs With Multiple Core Course Offerings in Social Justice and Leadership

	Institution	Program	Courses
1	American University	Women, Policy, and Political Leadership Undergraduate Certificate	Women and Politics; Women, Politics, and Public Policy; Women and Political Leadership; Introduction to Women and Politics; Topics in Women and Politics
2	Antioch University	Women and Leadership Certificate	The Influence of Gender on Leadership: Case Studies of Female Leaders, Past & Present Part I & II; Gender Related Challenges of Leadership
3	Columbia College	Minor in Leadership Studies	The Sophomore Experience: Gender, Diversity & Social Justice; Women, Leadership, & Social Change
4	Creighton University	BS in Leadership	Leadership and Social Justice: Faith Traditions and Global Perspectives; Social Justice: In Thought and Action
5	Florida State University	Undergraduate Certificate in Leadership Studies	Leadership in Groups and Communities; Leadership and Complexities
6	Loyola Chicago–Illinois	BA in Pastoral Leadership	Social Justice Foundations; Diversity and Equity; Leadership in Social Justice Organizations
7	Metropolitan State College of Denver	Minor in Leadership Studies	Leadership and Social Change; Perspectives on Leadership
8	The College of New Jersey	Women Learning and Leadership Program	All coursework focused on women, gender, and leadership
9	University of St. Thomas–Minnesota	BA in Justice and Peace Studies—Concentration in Leadership for Social Justice	Leadership for Social Justice; Social Problems; one required cultural awareness course

HOW IS SOCIAL JUSTICE BEING TAUGHT IN LEADERSHIP EDUCATION?

Leadership education occurs in an interdisciplinary arena, with programs and courses being taught in and across a multitude of disciplines depending on the campus environment, the development of the program, and the opportunity for funding and support (Andenoro et al., 2013; Guthrie et al., 2018; ILA, 2016). Successful implementation of high-quality pedagogical practices can come from reviewing current programs exhibiting tremendous methods for leadership learning engagement. I will review three leadership studies programs that weave social justice into leadership. A diverse group has been selected to provide a broader perspective on how different types of institutions and programs are tackling this challenge. I will consider two leadership studies minors and a certificate program from two public and one private institution. I will provide an overview of the basic components of the course or program, key assignments or elements, and further challenges or considerations for implementation of the ideas from these examples.

Kansas State University: Core Course

The leadership studies minor at Kansas State University includes a core class in the students' second year focusing on culture and context in leadership (Kansas State University, n.d.). The course is taught with an integration of academic content surrounding the understanding of social identities and complex social problems and the practical engagement of these problems in the community. The course focuses on storytelling; students share their stories and hear from others different from them. This storytelling framework provides a foundation for students' consciousness raising for understanding and considering the world from a lens of social justice. This consciousness raising encourages students to consider where they hear examples of privilege and oppression within the stories from class and beyond to their interactions with others outside of the academic setting.

Subsequently, using the tools provided in the social change model of leadership development (Higher Education Research Institute, 1996), the course engages students in social action to generate change. The community-based action research project is a semester-long undertaking in small groups requiring students to identify a challenge connected with a particular social issue or identity, connect with people or organizations in the community who work with this issue, and learn more. Using ethnographic qualitative methods, students are challenged to identify their issue from a lens of inclusion. From this investigation, they discover ways to work with community partners to further understand the issue and identify leadership opportunities. This process culminates in a final presentation of the student groups on their learning and any positive change action or possibilities that can be an outcome of the project (L. Fine, personal communication, December 1, 2016).

The Kansas State example provides leadership educators with a model of incorporating one core course within the program focused on how leadership practice is engaged in context with complex social identities and challenges. This represents an example of the experiential learning endeavor advocated by a multitude of leadership educators (Allen & Hartman, 2008). An important consideration when implementing this type of community connection project is supply students with the foundational tools, including personal introspection and reflection on their privileged identities and socialized assumptions (Harro, 2000) before going out to work with the community. Service-learning activities focused on social change generally have the best of intentions but can be excluding and damaging (Davis, 2006). By including thoughtful, reflective, critical discussions about intention versus impact (Arao & Clemens, 2013) and asset/collaborative rather than deficit/savior mentality regarding marginalized communities (Davis, 2006), courses such as Kansas State's Culture and Context in Leadership can provide avenues for social justice education and action in leadership education.

Columbia College: Holistic Identity-Based Program

Columbia College is a small, private, Methodist affiliated women's college located in South Carolina. They offer a 16-credit hour minor in leadership studies with an emphasis on cultivating women leaders (Columbia College, n.d.). The four core courses of the program, leadership in context; gender, diversity, and social justice; women, leadership, and social change; and leadership in action, focus on how students become leaders through social change in their communities (Columbia College, n.d.). The minor emphasizes relationship building as a key element of leadership development and infuses exploring identity in personal and systemic perspectives into all courses in the curriculum (L. Fleming, personal communication, December 2, 2016). The program also integrates service learning as an essential element. Students consider community issues and how understanding community needs and working as active collaborators can help create real connections and change for both students and community members.

The Columbia College model presents leadership educators with a particular framework for infusing concepts of social justice throughout the program. This minor connects with the identity of the population of the institution and situates all of its coursework on the development of women in leadership through relationship building in the community. This moves beyond the previous example by highlighting a particular identity and integrating all elements of the program into the intricacies of understanding that identity in connection with the students' growing leadership identity, capacity, and efficacy.

Florida State University: Core and Identity-Based Courses With Collaborative Integration

The undergraduate certificate in leadership studies at Florida State University (FSU) was developed in 2005 as a collaborative partnership between the college of education's higher education program and the Center for Leadership and Social Change (Guthrie & Bovio, 2014). Support from these two entities, from the academic and student affairs areas, allows for a unique blending of curricular course offerings grounded in experiential frameworks. Requiring 18 hours, with five core courses and an elective, the certificate allows students from a variety of majors to complete the process. The location of the certificate, both figuratively in partnership with and literally in the shared physical space with the Center for Leadership and Social Change allows for an inimitable connection to the center's theoretical groundings in diversity, service, leadership, and student development (Center for Leadership and Social Change, n.d.).

Core and Identity Specific Courses

The certificate incorporates learning objectives for each course inclusive of theoretical understanding, skill development, personal reflection, and theoretical application. Concepts of social justice are fused specifically into two of the core classes, Leadership in Groups and Communities and Leadership and Complexity, through readings, activities, reflection, and discussion. Students also have the opportunity to take elective courses grounded in specific identities or social issues including: Black Male Leadership, Gender and Leadership, Leadership Through Intergroup Dialogue, Latinx Leadership, Poverty and the Working Poor, and Leadership for Social Justice.

The inclusion of a broad variety of identity and issue focused courses allows for students to select from an array of social justice issues within their leadership education experience. This example provides a route for programs to expand their curriculum to consider intensive perspectives from the narrative voices of historically marginalized populations; a key tenant of critical race theory (McCoy & Rodricks, 2015). While creating identity and issue focused electives can be positive for social justice integration, leadership educators should be cautious of focusing only on the development of elective courses. If elective courses are the sole place social justice concepts are considered, this does not meet the need of infusing social justice consciousness into the leadership education program as a whole.

Collaborative Integration

The Leadership for Social Justice and Leadership through Intergroup Dialogue courses represent further examples of the collaborative model of the leadership certificate within the cocurricular design of a living learning community. Students in the Social Justice Living Learning Community (SJLLC), a first-year, residential community supported through staff from the Center for Leadership and Social Change, must take both the Leadership for Social Justice and Leadership Through Intergroup Dialogue courses in addition to attending cocurricular programming experiences. The in-classroom curriculum is foundational to allow instructors to inform the cocurricular programming needs of the SJLLC cohort. SJLLC program coordinators can expand upon issues or topics addressed in class in a more comprehensive, intentional format in the cocurricular programs based on what students express they understand and are prepared to explore further in the classroom setting (B. Albrecht, personal communication, December 1, 2016).

This model also integrates social justice education into leadership education through collaborative partnerships with academic and student affairs. While a more complex endeavor, the connection of learning for students from both in and outside of the classroom can be a powerful tool for growth. However, challenges of clear shared goals and vision for the program can arise in this type of venture. The FSU example utilizes the program coordinator and other staff directly connected with all elements of the SJLLC as instructors for the two required courses. This allows for the instructors to be informed by the conversations in the classroom for their cocurricular development.

RECOMMENDATIONS FOR FUTURE DIRECTIONS

In addition to exploring the practices of various programs, it is imperative for leadership educators to expand their knowledge of teaching to include critical pedagogies which disrupt normalized understandings from the perspective of the privileged groups as the overall narrative of leadership. Educators can utilize tenants from critical race theory and critical leadership pedagogy (Mahoney, 2016; McCoy & Rodricks, 2015; Pendakur & Furr, 2016) to allow for counter storytelling, acknowledgment of diverse voices, and critique of colorblind (Bonilla-Silva, 2006), non-inclusive ideology in texts, discussions, and learning environments. "High-impact learning pedagogies empirically proven to make a difference in leadership development should be integrated into educational interventions" (Dugan, 2011, p. 81). Integration of experiential and critical leadership pedagogy can allow educators to engage students in these difficult conversations in a meaningful way. See this volume, Chapter 20 for further exploration of this topic.

Structural Integration

A progression of social justice concepts for leadership education programs must include structural concepts of how our overarching systems reify dominate groups (Mahoney, 2016). These structures are steeped in the frameworks of patriarchy and Whiteness to such a degree that it is difficult to see and reform how we are taught (Brunsma et al., 2012). Socially just leadership educators consider how patriarchy and Whiteness, as well as other forms of systemic oppression, influence the spaces, curriculum, courses, and persons who are within a program (Beighley, Simmons, & West, 2014). By thinking through these elements, educators can disrupt normative assumptions through incorporation of diverse instructors, authors, and conversations in the classroom. The following sections identify recommendations regarding theoretical framing and useful readings which could be included in courses.

Theories

Theoretical foundations are crucial to curricular success. The theories which can be utilized with social justice and leadership learning include Roberta Harro's (2000) cycles of socialization and liberation; critical race theory (McCoy & Rodricks, 2015); intersectionality (Mitchell et al., 2014) which stems from Black feminist theory (Hill Collins, 2000; hooks, 1994); the social change model of leadership development (Higher Education Research Institute, 1996); the multiple dimensions of oppression model (Hardiman, Jackson, & Griffin, 2016); and Juana Bordas' (2012) multicultural collaborative leadership. Each of these theories allows for academic engagement in complex social issues which engage students in the challenges of understanding social justice issues beyond simply their own personal experiences.

Books and Readings

Exploring diverse voices and expanding beyond the White, Western narrative of leadership allows for inclusion of accounts of people of color (McCoy & Rodricks, 2015), and diverse expansion of the leadership cannon. In order to incorporate social justice concepts into leadership education, leadership educators must be familiar with social justice education and have access to resources to further expand their own understanding and personal growth. Books and readings focused on further educating the educator are useful tools for those who teach leadership. Additionally, a host of books and readings are excellent to use in the leadership classroom to integrate social justice concepts. These readings allow for inclusion of diverse voices, and represent a broader perspective of leadership from various cultural and contextual lenses. Table 2.2 provides recommendations on possible

TABLE 2.2   Selected Resources for Leadership Training and Development

Resource Title	Author(s), Year	Useful in Training and Development or Curriculum
Intersectionality and Higher Education: Theory, Research, and Praxis	Mitchell, Simmons, & Greyerbiehl, 2014	Training and Development
Is Everyone Really Equal: An Introduction to Key Concepts in Social Justice Education	Sensoy & DiAngelo, 2012	Curriculum
New Directions for Student Leadership: No. 152. Developing Culturally Relevant Leadership Learning	Guthrie, Bertrand Jones, & Osteen, 2016	Training and Development
New Directions for Student Leadership: No. 154. Gender and Leadership	Haber-Curran & Tillapaugh, 2017	Training and Development
Readings for Diversity and Social Justice	Adams, Bell, & Griffin, 2016	Curriculum
Salsa, Soul, and Spirit: Leadership for the Multicultural Age	Bordas, 2012	Curriculum
Teaching for Diversity and Social Justice (3rd ed.)	Adams, Bell, Goodman, & Joshi, 2016	Training and Development
The Art of Effective Facilitation: Reflections of Social Justice Educators	Landreman, 2013	Training and Development
The Power of Latino Leadership: Culture, Inclusion, and Contribution	Bordas, 2013	Curriculum

books to use as training and development for leadership educators and/or readings to be implemented in the leadership learning curriculum.

Theoretical foundations and essential resources are crucial ingredients to framing a leadership program within social justice. I encourage leadership educators to further explore helpful tools to expand their own knowledge and the concepts shared in the leadership classroom.

CONCLUSION

Leadership education stands at a juncture; either responding to the massive rift in understanding among people who have different backgrounds, stories, and perspectives, or perpetuating a history of marginalization and oppression. This crossroads allows leadership educators the opportunity to see how the curriculum can assist future leaders to expand beyond oppressive rhetoric and divisive actions to build meaningful, collaborative coalitions (Harro, 2000). A significant shift needs to occur in undergraduate leadership education to ensure a foundation of social justice education is included in the leadership classroom. This reframing will expand and engender leadership learning and development to be cognizant of the complex and difficult past, as well as the challenging and inequitable current reality of access to leadership in our world (Bertrand Jones, Guthrie, & Osteen, 2016). Social justice consciousness does not develop without interacting with and reflecting upon individual social identities and overarching systems of power and oppression that shape our society (Noble, 2015). "Imbued with a solid understanding of the past, an increased awareness of the nuances of the present, and with a watchful and curious eye on the future, such [leadership education] programs can be transformational as they lead efforts toward social justice..." (Noble, 2015, p. 51). When the current reality of leadership in the United States and the world discounts the importance of understanding and dismantling systems of power, privilege, and oppression, a foundational insertion of conversations about identity, dialogue, and shared understanding for social justice and change is imperative to leadership education. The future of leadership depends on leadership education which integrates social justice consciousness and competency to create inclusive, collaborative, future leaders prepared to engaged in the complex challenges of our world.

REFERENCES

Adams, M., Bell, L., Goodman, D. J., & Joshi, K. Y. (2016). *Teaching for diversity and social justice*. New York, NY: Routledge.

Allen, S. J., & Hartman, N. S. (2008). Leadership development: An exploration of sources of learning. *S.A.M. Advanced Management Journal, 73*, 10–19.

Allen, S. J., & Roberts, D. C. (2011). Our response to the question: Next steps in clarifying the language of leadership learning. *Journal of Leadership Studies, 5*(2), 63–69.

Andenoro, A. C., Allen, S. J., Haber-Curran, P., Jenkins, D. M., Sowcik, M., Dugan, J. P., & Osteen, L. (2013). *National leadership education research agenda 2013–2018: Providing strategic direction for the field of leadership education*. Retrieved from http://leadershipeducators.org/ResearchAgenda

Arao, B., & Clemens, K. (2013). From safe space to brave space: A new way to frame dialogue around diversity and social justice. In L. Landreman (Ed.), *The art of effective facilitation: Reflections from social justice educators* (pp. 135–150). Terre Haute, IN: Stylus.

Astin, A. W., & Astin, H. S. (2000). *Leadership reconsidered: Engaging higher education in social change*. Battle Creek, MI: W. K. Kellogg Foundation.

Beighley, C. S., Simmons, C., & West, E. (2014). Beyond identity politics: Equipping students to create systemic change. In D. Mitchell, Jr., C. Y. Simmons, & L. A. Greyerbiehl, (Eds.), *Intersectionality and higher education: Theory, research, and praxis* (pp. 269–279). New York, NY: Peter Lang.

Bertrand Jones, T., Guthrie, K. L., & Osteen, L. (2016). Critical domains of culturally relevant leadership learning: A call to transform leadership programs. In K. L. Guthrie, T. Bertrand Jones, & L. Osteen (Eds.), *New directions for student leadership, No. 152: Developing culturally relevant leadership learning* (pp. 9–21). San Francisco, CA: Jossey-Bass.

Bonilla-Silva, E. (2006). *Racism without racists: Colorblind racism and the persistence of racial inequality in the United States.* Oxford, England: Rowman & Littlefield.

Bordas, J. (2012). *Salsa, soul, and spirit: Leadership for a multicultural age.* San Francisco, CA: Berrett-Keohler.

Bordas, J. (2013). *The power of Latino leadership: Culture, inclusion, and contribution.* San Francisco, CA: Berrett-Koehler.

Brown, K. M. (2004). Leadership for social justice and equity: Weaving a transformative framework and pedagogy. *Educational Administration Quarterly, 40,* 77–108.

Brungardt, C. (1997). The making of leaders: A review of the research in leadership development and education. *Journal of Leadership & Organizational Studies, 3,* 81–95. doi:10.1177/107179199700300309

Brunsma, D. L., Brown, E. S., & Placier, P. (2012). Teaching race at historically white colleges and universities: Identifying and dismantling the walls of Whiteness. *Critical Sociology, 39,* 717–738.

Center for Leadership and Social Change. (n.d.) *Our beliefs and theoretical groundings.* Retrieved from http://thecenter.fsu.edu/About-Us/Our-Beliefs-and-Theoretical-Groundings

Columbia College. (n.d.). *Leadership studies.* Retrieved from https://www.columbiasc.edu/program/leadership-studies

Davis, A. (2006). What we don't talk about when we don't talk about service. In A. Davis & E. Lynn (Eds.), *The civically engaged reader: A diverse collection of short provocative readings on civic activity* (pp. 148–154). Chicago, IL: Great Books Foundation.

Dentith, A. M., & Peterlin, B. (2011). Leadership education from within a feminist ethos. *Journal of Research on Leadership Education, 6,* 36–58.

Dugan, J. P. (2011). Pervasive myths in leadership development: Unpacking constraints on leadership learning. *Journal of Leadership Studies, 5*(2), 79–84.

Freire, P. (1979). *Pedagogy of the oppressed.* New York, NY: Bloomsbury.

Guthrie, K. L., Bertrand Jones, T., & Osteen, L. (Eds.). (2016). *New directions for student leadership, No. 152: Developing culturally relevant leadership learning.* San Francisco, CA: Jossey-Bass.

Guthrie, K. L., & Bovio, B. (2014). Undergraduate certificate in leadership studies: An opportunity for seamless learning. *Journal of College and Character, 15,* 25–31.

Guthrie, K. L., Teig, T. S., & Hu, P. (2018). *Academic leadership programs in the United States.* Tallahassee: Leadership Learning Research Center, Florida State University.

Haber-Curran, P., & Tillapaugh, D. (Eds.). (2017). *New directions for student leadership, No. 154: Gender and leadership*. San Francisco, CA: Jossey-Bass.

Hardiman, R., Jackson, B., & Griffin, P. (2016). Conceptual foundations of social justice education. In M. Adams, L. A. Bell, & P. Griffin (Eds.), *Teaching for diversity and social justice* (pp. 35–66). New York, NY: Routledge.

Harro, B. (2000). The cycle of socialization. In M. Adams, W. Bluenfeld, R. Castenda, H. Hackman, M. Peters, & X. Zuniga (Eds.), *Readings for diversity and social justice* (pp. 45–51). New York, NY: Routledge.

Heifetz, R. A., & Linsky, M. (2002). *Leadership on the line: Staying alive through the dangers of leading*. Cambridge, MA: Harvard University Press.

Higher Education Research Institute. (1996). *A social change model of leadership development: Guidebook* (Version III). Los Angeles, CA: Author.

Hill Collins, P. (2000). *Black feminist thought: Knowledge, consciousness, and perspectives on empowerment (perspectives on gender)*. New York, NY: Routledge.

hooks, b. (1994). *Teaching to transgress: Education as a practice of freedom*. New York, NY: Routledge.

International Leadership Association. (2016). *Directory*. Retrieved from http://www.ila-net.org/Resources/LPD/index.htm

Inter-Association Leadership Education Collaborative. (2016). *Collaborative priorities and critical considerations for leadership education*. Hays, KS: Association of Leadership Educators. Retrieved from https://www.leadershipeducators.org/ILEC

Kansas State University. (n.d.). *Staley school of leadership studies: Minor in leadership studies*. Retrieved from https://www.k-state.edu/leadership/academics/index.html

Komives, S. R. (2011). Advancing leadership education. In S. R. Komives, J. P. Dugan, J. E. Owen, C. Slack, & W. Wagner (Eds.), *The handbook for student leadership development* (pp. 1–34). San Francisco, CA: Jossey-Bass.

Landreman, L. (Ed.). (2013). *The art of effective facilitation: Reflections from social justice educators*. Terre Haute, IN: Stylus.

Landreman, L., & MacDonald-Dennis, C. (2013). The evolution of social justice education and facilitation. In L. Landreman (Ed.), *The art of effective facilitation: Reflections from social justice educators* (pp. 3–23). Terre Haute, IN: Stylus.

Mahoney, A. (2016). Culturally responsive integrative learning environments: A critical displacement approach. In K. Guthrie, T. Bertrand Jones, & L. Osteen (Eds.), *New Directions for Student Leadership, No. 152: Culturally relevant leadership learning* (pp. 47–59). San Francisco, CA: Jossey-Bass.

McCoy, D. L., & Rodricks, D. J. (2015). *Critical race theory in higher education: 20 years of theoretical and research innovations. ASHE Higher Education Report*, 41(3), 1–117.

Mitchell, D., Jr., Simmons, C. Y., & Greyerbiehl, L. A. (2014). *Intersectionality and higher education: Theory, research, and praxis*. New York, NY: Peter Lang.

Noble, D. J. (2015). Leading for tomorrow in a world yearning for social justice. In M. Sowcik, A. C. Andenoro, M. McNutt, & S. E. Murphy (Eds.), *Leadership 2050: Critical challenges, key considerations, and emerging trends* (pp. 43–58). Bingley, England: Emerald Group.

Northouse, P. G. (2015). *Leadership: Theory and practice* (7th ed.). Thousand Oaks, CA: SAGE.

Oplatka, I., & Arar, K. H. (2016). Leadership for social justice and the characteristics of traditional societies: Ponderings on the application of western-grounded models. *International Journal of Leadership in Education, 19*(3), 352–369.

Pendakur, V., & Furr, S. C. (2016). Critical leadership pedagogy: Engaging power, identity, and culture in leadership education for college students of color. In K. L. Guthrie & L. Osteen (Eds.), *New Directions for Higher Education, No. 174: Reclaiming higher education's purpose in leadership development* (pp. 45–55). San Francisco, CA: Jossey-Bass.

Perruci, G., & McManus, R. M. (2013). The state of leadership studies. *Journal of Leadership Studies, 6,* 49–64.

Sensoy, O., & DiAngelo, R. (2012). *Is everyone really equal: An introduction to key concepts in social justice education.* New York, NY: Teachers College Press.

CHAPTER 3

MORE THAN *JUST* WORDS

Transforming Leadership Education Toward Liberty and Justice For All

Miguel Ángel Hernández

Throughout history, words have been used to deprive and destroy. The meaning of words can shape the morals, ideals, and principles of a people. Words have been used to rob people of humanity. But words have also been used to uplift and restore the dignity of people. This chapter will focus on exploring words intended to transform social, political, and economic systems from excluding marginalized identities toward inclusion. Specifically, the perspective is offered which states a relationship exists between the words and concepts related to *equity, diversity, multicultural,* and *social justice.* These words are framed as responses to both historic and modern elements of *nationalism* and as part of a movement toward *post nationalism.* We end with a discussion focused on the role *social justice leadership education* has in this movement toward inclusion.

The words and concepts included in this chapter have been with us for centuries. We join a conversation dating back to the days of historical philosophers such as Aristotle, Socrates, and Plato. Over the centuries the

Changing the Narrative, pages 27–40
Copyright © 2018 by Information Age Publishing

use of these words and concepts have held different meaning based on the influence of time, place, and world events. Before moving forward, it is important to acknowledge the challenge of presenting just one definition of any concept related to how individuals or communities perceived themselves or others. Over the past few centuries, there have been many interpretations of terms such as equity, diversity, and multiculturalism. For this reason, we draw from several areas of knowledge and are grounded in the context of higher education within the United States. This chapter will focus on both the meaning and practice of the terms introduced above.

NATIONALISM

From its humble beginnings as a British colony, these United States of America, and its citizens, have faced a national identity crisis. This journey has been more painful for some groups of Americans than others, but has nonetheless resulted in widespread nationalism. Hutchinson and Smith (1994) described American nationalism as "...a doctrine of popular freedom and sovereignty... [and] an ideology and discourse... [which]... became prevalent in North America in 1776... [through]... the American Declaration of Independence" (p. 5). Building from these ideas in the late 1700s, former President George Washington declared this country "...was open to receive not only the opulent and respectable stranger, but the oppressed and persecuted of all nations and religions" (Kunnan, 2009, p. 38). However, the contentious nature of the nascent American identity was made plainly apparent when the first congress, in defiance to this declaration, limited access to citizenship through the Naturalization Act of 1790 to free White men (Kunnan, 2009, p. 38).

Nationalism is not inherently a negative concept. Loyalty to a country whose philosophies, principles, and symbols align with all its people is a critical element in nation-building and ultimately necessary for its long-term survival. However, U.S. nationalism has a history of alignment with the exclusion of non-White individuals as set by the first Congress; opposing to the sentiments articulated by President Washington. In this way, White privilege was deeply embedded into the founding of this country, but significant steps can still be taken to realize a vision of liberty and justice for all. This visionary position can continue to inform the social changes modern-day leaders strive toward.

The first 200 years of U.S. governance was marked by the adoption of legislation aimed at excluding women, people of first nations, slaves and their descendants, people of Asian ancestry, and Méxicanos living on lands originally part of los Estados Unidos Méxicanos from fully participating in the political, economic, and social context of establishing this country.

Throughout history, this nation has wrestled with the challenge of how to establish a national identity while simultaneously deciding who should have access and freedom to pursue life, liberty, and the American dream. Each of these challenges are related to nationalism.

In many aspects, U.S. nationalism continues to be rooted in exclusionary practices and has served as a source of countless domestic riots, protests, movements and other forms of social unrest. Ultimately, this phenomena calls for citizens to "...see themselves as ethnically and linguistically homogeneous groups" and work tirelessly to "...protect their identity not only as an ethnic community but as a people forming a nation..." (Appiah et al., 1994, p. 118). This is incredibly difficult for people from historically marginalized groups to do as it would require them to adhere to rules and practices designed to keep them on the fringes of civic participation.

While nationalism aims to maintain and preserve, post-nationalism intends to broaden and redefine the meaning of symbols, traditions, and customs set by the original founders of America. This transformation, over the course of 200 plus years, has shifted from adopting exclusionary philosophies and policies targeting non-White communities to embracing inclusionary ideologies and practices. This process can be observed in Figure 3.1 which illustrates how key words and themes were used during specific moments in time influencing the transformation from exclusion to inclusion.

In Figure 3.1 the model holds the term nationalism at one end of this spectrum while illustrating the idea that movement toward post-nationalism shifts both philosophy and practice toward the full inclusion of non-White identified communities. The curved arrows connecting the terms across time represent critical incidents throughout history which influenced legal, political, and social behaviors. The primary terms, numbered two through five, also point to a strategic goal achieved during specific periods of time.

In Figure 3.1, exclusion of non-White identity is positioned between nationalism and equity. Exclusion refers to non-White groups who have historically not benefited from or had access to engage with the political, social, and economic systems and structures by intentional design. Exclusion of non-White identity was achieved, in part, through the creation of the institution of slavery, destruction of and war with first nation people, los Estados Unidos Méxicanos, and el Reino de España. These moments in U.S. history produced a legacy of genocide and annihilation committed against non-White communities. The effects of those irreversible violent acts, or trauma, have been passed from generation to generation as an inheritance of oppression and subordination. The practice of transferring trauma across generations via the oral traditions of marginalized communities in the form of hymns, poetry, and storytelling become sources of inspiration for many who yearn for a different reality.

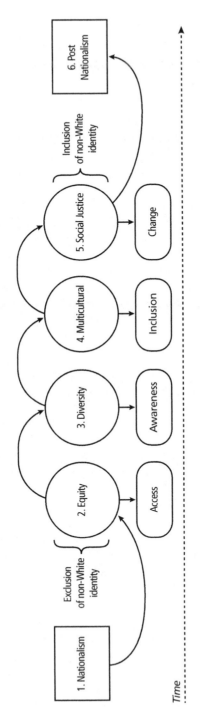

Figure 3.1 Transformation toward inclusion.

The beginning of progress toward a new reality of inclusion is illustrated in Figure 3.1 in the first arrow moving away from nationalism toward equity. This part of the model represents a shift from a foundation intentionally designed as an oppressive system targeting non-White communities toward post nationalism. After centuries of exclusion, non-White communities began to organize and fight for access to life, liberty, and freedom. Specific events throughout history serve as transformative moments ushering in equity as a new theme and access as its strategic goal.

EQUITY

One of the earliest uses of the word *equity* in the English language can be traced back to the writings of John Wycliffe's translation of *Malachi*, the 39th book of the Bible, "... to mean reasonableness between people, a quality of avoiding insisting on one's own rights or views too vigorously" (Unterhalter, 2009, p. 417). Based on this early use, equity referred to how people interact with and treat each other regardless of individual point of view or social differences. Within the context of the United States, the Merriam-Webster's Dictionary provided a modern definition, stating equity is "...justice according to natural law or right..." (Equity, n.d.). These definitions provide a foundation to explore both individual and collective responsibility related to promoting equity.

Although all humans may very well have been created equal, all people in the United States were not granted access to equal treatment in context of social, political, or economic resources. The chaos, hostility, and inhumanity manifested through the economic institution of slavery, the civil war, the women's suffrage movement and the civil rights movement, were historic events that led the United States to approach the word equity as both a goal and a process. As a result of these movements, equity called to question all traditions and environmental aspects of systems, including higher education, that have historically excluded marginalized communities.

Conflict breeds conflict. Equity and the pursuit of access was born from national conflict which resulted in the passing of desegregation laws, affirmative action policies, and title IX legislation. Harris (1995) stated, "affirmative action begins the essential work of rethinking rights, power, equity, race, and property from the perspective of those whose access to each of these has been limited by their oppression" (p. 288). Despite necessity, this shift to a mindset and practice of equity was disruptive and forced upon those in power, mostly White identified male individuals.

Court cases such as *Mendez et al. v. Westminster School District* (1946) and *Brown v. Board of Education* (1954), along with legislative acts such as *Title IX of the Education Amendments of 1972,* and executive orders promoting affirmative action and desegregation policies were necessary, nevertheless forced measures which yielded continuous resistance by disenfranchised members of the populace. As a result, the second arrow illustrated in Figure 3.1 shifts the model from equity toward diversity representing resistance and movements leading away from exclusion toward inclusion.

DIVERSITY

Diversity has been referred to as a replacement term for equity, which was associated with mandates, requirements, or regulations mostly focused on broadening political and social access, considered to be threatening to majority populations (Smith, 2009). To continue making progress toward postnationalism, framing needed to change. Ahmed (2012) explained "...the shift from [equity] to the language of diversity becomes linked to a shift from confrontational to a collaborative working model, to sharing rather than enforcing values" (p. 64). Historically, the term diversity is believed to have originated with Chaucer in 1386 and was used in comparisons of the laws in different countries. Wood (2003) highlighted how diversity was present in the United States throughout "...the early republic, the Civil War, emancipation, the great waves of immigration, and on up through the Civil Rights struggle..." (p. 8). A simple way to define the word diversity involves noticing, acknowledging, or being aware of difference.

Beyond definitions, research provides dimensions or perspectives to examine how the concept of diversity has evolved. Four perspectives on the impact of diversity within higher education are framed as structural diversity, interactional diversity, cocurricular diversity, and curricular diversity (Harper, 2008, p. 6). The first perspective is structural diversity, which refers to the frequency of representations of different social identities within a given population (e.g., racial or ethnic categories). Next, interactional diversity refers to experiences individuals have with others who possess different social identities. Cocurricular diversity, the third perspective, focuses on the opportunities and experiences taking place outside the classroom. Finally, curricular diversity involves the academic agendas, class content, and source of knowledge included in the curriculum by the faculty (Harper, 2008, p. 6). Taken together, these ways of operationalizing diversity within higher education are helpful in understanding the broader landscape of the term, and why so much ambiguity exists across the academy; often, individuals are not explicitly clear about which form(s) of diversity they are referencing when articulating missions, visions, and strategic plans.

The language of diversity represented a shift from forced equity toward more passive approaches to gaining awareness and knowledge related to appreciation for diversity, framed as a benefit to the majority of power structures. In the course of healing from the Great War, many institutions experienced significant social, political, and economic shifts throughout the 1950s. Colleges and universities were no exception to these influences, and continued to provide fertile grounds for diversity as a social phenomenon to plant roots. La Belle and Ward (1996) highlighted examples of structural diversity as they shared how, "...demographic changes propelled a dramatic transformation of higher education in the 1950s...[through efforts] such as bilingual schools and denominational colleges that used education to preserve subordinate-group culture and language" (pp. 9–10).

The 1950s in the United States were marked by social resistance, political protests, and college students unapologetically claiming pride in marginalized identities across the nation. The assassination of a president, a failed domestic war on poverty, failed military operations in Vietnam, the civil rights movement, and the gay rights movement all targeted discriminatory social structures and practices throughout the decade. Social tensions on college campuses mirrored that of the rest of the country.

An example of how these movements shaped, and continue to shape, higher education is described by Banks and McGee Banks (2010) who stated, "...the consequences of the civil rights movement had a significant influence on educational institutions as ethnic groups...demanded that schools and other educational institutions reform curricula to reflect their experiences, histories, cultures, and perspectives" (p. 6). Simply noticing the existence of Black and Brown community members while dismissing their traditions, customs, rituals, and civil liberties would no longer be tolerated.

Ultimately, the word diversity was seen as less threatening to White-identified individuals and predominately-White institutions since practices related to diversity were largely suggestive and did not require systems to change. Ahmed (2012) remarked, "...diversity becomes identified as more inclusive language because it does not have a necessary relation to changing organizational values" (p. 65), although that is exactly what needed to happen. As the population continued to grow in structural diversity, the awareness phase was no longer enough. Community needs led to a new approach focused on the inclusion of different cultures, giving rise to the multiculturalism movement.

Returning to Figure 3.1, the third arrow shifting from diversity toward multicultural represents a new message or invitation for all Americans to actively participate in the movement. New traditions are adopted and observed across the country such as Native American Heritage Month, the Dr. Martin Luther King national holiday, Hispanic Heritage Month, and Women's History Month all aimed at increasing awareness of the benefits gained from embracing the nation's rich diversity. In the movement toward inclusion, the next era to emerge is multiculturalism, which emphasizes inclusion as its strategic goal.

MULTICULTURALISM

Concepts related to multiculturalism are not new. Museums around the world house artifacts depicting the ancient Egyptian civilization as a multicultural society. The Egyptian empire conquered many governments of other civilizations, yet allowed cultures to retain aspects of their language, religion, and customs. Today, multiculturalism is defined as "the existence, recognition, or preservation of different cultures or cultural identities within a unified society" (Books, 1997, p. 861). Beyond access and awareness, multiculturalism is focused on creating space for the inclusion of communities whose cultures are different from the majority.

Hong and Benet-Martinez (2014) differentiated the concept of multiculturalism from equity and diversity by highlighting, "...multiculturalism also requires intercultural contact and equitable participation of all cultural elements in the life of the larger society" (p. 39). Multiculturalism can be understood as both an internal cognitive process and an external phenomenon in practice. Similar to diversity, multiculturalism involves recognizing the values, beliefs, or convictions held by individuals that also allow those from other cultures to be seen and treated as equal. Unlike diversity, the externalized aspect of multiculturalism is related to behavioral practice; demonstrated in the ways people engage in experiences and create spaces to bring adherents of various cultures together for mutual learning and sharing.

Multiculturalism goes beyond simply noticing the existence of different cultures some may otherwise choose to keep at arm's length. Gollnick and Chinn (2013) stated, "...multiculturalism allows different cultural groups to maintain their unique cultural identity while participating equally in dominant culture" (p. 12). This approach requires individuals to be fully involved in supporting different cultures' preservation of their traditions, customs, rituals, and language throughout community and acknowledge these cultural identities as inalienable human rights.

Although this level of commitment has not been reached systemically, reflecting on how multiculturalism has evolved within higher education over time provides some hope of a brighter future. Student unrest across the nation placed colleges and universities on notice that curricula and space would need to reflect the multiple identities within the communities these institutions were charged to serve. In response, some institutions in the 1970s set goals designed "...to reorganize education for the benefit of minority students" (Gordon & Newfield, 1996, p. 77).

Moving into the 1980s, many institutions of higher education began establishing offices to enforce affirmative action policies, address discrimination issues, provide equal opportunity initiatives, and expand the diversity of their faculty, staff, and administrators. In many instances, directors of these offices reported directly to the college president or provost as positional power was needed to challenge the White, heterosexual, and male dominated academic environment. These changes were not limited to the administrative and academic side of the university. Professor Laura I. Rendón (1994) recognized that beyond access and awareness, the culture of colleges and universities in the United States had to change to meet the needs of the ever changing diverse campus communities. An example of this transition came about as a response to student protests across the country. Many institutions were simultaneously creating minority affairs offices under the dean of students or division of student affairs leadership.

La Belle and Ward (1996) spoke to the charge of these offices as they were focused on efforts outside the classroom environment by situating "...multiculturalism as a cover term for developments, movements, and points of view related to growing diversity, to an assumption that students will be employed in increasingly diverse environments, and to critiques of societal and educational power relations" (p. 51). Throughout the 1980s, minority affairs offices created cultural enrichment programs, developed academic support services, and established physical safe spaces for African American college students at historically White colleges and universities. Programs and services housed within minority student serving offices become a model for student affairs practice in providing support for students from underrepresented racial and ethnic groups.

Delgado and Sefancic (2012) shared the idea "...social institutions should reflect many cultures" (p. 168). Throughout the 1990's, universities begin to reflect more cultural diversity as student enrollment of those from marginalized populations such as Latinx, Asian, First Nation people, women, gay, and lesbian identified students increased. These various identities created the multicultural student body that continues to shape and redefine policies, pedagogies, and practices in higher education. One such redefined practice in academic affairs included the adoption of multicultural course requirements into the undergraduate curriculum throughout the country. In student affairs, services were redefined from minority to multicultural offices and were given new expectations to support other marginalized student populations.

These administrative decisions seem appropriate when institutions intend to "...allow different cultural groups to maintain their unique cultural identity while participating equally in the dominant culture" (Gollnick & Chinn, 2013, p. 12). Developing professional support services for underrepresented student populations became increasingly challenging as White administrators often did not understand that simply being a person of color does not qualify or equip professionals with the awareness, knowledge, and skills essential to supporting members of their own identity group, let alone create and hold space for multicultural communities.

As we move into the 2000s, the United States experienced historic moments such as the election of President Barack Obama and the appointment of Justice Sonia Sotomayor to the supreme court. These events influenced some college administrators to believe there no longer exist a need for ethnic or multicultural centers on their campuses. Such color-blind racial attitudes (Bonilla-Silva, 2017) are quite damaging to society in general, and higher education more specifically. Similar climate shifts in social and political communities began developing in response to the inclusion of multicultural identities in the highest levels of government.

The fourth arrow in Figure 3.1 illustrates a shift from multicultural toward social justice which represents an awakening that leads to a sense of urgency aimed at addressing systemic oppression focused on eliminating root causes of injustice and exclusion. As a result, the needs of underrepresented communities began to shift from greater inclusion to something more permanent, systemic change. The next concept introduced in this discussion is social justice and holds as its strategic goal—change.

SOCIAL JUSTICE

The purpose of social justice, as described by Jean-Marie, Normore, and Brooks (2009), is seeking "...to transform inequitable, undemocratic, or oppressive institutions and social relations" (p. 11) grounded in the ideals of fairness and respect for basic human rights (North, 2006; Sensoy & DiAngelo, 2012). The earliest use of this phrase dates back to the mid-1800s. Influenced by Catholicism, the term was first introduced by an Italian scholar and priest, Luigi Taparelli d'Azeglio (Behr, 2003). His early use of the term social justice was grounded in the idea of moral and spiritual responsibilities members of the church had to end poverty. Almost two hundred years later the ideals related to social justice is significantly broader, however the effort continues to invoke the responsibility individuals and groups have to take positive action toward creating change for the betterment of all.

Theoharis (2007) expanded the context of social justice from individual behavior or action to focusing on "...disrupting and subverting arrangements that promote marginalization and exclusionary processes" (p. 222) on systemic, organizational, or structural levels. This approach involves focusing efforts on identifying and addressing root causes of injustice within social systems and working toward "...eradicating all forms of oppression and differential treatment extant in the practices and policies of institutions..." (Hytten & Bettez, 2011, p. 8).

The approach used in pursuing the systemic level of change required to transform institutions toward a more social justice frame resemble the forced approach mentioned in the discussion related to equity. A positive difference in pursuing social justice is that efforts are built from a stronger foundation informed by access secured via equity, awareness gained through diversity and relationships established as a result of inclusion. The relationship between these transformative words has prepared communities to own and act on the shared responsibility described by Theoharis (2007) related to changing the political, social, and economic system "by actively engaging in reclaiming, appropriating, sustaining, and advancing inherent human rights...in social economic, educational, and personal dimensions" (p. 223). Recent examples of social justice efforts aimed at inclusion of marginalized identities include the *Affordable Care Act* (2010) expanding access to health care; the landmark U.S. Supreme Court decision in *Obergefell v. Hodges* (2015) which legalized same-sex marriages; and impacting higher education, the *Deferred Action for Childhood Arrivals* (DACA; 2012) executive order targeting undocumented youth.

The work of social justice is complex. To do this work well, individuals must be willing to deeply reflect on themselves and identify ways in which they consciously and unconsciously benefit from and perpetuate oppression. For leaders interested in acquiring social justice knowledge and skills, it is important to intentionally prepare for this work. Therefore, a need exists to educate scholars and practitioners to fully engage in disrupting and dismantling policies and practices created to further marginalize underrepresented communities. On the topic of preparation, Jean-Marie et al. (2009) suggested engaging in intentional programming designed to "...teach, model, and cultivate the necessary behaviors, attitudes, and knowledge to help shape the social justice value stances and skills of practicing and future administrators" (p. 11). Leading this work are a growing number of leadership educators who have committed to incorporating social justice into their scholarship and practice.

SOCIAL JUSTICE LEADERSHIP EDUCATION

The goal of social justice leadership education is centered on the need to formalize the learning process arming participants with the knowledge, awareness, and skills necessary to fully engage in socially just leadership practices. This role and responsibility is described further by Evans (2007) who stated, "...the scholarship of social justice supports the notion that educational leaders have a social and moral obligation to foster equitable practices, processes, and outcomes" (p. 250).

Social justice leadership education can be conceptualized as an educational reform movement to produce leaders with the ability to transform oppressive systems and organizations. As a social justice leadership educator I have engaged in formalizing both cocurricular and curricular learning opportunities for college students, administrators, and faculty over the past 15 years. Through various training sessions, workshop series, and academic courses my goal has been to further develop participants who engage in socially just leadership practices.

One example of a formal curricular program designed for first-year undergraduate college students is our social justice living learning community. This residential program engages 30 students who live together and are required to enroll in a shared three credit academic course per semester focused on leadership and social justice. As one of the instructors for this program, I begin with providing a theoretical foundation for students to engage critically with concepts related to identity development, social justice activism, and leadership education. Next, students examine forms of oppression from a historical, political, social, and economic context. Throughout the semester, students engage with various self-reflection prompts aimed at exploring the complexity and intersection of their identity. Finally, a critical component of the course is to develop and practice skills aimed at disrupting dominant ideology.

A second example of a formal cocurricular program designed for staff, administrators, and faculty at Florida State University is our diversity and inclusion certificate program. This professional development series creates an opportunity for staff, administrators, and faculty to explore strategic areas related to leadership and social justice. Successful completion of the certificate requires completion of three core sessions, three elective sessions, and one theory to action project within an 18 month time frame.

The diversity and inclusion certificate program is in its fifth year and currently has approximately 200 participants. As the director for the certificate program, my overall goal is to engage staff, administrators, and faculty in developing socially just leadership practices. Similar to my approach with students, the certificate is designed to provide multiple theoretical foundations for participants to explore how diversity and social justice show up in their leadership, research practices, and service to the campus community. Discussions are framed from a broad historical, political, social, and economic context and gradually transition to exploring connections to specific colleges, departments, and roles on campus. Throughout the program, various assessment tools are used to gauge how participants rate their understanding of curriculum. Lastly, the theory to action project allows participants to practice using the awareness, knowledge, and skills gained throughout the curriculum.

In both the curricular and cocurricular examples discussed, social justice leadership education intentionally positions "issues of race, class, gender, disability, sexual orientation, and other historically and currently marginalizing conditions in the United States central to [one's] advocacy, leadership practice, and vision" (Theoharis, 2007, p. 223). My vision for participants in both programs is to emerge from these formal social justice leadership education initiatives well prepared to move beyond *just* words, fully engaged in socially just leadership practices that embrace inclusion of all identities. As this chapter discussed, understanding the difference in concepts such as equity, diversity, multicultural, and social justice and the role social justice leadership education has in this movement toward inclusion is critical.

REFERENCES

Ahmed, S. (2012). *On being included racism and diversity in institutional life.* Durham, NC: Duke University Press.

Appiah, K. A., Taylor, C., Habermas, J., Rockefeller, S. C., Walzer, M., & Wolf, S. (1994). *Multiculturalism.* Princeton, NJ: Princeton University Press.

Banks, J. A., & McGee Banks, C. A. (Eds.). (2010). *Multicultural education: issues and perspectives* (7th ed.). Hoboken, NJ: Wiley.

Behr, T. C. (2003). Luigi taparelli d'azeglio, S. J. (1793–1862) and the development of scholastic natural-law thought as a science of society and politics. *Journal of Markets and Morality, 6*(1), 99–115.

Bonilla-Silva, E. (2017). *Racism without racists: Color-blind racism and the persistence of racial inequality in America.* Lanham, MD: Rowman & Littlefield.

Books, G. (1997). *Webster's universal college dictionary.* Random House Value Pub.

Brown v. Board of Education, 347 U.S. 483 (1954).

Delgado, R., & Stefancic, J. (2012). *Critical race theory: An introduction.* (2nd ed.). New York, NY: New York University Press.

Equity. (n.d.). In Merriam-Webster's online dictionary (11th ed.). Retrieved from https://www.merriam-webster.com/dictionary/equity

Evans, A. E. (2007). Horton, Highlander, and leadership education: Lessons for preparing educational leaders for social justice. *Journal of School Leadership, 17*(3), 250.

Gollnick, D. M., & Chinn, P. C. (2013). *Multicultural education in a pluralistic society* (9th ed.). Boston, MA: Pearson.

Gordon, A. F., & Newfield, C. (1996). *Mapping multiculturalism.* Minneapolis, MN: University of Minnesota Press.

Harper, S. R. (Ed.). (2008). *Creating inclusive campus environments for cross-cultural learning and student engagement.* Washington, DC: NASPA.

Harris, C. (1995). Whiteness as property. In K. Crenshaw, N. Gotanda, G. Peller, & K. Thomas (Eds.), *Critical race theory: The key writings that formed the movement* (pp. 276–291). New York, NY: The New Press.

Hong, Y., & Benet-Martinez, V. (2014). *The oxford handbook of multicultural identity.* Oxford, England: Oxford University Press.

Hytten, K., & Bettez, S. C. (2011). Understanding education for social justice. *Educational Foundations, 25*(1), 7–24.

Jean-Marie, G., Normore, A. H., & Brooks, J. S. (2009). Leadership for social justice: Preparing 21st century school leaders for a new social order. *Journal of Research on Leadership Education, 4*(1), 1–31.

Kunnan, A. J. (2009). Politics and legislation in citizenship testing in the United States. *Annual Review of Applied Linguistics 29,* 37–48. doi:10.1017/S02671905 09090047

La Belle, T. J., & Ward, C. R. (1996). *Ethnic studies and multiculturalism.* Albany: State University of New York Press.

Mendez v. Westminster School District, et al., 64 F. Supp. 544 (S.D. Cal. 1946).

Napolitano, J. (2012). *Exercising prosecutorial discretion with respect to individuals who came to the United States as children.* Memorandum, June, 15.

North, C. E. (2006). More than words? Delving into the substantive meaning(s) of "social justice" in education. *Review of Educational Research, 76*(4), 507–535.

Obergefell v. Hodges, 135 S. Ct. 2584, 2589 (2015)

Protection, P., & Act, A. C. (2010). Public Law 111-148. Title IV, x4207, USC HR, 3590, 2010.

Rendón, L. I. (1994). Validating culturally diverse students: Toward a new model of learning and student development. *Innovative Higher Education, 19*(1), 33–51.

Sensoy, O., & DiAngelo, R. (2012). *Is everyone really equal? An introduction to key concepts in social justice education.* New York, NY: Teachers College Press.

Smith, D. G. (2009). *Diversity's promise for higher education: Making it work.* Baltimore, MD: Johns Hopkins University Press.

Theoharis, G. (2007). Social justice educational leaders and resistance: Toward a theory of social justice. *Educational Administration Quarterly, 43*(2), 221–258.

Unterhalter, E. (2009). What is equity in education? Reflections from the capability approach. *Studies in Philosophy and Education, 28*(5), 415–424.

Wood, P. (2003). *Diversity: The invention of a concept.* San Francisco, CA: Encounter Books.

CHAPTER 4

INTERSECTING ACTIVISM AND SOCIAL JUSTICE IN LEADERSHIP EDUCATION

Marshall Anthony Jr.

Historically, activism has served as a tool to address a myriad of economic, political, and social issues such as civil and human rights, hunger, poverty, and world peace. Bell (2010) described social justice as a process and a goal to ensure (a) full and equal participation of all members in society, (b) the physical and psychological safety of all members, and (c) the equitable distribution of resources. Scholars, like Brennan and Naidoo (2008) have discussed higher education's role in advancing a social justice agenda, but the academic preparation of leadership for these changes is notably absent from their work. In the context of U.S. leadership education, Guthrie, Bertrand Jones, and Osteen's (2017) culturally relevant leadership learning (CRLL) model is foundational; calling for CRLL environments. The purpose of this chapter is to explore the intersection of activism and social justice in order to provide educators with the tools to (a) develop CRLL environments, and (b) dismantle the culture of Eurocentrism in U.S. leadership education. Together, the strategies discussed can serve as tools to

Changing the Narrative, pages 41–56
Copyright © 2018 by Information Age Publishing
41

dismantle Eurocentrism in leadership education and replace it with an intersecting representation of activism and social justice.

CULTURALLY RELEVANT LEADERSHIP LEARNING: THE FOUNDATION

A fundamental component of globalization, Quijano (2000) defined Eurocentrism as "the social classification of the world's population around the idea of race, a mental construction that expresses the basic experience of colonial domination and pervades the more important dimensions of global power, including its specific rationality" (p. 533). Sayyid (2015) framed Eurocentrism as the result of discourse emerging between disarticulating and rearticulating the relationship between Western culture and universalism (i.e., domination). Furthermore, Sayyid posited Eurocentric logic is sustained by Western culture being accepted as the center (i.e., the universal example), and is dismantled when the West is not acknowledged as a universal truth. Adopting Guthrie et al.'s (2017) CRLL house as the foundation in exploring the intersection of activism and social justice, this chapter attempts to dismantle Eurocentric ideology as a way of knowing in U.S. leadership education.

Guthrie et al. (2017) described the CRLL house (Figure 4.1) as having three main components: (a) windows, (b) the door, and (c) the foundation.

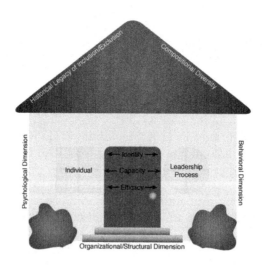

Figure 4.1 Culturally relevant leadrship learning house. Reprinted with permission from Guthrie et al., 2017.

Windows and Door

The windows represent an individual's *intrapersonal* experiences in the leadership process. Intrapersonal experiences are ongoing interactions of an individual's identity, capacity, and efficacy in the leadership process—encompassed within the door of the house. Identity describes an individual's self-portrait, most commonly addressed by the question: *Who am I?* An individual's identity determines their leadership identity, "A building block that creates meaning and organizes new leadership knowledge" (Bertrand Jones, Guthrie, & Osteen, 2016, p. 13). Capacity relates to an individual's knowledge, attitudes, and skills. Leadership capacity integrates an individual's knowledge, attitudes, and skills "reflecting their overall ability to behave effectively in the leadership process" (Bertrand Jones et al., 2016, p. 14). Generally, efficacy refers to an individual's belief of successfully performing and/or completing an activity (Bandura, 1997). Leadership efficacy describes an individual's belief in successfully navigating the leadership process (Bertrand Jones et al., 2016). In order for the intersection of activism and social justice to be leveraged toward dismantling Eurocentrism, leadership educators must be cognizant about themselves and effectively assist students' through their identity, capacity, and efficacy development.

Foundation

The windows and door of the CRLL house describe the intrapersonal experiences of an individual in the leadership process (Guthrie et al., 2017). Alongside the intrapersonal experiences, an individual simultaneously navigates through an *interpersonal* journey. The foundation of the CRLL house characterizes an individual's interpersonal experiences with (a) the historical legacy of inclusion and exclusion, (b) compositional diversity, (c) the psychological dimension, (d) the behavioral dimension, and (e) the organizational/structural dimension (Guthrie et al., 2017). Each component establishes the foundation of intersecting activism and social justice in U.S. leadership education.

Historical Legacy of Inclusion and Exclusion
In leadership education, understanding the historical role of Eurocentrism within our institutions is essential. Eurocentric leadership theories, pedagogies, and practices, served and promoted those in power (i.e., dominant groups) and disenfranchised traditionally marginalized groups. Left unchallenged, these dangerous social dynamics continue to shape the modern leadership education landscape. These imbalances of power have minimized the experiences of members of marginalized groups from existing

literature and in leadership education, including curriculum development (Bertrand Jones et al., 2016). According to Bertrand Jones et al. (2016), "It is simply not enough to acknowledge that these patterns of exclusion and inclusion exist(ed); leadership educators must then develop intentional ways to respond to such history" (Bertrand Jones et al., 2016, pp. 16–17). Effective responses cannot be formulated in the absence of understanding the path that has led us to where we are now.

Compositional Diversity

Eurocentrism has also contributed to the disproportionate admission, enrollment, persistence, retention, and graduation trends of members of historically marginalized populations in U.S. postsecondary education, especially at predominantly White institutions (Tinto, 1993). However, compositional diversity is more than just the numbers of people from marginalized groups on college campus and in leadership settings. While one aspect of compositional diversity relates to enrollment increases of those from marginalized populations, it also calls for the *intentional* appreciation, respect, and incorporation of various perspectives in leadership learning environments (Bertrand Jones et al., 2016). In this way, considerations related to the compositional diversity of our institutions, our programs, and our classrooms depend on both the *numerical* representations of students from diverse backgrounds, and the *quality* of the experiences they have on our campuses.

Psychological and Behavioral Dimensions

The psychological and behavioral dimensions of the CRLL house have both intrapersonal *and* interpersonal characteristics (Guthrie et al., 2017). An individual's leadership identity, capacity, and efficacy are shaped by psychological characteristics, such as cognitive ability, motivation, and potential for personal growth, as well as particular leadership behaviors and behavioral patterns. However, individuals must also navigate their psychological and behavioral experiences by interacting with others in the leadership process (i.e., students' actions). According to Bertrand Jones et al. (2016), the psychological dimension ". . . emphasizes individual views of group relations, perceptions of discrimination or conflict, attitudes about difference, and institutional responses to diversity" (p. 17). When students from marginalized backgrounds share their perceptions in a learning environment, more privileged students validate or invalidate marginalized students' perspectives (Bertrand Jones et al., 2016). Moreover, the behavioral dimension ". . . focuses on the interactions between all students and the quality of interaction within culturally diverse groups" (Bertrand Jones et al., 2016, p. 18). Intentionally or unintentionally, White or otherwise privileged educators and students might reinforce Eurocentric ideology and reasoning in U.S. leadership learning environments. Therefore, socially just leadership educators actively dismantle Eurocentrism by (a) being aware of student dynamics and (b) promoting psychologically and behaviorally safe environments, especially for marginalized students.

Organizational and Structural Dimension

The organizational and structural dimension of CRLL centers leadership learning in the daily operations of an institution (Milem, Dey, & White, 2004). Policies are an essential component of the organizational/structural dimension, in terms of whether or not they are equitable. For example, securing a location for student groups to protest can be an easy process or one defined by complex rules and regulations. Does a diverse representation of teaching and research assistants exist in your program? Are marginalized students represented on institutional committees such as an honors (conduct) council or a tuition board? The answers to these questions, as perceived by students from diverse backgrounds, are strong indicators of the socially just policy environment in which leadership education occurs. Another example of how to leverage the organizational and structural dimension in leadership learning, Bertrand Jones et al. (2016) posited, "Educators can scrutinize the course reading lists for diverse authors that represent the breadth of thinking about leadership in a variety of social contexts" (p. 19). While the organizational and structural dimension should apply across institutional settings, its representation will be unique to each institution.

Guthrie et al.'s (2017) CRLL house provides a social justice lens to dismantle Eurocentrism in U.S. leadership education. The house grounds this chapter's discussion on four proposed approaches for intersecting activism and social justice in leadership education: (a) activism appreciation, (b) activism heterogeneity, (c) activism psychology, and (d) activism behavior. In the following sections, I will provide a definition of each approach; describe each approach's intersection with culturally relevant leadership learning; and, connect the role of each approach to constructing non-Eurocentric, socially just leadership learning environments.

ACTIVISM APPRECIATION

Activism has a long, and often complex, tradition in the history of American higher education. Activism is inevitable and has changed the face of both U.S. postsecondary education and greater society. At the intersection between activism and social justice resides an authentic appreciation of productive conflict and its role in advancing society.

Some argue activism has always been a part of the fabric of college campuses, especially at U.S. postsecondary institutions. In 1638, Harvard (America's first institution of higher education) students expressed their dissatisfaction with disciplinary procedures (Ellsworth & Burns, 1970). Moreover, in 1766, Harvard students participated in the infamous Butter Rebellion food fight as a result of bad butter served in the common areas (Ellsworth & Burns, 1970). In 1807, at Princeton, the Presbyterian faculty and trustee members suspended students for violent protest on the basis of "Deism, irreligion, and false notions of liberty" (Ellsworth & Burns, 1970, p. 9). The rise of Greek-letter fraternities and student literary publications (e.g., *Yale Literary Magazine*), from the mid- to late 19th century, saw a rise in student protests calling for collegiate reformation (Ellsworth & Burns, 1970). This history of activism resonated well into the 20th and 21st centuries, too.

In the 1960s, at the University of California, Berkeley, Mario Savio and the free speech movement made international headlines and ignited conversations about students' rights to use campus spaces for political activity and debate (Freeman, 2004). On February 1, 1960, at North Carolina Agricultural and Technical State University, four Black first-year students—Joseph McNeil, Franklin McCain, Ezell Blair Jr., and David Richmond—sat at the Whites-only Woolworth's lunch counter, in Greensboro, NC, igniting similar sit-in movements across the country. In 2014, Emma Sulkowicz, a student at Columbia University, carried the mattress she reported being raped on around campus in response to the university's lack of action regarding the incident; other students soon joined and also carried mattresses in support (Izadi, 2015). In December 2014, University of Texas at Austin students, along with students around the country, held die-ins to protest the killings of countless Black women and men, including transgendered persons, by law enforcement agents ("UT students hold 'die in' to protest Eric Garner's death," 2014).

Activism Appreciation and Culturally Relevant Leadership Learning

Activism appreciation exudes the qualities described in the historical legacy of inclusion and exclusion dimension in Guthrie et al.'s (2017) CRLL house. The historical legacy of inclusion/exclusion calls for (a) an acknowledgement of systemic patterns of injustice and (b) leadership educators to respond to these patterns, intentionally (Bertrand et al., 2016). Around the world, but especially in the United States, systemic Eurocentric oppression continues to serve and promote dominant groups and disenfranchise marginalized populations. Ellsworth and Burns (1970) noted, "A clearer perception of historical events in the activist movement is necessary for an understanding of present and future student activism" (p. 17). Activism appreciation (a) acknowledges Eurocentrism has historically benefited some groups while oppressing others and (b) recognizes students from *all* social identities have participated in activist efforts as a result of their voices being actively or passively invalidated.

Socially Just Leadership Education Appreciates Activism

The inescapable nature of Eurocentrism should motivate leadership educators to design intentional learning environments to acknowledge these injustices and support activism as a *valid* form of response. Ellsworth and Burns (1970) asserted, "To ignore student unrest in American history is to deny a fact in the development of higher education" (p. 5). Before helping students understand the importance of activism, socially just leadership educators investigate instances of student activism themselves. When leadership educators struggle to find the value in student activism, critical self-reflections on the dynamics of power, privilege, and oppression may be necessary. Activism often emerges from members of marginalized groups not being heard or validated by those in power. Whether they agree or disagree with the cause at hand, socially just leadership educators emphasize students' voices. Once leadership educators value activism, they can begin incorporating the role of activism in transforming college campuses and the world into their practice of leadership education. According to Ellsworth and Burns (1970), "Respecting the fact that unrest is not a new phenomenon but an insistent restatement of the need for both societal and institutional reform, the academic community can then address itself to the causes of activism and its place in the education framework" (p. 17). Therefore, in order to use activism as a resource for enacting social justice, leadership educators place value on its historical contributions to society and make those contributions clear and relevant to their students.

ACTIVISM HETEROGENEITY

The root word of activism comes from the verb "to act." General agreement exists that in order to perform activism, one must indeed act or move in some way. However, acting means different things to different people. For example, while one may perceive culturally relevant academic or policy work as activism, another may believe rallying is the only form of activism. To combat dissension of what may constitute as activism, socially just leadership educators value the heterogeneity of ways one might act, or not act; such as in the case of boycotts as activism.

Reconsidering Oxford Living Dictionary's definition of activism as, "the policy or action of using vigorous campaigning to bring about political or social change" (activism, n.d.), Strange and Banning (2001) further elucidated the heterogeneity of involvement by stating, "[i]nvolvement is most clearly manifested in actions such as joining, participating, attaching, committing, engaging, immersing, and volunteering" (p. 139). Together, Oxford Living Dictionaries' definition of activism and Strange and Banning's operationalization of involvement provides credence for *activism as a form of involvement*. Astin (1984) noted involvement as an integral part of student development linked to positive qualitative and quantitative student outcomes (e.g., healthy physical and psychological energy, commitment to curricular and cocurricular activities, etc.). To dismantle Eurocentrism, activism, in its many forms, must be valued. To that end, the following example is provided.

Minnesota Campus Compact's (1996) Social Change Wheel

While the Minnesota Campus Compact's (MCC: 1996) Social Change Wheel (Figure 4.2) is a little over 20 years old, it is the most useful resource in understanding some of the many forms of activism. MCC's (1996) Social Change Wheel highlighted six ways to enact social justice:

1. *Charitable volunteerism:* Involvement aimed to serve immediate needs, but not the root causes of those needs (e.g., feeding homeless individuals; fundraising for research efforts to find a cure for a disease; mentoring and tutorial services for youth);
2. *Community/economic development:* Involvement aimed to boost the economic and human capital in a community (e.g., placing career development programs in communities with high unemployment rates like the Job Corps Centers);
3. *Voting/formal political activities:* Involvement aimed to educate communities about political candidates and public policies and to encourage participation in the political process (e.g., arranging for political candidates to discuss their platforms; hosting town hall meetings with elected officials to speak about the legislative process; planning voter registration drives);
4. *Confrontational strategies:* Involvement aimed to confront those in power and encourage public disobedience to formulate or change a controversial issue or policy (e.g., coordinating local, state, and national marches like the Women's March on Washington; using social media to mobilize public dissatisfaction like Occupy Wall Street; Gismondi & Osteen, 2017);
5. *Grassroots political activity/public policy work:* Involvement aimed to mobilize individuals (from the ground-up) around a common issue in order to change policy (e.g., employing a viral short, catchy, yet impactful social media hashtag like #BlackLivesMatter to raise

Figure 4.2 Social change wheel. *Source:* Adapted from Minnesota Campus Compact, 2016.

> awareness about police brutality on Black and Brown bodies; Gismondi & Osteen, 2017);
6. *Community building:* Involvement aimed to foster trusting relationships among multiple parties and stakeholders (e.g., encouraging community members and local small business owners to express their concern to elected officials about gentrification efforts).

Although the essence of activism should not be restricted to six components, leadership educators can use MCC's (1996) Social Change Wheel as a guide to understand some of the most commonly used forms of activism.

Activism Heterogeneity and Culturally Relevant Leadership Learning

Activism heterogeneity is exhibited in the compositional diversity component of Guthrie et al.'s (2017) CRLL house. Compositional diversity relates to the physical makeup of marginalized populations as well as the intentional appreciation, respect, and incorporation of various perspectives in leadership learning (Bertrand Jones et al., 2016). Institutions of higher education are microcosms of the larger society; as society grows increasingly diverse (and away from Eurocentric ideology), those institutions will do so as well. Moreover, as the student body grows more diverse, institutions will experience a rise in a heterogeneity of perspectives—potentially conflicting with Eurocentric thought. Students' expression of their views will continue to vary, especially when combating injustice and Eurocentrism. Institutions must be prepared to understand the various faces of activism. Socially just leadership educators inform students how and why a one-size-fits-all approach to creating social change does not exist.

Socially Just Leadership Education Affirms Activism Heterogeneity

Astin (1984) posited, "The greater the student's involvement in college, the greater will be the amount of student learning and personal development" (p. 528). Leadership educators serve as facilitators of students' learning and personal development. Therefore, socially just leadership educators teach students a plethora of ways to enact egalitarian change in society. For example, leadership educators can create workshops or curricula on each of the six components of social change (MCC, 1996). In these sessions, leadership educators can provide examples of activism throughout history (i.e., activism appreciation) and have students match the type of social change involvement activity to the historical scenario. Leadership educators can discuss the strengths and weaknesses of each social change involvement activity and challenge students to reflect on additional ways to enact social justice in their local and greater communities. Participation in activist efforts aids in students' learning and personal development. For leadership educators, understanding the heterogeneity of activism allows students to see that everyone has a place in activism and anyone can play a role.

ACTIVISM PSYCHOLOGY

Posited by Rosch and Anthony (2012) as one of the most frequently used leadership theories, the Higher Education Research Institute's (Higher Education Research Institute, 1996) social change model of leadership development can help leadership educators understand the interaction of three key values to enact social change: (a) individual, (b) group, and (c) community/societal. Individual values, specifically, emphasize the importance of developing personal qualities and self-awareness through the sub-values of consciousness of self, congruence, and commitment (Higher Education Research Institute, 1996). While Higher Education Research Institute (1996) highlighted some general traits of valuing social change at the individual level, the psychology of activism is a much more complex process. In fact, according to Ellsworth and Burns (1970), "after inspecting the state of student activism . . . internal and external factors affecting a student activist can be schematically drawn" (p. 19). The following subsection examines the schematic internal and external psychological factors of student activists.

Activism Psychology and Culturally Relevant Leadership Learning

Activism psychology relates to the psychological and organizational/structural dimensions of the CRLL house (Guthrie et al., 2017). The psychological dimension emphasizes an individual's *cognitive* process about their external environment (Bertrand et al., 2016). Moreover, the organizational/structural dimension describes an institution's (i.e., external environment) daily operations and processes (Bertrand et al., 2016). Activism psychology can describe an individual's *internal* feelings about their *external* environment. Ellsworth and Burns (1970) Factors Affecting Student Activism diagram (Figure 4.3) is helpful for leadership educators to understand an individual's psychological process of enacting social justice in the external environment.

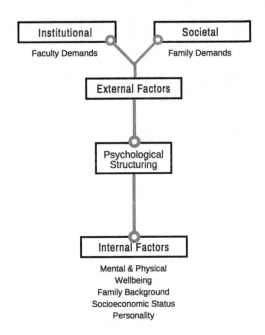

Figure 4.3   Factors affecting student activism diagram.

According to the diagram, both institutional *and* societal factors influence the greater external environment. For example, faculty demands (i.e., an institutional factor) coupled with family demands of a faculty or staff member and/or the student (i.e., a societal factor) influence the overall external environment. While students are psychologically structuring their external environment, they are also processing a range of internal factors (e.g., their mental and physical well-being, family background, socioeconomic status, personality, etc.). In understanding and diffusing knowledge about the intersection of activism and social justice, leadership educators understand the complexity of interactions students' internally and externally experience in a predominantly Eurocentric environment.

Socially Just Leadership Education Validates Activism Psychology

Ellsworth and Burns (1970) Factors Affecting Student Activism diagram is a great resource for leadership educators to understand activism psychology. *Leader* development is vital for the student (internally) and *leadership* development is crucial for the institution and society (externally). The diagram highlights the dynamic interaction between an individual's psychological structuring with their external environment. While students are processing complex interactions between their internal and external environment, socially just leadership educators are experiencing this process, too. Therefore, justice-focused leadership educators are aware of the interplay between their internal and external environments, and recognize how their actions (resulting from their own psychological structuring) might show up for students in leadership learning spaces. The commonality of psychological structuring presents an opportunity for both leadership educators and students to understand and enact social justice. From this understanding, socially just leadership educators use privileges they hold to empathize with and validate marginalized students in an otherwise Eurocentric culture. Moreover, these leadership educators design activities allowing students to identify prominent and subtle internal and external influences. Students can then reflect on how these influences might directly and indirectly appear in their quest toward social justice.

ACTIVISM BEHAVIOR

The behavioral dimension of the CRLL house helps characterize activism behavior (Guthrie et al., 2017). According to Bertrand Jones et al. (2016), the behavioral dimension emphasizes the "interactions between all students and the quality of interaction within culturally diverse groups" (p. 18). Activism behavior closely relates to activism psychology. While activism psychology examines an individual's cognitive structuring of their external environment, activism behavior describes the *actions* an individual decides to take (or not take) based on their psychological processing. Moreover, activism behavior describes the *quality* of activists' interactions with other groups (e.g., peers, faculty/staff, administrators, community members, etc.).

Activism Behavior and Culturally Relevant Leadership Learning

Lewin (1936) is credited with creating one of the most fundamental formulas to understand an environment's influence on human behavior: $B = f(P \times E)$, where behavior (B) is a function (f) of a person (P) interacting with their environment (E). Newcomb's (1962) Schematic Diagram of Student Peer Groups Influences (Figure 4.4) places Lewin's (1936) heuristic behavior formula in the context of education.

The diagram assumes the interaction between a student's characteristics and their institution's characteristics determines the overall student experience (Newcomb, 1962). The student's experience, in turn, influences changes in the student's final characteristics (with a possibility that change might not occur; Newcomb, 1962). Tinto (1993) affirmed this assumption in his interactionist model of student departure, indicating a student's background shapes their academic and social integration (i.e., interaction)

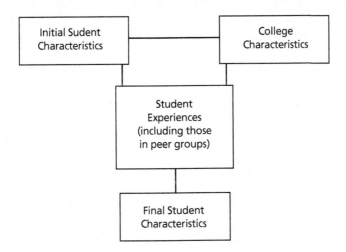

Figure 4.4 Student peer group influences. *Source:* Adapted from Newcomb, 1962.

within their college environment, which produces positive or negative effects on the student's outcomes (e.g., persistence or departure).

Socially Just Leadership Education Understands Activism Behavior

While students are cognitively processing their environment, leadership educators understand students are actively engaging, disengaging, or not engaging with their environment, as well. According to Newcomb (1962), one can understand the consequences of an event when one examines the factors causing the event. Socially just leadership educators understand how activism psychology translates to students' choices of enacting (or not enacting) social justice. Moreover, leadership educators understand the dynamics of interactions between each student and their environment might cause students to respond to their environment in different ways. For example, an oppressive, Eurocentric culture might motivate one marginalized student to enact social justice, while demotivating another marginalized student to disengage (or never engage at all). Socially just leadership educators design exercises for students to draw connections between their feelings (i.e., activism psychology) of social justice to their actions (i.e., activism behavior).

BRINGING IT ALL TOGETHER: ACTIVISM AND SOCIAL JUSTICE IN LEADERSHIP EDUCATION

Socially just leadership educators are prepared to serve students from an array of backgrounds. More importantly, socially just leadership educators support the navigation of marginalized students through systemically oppressive, Eurocentric environments. Activism has deep, historical roots in advancing social justice on college campuses and in society. When we reject an affinity for activism and social justice, we reject progress. Socially just leadership educators serve on the right side of progress, acknowledging Eurocentrism advantages dominant groups and disenfranchises marginalized populations. These educators can use the components of activism appreciation, heterogeneity, psychology, and behavior to create and sustain culturally relevant leadership learning environments. Formal and informal culturally relevant leadership learning spaces ensure all students, especially marginalized students, are (a) full and equal participants, (b) physically and psychologically safe, and (c) provided with equitable resources to enact social justice. Leadership educators empathize with and validate the voices of marginalized students for all students to know they each serve a unique purpose in advancing social justice.

REFERENCES

Activism. (n.d.). In *English Oxford Living Dictionaries.* Retrieved from https://en.oxforddictionaries.com/definition/activism

Astin, A. W. (1984). Student involvement: A developmental theory for higher education. *Journal of College Student Personnel, 25*(4), 297–308.

Bandura, A. (1997). *Self-efficacy: The exercise of control.* New York, NY: Freeman.

Bell, L. A. (2010). Theoretical foundations. In M. Adams, W. J. Blumenfeld, C. Castañeda, H. W. Hackman, M. L. Peters, & X. Zúñiga (Eds.), *Readings for diversity and social justice: An anthology on racism, antisemitism, sexism, heterosexism, ableism, and classism* (2nd ed., pp. 21–26). New York, NY: Routledge.

Bertrand Jones, T., Guthrie, K. L., & Osteen, L. (2016). Critical domains of culturally relevant leadership learning: A call to transform leadership programs. In K. L. Guthrie, T. Bertrand Jones, & L. Osteen (Eds.), *New directions for student leadership, No. 152: Developing culturally relevant leadership learning* (pp. 9–21). San Francisco, CA: Jossey-Bass.

Brennan, J., & Naidoo, R. (2008). Higher education and the achievement (and/or prevention) of equity and social justice. *Higher Education, 56*(3), 287–302.

Ellsworth, F. L., & Burns, M. A. (1970). Student activism in American higher education. In W. D. Martinson, D. A. Ambler, D. M. Knoell, N. K. Schlossberg, G. R. Scott, M. R. Smith, . . . L. C. Stamatakos (Eds.), *Student Personal Series* (No. 10, pp. 5–64). Washington, DC: American College Personnel Association.

Freeman, J. (2004). The Berkeley free speech movement. In Immanuel Ness (Ed.), *Encyclopedia of American social movements* (pp. 1178–1182). Armonk, NY: M.E. Sharpe.

Gismondi, A., & Osteen, L. (2017). Student activism in the technology age. In J. Ahlquist & L. Endersby (Eds.), *New directions for student leadership, No. 153: Going digital in student leadership* (pp. 63–74). San Francisco, CA: Jossey-Bass.

Guthrie, K. L., Bertrand Jones, T., & Osteen, L. (2017). The teaching, learning, and being of leadership: Exploring context and practice of the culturally relevant leadership learning model. *Journal of Leadership Studies, 11*(3), 61–67.

Higher Education Research Institute. (1996). *A social change model of leadership development guidebook* (Version iii). Los Angeles: University of California, Los Angeles.

Izadi, E. (2015, May 20). Columbia student protesting campus rape carries mattress during graduation. *Washington Post.* Retrieved from https://www.washingtonpost.com/news/grade-point/wp/2015/05/19/columbia-student-protesting-campus-rape-carries-mattress-during-commencement/?utm_term=.34ef099147ca

Lewin, R. (1936). *Principles of topological psychology.* New York, NY: McGraw-Hill.

Milem, J. F., & Dey, E. L., & White, C. B. (2004). Diversity considerations in health professions education. In B. D. Smedley, A. S. Butler, & L. R. Bristow (Eds.), *In the nation's compelling interest: Ensuring diversity in the health care workforce* (pp. 345–390). Washington, DC: National Academies Press.

Minnesota Campus Compact. (1996). *Social change wheel.* Retrieved from http://mncampuscompact.org/what-we-do/publications/social-change-wheel/

Newcomb, T. (1962). Student peer-group influence. In N. Sanford (Ed.), *The American college: A psychological and social interpretation of the higher learning* (pp. 469–488). New York, NY: Wiley.

Quijano, A. (2000). Coloniality of power, Eurocentrism, and Latin America. *Nepantla: Views from South, 1*(3), 533–580.

Rosch, D. M., & Anthony, M. D. (2012). Leadership pedagogy: Putting theory to practice. In K. L. Guthrie, & L. Osteen (Eds.), *New directions for student leadership, No. 140: Developing students' leadership capacity* (pp. 37–51). San Francisco, CA: Jossey-Bass.

Sayyid, S. (2015). *A fundamental fear: Eurocentrism and the emergence of Islamism.* London, England: Zed Books.

Strange, C. S., & Banning, J. H. (2001). *Educating by design: Creating campus learning environments that work.* San Francisco, CA: Jossey-Bass.

Tinto, V. (1993). *Leaving college: Rethinking the causes and cures of student attrition research* (2nd ed.). Chicago, IL: University of Chicago.

PART I

SOCIAL IDENTITY AND SOCIALLY JUST LEADERSHIP EDUCATION

CHAPTER 5

SOCIAL CLASS IDENTITY CONSCIOUSNESS IN SOCIALLY JUST LEADERSHIP EDUCATION

Sonja Ardoin

As we consider how to progress leadership education from a socially just frame, we need to be conscious of how individuals' identity impacts their perceptions about, opportunities for, and practice of leadership. While not given as much attention as some other dimensions of identity, social class impacts "nearly everything about [a person]," serving as a "script, map, and guide...tell[ing] us how to dress, how to hold ourselves, how to eat, and how to socialize" (Lubrano, 2004, p. 5). Institutions of higher education are not immune to these influences and the field is not as class neutral as some may believe. Classism is still pervasive in the academy and can, overtly and covertly, affirm and replicate social class distinctions (Hurst, 2010, 2012; Soria, 2015). Leadership education partakes in this classism because "leaders operate within larger structures of inequality" (Jones, 2016, p. 24) and students from middle- and upper-class backgrounds with

Changing the Narrative, pages 59–75

prior leadership experiences more readily seek, and often acquire, leadership opportunities and roles on campus (Barratt, 2011). This chapter will focus on the perspective of individuals from poor and working-class backgrounds, through Yosso's (2005) community cultural wealth model; highlighting their experiences in leadership education and underscoring ways we can work toward socially just leadership education through social class identity consciousness.

It is important to note my positionality here. I identify as a first-generation college student from a rural, working-class background, along with privileged identities as a White, Catholic, able-bodied, heterosexual, cisgender woman. I have worked in cocurricular leadership education through professional roles in higher education and facilitator roles with national nonprofit organizations. Additionally, I study and teach about social class and leadership, in various ways, in an academic classroom setting to undergraduate and graduate students. This is the collective perspective from which I share stories in this chapter about my experiences as a student, student affairs educator, faculty member, and person. Thus, depending on readers' perspectives, some of the stories may resonate and others may not; however, I hope people receive the information as at least my truth to consider as we work toward socially just leadership education, through this chapter's focus on including people from poor and working-class backgrounds.

THE COMPLEXITIES OF SOCIAL CLASS

Similar to other dimensions of social identity, class identity can be complex and ambiguous (Martin, 2015; Soria, 2015). While it is often relegated to an individual's or family's socioeconomic status—or financial capacity, social class involves money, wealth, and many additional aspects of how someone, or a group, experiences life. These additional aspects are frequently and collectively termed "capitals," which refer to one's knowledge, experiences, resources, and possessions. Because social class encompasses so many forms of capital, it can quickly become complicated to define—for oneself or in relationship to others—and may shift or change over time. Barrett (2011) offered three frames from which one can consider their social class identity; see Figure 5.1.

First, class of origin speaks to the background of the individual—how they grew up as a child and the resources that their family possessed; which remains influential throughout our lives (Barratt, 2011). Second, current, felt class is how the individual defines their social class in the present moment; how they assess their personal access to knowledge, experiences, and resources today. Finally, attributed class is how the individual believes others perceive their social class identity (Barratt, 2011); this is likely based on how

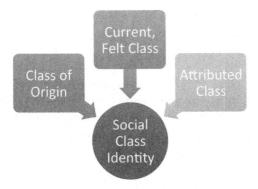

Figure 5.1 Three social class identities. *Source:* Adapted from Barratt, 2011.

one presents themselves (e.g., clothing, speech, etc.), others' knowledge of their possessions and resources, and the stereotypes about various social classes. Individuals may choose one of more of these frames to characterize their social class identity. However, for purposes of this chapter, social class identity is conceptualized as the confluence of all three frames.

Utilizing Yosso's (2005) Community Cultural Wealth Model

While much of the literature on social class focuses on poor and working-class students from a deficit perspective, scholars such as Hurst (2010, 2012) and Soria (2015) called for reframing these student populations and their backgrounds as assets to both themselves and their higher education institutions. Yosso's (2005) community cultural wealth model focuses on "the array of cultural knowledge, skills, abilities and contacts possessed by socially marginalized groups that often go unrecognized and unacknowledged" (p. 69). The model expands upon Bourdieu's (1986) concept of cultural capital into six forms of capital: (a) aspirational, (b) familial, (c) linguistic, (d) navigational, (e) resistant, and (f) social capital (Yosso, 2005). Aspirational capital is future-focused and resiliency-centered. Familial capital focuses on connections to one's family and community through kinship and culture. Linguistic capital is the ability to communicate in more than one language or dialect. Navigational capital "acknowledges individual agency within institutional constraints" (Yosso, 2005, p. 80). Resistant capital is the recognition of inequity and the drive to challenge it. Social capital is an individual's network of resources and the use of those resources to assist others. Yosso (2005) connected each of these forms of capital to the holistic wealth an individual possesses to highlight how people contribute to their communities; thus adding to the community's wealth through a multitude of ways—not only through one's financial wealth but also through one's beliefs, language(s), experiences, and actions.

Yosso's model has been showcased as a "vehicle to disrupt social stratification" in leadership education (Dugan, 2017, p. 41). When leadership educators design socially just leadership education through the asset-based lens of Yosso's (2005) model, poor and working-class students' perspectives and experiences are seen and appreciated differently and become more closely linked to leadership education and practice. This may create more space for poor and working-class students to see themselves in leadership education and to explore ways to both value and build upon their background and skill sets. This can also allow other educators and students to view poor and working-class students as more viable applicants for positional leadership roles on campus.

THE RELATIONSHIP BETWEEN SOCIAL CLASS AND SOCIALLY JUST LEADERSHIP EDUCATION

Social class identity and leadership are socially constructed concepts, meaning that both concepts "do not naturally exist...but [are] based on social interactions among people...co-created in terms of meaning" (Dugan, 2017, p. 7; Jones, 2016). The "story most often told" (Dugan, 2017, p. 58), or dominant narrative about leadership does not appear to embrace individuals from poor and working-class backgrounds; thus, socially just leadership education should acknowledge this shortcoming in its theories and representation, and work to make leadership education and practice more inclusive (Jones, 2016). Dugan (2017) noted "leadership is unequivocally learnable" (p. 17), which makes socially just leadership education vitally important. Essentially, leadership educators have the opportunity to affirm the existing narratives around social class and leadership or dismantle them, allowing poor and working-class students to see themselves as contributors to leadership education and practice in a society that may often send counter messages. Dugan (2017) called for leadership educators to strive for socially just leadership education by paying attention to "social location—or the position one holds in society based on a variety of social identities" (p. 39), including how individuals' identity, knowledge, and access to power influence their leadership opportunities, and "acknowledging...differences in how leadership is understood, experienced, and enacted" (p. 317). Social class identity and social location are inextricably tied to one another, making social class consciousness a core consideration of socially just leadership education.

SOCIALLY JUST LEADERSHIP EDUCATION
THROUGH THE CONSTRUCTS OF CAPITAL

One way to heed Jones' and Dugan's calls is to raise awareness of social class and incorporate the exploration of this identity, and its inherent forms of capital, in socially just leadership education. This chapter begins those processes by considering five of the forms of capital—(a) financial/economic capital, (b) social capital, (c) cultural capital, (d) linguistic capital, and (e) navigational capital—through descriptions and stories. Understanding these capitals can aid leadership educators in recognizing how social class can show up in leadership education and allow them to reflect on ways they might be able to progress toward more socially just leadership education.

Financial/Economic Capital

Financial, or economic, capital is individuals' available assets, including their incomes, savings, and wealth items (home, car, land, etc.) which can be turned into currency. Stuber (2011) explained how "extensive participation in the [co-curricular] requires financial capital" (p. 65). Students from poor and working-class backgrounds often have more financial capital restraints than their peers (Soria, 2015), influencing their campus engagement, including in leadership education. In higher education, we often attach prices to leadership education and participation—academic course tuition and fees for leadership majors, minors, and/or certificates; conference and institute fees, costs of specific attire (e.g., organizational polos, business casual, business, etc.), and books or codes for leadership assessments, among others. Socially just leadership educators should be aware of the financial requirements associated with their leadership education initiatives and actively work to reduce or eliminate economic constraints to engagement.

The Actual Costs of Positional Leadership

Positional leadership roles can add additional financial burdens as well. Barratt (2011) pointed out involvement is limited for those without liquid cash or credit. I found this out as an undergraduate student when I held a positional role with an extended orientation camp. In this role, I was planning and executing the activities that would occur at the camp, many of which required ample supplies and decorations. I inquired with the student executive director of the organization about how to cover these costs and he instructed me to just "front" the money and submit receipts to our advisor to get reimbursed. This created an uncomfortable situation for me. I did not have the money to front from my own checking account and the only credit card that I possessed was one that my parents firmly instructed me to use solely for dire emergencies. Thus, I felt faced with two choices: (a) ask my parents to make an exception that I knew they could not afford or (b) share with my peer that neither my financial situation nor that of my family allowed me to follow this common procedure of purchasing materials for the university's extended orientation camp. This situation made me question whether or not "someone like me" should be in the activities director role; if I could not provide what the organization needed—in this case, fronting funds—then maybe I was not capable of fulfilling the role. It also made me very aware that my social class background and current status were different than my peers who were also in positional leadership roles with the organization. Ultimately, I chose neither of the aforementioned options; rather, I bought the items from my personal checking account and immediately submitted receipts for reimbursement with the hope that it would be turned around in a timely fashion so I could still eat and pay rent. I was gambling on my basic needs in order to fulfill the positional leader expectations and mask that I was different from my peers.

I later saw similar social class-based financial issues as a student affairs educator. At one institution where I worked, students and advisors alike were, again, expected to purchase student organization items from their personal funds and, later, receive reimbursement from the university. I shared the challenges of this practice with my supervisor to no avail. This was the university's traditional practice and it was not up for reconsideration. Thus, I acknowledged the limitation to students in the organization, which I advised, and informed them that I was willing to assist if they needed something that they could not purchase with their personal funds. While this put financial strain on me as an advisor, I wanted to lessen the burden on students, particularly those from poor and working-class backgrounds, who may be limiting their participation in the organization for fear of being unable to purchase items necessary for the organization to function. However, the reality remained that we, as an institution, were sending the message that financial contributions were an expectation of involved students; a philosophy that I believe is both classist and in tension with stated institutional values.

These types of scenarios do not stop with students or student organization advisors either. It continues in the general practice of higher education by both institutions and national organizations and associations. Many of the opportunities to serve in leadership positions or gain leadership experiences come at a financial cost to the individual. Whether it is the pressure to contribute to the institutional capital campaign, the requirement to donate to the association in order to attain or maintain a board position, or the payment of travel expenses for the opportunity to facilitate leadership curriculum, many of the opportunities for professional engagement and development come with a price tag which constrains who can participate and how.

Social Capital

Social capital is one's connections—who you know and who knows you. Noted by both Bourdieu (1986) and Yosso (2005) as a critical component of social class identity, social capital allows one to collaborate with others, join resources, and network for opportunities and further resources. It is often who one knows—and not necessarily their knowledge or skill set—that influences their access to opportunities. The student who comes to campus as a first-generation college student from a rural, working-class town (e.g., me!) may not know anyone to "pipeline" them into campus engagement and leadership. The same is often true for student affairs educators and faculty members; collegial relationships with certain individuals can beget invitations for facilitation, writing, and positional roles. Socially just leadership education considers how poor and working-class students' engagement will build upon their existing social capital and "connect them to a diverse set of students, community leaders, college faculty, and alumni" (Stuber, 2011, p. 64).

Knowing People: The Snowball Effect

Whether it is framed through undergraduate student groups or professional associations, there is often a "snowball effect" with leadership education and practice. As an undergraduate student, I first became aware of this trend when I was interviewed by some upperclassmen for a first-year student government committee. All three of the interviewers were from larger cities in the state and seemed to know each other and many of the other applicants from prior leadership experiences; ones that people from my hometown did not have access (e.g., Hugh O'Brian Youth Leadership, American Legion Auxiliary's Girls State/Boys State, etc.). In fact, they had never heard of my hometown and asked me multiple questions about it, which resulted in my feeling like the "odd duck" of the applicant pool, realizing that I was the proverbial "small fish in the big pond" now, and concluding that my social circle back home did not translate to my university in any way. That interview was the only successful one I had during my first year of college. Those three men who interviewed me provided the opportunity to meet other first-year students through this student government committee—many of whom were from places like those men and several of whom went on to pursue, and attain, powerful positional roles at the university in student government, fraternities and sororities, orientation, student media, and ROTC. Those three men did not realize it, but what they did for me that day through that awkward interview broadened my social capital, which, in turn, expanded my opportunities for leadership learning and practice.

I also noticed this trend serving on membership committees for various student groups throughout my undergraduate experience. This always bothered me because I knew that people with backgrounds similar to mine did not always receive the same consideration; these folks did not know the "right" people or come from the right places, at least by membership committee members' definitions of right. Many times, those committees were less inclined to take the same chance on the unknown or unassociated individual than the three men who opened the student leadership door for me. Hurst (2010) recognized classism in student engagement too, noting student organizations were "plagued by internal class divisions" (p. 86), while Soria (2015) observed some working-class students "feel alienated at college" because they perceive themselves as beneath their peers (p. 43). I believe similar situations occur for higher education administrators and faculty as well. While the social circles may be more numerous and nuanced, in-groups can dominate professional organizations, allocate positional roles, and shape one's reputation in the field by association.

Cultural Capital

Cultural capital is the culmination of individuals' experiences—what they know, where they have been, how they spend their time, and which items they possess. Bourdieu (1986) acknowledged some types of cultural capital are considered more prestigious than others, noting "highbrow," or middle- and upper- class, experiences with higher education, museums, art galleries, fine dining establishments, and travel may be more highly valued in society than other types of experiences. Particular characteristics of cultural capital should not be assumed in the context of socially just leadership education. Rather, questions and discussion should be utilized to share the types of cultural capital that participants possess and thorough explanations should be provided for various types of knowledge—particularly in relationship to jargon terms or acronyms—prior to all activities or programs. This will not only benefit poor and working-class participants, but anyone who is involved with the leadership education, thus exercising social justice.

Using Utensils: Which Fork is For What?

Growing up in a small, rural town in a working-class household, our meals often consisted of simple dishes that could be eaten on one plate with, at most, two utensils and it was not unusual for someone to reach across your plate and grab something that they wanted to taste. We did not frequent "fancy" restaurants because there was only one in town and we could not afford such an experience. In fact, my community often hosted large gatherings, such as crawfish boils, where folks would literally stand

and eat with their hands from tables topped with newspaper. Thus, I was unfamiliar with formal place settings and silverware when I arrived at college. I could not wrap my mind around why there were so many different plates and utensils on the table for one person to use! Why would anyone need three forks for one meal? That created a lot of unnecessary dishes to wash, which I was very aware of because no one in my family had a dishwasher in their kitchen (meaning the machine; we had several humans, like me, who were assigned the task though).

Yet, many student organizations and campus departments hosted formal events, including etiquette dinners, at my undergraduate and graduate institutions that sent the message that formal meals were standard and something students needed to easily and expertly handle. The entire process made me uncomfortable—and still does—because it makes me feel unwelcome, nervous, and ill-equipped to do something as simple as eating. It also sent the message that the type of meals, dishes, and utensils that I enjoyed were not good enough for my middle- and upper-class collegiate peers, advisors, and faculty. The message that I had to learn to eat this way to be ready for interviews, meetings, or events made me question whether or not I wanted to live in "that world." I am not alone in this situation; participants in Hurst's (2010) study also shared their desire to take an etiquette class to acquire manners in which others already seemed well-versed. They too recognized that their practices were different than—and considered beneath—those of their peers. Socially just leadership educators carefully examine how their programs and curriculum favor certain forms of cultural capital over others, or teach that one way of being and doing is the right way to be appropriate or successful as a leader, and actively seek to recognize and present a multitude of cultural capital elements.

Linguistic Capital

Linguistic capital is comprised of language, dialect, speech patterns, and body language. Barratt (2011) advanced "accent, timing, vocabulary, grammar, word choice, and sentence construction are all...primary social class cue[s]" (p. 62). He also noted that nonverbal forms of communication—including "how you sit, how you move, what you do with your hands, and how you shake hands"—are tied to one's social class background (Barratt, 2011, p. 62). In short, linguistic capital is how individuals express themselves. Socially just leadership education, particularly if focused on communication, emotional intelligence, or relational leadership, should reflect on whether particular forms of expression are taught and esteemed and how that may influence engagement of those from poor or working-class backgrounds who may not choose or prefer those forms of expression.

Contesting Communication Choices

Growing up in rural, Cajun-country, everyone I knew talked like me, even the folks on the local news (we did not have cable television). Therefore, I never realized I had an accent until I arrived at my undergraduate institution, where I was made almost painfully aware that my dialect, word choice, and inflection were different than my peers from the larger cities within the state and certainly those from out of state or other countries. There were many instances where my peers treated me as their parrot of sorts, asking me to say two words that they believed sounded distinctly different but I happened to pronounce very similarly (e.g., pill and peel). My vernacular soon became simultaneously a point of pride and shame and I understood the "hidden curriculum" that was trying to "fix" how I spoke and wrote. One of my best friends, who also had similar linguistic capital, was blatantly told that she had to relearn English in a standard dialect and shift other elements of her communication if she wanted to be successful in her broadcast journalism pathway.

Later on in my educational and professional pursuits, I also learned that my tendency to be honest—and maybe a bit brash—was also peculiar in the academy. Lubrano (2004) discussed his own experiences with this, offering that "[poor and working class individuals] tell you what we feel rather than what you want to hear . . . the direct and honest approach . . . in some environments, that's not appreciated" (p. 131). He is right; in fact, my own approach was often viewed as unprofessional and undesirable. Supervisors and mentors cautioned me that my "say it like it is" approach and facial expressions needed some finessing if I wanted to progress in the higher education field. The message was clear that my forms of expression were deemed uncouth and a potential hindrance to advancement, particularly if I wanted to pursue senior-level leadership roles. I understood the feedback, yet I was—and am still—hesitant to change what I consider to be my authentic self-expression and communication. I value honesty and transparency; while those may not always be smooth, or calculated enough for others' liking, some people do appreciate my communication and find it refreshing.

Leadership educators may want to consider how they are framing communication and linguistic capital and if they are favoring certain communication styles over others or sending mixed messages about the need to communicate in specific ways while also encouraging students to be authentic; two things which may be in tension. In order to be socially just, leadership education should highlight the value of different forms of linguistic capital and celebrate when students can communicate in multiple languages, dialects, or nonverbal techniques.

Navigational Capital

Navigational capital is one's capability to understand and experience processes embedded in a place or system (Yosso, 2005). For example, growing up with grandparents who were farmers, I understood and experienced the process of, what is now known as, "farm to table." I had been present on the literal farm for the planting of seeds, caretaking of land and providing of nutrients, cutting of the crop, and preparing the crop for either personal meals or external sale. This navigational capital was crucial in my hometown, and to the economic vitality of my entire extended family, but not as helpful when I became a college student. While it may have been useful in a few courses, my ability to navigate farms and other rural systems was no longer applicable or valued. Socially just leadership education considers whether its system of learning is creating processes that will be more challenging to navigate for some students over others and if those processes negate the navigational capital that poor and working-class students possess or deter them from engaging in leadership education.

Encountering New Systems

At the end of my junior year in college I was elected president of a senior-level honor society chapter on my campus. I was excited about the role because the organization's mission combined scholarship, leadership, and service, all of which I valued (and still do today). However, I was nervous as well. This role required the chapter president to attend the national conference each year and, although there were no personal costs to attend, that meant I would have to travel to Ohio, which also meant I would have to fly. This was concerning and exhilarating for me because, at the age of 21, I had never flown. In fact, I had never been to an airport at all. My advisor assured me that it would all be fine and that she would be attending the conference as well and could "show me the ropes" of air travel. This helped to ease my anxiousness, until the night before the flight. That is when my advisor called me to share that she was quite ill and could no longer attend the conference with me. I suppressed my emotional reaction while on the phone with her because I understood it was not her fault and I would have to manage, but after the call I freaked out. Now, I would have to not only fly alone for the first time but also navigate the conundrum of the airport by myself. Like most folks navigating new systems for the first time, I experienced uncertainty, fear, and triumph as I found my way through check in, security, boarding, the actual flight, and, finally, baggage claim. There were many moments where I wanted to cry and laugh, sometimes simultaneously, like when my carry-on duffle bag was overweight, did not fit in the overhead or under the seat, nor had wheels to ease the hauling of it between gates. And, I still have deep appreciation for the kindness of the stranger who happened to sit next to me that first flight and had the patience and grace to explain every sound and bump to me because he could see the trepidation on my face.

I share this story because it is one example of how leadership opportunities may require folks from poor and working-class backgrounds to navigate new spaces and practices that others may assume everyone has experienced or knows how to approach. Later, I volunteered for that senior honor society conference and I always asked to work registration so I could connect with other chapter delegates who had experienced their first flight to travel to the conference. I wanted them to know that they were not alone and have someone to connect with about their new navigational capital and all the corresponding emotions. If leadership education is going to be socially just, it needs to consider the processes and systems it expects participants can decipher, then, if those are necessary or unavoidable, offer resources that assist students in building the navigational capital it involves.

CLASS CONSIDERATIONS IN SOCIALLY JUST LEADERSHIP EDUCATION: SUGGESTIONS FOR PRACTICE

Considering the five aforementioned forms of capital, along with the others not explicitly explored in this chapter, can serve as a first step toward socially just leadership education. If educators can critically reflect on how social class may be showing up in leadership education—"the broad understanding of leadership knowledge, skills, and values" (Bertrand Jones, Guthrie, & Osteen, 2016, p. 11)—then, they can assess how to re-envision it to be more inclusive of social class and, thus, move toward a more socially just form. Four suggestions for creating socially just leadership education for poor and working class students include (a) talking about social class utilizing asset-based frameworks, (b) inventorying and reducing engagement barriers, (c) marketing the value of socially just leadership education, and (d) showcasing leaders from all walks of life.

Talk About Social Class Utilizing Asset-Based Frameworks

Hurst (2010) noted that poor and working-class experiences are not often presented in higher education and, even when they are, can be "romanticized or mythologized...always the 'other'" (p.118). hooks (2000) contended social class conversations remain at the periphery of campus consciousness and typically conjure negative connotations. Both Hurst and hooks challenge us to break the silence around the taboo topic of social class—in short, to talk about class identity realities. While that may sound simple to some, engaging in such conversations can be complex, since social class identity itself is multifaceted and because most of us are socialized to not talk about money, which is often conflated with social class. Still, we have to unlearn these elements of socialization to explore social class identities and how they influence how we perceive, receive, learn, and practice leadership. This likely means leadership educators will need to explore their own social class identities and learn how to generate and facilitate discussions on social class and how it relates to leadership.

Jones and McEwen's (2000) model of multiple dimensions of identity may be helpful in facilitating discussions about social class identity. The model invites individuals to consider the various dimensions of their identity to determine which dimensions are most significant to them and how the dimensions interact with one another. It also frames identity in relation to one's "family background, sociocultural conditions... current experiences, and career decisions and life planning" (Jones, 2016, p. 28). This framing can be helpful in inviting poor and working-class students to share their backgrounds and how those may differ from their current, collegiate experiences. It may also encourage conversation about if, or how, poor and working-class students perceive the campus' leadership education as supportive or hostile to their social class identity (Jones, 2016). It would also be helpful to combine use of Jones and McEwen's (2000) model, and other forms of social class identity conversations, with asset-based frameworks, such as Yosso's (2005) community cultural wealth model, to allow all leadership education participants to see their identity and knowledge and skill sets—their forms of capital—as valuable and a base on which to build. Additionally, if leadership educators can utilize asset-based frameworks for program and curriculum creation, leadership education will become more socially just.

Inventory and Reducing Engagement Barriers

When was the last review of the leadership education curriculum or programming design through a social justice lens, or one focused on social class identity? It may be beneficial to critically evaluate the program to inventory any financial, time, or other capital barriers, which may be limiting poor and working-class students' engagement. Bertrand Jones et al.'s (2016) culturally relevant leadership learning model can serve as a framework from which to perform the critical evaluation. Particularly, three of their five domains of cultural relevant leadership learning, including "historical legacy of inclusion/exclusion, compositional diversity, and the organizational/structural dimension" (Bertrand Jones et al., 2016, p. 16), may be helpful. First, educators can evaluate "who has traditionally participated in leadership learning opportunities on campus" (Bertrand Jones et al., 2016, p. 16), which is the historical legacy, and compare that to the institution's compositional diversity, or proportion of poor and working-class students. This will provide information on whether individuals from poor and working-class backgrounds are participating at all and if so, to what degree. After this broad evaluation, educators can more critically assess their own "structures and processes that guide day-to-day 'business'" of leadership education to determine if their "curricula, budget allocations, recognition or award practices, and other policies" (Bertrand Jones et al., 2016, p. 18) benefit certain social classes or capitals over others.

A starting place, if one is helpful, may be to simply track how much financial capital the leadership education opportunities cost students, then follow the recommendations of Soria (2015), Martin (2015), and Ardoin (2017), who all suggest offering financial scholarships or eliminating or subsidizing participation fees as an approach to reduce economic barriers to engagement. A second task could be to assess when leadership education is happening; if leadership education opportunities only occur on nights or weekends, for example, that may inhibit poor and working-class students from participating because they may be working or caring for family. These kinds of reflections, followed by actions to reduce barriers, can shift the leadership educational program's organizational/structural dimension and facilitate more inclusion of poor and working-class individuals, thus increasing compositional diversity and overcoming a historical legacy of class-based exclusion.

Market the Value of Socially Just Leadership Education

Once barriers have been reduced, leadership educators should consider how to market the value of leadership education for poor and working-class students. Sometimes "traditional" marketing techniques only reach students who are already looking for leadership education opportunities, who are typically from middle or upper classes (Barratt, 2011). Students from poor and working-class backgrounds are not always aware of, or privy to, cocurricular engagement's value (Barratt, 2011; Stuber, 2011). Stuber (2011) suggested students need more customized information and to know or see others, particularly with those who share their identities, transferring this information knowledge into participatory action. It may be helpful to market leadership education as opportunities to advance the "distinguishing features of working class culture," including "hard work, a strong moral core, and a sense of authenticity" (Stuber, 2011, p. 74). Leadership educators should brainstorm and benchmark methods of marketing that could reach poor and working-class students—particularly those who are also students with jobs, part-time students, off-campus residents, or parents or caretakers—and highlight the value of leadership education and how it can build on students' existing capitals and apply to both students' present and future endeavors.

Showcase Leaders From All Walks of Life

When leadership education programs are created or revised, are we conscious of who is being showcased as a leader? Do we consider social class as a component of diverse identity? I would argue we often highlight examples of people who either originate from middle- and upper-class backgrounds or who currently identify that way—folks who are in positional roles in "white collar" careers. That may limit poor and working-class students' ability to see themselves, or their families and communities, represented in leadership education. We need to broaden our illustration of what leadership is, who can be involved, and how it can be practiced.

Magolda (2016) provided insights into how campus custodians exercise leadership through their roles at colleges and universities. While this population may not be the first to arise in a conversation or program on leadership, the ethnography provides multiple leadership counter-stories that broaden how leadership is viewed in higher education. Leadership education can also feature small-business owners (without college business degrees), farmers, postal workers, and other populations who contribute significantly to the community through their own forms of leadership, whether or not they have perceived occupational prestige. It is a responsibility of socially just leadership education to both consider and offer wideranging examples of leadership to allow all students the potential to see themselves—and those they know and love—as capable of leadership.

While leadership educators may encounter some resistance from students, colleagues, or supervisors about this approach, it is important to combat the stereotypes of what leadership is and who can practice it. A tactic for gathering support may be to inquire with students, formally or informally, about who they see as leaders in their lives and on the campus. Students will often name individuals without formal titles and from different social class identities who impact their lives. Personally, I have heard students name grandparents, parents, peers, campus security guards, and dining hall staff as leaders and mentors just as often as, or even more often than, faculty, administrators, or other "white collar" title holders. Gathering information like this can illuminate how students see leadership through everyday interactions and garner support for showcasing leadership through various lenses, definitions, and examples. Another approach is to invite students to nominate individuals for leadership panels and lectures, which would hopefully bring a variety of identities and perspectives to the forefront. If we as leadership educators cannot highlight how leadership happens daily and without fanfare, how can we expect all students to see themselves as capable of leadership?

CONCLUSION

Socially just leadership education involves social class identity consciousness. In fact, leadership education itself is a form of capital that is acquired at varying levels and perceived in different ways depending on one's social class identity. For example, a farmer or sanitation worker may need and use different forms of leadership practice to serve their community than a teacher or doctor applies; however, if we only teach the latter as leadership then we are negating the contributions and impact of many individuals. Viewing and teaching leadership from only the middle- and upper-class lenses is classist and a form of social reproduction, shaping how one might view themselves and others in relation to leadership.

My own stories in this chapter showcase how I have struggled to view myself within the status quo perspective of leadership because of financial, social, cultural, linguistic, and navigational capital expectations that frame my working-class forms of capital as inferior and middle- and upper-class forms as superior. It has taken me much time, reflection, and acceptance to recognize that I can practice leadership in ways that both honor and value my poor and working class background and forms of capital while also acquiring additional forms of capital that enhance my ability to lead. It is a both/and not an either/or, meaning that I can utilize both working- and middle-class capitals in my leadership practice but do not have to replace one with the other in order to be a "good" or "successful" leader.

Furthering social class consciousness in socially just leadership education includes but is not limited to recognizing the complexity of social class identity, and its inherent forms of capital, modifying the messaging poor and working-class individuals receive about their capacity to learn and practice leadership, and considering how to include and celebrate social class identity as part of leadership education. Educators can advance both class consciousness and socially just leadership education by talking about social class utilizing asset-based frameworks, inventorying, and reducing engagement barriers, marketing the value of socially just leadership education, and showcasing leaders from all walks of life. Engaging in these conversations and perspective shifts can allow leadership educators to become agents of social change and social justice.

REFERENCES

Ardoin, S. (2017). Priced out: Considerations for increasing low-income students' ability to engage on campus and increase cultural and social capital. [*NASPA Knowledge Community Online National Conference Publication*]. Washington, DC: NASPA. Retrieved from https://www.naspa.org/images/uploads/events/2017-naspa-final.pdf

Barratt, W. (2011). *Social class on campus: Theories and manifestations.* Sterling, VA: Stylus.

Bertrand Jones, T., Guthrie, K. L., & Osteen, L. (2016). Critical domains of culturally relevant leadership learning: A call to transform leadership programs. In K. L. Guthrie, T. Bertrand Jones, & L. Osteen (Eds.), *New directions for student leadership, No. 152: Developing culturally relevant leadership learning* (pp. 9–21). San Francisco, CA: Jossey-Bass.

Bourdieu, P. (1986). The forms of capital. In J. G. Richardson (Ed.), Handbook of theory and research for the sociology of education (pp. 241–258). New York, NY: Greenwood.

Dugan, J. P. (2017). *Leadership theory: Cultivating critical perspectives.* San Francisco, CA: Jossey-Bass.

hooks, b. (2000). *Where we stand: Class matters.* New York, NY: Routledge.

Hurst, A. L. (2010). *The burden of academic success: Loyalists, renegades, and double agents.* Lanham, MD: Lexington Books.

Hurst, A. L. (2012). *College and the working class: What it takes to make it.* Rotterdam, The Netherlands: Sense.

Jones, S. (2016). Authenticity in leadership: Intersectionality of identities. In T. Bertrand Jones, K. L. Guthrie, & L. Osteen (Eds.), *New directions for student leadership, No. 152: Developing culturally relevant leadership learning* (pp. 23–34). San Francisco, CA: Jossey-Bass.

Jones, S. R., & McEwen, M. K. (2000). A conceptual model of multiple dimensions of identity. *Journal of College Student Development, 41,* 405–414.

Lubrano, A. (2004). *Limbo: Blue-collar roots, white-collar dreams.* Hoboken, NJ: Wiley.

Magolda, P. (2016). *The lives of campus custodians: Insights into corporatization and civic disengagement in the academy.* Sterling, VA: Stylus.

Martin, G. L. (2015). "Tightly wound rubber bands": Exploring the college experiences of low income, first-generation white students. *Journal of Student Affairs Research and Practice, 52*(3), 275–286.

Soria, K. (2015). *Welcoming blue-collar scholars into the ivory tower: Developing class-conscious strategies for student success.* Columbia, SC: National Resource Center for The First-Year Experience and Students in Transition.

Stuber, J. M. (2011). *Inside the college gates: How class and culture matter in higher education.* Lanham, MD: Lexington Books.

Yosso, T. (2005). Whose culture has capital? A critical race theory discussion of community cultural wealth. *Race Ethnicity and Education, 8*(1), 69–91.

CHAPTER 6

BEYOND THE BINARY

Advancing Socially Just Leadership Through the Lens of Gender

Paige Haber-Curran and Dan Tillapaugh

We must only open our eyes and ears to everyday interactions and messages to recognize the society in which we live in is quite gendered. From an early age we are taught, albeit not always directly, what is feminine and what is masculine, how girls should behave and how boys should behave, and the positive or negative repercussions that come from *obeying* or *disobeying* these gendered expectations. Society categorizes individuals from birth into rigid boxes of gender identity and expects conformity and adherence to those assigned identities. These messages and expectations are so powerful and ingrained that often we are not aware of them or how they impact our thoughts, feelings, and behaviors, or our expectations of others. More often than not, these messages and expectations are unquestioned and taken as objective truth rather than understood as socially constructed. From a standpoint of advocating for socially just leadership, we argue that failing to critically examine gender is dangerous. Leadership educators play a crucial

Changing the Narrative, pages 77–92
Copyright © 2018 by Information Age Publishing
All rights of reproduction in any form reserved.

role in helping individuals critically examine and problematize the constructs of gender and leadership.

Reinforced through many dynamics such as families, schools, media, faith communities, social networks, and professional arenas, gendered messages and expectations affect individuals, organizations, and communities. These messages and expectations are often rooted in patriarchal and hegemonic ideals, creating a hierarchy of power, privilege, and oppression. Individuals who uphold traditional, socially acceptable gender norms and expectations are rewarded with privilege. Those who do not uphold these norms may find themselves marginalized, oppressed, and/or punished through gender policing.

Although the topic of gender has somewhat been examined in conjunction with the topic of leadership, much of the focus has been on examining gender differences in leadership outcomes, such as leadership style or behavior, often within a professional or corporate context. In fact, very little emphasis has been placed on examining the role of gender within leadership education and even less on examining gender as a social justice issue within the context of leadership (see Tillapaugh & Haber-Curran, 2017 for a more in-depth exploration of this topic).

With the aim of advancing social justice on our campuses and in our world, the purpose of our chapter is to critically examine gender and leadership to help inform and advance leadership education. We argue that it is a social justice imperative to understand and challenge the traditionally-held and restrictive notions of gender in society, and how those ideas are reinforced in higher education, with a specific focus on leadership development and education. To do so, we focus on the historical and current context of gender and leadership, provide a brief overview and critique of the research on gender and college student leadership, and suggest key commitments and offer key areas of knowledge, skills, and values critical for advancing socially just leadership education through the lens of gender. Throughout the chapter, we emphasize the responsibility leadership educators have in educating themselves and engaging in self-work and critical self-reflection on these topics in order to advance socially just leadership education.

GENDER AS A SOCIAL JUSTICE ISSUE

Gender plays a significant role in our lives, often before we are even born. One of the first questions asked about a baby in utero is: "Is it a boy or a girl?"; with the answer drawing up images and expectations instantaneously about who the child will be. Different from assigned birthsex, which is determined by biological criteria such as genitalia or chromosomal makeup, gender is socially constructed within society as "the range of mental or behavioral characteristics pertaining to, and differentiating between and across, masculinity and femininity" (West & Zimmerman, 1987, p. 126). In this dichotomy, masculinity and femininity are on opposite ends of the continuum, and society overwhelmingly expects and rewards gendered characteristics and behaviors when they align with one's biological sex (e.g., female and feminine, male and masculine). As a result, this perspective privileges and oppresses individuals based on their gender identities and expressions. Yet, these ideas are limiting because not everyone identifies as either a man or woman.

Gender exists well beyond the dichotomy of man and woman or masculine and feminine. In fact, more students arrive on college and university campuses today identifying as transgender or gender nonconforming (Nicolazzo, 2017; Renn, 2010; Stolzenberg & Hughes, 2017). These students do not necessarily subscribe to the aforementioned gender binary; they instead reject these restrictive terms to represent the robustness and fluidity of their gender identity. Often, these students experience genderism in their daily lives, both on- and off- campus, whereby the binary of man/woman is systemically privileged and reinforced as the status quo within society (Hill, 2003; Wilchins, 2002). Genderism plays a significant role in human interactions within society and our environments, including college and university campuses (Bilodeau, 2009). Individuals, as well as organizations, systemic rules, policies, and regulations reinforce genderism. Examples of genderism in higher education abound, including campus record-keeping systems which do not allow students to choose a gender identity beyond man/woman or a name that reflects their gender identity that may be different than their legal name, restroom facilities designated only for men or women rather than being gender-inclusive spaces, or health care professionals on-campus who are not familiar with care needs of trans* or gender nonconforming students. These issues play a large role in the daily functioning of these students, and when they are not able to access facilities or campus resources that are needed to support their health and well-being, administrators at these institutions underserve all of our students and hinder their abilities to be successful.

Although these issues may not readily be seen as connected to socially just leadership, we argue these issues are inherently about social justice. When our educational institutions and the administrators who work in these institutions uphold policies, rules, and regulations that are embedded in genderism, we fail to engage in socially just leadership ourselves. We believe encouraging and teaching socially just leadership as professionals requires us to be congruent in our values and actions as well as considering how these issues of daily life directly affect our students' abilities to practice leadership. Socially just leadership, at its heart, requires each of us to be proactive in our own education around issues of power, privilege, and oppression and critically examine the ways genderism (and other forms of "isms") permeates our lives.

As many of our students, as well as campus administrators and faculty, adopt language around gender that is fluid, dynamic, and ever-changing, we acknowledge the research and scholarship that exists on gender has struggled to keep pace. In fact, there is a great deal of research upholding genderism and cissexism, thereby erasing individuals who exist outside of the binary of men/women. In fact, in much of the scholarship on gender, scholars tend to still use "gender" as a coded term for only women (Bannon & Correia, 2006), due to the issues of discrimination and marginalization women face as a subordinated group in society. Yet, the use of gender as a synonym for women becomes problematic considering everyone has a gender identity, not just girls and women. For example, when looking at contemporary texts on leadership and gender, many scholars' work frames gender only around women (Hoyt & Simon, 2017; Madsen, 2017; Werhane & Painter-Morland, 2011). This omits focusing on the leadership practices of men, transgendered, and agender individuals. How does their gender identity and expression play a role in their leadership? These issues will be discussed further in the following section.

Finally, our collective understanding of gender beyond the binary is a social justice issue and a social justice imperative. Each of us has a gender, and our gender converges with all of the other social and personal identities we have, shaping our worldviews and interactions. The societal systems in which we participate inform how we hold power and privilege, and the ways in which we are subordinated and oppressed. Given this connection to power, gender as a social justice concept also influences one's leadership practice and the ways in which we are seen, heard, and perceived. As a result, one's gender is often connected with one's understanding of leadership (Haber-Curran & Tillapaugh, 2017).

HISTORICAL AND CURRENT CONTEXT OF GENDER AND LEADERSHIP

Leadership has historically been conceptualized, studied, and promoted in the Western world as an inherently masculine concept; often signified by positional roles and authority. As such, it was predominantly White men from socioeconomically privileged backgrounds who held such roles and were deemed as leaders (Dugan, 2017). Stemming from this strong focus on position and authority, leadership came to be viewed within dominant culture as involving hierarchical, top-down, and authoritative behaviors, further masculinizing the concept of leadership, and the designation of who was considered a leader—and who wasn't considered a leader—across many sectors of society. Individuals and groups who were affecting positive change and organizing others in less visible roles or through alternative means and individuals from underrepresented groups (i.e., not White, privileged men) were not included in the leadership conversation or the study of leadership (Komives & Dugan, 2010).

This historical context is helpful in understanding the landscape of leadership today and the challenges the field of leadership studies continues to face in promoting leadership as an inclusive process that moves beyond position and focuses on making a positive impact. The historical context is also important for understanding how often, still today, individuals from underrepresented groups, including women and trans* identified individuals, may resist the label of leader or may not see the work that they are doing as leadership (Arminio et al., 2000; Haber, 2011; Porter, 1998; Renn & Bilodeau, 2005a, 2005b). There is a long history, in fact centuries, of privileging certain identities and behaviors within society, not only within the context of leadership, but across many realms (e.g., individual, economic, social, educational, political), significantly impacting the landscape of our world today. It is easy to see how this historical context has not only excluded, but also discredited and even harmed, generations of individuals who made a significant impact in their communities and affected change; not to mention the individuals who never had the opportunity to do so. Furthermore, we believe the narrow and masculinized conceptualization of leadership has hurt everyone, even privileged White men, as this conceptualization does not allow for a wide range of attributes and behaviors and in many ways punishes those who don't follow the script. By limiting leadership to traditional, hierarchical, and masculine conceptualizations, our organizations, communities, and society at large have been slighted and harmed as the full human potential for leadership has been constricted.

Over the past 40 years, leadership scholars have sought to move the conversation and study of leadership beyond the constraining and restricting industrial conceptualizations of leadership. Unsurprisingly, many of the early scholars prominent within the field of leadership studies whose work is recognized as helping move the field forward were White men; notably Burns' (1978) work on transforming leadership, Greenleaf's (1977) work on servant leadership, and Rost's (1991) examination of industrial and postindustrial leadership. Although these scholars did not explicitly focus their work on including individuals from diverse and underrepresented backgrounds in leadership, they nonetheless advocated for new ways of thinking about leadership, challenging the inherently masculine historical context of leadership that dominated the field. This advocacy paved the path for further work to be done toward making the study of leadership and practice of leadership education more inclusive and socially just.

Since then, many other scholars have had a positive impact on the field of leadership studies, introducing new thinking on leadership (Avolio & Gardner, 2005; Bordas, 2007; Heifetz, 1994; Kouzes & Posner, 1987; Wheatley, 1994); some of whom focus specifically on college student leadership development (Higher Education Research Institute, 1996; Komives, Lucas, & McMahon, 1998; Shankman, Allen, & Haber-Curran, 2015). Many of these models promote leadership as a process and as a skill set or set of attributes that can be developed, emphasizing concepts such as collaboration, values, and positive change. Today, many of these democratic and process-oriented approaches to leadership are recognized, valued, and even promoted. Further, many of these approaches have come to be classified as feminine approaches to leadership, reflecting gendered language that distinguishes between feminine (i.e., contemporary and collaborative) and masculine (i.e., traditional and hierarchical) leadership (Eagly & Carli, 2007). The framework of feminine and masculine leadership is now fairly common language within the leadership literature, and although we understand why and how this language has come about, we also see this framework as limiting and problematic as we look to advance socially just leadership, which will be discussed later in the chapter.

RESEARCH ON GENDER AND COLLEGE STUDENT LEADERSHIP

When looking to the broader research base of gender and leadership, outside of the context of college students, there is a well-known and well-researched assumption that women tend to view, approach, and enact leadership that is more "feminine" (i.e., democratic, collaborative, and transformational), and men tend to view, approach, and enact leadership that is more "masculine" (i.e., authoritative, hierarchical, and transactional; Eagly & Carli, 2007; Haber-Curran & Tillapaugh, 2017). These differences in leadership, along with the significant underrepresentation of women in top leadership roles, have been the primary focus of the conversation about gender and leadership. Differences by gender are also present in the limited research base on gender and student leadership (Dugan & Komives, 2007; Dugan, Komives, & Segar, 2008; Haber, 2012; Haber-Curran & Tillapaugh, 2017; Kezar & Moriarty, 2000; Komives, 1992). Certainly understanding differences in leadership approaches, behaviors, and attitudes by gender is important to acknowledge, as is calling out and questioning the underrepresentation of women in leadership; yet, there is much more that can and should be included in the conversation about gender and student leadership and even more that is yet to be researched.

As we have critically examined the research base on gender and student leadership, we have identified areas that warrant consideration and additional research, particularly as we seek to advance leadership as a social justice imperative. First, we challenge the oversimplified narrative that women lead in a feminine way and men lead in a masculine way; and even further, we challenge the categorization of certain behaviors as feminine and others as masculine. This narrative further enforces a binary and sets up expectations for individuals based on binary genders. We also challenge the oversimplification of gendered ways of leading because our research on both college men (Tillapaugh & Haber-Curran, 2016) and college women (Haber, 2011) suggested both women's and men's leadership styles cross these socially constructed divides. Further, the research suggests college students not only embrace and practice leadership across a wide spectrum of behaviors, they also resist and challenge gendered binaries of leadership styles (Haber, 2011; Tillapaugh & Haber-Curran, 2016). Additionally, quantitative research demonstrating differences in leadership outcomes, approaches, and perspectives by gender are plagued by small effect sizes (Dugan et al., 2008; Haber, 2012), indicating that although statistically significant differences may exist, the magnitude of the practical differences are small and required in-depth examination. These research findings, both qualitative and quantitative, provide grounds from which we must challenge those gender binaries reinforced in scholarly work and in practice.

A second critique astutely follows, which is the dearth of research examining trans* and gender nonconforming students. Some recent research has emerged highlighting the leadership experiences of trans* students (Dugan, Kusel, & Simounet, 2012; Jourian, 2014, 2016; Jourian & Simmons, 2017), yet much remains unknown about the leadership identity, development, and experiences of members of this population. Much of how *leadership* is promoted and conceptualized within the research and leadership education, characterized often by on-campus student organization involvement and leadership positions, may marginalize trans* and gender nonconforming students by reinforcing dominant leadership narratives (Jourian & Simmons, 2017).

A third critique of the extant research is the relative absence of examining gender in relation to leadership, which we note as different from examining the leadership experiences or outcomes of individuals with a particular gender identity. In other words, very little research actually focuses on gender as an explanatory variable rather than merely as a demographic characteristic used to identify research participants. For example, examining individuals' views of themselves as men and as men engaging in leadership is different from studying how a group of men engage in leadership. As we advance our understanding of the role of gender in leadership development, with the goal of promoting social justice, it is important to also ask questions. These questions should grapple with both research and leadership education practice, about how one's gender plays a role in their leadership development.

ADVANCING SOCIALLY JUST LEADERSHIP
THROUGH THE LENS OF GENDER

Building from the critical examination of the historical and current context of gender and leadership and the limited research base on gender and leadership outlined in the previous sections, we offer three pivotal commitments for advancing socially just leadership. Discussed in further detail below are the three commitments of

1. challenging and unlearning,
2. promoting a wide range of leadership capacities that advance social justice, and
3. acknowledging students' multiple and interlocking identities.

Independently, each of these commitments represent avenues toward inclusivity in leadership education, and collectively, they represent a mechanism by which the field can become more socially just.

Challenging and Unlearning

In his book *Leadership Theory: Cultivating Critical Perspectives*, Dugan (2017) offered tools of deconstruction and reconstruction as helpful ways to view leadership theories and models. We find a great deal of utility in this idea of shifting mental models and engaging in unlearning from a critical perspective. Socially just leadership, particularly through the lens of gender, requires leadership educators and their students to challenge societal norms, mental models, and assumptions about what gender is and what leadership is. For example, higher education professionals often reinforce a hierarchy of positional leadership on campus, praising and rewarding students who are dedicated to positions of prestige such as student government, resident assistants, or orientation leaders. Yet, these same professionals often overlook grassroots activism and advocacy as leadership, particularly if that activism and advocacy is disruptive and uncomfortable for the status quo on campus.

Among many historically marginalized populations on campus (such as LGBTQ+ students, undocumented students, and students of color), activism and advocacy are used to challenge and disrupt chilly campus climates. Frequently, this climate is created through overlapping issues of hegemonic masculinity, patriarchy, genderism, sexism, and racism. As a result, we encourage leadership educators and students alike to consider the ways in which they uphold these ideas in conscious or subconscious ways. As we have engaged in more critical thinking about leadership, it is hard to acknowledge that many of the concepts around leadership inherently tend to center White, Western, male-dominated, middle-class norms that reinforce power, privilege, and formal authority. If we do not spend adequate time and energy considering and critiquing leadership and the concepts related to it, we potentially send dangerous and inappropriate messages to students who may be harmed by these very dominant ideas. From a gender perspective, this happens by reinforcing the myth that leadership styles are gendered.

As mentioned previously, much of the research and scholarship on gender and leadership has created a false binary of masculine versus feminine leadership styles. This creates a problematic divide given the fact that these gendered ideas of leadership are often embedded in sexist, patriarchal cultural norms and gender expectations. As a result, we advocate for leadership educators to take a more inclusive stance and embrace more so-called feminist leadership approaches where individuals practice leadership that is equitable across gender (Shea & Renn, 2017). This also allows for greater inclusivity for students who personally identify outside of the rigid binary of man or woman. We must acknowledge, anticipate, and support the fact that students entering higher education today are doing so with a greater array of gender identities and a more nuanced understanding of the fluidity of gender expression and performance; as a result, leadership educators must do the important work of educating themselves around these issues to be good models and stewards of the importance of self-work and unlearning of gender to best serve all of the students who enter their offices. Additionally, leadership educators must educate their students to do the same as they engage in the world and practice leadership.

Promoting a Wide Range of Leadership Capacities to Advance Social Justice

Engaging in socially just leadership requires a wide range of leadership capacities, behaviors, and approaches for people of all genders. For example, many believe students who practice leadership must be able to collaborate with others, assert themselves in healthy, appropriate ways, take action with a thorough understanding of one's values and ethics, and be able to take initiative to make positive social change in community with others. None of these practices are gendered; instead, all of our students, regardless of their gender identity and expression, should be encouraged to find those elements of leadership practice that work best for them personally.

Inherently, we believe everyone holds implicit biases that inform how we make meaning in our lives. These implicit biases can also be connected to assumptions around gender. We advocate that leadership educators consider the assumptions they have about their students and their leadership development needs based upon gender. Do we choose more relational models to use as a framework when we are speaking to an audience of women and more transactional or leader-centric models for men? Might we ignore or think critically about offering examples within our trainings and programs of leaders who may identify as trans* or gender nonconforming rather than always presenting examples of individuals who adhere to the gender binary of man and woman? How can we move beyond distinctions and dichotomies to recognize that all students regardless of gender identity need to have a wide range of leadership capacities, behaviors, and values that don't fall into gendered categories? Much of this requires a great deal of self-learning, personal, and professional development to promote greater consciousness about the role of gender socialization and how deeply embedded these ideas are within the constructs of our daily lives.

Acknowledge Students' Multiple and Interlocking Identities

As we consider individuals' gender identities, it is imperative to recognize that gender identity is just one of the multiple and interlocking identities that make up an individual and that not only shape their lives, but also influence their social positions in society (Jordan-Zachery, 2007). The model of multiple dimensions of identity (MMDI) highlights how other social identities, such as race, ethnicity, class, sexuality, physical ability, nationality, and religion, are experienced in connection with one's gender identity, and the intersection of these multiple identities in mutually reinforcing ways (Jones & Abes, 2013, p. 159). Structures of oppression and privilege influence how salient these multiple identities may be for an individual in a given context, whether the individual intends this to be the case or not (Jones & Abes, 2013). As we seek to understand individuals and their lived experiences through recognizing their multiple identities, it is crucial to recognize the existence of intragroup differences (Jones & Abes, 2013), acknowledging, for example, that the lived experiences of all Black women or all Latinx trans* individuals could have commonalities, yet are different.

Tillapaugh, Mitchell, and Soria (2017) used intersectionality as a lens through which to view gender and student leadership. Their discussion encourages leadership educators to help students critically examine and reflect upon their complexity of identity and their leadership development, posing questions for students to consider such as: "How do my social identities affect my personal leadership identity? In what ways do my social identities affect others' prescriptions, expectations, or assumptions about my leadership style or abilities[?]" (Tillapaugh et al., 2017, p. 28). Through awareness of one's own intersectional social identities, one can begin to gain a deeper understanding of the experiences of others (Tillapaugh et al., 2017), a capacity and outcome that is central to socially just leadership.

Knowledge, Skills, and Values for Socially Just Leadership Through the Lens of Gender

Below we propose some critical areas of knowledge, skills, and values in advancing socially just leadership education through the lens of gender. These areas are relevant for leadership educators in their own personal and professional development and are also relevant as key guideposts as leadership educators seek to develop students to be socially just leaders.

Knowledge

- The social construction of gender identity, gender expression, and gender roles and how privilege and oppression are connected to one's gender identity and expression.
- The fluidity of gender identity and gender expression, acknowledging an array of identities and expressions rather than rigid binaries.
- The limitations of the traditional, hierarchical, and authoritarian conceptualizations of leadership, acknowledging how these conceptualizations leave many individuals out and further reinforce gendered privilege and oppression.

Skills

- Awareness of one's own identities, biases, perspectives, and mental models of gender and of leadership.
- Ability to be open, authentic, and vulnerable.
- Awareness of others' identities and perspectives.
- Ability to empathetically listen in order to seek to understand and connect.
- Ability to act with agency and advocate with assertiveness to affect change.
- Ability to connect and collaborate with others across differences.
- Ability to engage in critical examination and inquiry at individual, group, and systemic levels.
- Ability to welcome, accept, and learn from feedback.
- Ability to challenge and interrupt exclusionary practices.

Values

- Justice, equity, and liberation with consideration of gender identity and gender expression.
- Inclusive feminism that seeks to end sexism, genderism, and cissexism.
- Empowerment of oneself and of others.
- Commitment to lifelong learning and continuous growth.

As the study and practice of leadership continues to advance and as the social constructs of gender continue to be critically examined and deconstructed, this compilation of key areas of knowledge, skills, and values will too need to adapt and evolve. It is important to acknowledge that the previously denoted knowledge, skills, and values ultimately play out on individual- and systemic-levels. Individually, those engaging in socially just leadership through the lens of gender must unlearn and challenge the traditionally-held gender norms and expectations that restrict human behaviors, including one's leadership practice. Systemically, we all live in a world and society largely influenced by interlocking power structures informed by patriarchy and hegemony through sexism, genderism, and cissexism. As a result, we encourage individuals to think critically about how they can galvanize socially just leadership through their sphere of influence and then act in accordance with that thinking. By focusing on making changes within one's own personal networks through one's involvement in organizations and institutions, there is the potential and possibility of working collaboratively with others through coalition building to positively impact the systems in which we all take part. Doing inner work and moving to action through that work, collaboratively with others, can lead to effective socially just leadership. These guideposts we have outlined are intended as responsive to the world in which we live and lead and are crucial for making the world a better and more equitable place.

CONCLUSION

In order to advance leadership for social justice through the lens of gender there is much work that needs to be done. As the study of leadership has shifted and evolved over the years, at its core, not much about how leadership is conceptualized has really changed. In fact, Dugan (2017) highlighted the idea of zombie theories, where concepts and ideas of leadership have just been repackaged in new theories or models and cannot be killed off. Ultimately, conceptualizations of leadership still continue to center Western dominant ideologies. Socially just leadership, as a response to this, is about moving the needle and advancing new, critical approaches and understandings of leadership that disrupt traditional views. It embraces critical approaches and lenses in a way that help leadership educators and their students engage in more inclusive practices of leadership to benefit equity across difference. As we note throughout this chapter, socially just leadership through the lens of gender is just one starting place leadership educators may consider using in their work. This work must happen on an individual level and, just as importantly, on a broader systemic perspective as well.

As described earlier, leadership educators' work is done in the context of larger institutional systems often informed by genderism, sexism, and cissexism. While there has been a great deal of attention to gender equity in the recent past, colleges and universities inherently operate in ways that advantage cisgender men (Allan, 2011). Therefore, genderism, sexism, and cissexism still contribute to women, trans* and gender non-conforming individuals, and agender students feeling marginalized or left out on their campuses. At a systemic level, higher education professionals need to work collaboratively through coalition building to shift their institutions and disrupt systems of genderism and sexism to create more equitable processes and outcomes for all, particularly across gender identities and expressions. However, this systemic work cannot be done without individuals engaging in their own inner work around these issues.

The commitments we provide in this chapter of (a) challenging and unlearning, (b) promoting a wide range of leadership capacities that advance social justice, and (c) acknowledging students' multiple and interlocking identities serves as a potential framework for engaging in self-work in order to develop as more socially just leaders and leadership educators. Critical self-reflection is a vital tool for self-work around socially just leadership. We argue just as leadership educators must consider unlearning and relearning about leadership through a critical lens, they must also do the same with their understanding of gender. As we have outlined within this chapter, our ever-evolving understanding of gender as a social construct means that there is always more to learn and examine around this concept. Our students are arriving to colleges and universities today with more sophisticated ideas and language around gender identity than ever before. In a world of changing pronouns, a rejection of rigid binary gender identification labels, and more forethought on gender as performance, leadership educators must think critically about their own views on gender and how those views inform their worldviews and thus, their interactions and relationships with students. We cannot uphold antiquated notions of gender and leadership with our students any longer. To do so, we violate the professional standards set forth for college student educators in our field. We must work collaboratively to educate ourselves and engage in proactive rather than reactive work. By doing so we begin to work across our field of leadership education to advance the necessary and critical work of social justice and operationalize this in our professional practice as socially just leadership.

REFERENCES

Allan, E. J. (2011). *Women's status in higher education: Equity matters: ASHE Higher Education Report, 37*(1). San Francisco, CA: Jossey-Bass.

Arminio, J. L., Carter, S., Jones, S. E., Kruger, K., Lucas, N., Washington, J., & Scott, A. (2000). Leadership experiences of students of color. *NASPA Journal, 37*, 496–510.

Avolio, B. J., & Gardner, W. L. (2005). Authentic leadership development: Getting to the root of positive forms of leadership. *The Leadership Quarterly, 16*, 315–338.

Bannon, I., & Correia, M. C. (Eds.). (2006). *The other half of gender: Men's issues in development.* Washington, DC: International Bank for Reconstruction and Development.

Bilodeau, B. L. (2009). *Genderism: Transgender students, binary systems and higher education.* Saarbrücken, Germany: VDM Verlag.

Bordas, J. (2007). *Salsa, soul, and spirit: Leadership for a multicultural age.* San Francisco, CA: Berrett-Koehler.

Burns, J. M. (1978). *Leadership.* New York, NY: Harper & Row.

Dugan, J. P. (2017). *Leadership theory: Cultivating critical perspectives.* San Francisco, CA: Jossey Bass.

Dugan, J. P., & Komives, S. R. (2007). *Developing leadership capacity in college students: Findings from a national student.* College Park, MD: National Clearinghouse for Leadership Programs.

Dugan, J. P., Komives, S. R., & Segar, T. C. (2008). College student capacity for socially responsible leadership: Understanding norms and influences of race, gender, and sexual orientation. *NASPA Journal, 45*, 475–500.

Dugan, J. P., Kusel, M. L., & Simounet, D. M. (2012). Transgender college students: An exploratory study of perceptions, engagement, and educational outcomes. *Journal of College Student Development, 53*, 719–736.

Eagly, A. H., & Carli, L. L. (2007). *Through the labyrinth: The truth about how women become leaders.* Boston, MA: Harvard Business School Press.

Greenleaf, R. K. (1977). *Servant leadership.* Mahwah, NJ: Paulist Press.

Haber, P. (2011). Iron sharpens iron: Exploring the experiences of female college student leaders. *Advancing Women in Leadership Journal, 31*, 86–101.

Haber, P. (2012). Perceptions of leadership: College students' understandings of the concept of leadership and differences by gender, race, and age. *Journal of Leadership Education, 11*(2), 26–51.

Haber-Curran, P., & Tillapaugh, D. (2017). Gender and student leadership: A critical examination. In D. Tillapaugh & P. Haber-Curran (Eds.). *New directions for student leadership, No. 154: Critical perspectives on gender and student leadership* (pp. 11–22). San Francisco, CA: Jossey-Bass.

Heifetz, R. A. (1994). *Leadership without easy answers.* Cambridge, MA: Harvard University Press.

Higher Education Research Institute. (1996). *A social change model of leadership development.* Los Angeles, CA: Higher Education Research Institute.

Hill, D. B. (2003). Genderism, transphobia, and gender bashing: A framework for interpreting anti-transgender violence. In B. C. Wallace & R. T. Carter (Eds.),

Understanding and dealing with violence: A multicultural approach (pp. 113–136). Thousand Oaks, CA: SAGE.

Hoyt, C. L., & Simon, S. (2017). Gender and leadership. In P. Northouse (Ed.), *Leadership: Theory and practice* (7th ed., pp. 397–426). Thousand Oaks, CA: SAGE.

Jones, S. R., & Abes, E. S. (2013). *Identity development of college students: Advancing frameworks for multiple dimensions of identity.* San Francisco, CA: Jossey-Bass.

Jordan-Zachery, J. S. (2007). Am I a Black woman or a woman who is Black?: A few thoughts on the meaning of intersectionality. *Politics and Gender, 3*(2), 254–263.

Jourian, T. J. (2014). Trans* forming authentic leadership: A conceptual framework. *Journal of Critical Thought and Praxis, 2*(2), 1–15.

Jourian, T. J. (2016). *"My masculinity is a little love poem to myself": Trans* masculine college students' conceptualizations of masculinities.* (Unpublished doctoral dissertation). Loyola University Chicago, Chicago, IL.

Jourian, T. J., & Simmons, S. L. (2017). Trans* leadership. In D. Tillapaugh & P. Haber-Curran (Eds.), *New directions for student leadership, No. 154: Critical perspectives on gender and student leadership* (pp. 59–69). San Francisco, CA: Jossey-Bass.

Kezar, A., & Moriarty, D. (2000). Expanding our understanding of student leadership development: A study exploring gender and ethnic identity. *Journal of College Student Development, 41,* 55–69.

Komives, S. R. (1992). Getting things done: A gender comparison of resident assistant and hall director achieving styles. *Journal of College and University Student Housing, 22,* 30–38.

Komives, S. R., & Dugan, J. P. (2010). Contemporary leadership theories. In R. A. Couto (Ed.), *Political and civic leadership: A reference handbook* (pp. 111–120). Thousand Oaks, CA: SAGE.

Komives, S. R., Lucas, N., & McMahon, T. R. (1998). *Exploring leadership: For college students who want to make a difference.* San Francisco, CA: Jossey-Bass.

Kouzes, J. M., & Posner, B. Z. (1987). *The leadership challenge.* San Francisco, CA: Jossey-Bass.

Madsen, S. R. (Ed.). (2017). *Handbook of research on gender and leadership.* Cheltenham, England: Elgar.

Nicolazzo, Z. (2017). *Trans* in college: Transgender students' strategies for navigating campus life and the institutional politics of inclusion.* Sterling, VA: Stylus.

Porter, J. D. (1998). *The contribution of gay and lesbian identity development to transformational leadership self-efficacy* (Unpublished doctoral dissertation). College Park, MD: University of Maryland.

Renn, K. A. (2010). LGBT and queer research in higher education: The state and status of the field. *Educational Researcher, 39*(2), 132–141.

Renn, K. A., & Bilodeau, B. L. (2005a). Leadership identity development among lesbian, gay, bisexual, and transgender student leaders. *Journal of Student Affairs Research and Practice, 42,* 342–367.

Renn, K. A., & Bilodeau, B. (2005b). Queer student leaders: An exploratory case study of identity development and LGBT student involvement at a Midwestern research university. *Journal of Gay & Lesbian Issues in Education, 2,* 49–71.

Rost, J. C. (1991). *Leadership for the twenty-first century.* Westport, CT: Praeger.

Shankman, M. L., Allen, S. J., & Haber-Curran, P. (2015). *Emotionally intelligent leadership: A guide for students* (2nd ed.). San Francisco, CA: Jossey-Bass.

Shea, H., & Renn, K. (2017). Gender and leadership. In D. Tillapaugh & P. Haber-Curran (Eds.), *New directions for student leadership, No. 154: Critical perspectives on gender and student leadership* (pp. 83–94). San Francisco, CA: Jossey-Bass.

Stolzenberg, E. B., & Hughes, B. (2017). The experiences of incoming transgender college students: New data on gender identity. *Liberal Education, 103*(2).

Tillapaugh, D., & Haber-Curran, P. (2016). College men's perceptions of their leadership practice: Unpacking power and influence. *Journal of Leadership Education, 15*(3), 131–150.

Tillapaugh, D., & Haber-Curran, P. (Eds.). (2017). *New directions for student leadership, No. 154: Critical perspectives on gender and student leadership.* San Francisco, CA: Jossey-Bass.

Tillapaugh, D., Mitchell, D., Jr., & Soria, K. (2017). Considering gender and student leadership through the lens of intersectionality. In D. Tillapaugh & P. Haber-Curran (Eds.), *New directions for student leadership, No. 154: Critical perspectives on gender and student leadership* (pp. 23–32). San Francisco, CA: Jossey-Bass.

Werhane, P., & Painter-Morland, M. (Eds). (2011). *Leadership, gender, and organization (Issues in Business Ethics).* Dordrecht, The Netherlands: Springer.

West, C., & Zimmerman, D. H. (1987). Doing gender. *Gender and Society, 1*, 125–151.

Wheatley, M. J. (1994). *Leadership and the new science: Learning about organizations from an orderly universe.* San Francisco, CA: Berrett-Koehler.

Wilchins, R. A. (2002). Queerer bodies. In J. Nestle, C. Howell, & R. A. Wilchins (Eds.), *Genderqueer: Voices from beyond the sexual binary* (pp. 33–46). Los Angeles, CA: Alyson.

CHAPTER 7

GETTING IN FORMATION TO LEAD

Black Female Student Leadership Development

LaFarin R. Meriwether

Be a leader not a follower! Parents, teachers, camp counselors, siblings, grandparents, and a multitude of other authoritative persons wag fingers or, in disciplinary tones, convey this message to children. Most often these messages are given after some unfortunate experience involving following the crowd that led to a phone call or note home. Guardians want their children to be able to think independently and make good decisions about the people they are around. In most Black families, however, the instructions are usually followed by additional advice around not embarrassing the family with your actions and remembering you are representing more than yourself.

When I think about the beginnings of life lessons and leadership development for Black children I have known, it has always been about more than the individual. Leffler (2014) wrote for Black leaders "... each individual is

Changing the Narrative, pages 93–108
Copyright © 2018 by Information Age Publishing
All rights of reproduction in any form reserved.

a representative of the whole and each carries a sense of collective responsibility. This extended definition of self-focusing on the 'we' rather that the 'I'—has profound implications for leadership within and beyond the Black communities" (p. 3). For Black women this is the essence of their development as women, and subsequently, as leaders. Most often, these lessons begin in the home. King and Ferguson (2011) explained how this leadership knowledge flows through the "motherline." The motherline are:

> Women who pass on the value of African-centered worldview, women who help daughters learn to read the social climate, heal from dominant culture oppression, fashion a culturally grounded identity, form and carry out resistance aimed at a particular social context or institution. (p. 23)

In conjunction with motherline ideology, the historical beginnings of Black female leadership in America cannot go overlooked. The role of Black women during slavery, after the civil war, during the reconstruction, and the civil rights movement and beyond has shaped the pillars of Black female leadership. Leffler (2014) suggested "...people are products of their cultures, heritage, and environments. The social fabric of people's lives matter profoundly" (p. 3). This chapter seeks to understand the leadership development of Black female student leaders through a social justice framework by examining how students understand leadership and the contextual implications of how to develop these young women into social justice leaders.

WHAT IS LEADERSHIP?

The narrative of leadership for Black women tends to appear distinct from their White peers and Black male counterparts. Parker (2005) argued "...in the leadership literature there exists two competing models of leadership, based almost exclusively on studies of White women and men, presented as race neutral and assumed generalized to all people" (p. xi). Leadership experiences and perceptions for women and men are very different. Add race to the mix and the narrative changes drastically. The complexity of the intersection of race and gender for Black women has major impacts on their leadership experience. More simply put, leadership looks different for Black women because Black women are different. They represent unique experiences unmatched by members of other marginalized populations (King & Ferguson, 2011).

As we understand the process of developing Black female student leaders, words like "leader" and "leadership" have to be defined. It is important to understand how these terms are defined in order to understand the context of those who are classified as leaders and those who are engaged in leadership. I define leadership as a contextual collaboration that influences a group of individuals towards a common cause, goal, or purpose facilitated by a group of leaders and followers. This definition is partly influenced by Joseph C. Rost. Rost (1991) defined leadership as "an influence relationship among leaders and followers who intend real changes that reflect their mutual purposes" (p. 102). For Black leaders the idea of *Ubuntu* contributes to the communal collectivist ascribed purpose of leadership for Black leaders. Schuyler (2014) explained ". . . in Ubuntu philosophy, one is seen to be a person through others focusing on serving others as a way of life" (p. 161); the idea of "we" versus "I." For most Black women, performing actions for the betterment of all is grounded in a communal understanding of group representation and collective success.

HISTORICAL PERSPECTIVE OF BLACK FEMALE LEADERSHIP

Black female narratives are missing in leadership literature. The failure to consider the experiences of Black female leaders presents several factors that contribute to how we understand Black woman leadership today. The existing narrative includes African village ideology that was brought to the Americas by the enslaved. Parker (2005) argued "African American women's survival, resistance, and strategies of change in response to this cultural text reflect a leadership tradition that is useful for re-envisioning leadership in the 21st century" (p. 31).

The history of Black female leadership is a story of finding voice through struggle. During slavery, as powerless as they may have seemed, Black women managed homes; nursed babies; tended the fields; traded goods; raised their own children, those of others, and children of slave owners. Leadership for Black people is frequently seen from the lens of social activism. The civil rights movements of the 1950s and 1960s, the Black power movement, and the women's movements of the 1970s were all heavily influenced by Black female leadership. However, as active as they were, Barnett (1993) reminded us "although seldom recognized as leaders, these women were often the ones who initiated protest, formulated strategies and tactics, and mobilized other resources (especially money, personnel, and communication networks) necessary for successful collective action" (p. 163).

Popular depictions of history vividly tell stories of Black men involved in civil rights and White women involved in the women's movement, but Black women are invisible in these narratives. Barnett (1993) noted "the invisibility of modern Black women leaders and activists is in part a result of gender, race, and class biases prevalent in both the social movement literature and feminist scholarship" (p. 163). Socially just leadership educators remember the history of Black female leadership contributions, and their seeming invisibility, as they develop future Black female leaders. Furthering this point, Livingston, Rosette, and Washington (2012) explained:

> "Black female" is not merely the additive combination of race and gender. Rather, their dual subordinate identities assign Black women to a unique space. Because the prototypical Black [person] is male, and the prototypical woman is White, Black women tend to be defined as non-prototypical, marginal members of both their racial and gender groups, and consequently are often rendered invisible. (p. 355)

These ideas force us to critically question the representation of Black female leaders, historically and in the modern day, beyond the tokenization of those who participate in leadership development opportunities. Subsequently, important questions emerge around how we, as leadership educators, are or are not developing diverse individuals and groups of student leaders. Do our leaders of color feel as though they are valued or simply part of a quota? What does the answer say about who we view and promote as leaders?

The extant scholarship strongly implies some are more inclined to lead through social justice lenses because of their own unique lived experiences. I argue Black women are inclined to lead from a social justice perspective, from communal, historical, social, and familial socialization.

How Do Black Female Students Define Their Leadership Experiences?

Challenging and exploring how Black women in general, and Black female student leaders specifically, define leadership is critical in order to understand their development as leaders through a social justice framework. Guthrie, Jones, Osteen, and Hu (2013) stated, "...many people of color rely on their cultural and life experiences to guide their leadership experience" (p. 43). To further understand how Black female student leaders define leadership, it was necessary to actually speak with Black female student leaders about their leadership experiences, with particular focus on how they define and understand leadership.

The data analyzed for this chapter came from individual interviews of Black female student leaders who are or have been participants in a leadership certificate program at a large Research I institution in the southeastern United States. Purposive sampling was used to select individuals for the study. Johnson and Christensen (2004) noted in purposive sampling, the researcher specifies the characteristics of a population of interest and then tries to locate individuals who have those characteristics. Due to the nature of the questions of interest, participants were identified through faculty from an undergraduate certificate in leadership studies. Invitations to participate were sent to nine eligible women. Six participants were interviewed and those interviews ranged from 30 to 45 minutes. The participants consisted of four juniors and two seniors. Four identified as Black American, one as Afro-Latina, and one as Haitian American.

DEVELOPMENTAL PROCESS OF BLACK FEMALE LEADERS

The lens used to understand the development process of Black female student leaders was a combination of Standpoint Theory and Black Feminist Thought (Collins, 1985), the culturally relevant leadership learning model (Bertrand Jones, Guthrie, & Osteen, 2016), and Black Womanist Leadership (motherline; King and Ferguson, 2011). Standpoint theory and Black feminist thought examines how Black women make meaning of their own experiences through the social and historical context of race and gender. Hallstein (1999) noted, "...feminist standpoint theorists view women as active agents who make sense of their own lives within particular social and historical contexts" (p. 37). Black female life experiences coupled with campus experiences affect and define opportunities they pursue and how they make meaning of those opportunities. Collins (1985) suggested:

> Black women's insistence on self-definition, self-valuation, and the necessity for a Black female-centered analysis is significant for two reasons. First, defining and valuing one's consciousness of one's own self-defined standpoint in the face of images that foster a self-definition as the objectified "other" is an important way of resisting the dehumanization essential to systems of domination. The status of being the "other" implies being "other than" or different from the assumed norm of white male behavior. (p. 18)

Rethinking how Black female leaders are developed is essential in forming an appropriate context to facilitate leadership development for these women outside of the generally assumed definitions of leadership. Once this occurs we can apply social justice values into development practices.

CRLL frames leadership development of diverse student groups by taking into consideration issues of identity, capacity, efficacy, and the environment in which leadership development takes place. Bertrand Jones et al. (2016) state "...culturally relevant leadership learning acknowledges power in leadership, specifically, the power of language and the power of the institutional culture/climate to influence students' identity, capacity, and efficacy to create social change" (p. 10). Understanding identity, capacity, and efficacy of Black female leaders, and their motivation for leadership, should guide how we implement social justice leadership development practices for these women. Guthrie et al. (2013) wrote "...the process includes an awareness of students' identities as racial, gendered, and cultured individuals. Each student brings himself or herself, actualized or not, to the leadership experience" (p. 40).

Black womanist leadership articulates how Black women learn leadership through the motherline. Through the motherline "...we learn not only how their mothers pushed the edges toward a more just world, but how their mothers influenced the daughters' life chances and prepared daughters to step into the struggle of dismantling systems of oppression" (King & Ferguson, 2011, p. 15). This perspective implies Black women do not have to be taught to be socially just, or how to operate from a social justice framework, because they are inherently socialized to do so. The motherline is made up of the collection of women, whether biologically related or by communal connection, who instill leadership values on Black women in their care.

It is important to keep in mind the discussion of *Ubuntu* which permeates how and why Black women choose to lead and or are a part of the leadership process. Guthrie et al. (2013) advocates understanding "...Bordas's (2007) descriptions of leaders from communities of color—collectivist, servant, and activist—provide a framework for understanding how students from diverse backgrounds craft leader identities" (p. 43). King and Ferguson (2011) echo these thoughts by noting "...our communal upbringing teaches us that everyone's contribution is necessary to the success of a venture: thus it is unfair to emphasize the organizer to the exclusion of the group, village, community, or team" (p. 6).

The importance of developing Black female student leaders, enhancing the environments in which this development is happening, as well as considering the world educators are preparing them for, cannot be understated. Environments and the perceptions of environments, campuses, or other leadership learning contexts have impact on how Black female students navigate leadership. Socially just leadership educators create spaces where students can develop and refine skills in navigating campus culture and dynamics (see Chapter 14).

LISTENING TO BLACK FEMALE LEADERS' VOICES

As we develop strategies and practices to develop Black female student leaders, we first must understand how they see themselves as leaders, as women, as Black, and as Black women. Guthrie et al. (2013) noted Day's et al. assertion "...leader identity is a student's own theory about who he or she is as a leader and how the student thinks of himself or herself and his or her role in relation to the world" (p. 30). Five major themes surfaced from the interviews: (a) leadership for Black women can be difficult, (b) leadership learning began at home and in their community, (c) being Black and female is beautiful but hard to navigate at times, (d) giving back to the community and helping others progress is why you lead, and (e) seeing other Black women leading was impactful for them and their belief that they could be leaders. These themes support how important it is for leadership educators to honor more than dominant perspectives of what it is to be a leader.

When asked to describe a leader in three words, the only term provided by participants more than once was "motivated/motivation." Other reports included, "challenge," "inspired," "direction," "communication," "compromise," "initiative," "dedication," "identity," "power," "authority," and "perseverance." One participant, referred to as "Asia," described "leader" as:

> . . . someone who perseveres as best as they possibly can when faced with several challenges and along the way influences other people to do the same by helping those people, showing those people, and allowing those people to take the lead.

Other definitions had similar tones of influence and emphasized the need to keep people informed and on-task to achieve the goals of the group or project. Of particular note, one participant described being a leader and leadership as an "inside out process"; meaning that leading people comes from within. There is something in you that makes you want to do the things you do as well as work to cause change. This account speaks to how some members of the sample saw leader as an internalized identity as well as leadership as a process, which begins within the individual who is leading.

Black and Female: Exploring the Intersection of Race and Gender

The intersectionality of race and gender are important considerations when seeking to understand how Black female students view themselves as social justice leaders. Being Black, and being female, are salient identities for most Black females. The saliency may affect how these women navigate different areas of their lives, and being a leader—or participating in leadership—are not exempt from these influences. Shorter-Gooden & Washington (1996) suggested:

> African-American women develop a sense of strength in reaction to struggling with two ascribed identities—race and gender—that are devalued; or alternatively, the more racism and sexism an African-American woman perceives, the more likely she is to have an identity that includes a sense of strength. (p. 473)

When asked how they defined being Black the young women provided varied responses. Some responses were characterized by both seemingly positive and negative perceptions of what it meant to be Black. Asia said,

> Well, to be Black is to see hardship after hardship and still find a way to persevere. To be Black is to work extremely hard to prove yourself, when you don't necessarily have to prove yourself. To be Black is to hear over and over again, that you're inferior, and not in those words, but, you know, the way in which your people are portrayed in the media. The way in which people talk about you. The list goes on. To be Black is also to be beautiful. It's to be strong, it's to be courageous. To be ongoing and everlasting. "Khloe" echoed similar thoughts in her response:

> To be Black is to be beautiful. It's to be, it's to be everything. It, it's everything. Growing up, as an African-American woman, you get put down a lot or you get, you get shaded a lot on a lot of things, but standing true, you're standing true in your natural hair. Standing true in your full lips, your curves, and doing, everything that, no one wants you to do is being African-American. Being aware of your culture, being like, I feel like being a family. That's what it is. I feel like all Africans are a family. Whether I know you personally or not, when I see you, you're my cousin.

As confident as these two women were in how they defined being Black, others struggled with putting it into words. Another participant, "Angel" felt caught between the different parts of her identity, as she identified as Afro-Latina. In the United States, it is common practice to assume that if you look Black or African American, then the Black experience in America is the narrative that is ascribed to you regardless of your ethnic and or racial identification. Another sample member, "Jade," had a hard time expressing what being Black meant to her. She explained that she had never really thought about what being Black meant for her. From these brief accounts, it became clear that the intersections of race and gender were not uniform across participants. This within-group variation is another important factor to consider when attempting to support Black female leaders; while many individuals in this population may appear outwardly similar, their internalized thoughts, feelings, and experiences can be quite different.

Socially just educators understand each of our students is different, even if we are not always privy as to how. Some share identities, which may lend themselves to similar experiences, but how they process and live out loud with their identities may be different. While they all identified it as the first thing other people see, being Black meant something nuanced to the Black female student leader participants. Therefore, helping members of this population explore the meaning of Blackness is critical to their overall, and leadership, development.

Exploring each component of intersecting identities can lead to more accurate understandings of how they interact and influence the lived experiences of our students. Shorter-Gooden and Washington (1996) reasoned, "given that being female is devalued in this society, how women handle or integrate the notion of being a woman into their identity is an important area of exploration" (p. 466). When identifying what it meant to be a woman, most of the participants spoke about the impact of seeing their mothers handle households. In explaining those experiences, they expressed that is where they learned leadership, Angel shared:

> Women multitask so much better than men. Women just, are phenomenal, to be honest. And I, I didn't know that for a long time I didn't, for a long time, I didn't see the value in femininity. And, because my parents are like...My mom doesn't know that much English. My dad does. And she would make simple mistakes, but now looking, I've noticed my mom has great networking abilities. My mom can meet someone at the store and they'll be, like, they're best friends, versus when I was a kid, I'd be like, "Why is she always talking with people?" I didn't realize how resourceful she was. She was able to just make those connections. And if we ever needed anything as a family, she was able to solve that for us versus my dad. He wasn't able to do that.

Similar stories were shared by the other young women. Seeing how their mothers ran their homes and took care of their family taught them lessons on selflessness, multitasking, planning, and budgeting. It was not until later in life that they were able to classify those skills as leadership. Khloe described being a woman as:

> To be a woman, I'm strong. It means to be strong, it means to, it's empowering. It's uplifting. It's everything they say it's not. I feel like being a woman is breaking those barriers. Breaking down a lot of, hardships and doing stuff out of the norm.

These young women had very strong perceptions of their identities as women. They identified the hardships and the barrier breaking that came with being women, but they also identified their pride and abilities to go against the grain as women due to lessons learned in the home. Bertrand Jones et al. (2016) noted, "...understanding how students with different identities define and learn about leadership helps educators appreciate the critical connection of leadership and diversity" (p. 9).

For some, it is impossible to separate race and gender in a society that often forces minoritized individuals to do so. Race is a social construct with major influence on how Black female students navigate different spaces and environments. Guthrie et al. (2013) noted "...social psychologist Henri Taijfel coined the term social identity, defining it as part of the individual's self-concept, which develops from his or her acknowledgement of membership in a social group and the significance of membership in that group" (p. 40). As an example of these notions, Asia stated:

> To be a Black women means to never give up. Ever. It's to understand that the world is always gonna give you so much but you still have to find a way to make it through and to see it through. To be a Black woman is to make sure that you give your family and your friends the love and support that they need. It's to teach those who will come after you to listen to those who have come before you. It's to exhibit strength and bravery, intelligence, but it's also to struggle.

Concepts of strength emphasized by the motherline (King & Ferguson, 2011) as well the communal aspects of leadership that exist in the *Ubuntu* philosophy (Schuyler, 2014) echoed in the responses of these young women. They expressed the influence of family on leadership style. Khloe spoke to the influence of her parents and being the oldest of her siblings. When asked about what it meant to be a Black women, she shared:

> I feel like that's the two, you come out with like two strikes. Two strikes against you. It's like, oh, you're Black. Oh, you're like a female. Now you're minority within a minority…because no matter what you do or what you say, you're always going to be, have those two notches against you. So, you have to be on your game all the time. Everyone is always like, it's always a set of eyes on you.

The idea of being a double minority and having to work twice as hard was a sentiment echoed by all of the women who participated. However, all identified that was not a reason to stop doing what they were supposed to do, nor did it stop them from being leaders. In all cases, these dynamics made them more determined to prove others' negative stereotypes wrong.

Understanding how members of this population see themselves, how they perceive how others see them, as well as how they navigate environments at the intersection of race and gender helps leadership educators determine how to best aid in the development of these individuals from a social justice lens.

IMPLICATIONS FOR BLACK FEMALE LEADERSHIP DEVELOPMENT

Given the findings of this study, how can we develop or nurture Black female leaders? The first step is acknowledging the difficulties of leading through the lens of social justice. For marginalized individuals, leading change efforts while being triggered by societal and campus climates occurs more often than not. Socially just leadership educators consider how traditional leadership experiences fail to instill the ideas of positive social change in Black female student leaders. Assumptions of how Black female leaders are already socialized to create change for others should be critically examined and confronted. As "Valarie" noted, "If I'm gonna make it, I'm gonna also look behind me to see how am I gonna make sure that they [other black women] also make it."

Socially just leadership educators should carefully consider teaching and developing curriculum around the aspects of the CRLL model. Through this model, we can help develop their identities, capacities, and efficacies around leading. Each of these factors can be considered individually, as well as in conjunction, toward helping these students believe in their ability to create social change through leadership. However, contextual and environmental factors in which leadership learning occurs also affects efficacy, as the CRLL model indicates. As Asia mentioned:

> There are some people who I feel I can be myself around and there are other people who I feel like I can't be myself around, and that could be for a number of reasons. If we're working, for example, if we're working towards a common goal for a group project in class, especially being Black, the odds of me being in a group with other Black people, other Black girls, other minorities, it's not very common. I'm not gonna necessarily express myself the way in which I would if I were working in another group.

Encouraging the development of leadership identity, capacity, and efficacy for Black female leaders, despite campus and other social climates, which indicate they should not, is a difficult, but important, tension for socially just leadership educators to recognize and resolve.

These frameworks provide substantial starting points to understand the process of leader development among Black female undergraduates. Socially just leadership educators understand Black female student leaders are inclined toward serving others, have a mentality to move forward, and have been taught to think of the betterment of others. Standpoint theory, coupled with Black feminist thought, highlights the historical and cultural implications on identity development for young Black women. The young women interviewed in this study identified their family structures, surrounding community, and motherline histories, in particular, shaped how they see themselves as individuals and as leaders.

Identity: Knowing Who I Am

When interviewing participants, it seemed important to ask questions about how the young women defined or understood who they were. Knowing who they were influenced how they saw themselves, others, and their leadership capabilities. The CRLL model seeks to create "... space for students to understand their identity within and through the lens of their multiple and complex layers of identity" (Bertand Jones et al., 2016, p. 13). Socially just leadership educators engage in activities and seek literature to help unpack and reflect on the multiple identity layers for Black female student leaders at all stages of development. They recognize the importance of asking questions, as I experienced in interviews, which require students to thoughtfully reflect on how they define themselves. Engaging in those conversations allow them to define who they are for themselves in order to not let others, or the environments in which they lead, define them through this process. Guthrie et al. (2013) suggested "... growth in leader identity often relies on the increasing fit between environmental requirements and self-concept. Individuals align and evaluate their role through an understanding of how they fit into the environment and how they are unique from it" (p. 32).

Capacity: What I Know I Can Do

As previously discussed, skills in leadership for Black women are often developed through their homes, understanding of their histories, and community environments. Parker (2005) noted how Black women find "... ways to negotiate and mediate among different groups—men, women, people of different races and nationalities—to affect change that affirmed the mutual purposes of those groups" (p. 53). Socially just leadership educators allow Black female leaders to take inventory of the skills they believe they have as leaders and affirm the value of this inventory as capacity-building. Some skills and knowledge they possess may not be classified as those of a leader; drawing those distinctions can be helpful in other areas of leader development as well. As King and Ferguson (2011) argued, "... in constantly meeting the demands of survival and fending off the noxious stimuli of discrimination it is altogether possible for black women to not be cognizant of their own performance as leaders" (p. 5). Socially just leadership educators strive to be helpful in dissecting those beliefs alongside students to fully develop their capacity as leaders. Connecting the dots between Black female leaders' identity and their leadership skills is a vital part of the formula in their development process.

Efficacy: Believing I Can Do What I Know

Black women have always been doers; whether on the front lines or in the background. The belief that they can do has not been questioned by them but by society. Among Black female student leaders, self-efficacy, while present, may look different from their White or male counterparts, even in similar environments. Avolio and Luthans (2006) explained "...self-efficacy refers to the probability you have in mind—your confidence—that you will be successful in taking on a particular task or challenge" (p. 71). Valerie, despite her belief in her capabilities, felt as though she still had to prove she could lead, in order to confront race- and gender-based stereotypes. She explained how

> [i]n predominantly Black communities, the only thing that really shows up is my gender. Like, that's the difference. In predominantly White communities, it's my gender and my race. So for gender and race in predominantly White communities, even if there's an opportunity even if people think okay, we can have a girl in this position. Most of the time, they're thinking "You can have a White girl in this position." So then it's just, jumping that other barrier of, not only am I having to fight to be a woman in this position, I also have to fight to be a Black woman in this position or a Black woman doing this thing.

Helping Black female student leaders navigate environments in which they lead with respect to their race and gender identities have implications for others' reception, perception, and willingness to follow. Conversely, those identities also affect how they perceive others and how others perceive them as Black women and the leader in a group. Parker (2005) recalled her study where "...the women perceived that their colleague's unspoken assumptions about their presence as African American women in a traditionally White male settings sometimes reinforced patterns of interaction that challenged or undermined the women's authority" (p. 62). Subsequently, socially just leadership educators are aware of, and engender awareness of others, how intersections of identity reciprocally influence leader efficacy.

BLACK FEMALE LEADERS AND SOCIAL JUSTICE

Reviewing the literature on Black women, and hearing the experiences of the Black female students who were interviewed, lead to the conclusion that leadership educators do not have to teach Black female leaders to lead from a social justice lens. Black female leaders are socialized to lead from that perspective. To that end, Leffler's (2014) discussion of how young people were exposed to the fight for equal rights in the 1950s and 1960s, wrote:

> Others too young to participate watched the resistance and the counter resistance on their television sets, they saw the police dogs, the high-power hoses, the angry whites who spat on children trying to enter school. They heard the

white supremacist statements...they also saw determination, courage, and resilience of those fighting back. (p. 143)

Hearing these stories and watching modern day activism on television and social media has also taught Black female student leaders how to work with others in order to create change. Leffler (2014) also noted emerging social justice leaders see how "Blacks and Whites could resist together by participating in Freedom Rides and people could resist by going to jail or supporting those unfairly jailed. And they too were inspired" (p. 143).

The fourth theme uncovered through interviews emphasized giving back to others, which reinforced ideas of Black women being socialized toward ways of leading through social justice. These women understood someone before them had considered their needs as they led and served. King and Ferguson (2011) distilled this notion, commenting "...the primacy of the collective exceeds personal preference" (p. 79) among Black female leaders.

CONCLUDING THOUGHTS

Black women are members of a unique group in society whose lives occur at the collision of marginalized race and gender identities. Their leadership, as well as any other endeavors they pursue, is impacted by that collision. Understanding how Black females are socialized in general, and within the realm of leadership in particular makes the task of developing them into authentic leaders one that requires great care.

The beauty of how young Black women come to understand leadership, and how to lead in order to affect social change, is intricate and nuanced. Socially just leadership educators recognize there are specific factors to consider and process with Black female student leaders that could frustrate them when leading. First, since they are socialized to always think of the "we" over the "I," at times they can become invisible and taken for granted in the process of leading. King and Ferguson (2011) described this phenomena as: "I learned also too well, to step aside, postponing my needs to attend to the needs of others" (p. 79). This stepping aside was also a theme among the interviews, as participants noted how things have to get done and so they just do them regardless if they get the credit or recognition. King and Ferguson (2011) also noted the risks of stepping aside as "...Black women readily demonstrate leadership abilities behind the scene, without becoming the public face of leadership" (p. 6).

Second, socially just leadership educators carefully consider the racial climate in society, and on campus, when engaging leadership education with Black female students. Being race conscious was a consistent theme in the interviews. Understanding how the effects of racial battle fatigue can hinder these women as they lead in social change efforts is vitally important. Racial battle fatigue has been defined as "…the result of constant physiological, psychological, cultural, and emotional coping with racial microaggressions in less-than-ideal and racially hostile or unsupportive environments" (Smith, Allen, & Danley, 2007, p. 555). Socially just leadership educators consider, when attempting to employ the components of the CRLL model, how racial battle fatigue affects identity, capacity, and efficacy development of Black female student leaders; ultimately resolving how to help them lead while being triggered.

Third, socially just leadership educators create leadership development experiences that are authentic for Black female student leaders. One participant mentioned enjoying formal leadership learning experiences. However, she noted they created unrealistic expectations about how others with different lived experience would respond to what she had been taught. She commented in reference to this:

> Even though there were so many people with so many different identities there, it was an environment in which everybody felt comfortable, everybody felt safe, you know, to share how they felt. It was very easy to, express myself and display my creativity and, give them exactly who I am. But in real life, we don't have environments like that.

In our efforts to create safe and brave spaces for our leaders to develop, we may be setting them up to be unsuccessful or disappointed outside of those spaces. Preparing them for a variety of probable realities, not just ideal ones, requires addressing when preparing Black female student leaders.

Finally, leadership educators maximize their impact when they are as diverse as the students they serve. As one participant mentioned:

> In terms of leadership educators, I just feel like, I wish I would have had more interaction with Black leadership educators. Every leadership class I have taken has been taught by a White woman. I just wish I would have had more of that education from someone who looked like me. It would have legitimized what I was learning.

This member also described benefitting from informal leadership learning by others on campus who shared in her salient identities as making up for the lack of diversity in her leadership classrooms. Increasing the odds for successful Black female student leaders requires educators to help this population unpack their identities; aid in building their capacity to lead people who share, and do not share, their social identities; and augment their efficacy to lead in varied environmental contexts.

REFERENCES

Avolio, B. J., & Luthans, F. (2006). *The high impact leader: Moments matter in accelerating authentic leadership development.* New York, NY: McGraw-Hill.

Barnett, B. M. (1993). Invisible southern black women leaders in the Civil Rights movement: The triple constraints of gender, race, and class. *Gender & Society, 7*(2), 162–182.

Bertrand Jones, T., Guthrie, K. L., & Osteen, L. K. (2016). Critical domains of culturally relevant leadership learning: A call to transform leadership programs. In K. L. Guthrie, T. Bertrand Jones, & L. Osteen (Eds.), *New directions for student leadership, No. 152: Developing culturally relevant leadership learning* (pp. 9–22). San Francisco, CA: Jossey-Bass.

Collins, P. H. (1985). Learning from the outsider within: The sociological significance of Black feminist thought theoretical standpoints on social problems. *Social Problems, 33,* S14–S32.

Guthrie, K. L., Jones, T. B., Osteen, L. K., & Hu, S. (2013). *Cultivating leader identity and capacity in students from diverse backgrounds: ASHE Higher Education Report, 39*(4). Hoboken, NJ: Wiley.

Hallstein, D. L. O. (1999). A postmodern caring: Feminist standpoint theories, revisioned caring, and communication ethics. *Western Journal of Communication, 63*(1), 32–56.

Johnson, R. B., & Christensen, L. B. (2004). *Educational research: Quantitative, qualitative, and mixed approaches.* Boston, MA: Allyn and Bacon.

King, T. C., & Ferguson, S. A. (2011). *Black womanist leadership: Tracing the motherline.* Albany: State University of New York Press.

Leffler, P. (2014). *Black leaders on leadership: Conversations with Julian Bond.* New York, NY: Palgrave Macmillan.

Livingston, R. W., Rosette, A. S., & Washington, E. F. (2012). Can an agentic Black women get ahead? The impact of race and interpersonal dominance on perceptions of female leaders. *Psychological Science, 23*(4), 354–358.

Parker, P. S. (2005). *Race, gender, and leadership: Re-envisioning organization leadership from the perspectives of African-American women executives.* Mahwah, NJ: Erlbaum.

Rost, J. C. (1991). *Leadership for the twenty-first century.* New York, NY: Praeger.

Schuyler, K. G. (2014). *Leading with spirit, presence, & authenticity.* San Francisco, CA: Jossey-Bass.

Shorter-Gooden, K., & Washington, N. C. (1996). Young, Black, and female: The challenge of weaving an identity. *Journal of Adolescence, 19*(5), 465–475.

Smith, W. A., Allen, W. R., & Danley, L. L. (2007). Assume the position . . . you fit the description: Psychosocial experiences and racial battle fatigue among African American male college students. *American Behavioral Scientist, 51*(4), 551–578.

CHAPTER 8

THE WORLD IS YOURS

Cultivating Black Male Leadership Learning

Dorsey Spencer Jr.

The future belongs to those who prepare for it today.
—Malcolm X

Black men have been leaders in the United States throughout its history. One need only take a glance to find evidence of the positive contributions Black men have made in society. Whether referring to prominent leaders, such as W. E. B. Du Bois, Marcus Garvey, Charles Hamilton Houston, A. Phillip Randolph, Thurgood Marshall, Dr. Martin Luther King Jr., and Malcolm X., or the lesser well-known every day Black male leaders, community activists, church leaders, businessmen, and educators, it is evident that Black men are leaders. Unfortunately, one would not always be able to identify Black male leadership based on societal and media depictions and assumptions associated with Black men. Often, stereotypes of Black men include being lazy, violent, absentee fathers, criminals, uneducated, employable only as entertainers or athletes, and coming from nontraditional homes (Hodge, Burden, Robinson, & Bennett, 2008). These perceptions persist despite the positive contributions of Black men in many aspects of society.

Changing the Narrative, pages 109–126
Copyright © 2018 by Information Age Publishing
All rights of reproduction in any form reserved.

At the end of the first decade of the 21st century, there was a major disruption to the negative narrative surrounding Black men in the United States. President Obama's election has, on multiple levels, changed what leadership looks like and how we perceive the capacity of Black male leaders. For the first time, among Black men and boys, the ultimate symbolic figure of global leadership looked like them. The most powerful man in the free world was a Black man with a Black family. The question for the United States and higher education institutions is, "Now what?" How do we as a society develop and educate the next generation of Black male leaders? One answer is to invest in the development of Black male leadership courses at colleges and universities. As Malcolm X suggested, if we are going to continue to have effective Black male leaders in the future, we need to prepare them today. Juana Bordas' (2012) multicultural leadership ideology stresses the importance of the development of the next generation of leaders. Bordas (2012) stated, "A core tenet of multicultural leadership is ensuring ongoing community progress, which necessitates an intergenerational approach" (p. 143). She provided the example of the relationship between Black male leaders during the civil rights movement, noting specifically Martin Luther King Jr., more seasoned leaders like Ralph Abernathy and A. Philip Randolph, and emerging leaders such as John Lewis and Jesse Jackson. The success of these leaders was possible because they all worked together. Their intergenerational bond secured the progression of the movement.

WHY FOCUS ON BLACK MEN?

Black men face challenges, tribulations, and inequities generally in society, and particularly in higher education. Frequently, Black male college students are less academically prepared than their otherwise comparable peers (Lundy-Wagner & Gasman, 2011; Palmer, Davis, & Hilton, 2009). In a 2012 study involving Black male students from four cohorts at public colleges and universities, Harper (2012) found a 33.3% 6-year graduation rate, whereas the 6-year graduation rate for all students was 48.1%. Through all levels of postsecondary education, the retention, persistence, and degree attainment of Black men is disturbingly low; particularly in contrast to Black women. In fact, when examining the various racial and ethnic groups across all sexes in higher education in the United States, Black men have the lowest graduation rates (Strayhorn, 2010).

However, there is one area of postsecondary education where Black males are disproportionately overrepresented—intercollegiate athletics—particularly on revenue-generating teams (Harper, 2012). In most other aspects of collegiate life, Black male undergraduate's achievements and sense of belonging are undermined by stereotypes and racial microaggressions regularly encountered at predominantly White institutions (Smith, Allen, & Danley, 2007; Smith, Yosso, & Solórzano, 2007). Black men are less involved in campus activities and hold fewer leadership positions on campus than Black women (Harper, Carini, Bridges, & Hayek, 2004). Each of these disparities is important, and when considered together, constitute a significant social justice issue higher education has yet to confront directly or effectively. However, it is equally important to acknowledge there are Black men in higher education who persist because they are academically strong, actively engaged in and out of the classroom, and as a result, graduate and continue onto advanced degree programs (Harper, 2012).

For Black male undergraduate students, there are numerous social, political, psychological, and personal benefits to active engagement. Engaged Black men develop strong positive Black identities, which fosters productivity and further involvement on the campuses of predominately White institutions (PWIs; Harper & Quaye, 2007). These identities serve as positive counters to racist stereotypes (Museus & Quaye, 2009). Through active engagement, Black male students cultivate political insight, allowing them to be successful in professional settings where they are also racial minorities (Harper, 2006). Through these gains, they are able to overcome mental struggles related to masculine identity (Harper, 2004) and thrive with the support of their peers (Harper, 2006). Furthermore, they are able to rise above prior educational and socioeconomic disadvantages (Harper & Griffin, 2011), as well as gain social capital and access to resources through integration into new networks (Harper, 2008).

LITERATURE ON LEADERSHIP AND STUDENTS OF COLOR

Similar to nearly all people of color, Black students have been left out or pushed to the margins of leadership literature. Very few studies have addressed the intersection of race and leadership (Reed, 1997), and even fewer have done so in the context of a campus environment (Arminio et al., 2000). According to Dugan, Komives, and Segar (2008), research on college student leadership development lacks cohesion. Varying approaches to this body of research causes an inability to broadly apply the findings. In an exploratory study, Dugan et al. studied college students' capacity for socially responsible leadership through lenses of race, gender, and sexual orientation. The project was framed within the social change model of leadership development, using a modified Socially Responsible Leadership Scale instrument, to provide an inclusive understanding of the leadership development needs of U.S. college students.

Results noted differences between racial-, gender-, and sexual orientation-based groups (Dugan et al., 2008). Most notably, Black students scored the highest of all racial groups, particularly in the values of *consciousness of self, congruence,* and *controversy with civility.* A theme of collectivism and collaborative leadership in Black students emerged from the findings. Black students in the sample also seemed to prefer education- and advocacy-based approaches to social change. The most relevant finding of this study was the significant difference in the leadership capacities of Black college students as compared to others.

After realizing the low number of student leaders of color engaged in the leadership development initiatives at their institutions, Arminio et al. (2000) inquired into the leadership experiences of students of color. They sought to determine how campus-based leadership programs and initiatives aligned with the values and experiences of students of color. Surprisingly, their findings were dissimilar to assertions in the extant leadership literature. Students in the study disliked being called leaders. They did not think of themselves as leaders. The students felt being a leader alienated them from their respective racial group. For some students the word "leader" was not negative, just not a term that was used. Most of the students in the study discussed "hidden costs" associated with being a positional leader, including loss of relationships and concerns over personal privacy. Participants understood the importance of role models, but struggled to find role models on campus. Most students who were a part of several types of groups preferred multiracial or same-identity groups to groups that were predominantly White peers. Students also expressed a strong sense of group responsibility.

The researchers also highlighted differences between these students' ideas vis-à-vis conventional notions of leadership. They suggested incorporating cultural competency training among educators in leadership programs. They also recommended regularly and critically reviewing leadership initiatives to assess if and how students of color are being appropriately served. These findings showcase how students of color experience leadership in higher education and underscores the experiential differences among students of color.

Refocusing on Black students in particular, Beatty et al. (2010) examined the experiences of Black student leaders through the lens of social climate; specifically in student organizations. Findings of this study indicated students' understanding of the organization's mission and principles influenced how they performed the duties of their role. Participants reported experiencing relationships that were both supportive and unsupportive, and commented on how both shaped their experiences. Students also discussed how diverse organization involvement enhanced their growth. The researchers concluded Black student leaders' experiences could be meaningfully shaped by the social climate within student organizations (Beatty et al., 2010). Realizing and leveraging these influences empowers socially just leadership educators to carefully attend to and shape the social climate toward Black male student success.

Leadership Literature on Black Males

There is a scarcity of literature on leadership prospects for Black men at U.S. colleges and universities; nearly all of what exists focuses on positional leadership. Sutton and Terrell's (1997) research examined the benefits of leadership in student organizations; leaders in minority-focused organizations and historically Black fraternities. There were several notable findings. Black men in Black fraternities saw themselves as leaders within the Black student community. The men who were positional leaders in Black fraternities were also involved with campus-wide student organizations (Sutton & Terrell, 1997). According to the study, at PWIs, many Black men's first leadership experience was in a minority student organization. The participants felt that majority organizations provided less favorable environments for leadership development for Black men. The respondents felt the reason for the lack of Black men in leadership roles in campus-wide student organizations was a failure to provide leadership development initiatives. The researchers concluded by making several suggestions, one of which was establishing leadership development programs to address the needs of Black male student leaders.

Harper and Quaye (2007) examined identity development and expression among Black male college student leaders. The researchers used student organizations as the venue for students' identity development. Students expressed a duty to advancing the Black community on and off campus (Harper & Quaye, 2007). Participants also dedicated time to invalidating stereotypes, destroying barriers, and providing opportunities for their Black peers. Engagement with people from various cultures and backgrounds arose as a common theme, and the students felt compelled to advocate on behalf of marginalized people at their universities. The study provided further insight into the Black male experience and highlights issues of social justice.

Preston-Cunningham, Boyd, Elbert, Dooley, and Peck-Parrott (2016) sought to understand Black male students' perceptions of leadership. Due to the prevalence of deficit-model research, there is very little research on Black undergraduate men in leadership roles. The researchers argued that Black male leadership might present an opportunity to positively influence persistence and retention. The study focused on how Black male students define and understand leadership.

According to the participants, leaders need to motivate and influence others. Leaders should be engaging, selfless, and have a sense of responsibility. Leaders need to have an awareness of self and their followers. There are also leadership behaviors and traits (e.g., active listening and decisiveness) that are necessary for leaders to be effective. The researchers felt there was a theme of collectivism in the findings. This is another example of research emphasizing the collaborative/collective nature of leadership among Black male students, which is in line with literature on Black leadership (Walters & Smith, 1999). Additionally, a recommendation that leadership programs address identity development and servant leadership was prescribed (Preston-Cunningham et al., 2016).

LEADERSHIP LEARNING

Leadership has been deemed an important outcome of higher education (Chunoo & Osteen, 2016). Many colleges and universities provide students formal and informal opportunities to enhance leadership skills (Pascarella & Terenzini, 2005). Higher education has been charged with developing competent leaders with strong character (Nohria & Khurana, 2010). These factors, coupled with higher education's recognition of the need to explore the intersection of diversity and leadership development (Guthrie, Bertrand Jones, Osteen, & Hu, 2013), make it imperative to have a comprehensive understanding of how Black male student leaders develop, understand, and experience leadership while enrolled at a college.

Munin and Dugan's (2011) research supported style of delivery being as important as the content circulated in leadership programs. Leadership learning is the means of comprehending the process of leadership (Guthrie et al., 2013). Guthrie and Jenkins (2018) proposed a leadership learning framework that consists of six aspects of learning leadership. These aspects include leadership knowledge, leadership development, leadership training, leadership observation, leadership engagement, and leadership metacognition. Socially just leadership learning strategies enable and empower students through a holistic approach, taking into consideration all of these aspects. Leadership knowledge is the acquisition of knowledge and can occur in many different formats. Leadership development is the reflective and integrative approach to feedback and assessment. Leadership training is focused on enhancing leader skills, behaviors, and strategies; it can be done through programs, retreats, or workshops. Leadership observation is where the learner is passive and observes interaction of leaders and followers. Leadership engagement is how leaders apply what they have learned about leadership. Finally, leadership metacognition is making meaning of leadership experiences (Guthrie & Jenkins, 2018). All of the strategies build upon each other, and differentially contribute to students' leadership learning.

In order to develop the next generation of Black male leaders, socially just leadership educators strive to understand leader identity and leadership capacity. According to Guthrie et al. (2013), "... [u]nderstanding how students develop leader identity and capacity is fundamental to our ability to meet students where they are in the development cycle while challenging and supporting their leadership growth" (p. 30). Leader identity is how an individual sees themselves as a leader and their relation to society (Day, Harrison, & Halpin, 2009). Leader identity develops throughout the lifespan. It is promoted through activities such as facilitating self-awareness, reflection, and new experiences (Guthrie et al., 2013). Leader capacity is a leader's ability to draw upon their knowledge and skills in order to be an effective leader (Guthrie et al., 2013). Leader capacity is developed through learning and doing. Developing capacity can come from positional and non-positional, as well as formal and informal, leadership experiences. The development of Black male leader identity and capacity is vital to preparing them to be leaders. Black male leadership development and education help foster supportive learning communities, build upon assets Black male students possess, creating a gamut of leadership skills with positive practical impact on their college experiences, the attainment of their intended degrees, and the contributions to their local communities.

Critical and Culturally Relevant Approaches to Leadership Learning

Academic coursework is one mechanism to foster the development of leaders. A "one-size-fits-all" approach to leadership education may not the most effective strategy for establishing a leadership-learning environment (Rosch & Meixner, 2011). Furthering this perspective, Mahoney (2016) reasoned, "If college leadership educators hope to nurture the development of diverse students and foster transformative learning environments, educators must consider pedagogical strategies that are able to challenge and reconfigure dominant paradigms of knowing, being, and doing" (p. 48). Acknowledging how oppressive systems and structures in society hamper learning, critical pedagogy emerges as a practical learning theory, which strives to emancipate the student (hooks, 1994).

Culturally Relevant Leadership Learning

Ladson-Billings (1995) initially presented culturally relevant pedagogy to oppose the marginalizing and ostracizing influences faced by students of color in Western educational contexts. By doing so, Ladson-Billings (2014) challenged instructors to implement assets-based pedagogical approaches, specifically when working with culturally diverse students (p. 75). Generally, the history and experiences of students of color are framed from a deficit perspective, rather than an asset-based one, in many learning environments (Bertrand Jones, Guthrie, & Osteen, 2016; Ladson-Billings, 2014). In order to successfully apply culturally relevant pedagogy, instructors must operate within three domains: (a) academic success, (b) cultural competence, and (c) sociopolitical consciousness (Ladson-Billings, 2014; Bertrand Jones et al., 2016). Operating in these three spheres enhances the social justice mission of leadership education.

The culturally relevant leadership learning (CRLL) model is a framework for equipping leadership programs to embrace the challenges diversity generates (Bertrand Jones et al., 2016). CRLL urges leadership educators to think of new ways to educate students and produce leaders who are prepared to challenge social disparities and foster social change. This model encourages leadership educators to critique historical models of teaching leadership and conventional methods of leadership learning. Additionally, it calls for educators to develop innovative approaches to educating students and cultivating leaders capable of challenging the status quo. CRLL acknowledges the presence of power and oppression in leadership and their influences on students, ultimately impacting the ability to effectively produce transformation in society (Bertrand Jones et al., 2016).

Critical Leadership Pedagogy

Critical leadership pedagogy is a recent and emerging approach. It advocates for a critical pedagogical approach to leadership programs through curricular and cocurricular lenses (Pendakur & Furr, 2016). Similar to critical race theory (CRT), it relates leadership learning to the inequitable social construction of the world in which we all live. CRT challenges leadership educators and practitioners to move beyond basic understandings of leadership development and student identity to examine the numerous uneven and unjust ways educational spaces are developed and maintained (McCoy & Rodricks, 2015).

All of the aforementioned approaches to leadership learning are vital. As the United States becomes more diverse (Colby & Ortman, 2015) and increasing amounts of students of color enroll in postsecondary institutions (National Center for Education Statistics, 2013), these students reasonably expect colleges and universities to address their needs; especially given the increasing costs of tuition. Students of color deserve inclusive classrooms and curricula. Being engaged in classrooms fostering socially just leadership learning, while simultaneous accounting for social inequities, may be a resolution to building leader identity, capacity, and efficacy for Black men, with implications for their widespread success in higher education. The development of these individuals will have positive implications for the Black community and larger society. Thankfully, some institutions have heard the call and are taking action. Florida State University, University of Louisiana at Lafayette, and The Ohio State University have each created Black male leadership courses to provide safe and welcoming environments for Black men to holistically and authentically engage leadership learning.

BLACK MALE LEADERSHIP COURSES AS VEHICLES OF DEVELOPMENT

Undergraduate courses focused on Black male leadership are rare. There are some courses that focus on Black or African American leadership development, but courses that solely focus on Black men are uncommon. Black male leadership development programs and initiatives tend to take the form of conferences, retreats, summits, or institutes. For example, Louisiana State University and Northern Kentucky University have a Black Male Leadership Institute and LeaderShape has hosted Black male session for their Institute program. There are also Black male classes and programs that focus on encouraging academic retention and persistence from the lens of being a Black man in higher education. These Black male initiatives are important, but do not focus on Black male leadership development in a curricular context and are therefore not within the scope and analysis of this discussion. I am specifically focused on Black male leadership courses with a foundation in leadership theory and a focus on the perspectives, experiences, triumphs, and challenges of being a Black male. The following are descriptions of several Black male leadership courses and a document analysis of their syllabi. The structure of each course is different, but the intention here is to identify commonalities.

Florida State University

Florida State University has a Black male leadership course open to all students. It is offered as part of the undergraduate leadership education certificate offered by the College of Education and the Center for Leadership and Social Change. The course is 3-credits and counts as a supporting course—essentially an elective—toward the certificate. It can also be used as a leadership elective for university-wide cocurricular and experiential programs. The guiding theory in the class is the social change model of leadership (Higher Education Research Institute, 1996). The class uses books, articles, and videos to frame leadership from a Black male perspective, or at minimum, a Black perspective. The class occurs twice a week and has an enrollment limit of 25 students. The limited class capacity not only allows for the course to be manageable for the instructor but also the size permits the instructor the opportunity to get to know the students individually to build deep relationships. The course at Florida State University can be associated with fulfilling the mission of institutions of higher learning, to develop the next generation of leaders (Chunoo & Osteen, 2016). This course exemplifies an institution acting upon a commitment to Black men.

University of Louisiana at Lafayette

The Black male leadership course at the University of Louisiana at Lafayette was established as a 3-credit section of the institution's first year experience program. It covered learning outcomes set by the overseeing office, including "...critical thinking and problem solving..." and "...community engagement and service learning..." (University of Louisiana at Lafayette, 2016, p. 1). The course used two textbooks, *The College Experience for Men of Color* (Baldwin, Tietje, Fellinger, Lemelle, & Moore, 2014) and *The Black Male Handbook* (Powell & Harper, 2008). The course utilized student leadership competencies from *The Student Leadership Challenge* (Kouzes & Posner, 2008). It took place three times a week and also had a limit of 25 students. The purpose of this course is connected with retention of Black men.

Ohio State University

The Ohio State University's Black male course is called the Bell National Resource Center Leadership Institute. The course took place once a week for an hour and a half. Required readings include *Black Leadership* (Marable, 1998), *Student Leadership Challenge* (Kouzes & Posner, 2008), and *The Art of Followership: How Great Followers Create Great Leaders and Organizations* (Riggio, Chaleff, & Lipman-Blumen, 2008). The class encouraged leadership practices, ideologies, and procedures to develop students and provided tools for success on an individual and organizational level. The outcomes of the course were to develop and self-evaluate leadership skills, practice authentic leadership, and build social capital with peers and institutions. The mission of the course was to engage on the issues and challenges that Black men face throughout their life. The purpose of this course is associated with Black men's persistence and belonging.

Common Themes

According to their syllabi, the three courses shared commonalities. The minimum criteria for identifying themes included common texts and similar practices, topics, or ideas in two or more syllabi. Five prominent themes emerged from the review of the three syllabi or from additional information and context provided by the instructors. The themes from this analysis included (a) historical context, (b) understanding leadership theory, (c) self-assessment and reflection, (d) engaging with Black male leaders, and (e) community service/civic engagement.

Historical Context

All of the courses discussed a historical context of Black leadership and included discourse on leaders such as W. E. B. Du Bois, Frederick Douglas, Booker T. Washington, Martin Luther King Jr., and the other civil rights activists involved in the marches in Selma, AL. From my experience as one of the instructors of the course, a majority of the students did not have a foundational understanding of Black history or the history of Black leadership in the United States. This is not surprising since most primary and secondary school students do not learn much about African American history. Including historical context in the courses is evidence of the CRLL model's requirement to account for the past legacies of leadership in communities of color (Bertrand Jones et al., 2016). It allows students to understand how traditionally Black male leaders have engaged with, or are currently engaging with, leadership. A historical look at Black male leadership is an acknowledgement of the minimization of Black men in leadership scholarship and theory.

Leadership Theory

Another theme is the prevalence of leadership theory in the course. People of color did not develop any of the theories taught in any of the courses. The theories taught to the students were transactional leadership, transformational leadership, the great man theories, servant leadership, the social change model of leadership, and the leadership engagement model. The use of the social change model of leadership seems reasonable, especially because Black student leaders are more connected to the ideals of the social change model of leadership compared to other racial groups (Dugan et al., 2008). Teaching various leadership theories aligns with one of the components of leadership learning, leadership education (Guthrie et al., 2013). Learning theory enhances students' leadership capacity (Guthrie et al., 2013).

Reflection

Self-assessment and reflection are other themes that emerged. All of the courses included self-assessment and/or reflection, and these were accomplished through journals and written reflections, personal leadership philosophies, and assessment tools such as StrengthsFinder (Rath, 2007). The presence of self-assessment and reflection in the courses is backed by the literature on leadership. Reflection is an important aspect in the process of meaning making as it aids in guiding potential conduct. According to Chickering (2008), learning cannot be sustained apart from critical reflection. Reflection supports the development of students' identity, cognitive, and moral growth (Strain, 2005).

Engagement With Black Male Leadership

Engaging with Black male leaders also arose as a theme. These leaders came from the campus and local community. The engagement took the form of students interviewing the Black male leaders, then writing and/or presenting about the individual. Furthermore, all of the courses brought in Black men as guest speakers and presenters. An individual's definition of a leader illustrates whom they do or do not see as a leader (Kezar, 2000). This is why it was essential to have the student see and engage with Black male leaders. These interactions assisted the student in defining "leader," and it was important for them to see leaders who look like them. This is an important aspect of the course, particularly because Black male students may not see or interact with Black male leaders at the college, university, or local community.

Community Service

Civic engagement or service is the final theme that emerged. Two of the courses required students to participate in community service. Specifically, one of the courses required students to participate in a service project and develop a grant proposal for a community improvement project. The two classes that required service connected students to major service events that occur on their campus (e.g., Martin Luther King Jr. Day of Service). The course that does not require participation in service brings in a speaker to talk about the importance of civic engagement on multiple levels. Requiring students to engage in community service or discussing civic engagement aligns with Walters and Smith's (1999) definition of Black leadership, which is a form of community-centered leadership.

Participation in service positively correlates with improved writing, critical thinking skills, and grade point average (Astin, Vogelgesang, Ikeda, & Yee, 2000). Students engaged in service show a commitment to activism and to fostering racial understanding (Astin et al., 2000). They also display a strong sense of self-worth, strong interpersonal skills, and increased leadership ability. Furthermore, students engaged in service are more inclined to participate in service after graduation and may even choose a service career (Astin et al., 2000). Incorporating service learning and civic engagement into courses addresses many challenges Black males face and furthers their growth as leaders.

The document analysis of the three Black male leadership courses' syllabi supports the inclusion of these various pedagogical approaches to touch on several aspects of leadership learning (Guthrie & Jenkins, 2018). These courses can assist in the development of future Black male leaders and address some of the challenges and inequities Black men face in higher education. Students taking Black male leadership courses are making investments in their community cultural wealth (Yosso, 2005).

IMPLICATIONS

There are several implications from the reviews of the leadership literature and the Black male leadership course syllabi. First, there is a need for more research on how Black male students experience leadership learning. Understanding this experience will better prepare institutions to develop leadership initiatives that are appealing and engaging for Black males. There is a need for leadership educators to review how they outreach to Black males to encourage them to participate in their programs. Ideally, institutions would develop similar courses to those reviewed in this chapter, but minimally, it is necessary to acknowledge the importance of developing Black male student leaders. Colleges and universities should take an active role in developing Black male leadership educators. Subsequently, Black male student leaders will have the opportunity to see and engage with professionals who share similar identities.

Preferably, though not mandated, Black men should teach Black male leadership courses. Instructors should have an interest in working with Black men and leadership learning. This could potentially assist in addressing the lack of mentors and role models on campus. In the event there are no Black men available to teach the course, institutions should consider broadening the scope of the course to be a Black leadership or multicultural leadership course. Both of the alternative classes ought to have components of the previously mentioned themes of Black male leadership courses. Black male leadership courses should be easily accessible. The courses should be structured and classified in a manner that allows for all Black men to take the class with minimal obstruction. Examples of these barriers include rigid programs of study that have numerous prerequisites and do not allow the student to choose from the breadth of courses offered at the University, excess credit penalties, or financial resources.

A combination of the aforementioned ideas would be the best logistical and pedagogical approach to conducting a successful Black male leadership course. Curriculum should be built around the CRLL model to ensure it is critical and culturally relevant. Leadership programs need to consider and challenge historical, structural, and organizational components that perpetuate systems of oppression, power, and privilege. Socially just leadership educators take advantage of the opportunity to create courses, curriculum, and environments representative of the experiences, viewpoints, and voices of Black people, but more specifically Black men. Inspecting syllabi and course reading materials are steps in the right direction, as is seeking out diverse educators. In courses and programs, it is important to address the connection between leadership and identity, particularly social identity. This discussion is a gateway into considering how higher education engages students of color in leadership learning.

RECOMMENDATIONS

After reviewing the literature and analyzing several Black male leadership courses, the following recommendations for implementation arise. Researchers should conduct more quantitative and qualitative research on Black men and leadership learning. Scholars should seek to understand the differences between Black men in leadership programs and those of other social identities. Research should examine how Black men's leadership leading is impacted by the type of institution they attend. The leadership learning of Black student leaders should also be explored. All of this research should be shared with the masses and not just those in higher education. Institutions should review their recruitment, hiring, and reward structures to attract and retain more Black men to fill staff, faculty, and administrative roles.

Furthermore, leadership education offices, departments, and programs should be intentional in their development and support of Black male leadership educators. Offering teaching assistantships and sending these individuals to professional development opportunities that center around leadership education can help accomplish this objective. Encouraging and supporting Black male graduate students to conduct research on Black male leadership learning is a worthwhile approach. Institutions should also forge strong relationships with Black male alumni and community leaders. This will make it easier to bring in Black male leaders for the course. These relationships would also encourage coalition building through community.

From an academic policy perspective, socially just colleges and universities regularly review the organization and cataloging of leadership courses; especially identity-based leadership classes. When leadership education is important to an institution, it ensures leadership courses qualify as general education or liberal studies requirements. Another option, similar to the way internship courses are managed at some institutions, is making leadership courses exempt from counting towards excess credit policies and penalties. When examining accessibility of the courses, socially just college and universities consider making courses accessible to dual enrollment students. This would allow high school and community college students greater access to the class. Another opportunity is to offer the course online (without additional distance learning fees) and to use video conferencing for the guest speakers and panels. While not the most ideal, institutions may want to offer non-credit weekly cocurricular versions of such a course. This version of the course would assist those who may not have the financial resources necessary to pay for courses that are not in their program of study.

CONCLUSION

The importance of developing Black male leaders is undeniable. Black men face a myriad of challenges and inequities. Higher education has been charged with developing the nation's next generation of leadership. The research on Black students' experiences with leadership learning, particularly the experiences of Black males, is paltry at best. Some institutions have taken on this challenge by developing Black male leadership classes. Common themes within the pedagogy of these courses include (a) historical context, (b) understanding leadership theory, (c) self-assessment and reflection, (d) engaging with Black male leaders, and (e) community service/civic engagement. Supported by scholarship, all of these themes are ways to develop Black male student leaders and combat some of the challenges experienced by Black males. From a social justice perspective, higher education must do more to engage people of color overall, and Black males more specifically, in leadership learning. The historical neglect of Black male leadership development on most college campuses in the United States is inexcusable. Higher education must assist in developing the next generation of Black male leaders and college graduates. Black male leadership courses assist in enhancing Black men's community cultural wealth. It is this wealth that helps Black men understand the world is theirs.

REFERENCES

Arminio, J. L., Carter, S., Jones, S. E., Kruger, K., Lucas, N., Washington, J., & Scott, A. (2000). Leadership experiences of students of color. *NASPA Journal, 37*, 496–510.

Astin, A. W., Vogelgesang, L. J., Ikeda, E. K., & Yee, J. A. (2000). *How service learning affects students.* Los Angeles, CA: Higher Education Research Institute.

Baldwin, A., Tietje, B., Fellinger, A., Lemelle, D., & Moore, D. (2014). *The college experience for men of color.* Boston, MA: Pearson Education.

Beatty, C. C., Bush, A. A., Erxleben, E. E., Ferguson, T. L., Harrell, A. T., & Sahachartsiri, W. K. (2010). Black student leaders: The influence of social climate in student organizations. *Journal of the Indiana University Student Personnel Association, 43*, 48–63.

Bertrand Jones, T., Guthrie, K. L., & Osteen, L. K. (2016). Critical domains of culturally relevant leadership learning: A call to transform leadership programs. In K. L. Guthrie, T. Bertrand Jones, & L. Osteen (Eds.), *New directions for student leadership, No. 152: Developing culturally relevant leadership learning* (pp. 9–22). San Francisco, CA: Jossey-Bass.

Bordas, J. (2012). *Salsa, soul, and spirit: Leadership for a multicultural age.* San Francisco, CA: Berrett-Koehler.

Chickering, A. W. (2008). Strengthening democracy and personal development through community engagement. *New Directions in Adult and Continuing Education, 118*, 87–95.

Chunoo, V., & Osteen, L. (2016). Purpose, mission, and context: The call for educating future leaders. In K. L. Guthrie & L. Osteen (Eds.), *New directions for higher education, No. 174: Reclaiming higher education's purpose in leadership development* (pp. 9–20). San Francisco, CA: Jossey-Bass.

Colby, S. L., & Ortman, J. M. (2015). Projections of the size and composition of the U.S. population: 2014 to 2060. *Current Population Reports.* Retrieved from https://www.census.gov/content/dam/Census/library/publications/2015/demo/p25-1143.pdf

Day, D. V., Harrison, M. M., & Halpin, S. M. (2009). *An integrative theory of leadership development: Connecting adult development, identity, and expertise.* New York, NY: Psychology Press.

Dugan, J. P., Komives, S. R., & Segar, T. C. (2008). College student capacity for socially responsible leadership: Understanding norms and influences of race, gender, and sexual orientation. *NASPA Journal, 45*, 475–500.

Guthrie, K. L., Bertrand Jones, T., Osteen, L. K., & Hu, S. (2013). *Cultivating leader identity and capacity in students from diverse backgrounds: ASHE Higher Education Report, 39*(4). New York, NY: Wiley.

Guthrie, K. L., & Jenkins, D. M. (2018). *The role of leadership educators: Transforming learning.* Charlotte, NC: Information Age.

Harper, S. R. (2004). The measure of a man: Conceptualizations of masculinity among high achieving African American male college students. *Berkeley Journal of Sociology, 48*(1), 89–107.

Harper, S. R. (2006). Enhancing African American male student outcomes through leadership and active involvement. In M. J. Cuyjet (Ed.), *African American men in college* (pp. 68–94). San Francisco, CA: Jossey-Bass.

Harper, S. R. (2008). Realizing the intended outcomes of Brown: High-achieving African American male undergraduates and social capital. *American Behavioral Scientist, 51*(7), 1029–1052.

Harper, S. R. (2012). *Black male student success in higher education: A report from the National Black Male College Achievement Study.* Philadelphia, PA: Center for the Study of Race and Equity in Education.

Harper, S. R., Carini, R. M., Bridges, B. K., & Hayek, J. C. (2004). Gender differences in student engagement among African American undergraduates at historically Black colleges and universities. *Journal of College Student Development, 45*, 271–284.

Harper, S. R., & Griffin, K. A. (2011). Opportunity beyond affirmative action: How low-income and working class Black male achievers access highly selective, high-cost colleges and universities. *Harvard Journal of African American Public Policy, 17*(1), 43–60.

Harper, S. R., & Quaye, S. J. (2007). Student organizations as venues for Black identity expression and development among African American male student leaders. *Journal of College Student Development, 48*, 127–144.

Higher Education Research Institute. (1996). *A social change model of leadership development* (3rd ed.). Los Angeles, CA: Higher Education Research Institute.

Hodge, S. R., Burden, J. W., Robinson, L. E., & Bennett, R. A. (2008). Theorizing on the stereotyping of Black male student-athletes: Issues and implications. *Journal for the Study of Sports and Athletes in Education, 2*, 203–226.

hooks, b. (1994). *Teaching to transgress*. New York, NY: Routledge.

Kezar, A. (2000). Pluralistic leadership: Incorporating diverse voices. *Journal of Higher Education, 71*(6), 722–743.

Kouzes, J. M., & Posner, B. Z. (2008). *The student leadership challenge: Five practices for exemplary leaders*. San Francisco, CA: Jossey-Bass.

Ladson-Billings, G. (1995). Toward a theory of culturally relevant pedagogy. *American Educational Research Journal, 32*(3), 465–491.

Ladson-Billings, G. (2014). Culturally relevant pedagogy 2.0: aka the remix. *Harvard Educational Review, 84*(1), 74–84.

Lundy-Wagner, V., & Gasman, M. (2011). When gender issues are not just about women: Reconsidering male students at historically Black colleges and universities. *Teachers College Record, 113*(5), 934–968.

McCoy, D. L., & Rodricks, D. J. (2015). Critical race theory in higher education: 20 years of theoretical and research innovations. *ASHE Higher Education Report, 41*(3), 1–117.

Mahoney, A. D. (2016). Culturally responsive integrative learning environments: A critical displacement approach. In K. L. Guthrie, T. B. Jones, & L. Osteen (Eds.), *New directions for higher education, No. 152: Developing culturally relevant leadership learning* (pp. 47–60). San Francisco, CA: Jossey-Bass.

Marable, M. (1998). *Black leadership*. New York, NY: Columbia University Press.

Munin, A., & Dugan, J. P. (2011). Inclusive design in leadership program development. In S. R. Komives, J. P. Dugan, J. E. Owen, W. Wagner, C. Slack, & Associates (Eds.), *Handbook for student leadership development* (pp. 157–176). San Francisco, CA: Jossey-Bass.

Museus, S. D., & Quaye, S. J. (2009). Toward an intercultural perspective of racial and ethnic minority college student persistence. *The Review of Higher Education, 33*(1), 67–94.

National Center for Education Statistics. (2013). Percentage of 18- to 24-year-olds enrolled in degree-granting institutions, by level of institution and sex and race/ethnicity of student: 1967 through 2012. *Digest of Education Statistics.* Retrieved from http://nces.ed.gov/programs/digest/d13/tables/dt13_302.60.asp

Nohria, N., & Khurana, R. (2010). Advancing leadership theory and practice. In N. Nohria & R. Khurana (Eds.), *Handbook of leadership theory and practice: A*

Harvard Business School centennial colloquium (pp. 3–26). Boston, MA: Harvard Business Press.

Palmer, R. T., Davis, R. J., & Hilton, A. A. (2009). Exploring challenges that threaten to impede the academic success of academically underprepared African American male collegians at an HBCU. *Journal of College Student Development, 50,* 429–445.

Pascarella, E. T., & Terenzini, P. T. (2005). *How college affects students* (2nd ed.). San Francisco, CA: Jossey-Bass.

Pendakur, V., & Furr, S. C. (2016). Critical leadership pedagogy: Engaging power, identity, and culture in leadership education for college students of color. In K. L. Guthrie & L. Osteen (Eds.), *New directions for higher education, No. 174: Reclaiming higher education's purpose in leadership development* (pp. 45–56). San Francisco, CA: Jossey-Bass.

Powell, K., & Harper, H. (Eds.). (2008). *The Black male handbook.* New York, NY: Atria Books.

Preston-Cunningham, T., Boyd, B. L., Elbert, C. D., Dooley, K. E., & Peck-Parrott, K. (2016). What's up with this leadership thing? Voices of African American male college undergraduates. *Journal of Leadership Education, 15*(3), 53–74.

Rath, T. (2007). *StrengthsFinder 2.0.* New York, NY: Gallup Press.

Reed, C. R. (1997). *The Chicago NAACP and the rise of Black professional leadership, 1910–1966.* Bloomington, IN: Indiana University Press.

Rosch, D., & Meixner, C. (2011). Powerful pedagogies. In S. R. Komives, J. P. Dugan, J. E. Owen, W. Wagner, C. Slack, & Associates (Eds.), *Handbook for student leadership development* (pp. 307–337). San Francisco, CA: Jossey-Bass.

Riggio, R. E., Chaleff, I., & Lipman-Blumen, J. (Eds.). (2008). *The art of followership: How great followers create great leaders and organizations.* San Francisco, CA: Jossey-Bass.

Smith, W. A., Allen, W. R., & Danley, L. L. (2007). Assume the position . . . you fit the description: Psychosocial experiences and racial battle fatigue among African American male college students. *American Behavioral Scientist, 51*(4), 551–578.

Smith, W. A., Yosso, T. J., & Solórzano, D. G. (2007). Racial primes and Black misandry on historically White campuses: Toward critical race accountability in educational administration. *Educational Administration Quarterly, 43,* 559–585.

Strayhorn, T. L. (2010). When race and gender collide: Social and cultural capital's influence on the academic achievement of African American and Latino males. *The Review of Higher Education, 33,* 307–332.

Strain, C. R. (2005). Pedagogy and practice: Service-learning and students' moral development. *New Directions for Teaching and Learning, 103,* 61–72.

Sutton, E. M., & Terrell, M. C. (1997). Identifying and developing leadership opportunities for African American men. *New Directions for Student Services, 80,* 55–64.

University of Louisiana, Lafayette (2016). *Black male leadership course syllabus.* Lafayette, LA: Author.

Walters, R., & Smith, R. (1999). *African American leadership.* Albany, NY: State University of New York Press.

Yosso, T. J. (2005). Whose culture has capital? A critical race theory discussion of community cultural wealth. *Race ethnicity and education, 8*(1), 69–91.

CHAPTER 9

¡PA'LANTE SIEMPRE PA'LANTE!

Latina Leader Identity Development

Maritza Torres

Some of the most widely used practices in leadership development and education originated from theories and models created by White men (Dugan & Komives, 2011). However, these frequently employed practices rarely focus on the intersectionality of multiple identities or how these intersections influence students' leader identity development. As students crystallize their leader identities, it is possible that other aspects of their lives become less salient. This development can take place in curricular and cocurricular environments. In hooks' (1994), *Teaching to Transgress,* she advocated for the use of classroom environments as spaces for inclusive and holistic education. She wrote, "Since the vast majority of students learn through conservative, traditional educational practices and concern themselves only with the presence of the professor; any radical pedagogy must insist that everyone's presence is acknowledged" (hooks, 1994, p. 8). Leadership educators have the unique responsibility to aid the leader identity development of students by acknowledging their presence and honoring their experiences.

The purpose of this chapter is to discuss how socially just leadership educators can integrate and validate students' various identities into leader identity development. I will focus specifically on Latina college students, due to their increasing prevalence and marginalization in institutions of American higher education. "The numbers of Latinas alone—more than 26 million—make them a critically important group today, but projections are that by 2060 they will form nearly a third of the female population of the nation" (Gándara, 2015, p. 7). This population is going to continue to grow and will undoubtedly have an impact beyond their numbers at postsecondary institutions across the country; this is a matter of *when*, not *if*. Members of this population deserve particular consideration due to their comparatively low degree attainment.

> Although Latinas are going to college in record numbers, they are significantly less likely to actually complete a degree, compared to all other major groups: in 2013, almost 19 percent of Latinas between 25 and 29 years of age had completed a degree, compared to 23 percent of African American women, 44 percent of white women, and 64 percent of Asian women. (Gándara, 2015, p. 10)

Socially just leadership educators play a critical role in retaining and developing Latina students through leadership classes. However, the challenge they face involves balancing inclusive ways to empower Latinas to formulate their leader identity without negating their Latina identity in the process. The following narrative attempts to highlight the issues relevant to resolving this tension, as well as offer suggestions toward striking a careful balance between these factors.

BARRIERS FOR LATINAS IN HIGHER EDUCATION

Latina college students, and their Latino counterparts, are underrepresented at all levels of higher education and have lower persistence, retention, and graduation rates in postsecondary institutions. "Soon to be the numerical majority in the United States, it is critical that higher education institutions be accountable for understanding, recruiting, retaining, and matriculating Latina/o students" (Castellanos & Jones, 2003, p. 4). According to Castellanos and Jones (2003), the major contributing factors to the retention of Latina/o students include: cultural and personal background variables, socioeconomic status, academic and acculturative stress, family support, campus climate and cultural congruity, and faculty mentorship. Cultural and background variables include limited knowledge of the English language, living in single-parent homes, irregular attendance patterns, and parental education (Castellanos & Jones, 2003). Latina undergraduates may be the first in their family to attend college and most likely lack the social and cultural capital of their peers from majority identities. Socioeconomic deficits are often associated with attrition due to lack of financial aid resources. Also, some Latina students may be full- or part-time employed while enrolled as full- or part-time students to pay the rising cost of tuition while contributing to the financial needs of their families (Castellanos & Jones, 2003). The type of academic stress Latina students face also intersects with their identity; approaching faculty members, taking tests, writing papers, and meeting academic expectations can act as elevated stressors for Latina students (Castellanos & Jones, 2003) who may come from academic backgrounds that underprepared them for college life. Collegiate Latinas may be differentially impacted by racial campus climates, their minority status, and the lack of positive role models (Castellanos & Jones, 2003) in the academy.

Relatedly, familial support is of particular cultural value for Latinas, with important implications for their academic pursuits. Latina students are more inclined to achieve academically if they are presented with support mechanisms at home (Castellanos & Jones, 2003). First-generation students may have difficulty finding support due to their families' lack of knowledge of higher education and its mechanisms. Campus climate concerns and cultural incongruity result in Latinas not having a sense of belonging (Castellanos & Jones, 2003). Those attending predominantly White institutions face difficulties getting acclimated to the college environment due to their minority status. This is evident in classrooms as some Latinas may be the only ones within their ethnic group. Faculty mentors are incredibly important for all students in higher education, but especially for Latinas. These relationships provide Latina students with a person who is able to provide valuable resources and advice that can enhance their college experience. Representation of faculty and staff of color is especially needed because these students may be more inclined to connect with someone who shares the same identity.

According to Castellanos and Jones (2003), "Similar to other ethnic and racial groups, a larger number of Latina women attend college than do [Latino] men, though their numbers are low in comparison to other ethnic and racial groups" (p. xvii). While Latina undergraduates are faced with the barriers previously listed, they also have a set of unique circumstances affecting their persistence in higher education in comparison to their male counterparts. One of these circumstances is the decision of whether to attend college or not (Castellanos & Jones, 2003). Some Latino families expect women to get married, have children, and stay at home; "Gender-role stereotypes of Latinas suggests that they should be submissive and docile, and that their main purpose is to produce children" (Castellanos & Jones, 2003, p. xvii).

The second circumstance affects a "new generation" of Latinas. According to Castellanos and Jones (2003), new generation Latinas are expected to stay geographically close to home, resulting in them becoming commuter students who do not live on-campus, or attending local community colleges instead of 4-year institutions which they may qualify for, but are further away. Latina students face barriers as they navigate institutions of higher education, especially within their cultural identities. Socially just leadership educators must understand how Latina students' cultures and backgrounds affect their decisions and behaviors. With this knowledge, socially just leadership educators will be well equipped to tailor specific programs and resources, especially in leadership learning, to reflect the cultural values and needs of this population.

LATINO/A, HISPANIC, OR LATINX?

Latino/a, Hispanic, or Latinx are just some of the terms individuals from predominantly Spanish or Portuguese speaking countries may identify or be identified by others. Twenty-six sovereign states and territories make up what is often referred to collectively as "Latin America" (Countries That Make Up Latin America, 2016). Each of these states and territories have idiosyncratic cultures, identities, and traditions. However, terms such as "Latino/a" or "Hispanic" are used, especially in the United States, in order to classify them into an aggregate grouping. This can be problematic because these terms do not reflect how individuals choose to self-identify. The term "Latino" is defined as "...any person of Latin American descent residing in the United States" (Garcia-Navarro, 2015, para. 7). This is to not be confused with the term "Latin American" which defines people from Latin American countries (Garcia-Navarro, 2015). The term "Hispanic" refers to people who share Spanish as common ancestral language (Garcia-Navarro, 2015). Although often used interchangeably, these social identity terms mean different things, and have differential impacts on the lives of the individuals to whom they are pinned.

The term "Latinx" gained prominence in 2004 via queer internet communities and rose in popularity in late 2014 (Ramirez & Blay, 2016). Latinx is described as: "...the gender-neutral alternative to Latino, Latina and even Latin@. Used by scholars, activists and an increasing number of journalists, Latinx is quickly gaining popularity among the general public" (Ramirez & Blay, 2016, para. 7). This term accounts for transgendered, queer, agender, non-binary, and gender non-confirming individuals (Ramirez & Blay, 2016). See Chapter 6 for more information on discussion on gender. The Spanish language uses the masculine version of words for groupings of male- or mixed-gendered nouns (almost all nouns in Spanish and its dialects are gendered). However, this use of language does not acknowledge the range of possible gender identities. "The "x," in a lot of ways, is a way of rejecting the gendering of words to begin with, especially since Spanish is such a gendered language" (Ramirez & Blay, 2016, para 8.) The term Latinx is meant to reflect the inclusion and intersectionality of ethnic and gender identity.

IDENTITY

Knowledge of Latino identity development models and theories help leadership educators understand the Latina students. Developing this understanding begins by researching racial and ethnic identity development theories. "Racial identity theories focus on the role of race and the extent to which it is incorporated into identity or self-concept" (Evans, Forney, Guido, Patton, & Renn, 2010, p. 254). These theories inform socially just leadership educators about how racial and ethnic identities intersect with students' sense of self. "Ethnic identity models enhance an understanding of the process that individuals go through as they explore their own ethnicity and learn to navigate multiple cultures" (Case & Hernandez, 2013, p. 76). Socially just leadership educators invest in understanding the racial and ethnic identity process for Latina students to create trainings and environments in which these students' needs and experiences are validated.

Latino Identity Development

Ferdman and Gallegos' (2001) model of Latino identity development contains six orientations Latinos encounter in life (Evans et al., 2010). Latinos may experience any of these orientations at any time as they are not in any particular order. *Latino-integrated* is when Latino identity is integrated into their other identities (Evans et al., 2010). *Latino-identified* individuals see the Latino community as one race regardless of a person's skin color (Evans et al., 2010). *Subgroup-identified* Latinos only identify within their subgroup (Evans et al., 2010). For example, a Latino in this orientation may identify as Puerto Rican American instead of just American. *Latino as other* is when persons who have a mixed identity do not put themselves in a specific group due to lack of knowledge of their own heritage (Evans et al., 2010). *Undifferentiated/denial* Latinos do not identify with other Latinos and claim that race does not matter (Evans et al., 2010). Lastly, *White identified* are individuals who adopt a White identity and live their lives as White people while seeing other Latinos as inferior (Evans et al., 2010).

Ferdman and Gallegos (2001) provided some considerations on how Latinos experience race and racism (Evans et al., 2010). First, aspects of racism may manifest in the context of skin color (Evans et al., 2010). Those of darker skin may be discriminated against more than those with lighter skin. Second, Latinos represent a variety of skin colors and mixed heritages so it is not possible to put them in one category (Evans et al., 2010). Third, Latinos respond in various ways to the racial categories they are classified as in the United States (Evans et al., 2010). Some Latinos may identify as White, Hispanic, or Afro-Latino. These self-identifications may be influenced by friends, family, and their community.

Leader Identity Development

Leadership educators leverage leader identity models to understand the leader development of their students. According to Priest and Middleton (2016), "... individuals with a strong and integrated leader identity would be more motivated to engage in leader development and to exercise leadership than individuals not holding a leader identity, or those whose leader identity is less important to them" (p. 39). By having a strong sense of leader identity, students can embrace the work of leadership with or without designated positions or roles.

The Leadership Identity Development model was created by Komives, Owen, Longerbeam, Mainella, and Osteen (2005) to understand the process in which students develop their leadership identity. The six stages of this model include: awareness, exploration/engagement, leader identified, leadership differentiated, generativity, and integration/synthesis (Komives et al., 2005). Leadership identity can develop and change over time due to new identities or contexts that influence students' sense of identity (Komives et al., 2005). Transition to each stage occurs when students undergo an experience or develop new ways of thinking in their leadership identity development.

A CRITICAL LOOK AT LATINA IDENTITY DEVELOPMENT

Even though there are positive leadership outcomes for Latina students along intersecting dimensions of identity, significant barriers require management in the process. "In spite of a myriad of barriers, Latinas have made significant progress over the last decade, yet not all are faring as well as they must if they are to be able to realize their aspirations and continue to make important contributions to society and the economy" (Gándara, 2015, p. 7). This next section pinpoints how tenets of critical race theory (CRT) and Latino critical theory (LatCrit) confront and expose the invalidation members of underrepresented groups face in society and higher education. Also, this section highlights the influence of White privilege and oppression within leadership education.

Critical Race Theory

Gloria Ladson-Billings and William Tate asserted CRT could be used to examine the issues of races and inequities in education (Dixson & Rousseau, 2006). "In particular, they detailed the intersection of race and property rights and how this construct could be used to understand inequity in schools and schooling" (Dixson & Rousseau, 2006, p. 32). CRT can be used as a theoretical framework in describing the feelings of isolation some Latina students may have in creating their leader identity. The theme of voice in CRT, when applied to Latina students, requires others to hear their stories and histories in order for their development to take shape. "[T]he essence of 'voice' . . . [is] . . . the assertion and acknowledgement of the importance of the personal and community experience of people of color as sources of knowledge" (Dixson & Rousseau, 2006, p. 35).

The ability to provide spaces where Latinas share their thoughts and opinions is incredibly valuable to their identity development and their sense of belonging. All too often, ". . . students of color [who] are holders and creators of knowledge . . . feel as if their histories, experiences, cultures, and languages are devalued, misinterpreted, or omitted within formal educational settings (Delgado Bernal, 2002, p. 106). Socially just leadership educators reinforce the idea of students of color, specifically Latina students, as holders and creators of knowledge. These students have the capacity to further enhance leadership classrooms into places where students authentically learn from each other's experiences.

Latino Critical Theory

LatCrit is similar to CRT; it is, ". . . concerned with a progressive sense of coalitional Latina/Latino pan-ethnicity" (Valdes, 1996, p. 24) and "it addresses issues often ignored by critical race theorists" (Delgado Bernal, 2002, p. 108). Issues of oppression and marginalization of Latinos within a societal context are central to this framework. "LatCrit is a theory that elucidates Latinas/Latinos' multidimensional identities and can address that intersectionality of racism, sexism, classism, and other forms of oppression" (Delgado Bernal, 2002, p. 108). The implications of LatCrit are especially important within leadership learning environments because it helps frames dynamics of discrimination or bias. Latina students may be placed into environments characterized by these power dynamics with little to no knowledge regarding how to best address these situations.

Educational systems are rooted in ideas and ideologies grounded in socially constructed norms and practices which uphold constructs of Whiteness and masculinity at the detriment of others. In these environments, the voices of Latina students may be silenced implicitly or explicitly. Socially just leadership educators take active steps to be knowledgeable about how race- and gender-based socially constructed norms and values impede the success of Latinas in their classroom. Latina students benefit from opportunities to express how they see themselves within their campus and global environment. Providing this voice and these platforms in leadership classrooms motivate reflections on how their leader and Latina identities intersect in meaningful ways.

Oppression and White Privilege

A major portion of Bordas's (2012), *Salsa, Soul, and Spirit: Leadership for a multicultural age*, focuses on issues of oppression and White privilege. In sharing the perspectives of Paulo Freire, Bordas (2012) stated he, "...observed that as social mechanisms bombard the oppressed with negative messages and stereotypes about themselves, they begin to believe these to be true and to internalize them" (p. 108). Latinas may be victims of the internalized oppression described, especially when they feel as if their environments constantly marginalize and silence them, leading to the internalization of anger and pain. Bordas (2012) furthered Freire's ideas by claiming those who internalize their oppression are held hostage by their own minds. The impacts of internal oppression are compounded by external systemic marginalization due to the obstacles members of communities of color face when dealing with issues of racial discrimination (Bordas, 2012). "Dealing with oppression, people's lack of belief in their abilities, and the cold facts of discrimination is a central charge of leadership programs in communities of color" (Bordas, 2012, p. 108). This is an area where the Latino leadership principle of a collectivist culture is important to create and maintain, especially within Latina communities.

Conversations at the National Hispana Leadership Institute (NHLI) center on how forms of oppression manifest when successful Latinas do not support one another (Bordas, 2012). "For a Latina, garnering a good education, learning to maneuver through Anglo institutions, and developing the skills and talents to surface as a leader is a rare feat" (Bordas, 2012, p. 110). These are significant accomplishments for many Latinas considering how detrimental systemic and internalized oppression can be to the resilience and motivation both necessary and sufficient to attain them. When

Latinas gain success, it often comes at a cost to their connection to their roots; older ways of being begin to diminish or grow more distant (Bordas, 2012) as they adopt the thinking, feeling, and actions necessary to attain those successes. Bordas (2012) noted one way to detect oppression is by the expression of *envidia*, or envy, among Latinas. An example of envidia is inappropriately attributing negative qualities to successful others, which has the potential to exacerbate feelings of self-doubt (Bordas, 2012).

Bordas (2012) presented another form of oppression called "the crab syndrome" (p. 111). The crab syndrome is the tendency to hold on to people for safe-keeping and preventing them from leaving (Bordas, 2012). For example, a young Latina may be dissuaded by her parents to attend college in another state because they are scared for their daughter to be away from home. Although, Bordas does not mention Latino leadership and gender in this portion of the chapter, one can come to same conclusion that within Latino culture, there are issues of masculinity being seen as dominant culture which may run counter to a Latina's value system. Bordas, cited the work of Peggy McIntosh, when discussing the advantages of White privilege. In particular to women, men acknowledged that women were disadvantaged, but failed to recognize their own male privilege (Bordas, 2012).

This ideology of social hierarchy and privilege have a similar dynamic within race (Bordas, 2012). As a collectivist culture, Latinos struggle to keep their groups united when they are placed in a society dominated by the individualism present in many White cultural value systems (Bordas, 2012). Latinos must assimilate in order to be acknowledged, but acknowledgment is not guaranteed when they do. This causes identity dissonance for some Latinos as they struggle to maintain their ethnic identity but also operate within the rules of the larger society. To resolve this tension, Bordas (2012) recommended,

> Leaders in communities of color must reveal how the internalization of the psychology of oppression has affected them personally. They must help people become aware of how envidia, the crab syndrome, and the lack of support for others can impede community progress. (p. 111)

This is an enormous undertaking for leaders, especially Latinas, because it involves overcoming their own internalized oppression and their personal version of systemic barriers in order to help others do the same. This is how Latina leaders may feel when trying to maintain their own ethnic and cultural identities while fighting for causes or organizations which challenge the status quo.

In order to remedy the cycle of internalized oppression, Bordas (2012) recommended group introspection. This entails recognizing the personal emotional reactions to oppression and learning to let go of the bitterness and anger (Bordas, 2012). As this is done, Latinas are better able to refocus their energies, identities, and agency toward become agents of social change.

The privileges associated with being White or male, or both, are inescapable in Western society. Bordas (2012) stressed "White privilege, similar to the male advantage, is unconscious and invisible. Like the air around us, it cannot be seen or touched, but it is pervasive and always present" (p. 112). Individuals who are identified as racially White obtain access to resources not as readily available to members of communities of color. It is imperative for all leaders to be aware of the inequalities and inequities present in society so they may create ideologies, frameworks, and action plans combat those issues (Bordas, 2012). As asserted by Bordas (2012), "...only by becoming aware of how society is structured to perpetuate the dominance of some groups and to limit access for others will leaders be able to create the framework for the just and equal society in which diversity can flourish" (p. 112). Bordas challenged White leaders, and male leaders of all races, to recognize and confront how their privileges damage communities of color and perpetuate inequality. According to Bordas, successfully dismantling historic systems of race- and gender-based privileges will require a higher standard of leadership, where care and concern for everyone are linked, regardless of background.

LATINO LEADERSHIP DEVELOPMENT

In *The Power of Latino Leadership: Culture, Inclusion, and Contribution,* Bordas (2013) provided 10 principles of Latino leadership. Latino leadership is framed as the integration of Latino culture and influence on leadership processes. Her 10 principles consist of: the character of the leader (personalismo), knowing oneself and personal awareness (conciencia), personal and collective (destino), culturally based leadership (la cultura), inclusiveness and diversity (de colores), collective community stewardship (juntos), global vision and immigrant spirit (¡adelante!), social activism and coalition leadership (si se puede), leadership that celebrates life (gozar la vida), and sustained by faith and hope (fe y esperanza; Bordas, 2013, pp. 15–16).

These principles are rooted in the traditions and rituals that are part of the collective Latino community. Bordas (2013), asserted Latinos "...have built a legacy of inclusive community leadership based on cultural values and traditions that has as its purpose to uplift people" (p. x). Her book highlighted the leadership contributions of Latinos and integrated the principles into leadership learning, serving as one of the very few shining examples of the intersectionality of leadership learning and Latino identity. It is necessary at this point to focus more narrowly on the principles of culturally based leadership (la cultura) and social activism and coalition leadership (si se puede) with respect to socially just leadership education.

La cultura describes the five pillars of Latino leadership, namely, "...treating people like familia, being generous, having respeto for everyone regardless of status or position, always keeping one's word, and being of service" (Bordas, 2013, p. 110). These pillars unite communities even during times of hardship (Bordas, 2013). From these pillars we see how social change values of community and common purpose are prevalent in Latino culture, with important implications for leadership education and development. Socially just leadership educators use these pillars appropriately as a foundation when working with Latina student leaders. An example of this could entail how Latina leaders encourage their organizations to work with one another towards their organizations' common purpose or mission. Many Latina students may not see the connection of the Latino culture in leadership practices, especially if the literature informing practice is scarce.

The principle of social activism and coalition leadership (si se puede) sheds light on the history of Latinos experiencing discrimination and exclusion and how they have come together through collective forms of resistance. "Leaders become activists because of the economic discrepancies and inequities that exist in their own families and communities" (Bordas, 2013, p. 167). When faced with issues negatively affecting community or family, there is a rich Latino history of active social justice advocates and activists. Bordas (2013), stressed leadership and social justice as naturally interconnected for collective cultures since they both involve protecting vulnerable communities and their members. This way of thought directly contrasts western culture where individualized needs and concerns are given priority (Bordas, 2013). This type of leadership stems from a collectivist approach where the needs of many are acknowledged. Activist leadership requires the strength and courage of many people in order for positive change to occur (Bordas, 2013). "We need to express and develop a new style of leadership that is much more inclusive. We need to be prepared to provide leadership not just for Latinos but for everybody—this is the new frontier" (Bordas, 2013, p. 175). This is another example of the collective spirit of Latino leadership. Not only are the voices of Latinos need to be heard, but the voices of everybody should be part of that initiative. Latino leadership embodies the idea of a bienvenido spirit, in which inclusiveness is a strong core value. Through bienvenido, Latino leaders are able to build coalitions and reach out to other groups (Bordas, 2013).

INTERSECTIONALITY AND LEADERSHIP LEARNING

Aspects of a Latina's leader identity development impact how she sees herself as a leader and leads others. Latina students use characteristics of their race and ethnic identity in their leadership style. However, there can also be instances in which Latina leaders may feel that they must conform to the dominant leader identity characteristics that historically did not represent underrepresented and marginalized student populations. "There is very little research that examines Hispanic women's leadership development either in predominately White environments or minority-dominated environments" (Onorato & Musoba, 2015, p. 15). Leadership educators underserve Latina students by pushing them to pick an identity and not being aware how this might invalidate a Latina student and their ability to lead. The following section will introduce pedagogical practices for socially just leadership educators who are trying to find methods to integrate Latina leader identity development in a leadership classrooms.

Culturally Relevant Leadership

The CRLL model (Bertrand Jones, Guthrie, & Osteen, 2016), is a framework addressing experiences and backgrounds of marginalized and underrepresented groups in leadership learning. The CRLL has five domains: historical legacy of inclusion/exclusion, compositional diversity, as well as behavioral, organizational and structural, and psychological dimensions (Bertrand Jones et al., 2016). According to it's authors, "These domains of culturally relevant leadership learning propel leadership educators to consider the importance of students' experience of broader campus climate and how students engage in the leadership learning context of the campus" (Bertrand Jones et al., 2016, p. 15). Socially just leadership educators incorporate diverse authors and lessons within their curriculum.

They also establish learning environments where students are encouraged and affirmed in sharing their experiences. It is also the role of the leadership educator to be aware of how their identities are perceived in the classroom. For example, an instructor who identifies as Latina may be perceived by other Latinas as someone they can trust or emulate because they share a common identity. This connects to the value of recruiting diverse faculty and staff to create welcoming and inclusive environments on college campuses.

Teaching to Transgress

According to hooks (1994), engaged pedagogy is open to student expression and the empowerment of students. Furthermore, "[a]ny classroom that employs a holistic model of learning will also be a place where teachers grow, and are empowered by the process" (hooks, 1994, p. 21). However, this is not possible without instructors being vulnerable and encouraging their students to take risks (hooks, 1994). Socially just leadership educators role model the modes of behavior they expect from their students. By being vulnerable and appropriately sharing experiences, Latina students may be inclined to share their experiences in the classroom. Engaged pedagogy's holistic and inclusive emphasis is stated clearly by hooks (1994) in her assertion, "[t]o educate as the practice of freedom is a way of teaching that anyone can learn" (p. 13). Socially just leadership educators are careful and aware of how they approach curricula to create spaces where students are respected and validated as knowers.

hooks (1994) affirmed classroom culture changes are challenging when teaching in diverse settings, arguing, "[o]ften, if there is one lone person of color in the classroom she or he is objectified by others and forced to assume the role of 'native' informant" (hooks, 1994, p. 43). Latina students are often paradoxically placed in college environments; they are in the numerical minority but simultaneously expected to be the expert in Latino issues. By tokenizing Latina students, they may be less inclined to share their thoughts and perspectives for fear of being essentialized or fetishized. Framing Latinas as the other in educational settings actively works against the goals of learning; curtailing individual expression, squashing personal agency, and flattening Latinas' robust identities into caricatures of the real world.

Sentipensante Pedagogy

Laura Rendón's (2009) *Sentipensante Pedagogy* introduced a pedagogical approach which encompasses and embraces holistic learning. Sentipensante means sensing/thinking and encourages the intersection of both in learning experiences. According to Rendón (2009), sentipensante pedagogy is a "...teaching and learning approach based on wholeness, harmony, social justice, and liberation" (p. 132). Sentipensante pedagogy encourages teachers to treat their students as whole individuals via intellectual, social, emotional, and spiritual dimensions (Rendón, 2009). Classrooms constructed using this approach encapsulate group work, collaborative assignments, academic and interpersonal validation, relationship-centered interactions, community, and a caring and supportive climate which is open to emotion, and encourages students to bond with one another (Rendón, 2009).

Socially just leadership instructors play active and pivotal roles in creating these learning environments alongside their students who are partners in community building processes. Three goals are associated with this pedagogical approach: challenging aspects of traditional notions of teaching and learning, building well rounded and educated individuals, and instilling the importance of positive social change within the world (Rendón, 2009). Curriculum is viewed from a multi-human approach which is "...multicultural and humanistic in nature" (Rendón, 2009, p. 138). This type of curriculum contains examples from and dialogue regarding traditionally disadvantaged groups, diverse perspectives, feminist and masculine ways of knowing, personal teachings, and the wisdom of indigenous peoples (Rendón, 2009).

Sentipensante pedagogy challenges traditional forms of classroom teaching and learning. A traditional classroom would consist of lecture style teaching in which students are not given opportunties to interact with one another. The students would act as receivers of knowledge instead of contributors. Faculty have key roles in Sentipensante pedagogy: teacher/learning, artist, healer/liberator/humanitarian, and activist/social change agent (Rendón, 2009). Within these roles, leadership educators have the capability to fully embrace and acknowledge the students in their classroom, especially those struggling with issues of identity invalidation and self-doubt.

According to Rendón (2009), sentipensante pedagogy,

> ...is not for those who are uncomfortable with expressing emotions in class, do not wish to have extensive contact with students, are not open to collaboration and transdisciplinary learning, do not wish to employ strategies other than lectures, or are unwilling to share power with students in the classroom. (pp. 136–137)

This is an approach to learning and teaching where educators fully immerse themselves in building curricula and classrooms. This approach requires instructors to also do some self-work to determine if they are open to challenging the status quo of leadership learning and teaching.

MOVING FORWARD

The purpose of this chapter was to start a discourse on the intersectionality of leader and Latina identity development in leadership education. Socially just leadership educators employ various means to encouraged Latina students' development of their leader identity without negating their ethnic identity. While there are cocurricular programs that may address this issue, it is important to look at the curricular aspect of leader identity development. Many of the life experiences Latina students possess can be integrated within class discussions and coursework.

One recommendation is for leadership classes to incorporate leader and identity development within the curriculum. Leadership learning can incorporate culturally relevant, in this case Latina-relevant, curriculum into the classroom (Bertrand Jones et al., 2016). Leadership educators must be aware that Latina students may define leadership and leader identity that differ from the traditional models that are taught in the classroom.

By encouraging Latinas to use their voice and sharing their thoughts and perspectives on leader identity development.

A variety of techniques can be used in the classroom to help encourage this type of learning and engagement. Auditing course syllabi to make sure authors are representative of various identities and backgrounds is important (Bertrand Jones et al., 2016). Case studies could be used to highlight student's real life experiences and apply various cultural aspects (McCain, 2016). For students who are not as willing to talk in the classroom, class discussions can be done in small groups to encourage team thought processes. Guest speakers should consist of community leaders from Latino backgrounds in order to provide a role model who are able to share their leadership experiences. Reflective journaling can provide students the opportunity to clarify and think critically about their experiences and how they intersect within their leader and ethnic identity. Lastly, parallel blogging is a technique in which students have to read and analyze an article and apply the key points to their own experiences (McCain, 2016). This process will encourage students to think critically of the materials they are reading and will encourage them to make connections with their lived experiences.

Institutions of higher education should make the recruitment of a diverse faculty and staff a priority. Latina faculty and staff are often not as visible as their White and/or male colleagues in institution of higher education. In circumstances where only one, or a small group, is present, they tend to become the "go-to" persons for all students of color. These students may look up to the faculty/staff member because they share the same identity and can be a potential support system on campus. In accordance with findings from Arminio et al. (2000), ". . . campuses should assess their efforts in facilitating students meeting potential role models, especially at large institutions" (p. 505). In the classroom, a Latina faculty member may inspire Latina students to share their own experiences and become more comfortable in being vulnerable within the environment. However, this can only be done if the Latina faculty member mirrors that behavior and shares her vulnerability with her students. These mentors and role models have the capacity to inspire Latina leaders to participate in leadership activities and programs that may be influential in their leader identity development.

Leadership educators should be cognizant of the use of language when teaching leader identity. For some, the term leader may mean something entirely different to one student than the other. Armino et al. (2000), addressed ". . . by using the leader label and by extolling the individual benefits of serving in a leadership role, students of color may be turned away from taking advantage of opportunities" (p. 505). Socially just leadership educators emphasize the individual benefits of being a leader as well as the benefits leadership has amongst a group and community. Some recommendations provided by the literature include active use of language to emphasize group dynamics and collaboration. Also, when teaching leadership, provide moments when students are able to reflect on their experiences and backgrounds through a leader identity lens. This can be done through the use of reflection journals, one-minute papers, or incorporating reflection pieces into existing assignments.

Another recommendation involves collaborating with campus partners in divisions of student affairs and discussing curricular and cocurricular ways to teach leader identity. These valuable partnerships have the potential to create a holistic learning experience for Latina students. While traditionally student and academic affairs have faced challenges working collaboratively, it is incredibly important to bring each side to the table and talk about ways to support Latina students.

Leadership educators must be well equipped to teach college student populations that are becoming increasingly diverse. This is just one small step in creating change. It is my hope that this step may encourage discourse and action in order to create learning environments in which the saliency of multiple identities and how they intersect with leader identity development are critically examined and valued. It is my hope that this chapter can be used as a call to action for all leadership educators to reassess how their leadership programs can be reflective of our global society.

REFERENCES

Arminio, J. L., Carter, S., Jones, S. E., Kruger, K., Lucas, N., Washington, J., Young, N., & Scott, A. (2000). Leadership experiences of students of color. *NASPA Journal, 37*(3), 496–510.

Bertrand Jones, T., Guthrie, K. L., & Osteen, L. (2016). Critical domains of culturally relevant leadership learning: A call to transform leadership programs. In K. L. Guthrie, T. Bertrand Jones, & L. Osteen (Eds.), *New directions for student leadership, No. 152: Developing culturally relevant leadership learning* (pp. 9–21). San Francisco, CA: Jossey-Bass.

Bordas, J. (2012). *Salsa, soul, and spirit: Leadership for a multicultural age.* Oakland, CA: Berrett-Koehler.

Bordas, J. (2013). *The power of Latino leadership: Culture inclusion, and contribution.* San Francisco, CA: Berrett-Koehler.

Case, K. F., & Hernandez, R. (2013). "But still, I'm Latino and I'm proud": Ethnic identity exploration in the context of a collegiate cohort program. *Christian Higher Education, 12*(1–2), 74–92.

Castellanos, J., & Jones, L. (Eds.). (2003). *The majority in the minority: Expanding the representation of Latina/o faculty, administrators, and students in higher education.* Sterling, VA: Stylus.

Countries that make up Latin America. (2016). *worldatlas.* Retrieved from http://www.worldatlas.com/articles/which-countries-make-up-latin-america.html

Delgado Bernal, D. (2002). Critical race theory, Latino critical theory, and critical raced-gendered epistemologies: Recognizing students of color as holders and creators of knowledge. *Qualitative Inquiry, 8*(1), 105–126.

Dixson, A. D., & Rousseau, C. K. (2006). And we are still not saved: Critical race theory in education ten years later. In A. D. Dixson & C. K. Rousseau (Eds.), *Critical race theory in education: All God's children got a song* (pp. 31–54). New York, NY: Routledge.

Dugan, J. P., & Komives, S. R. (2011). Leadership theories. In S. R. Komives, J. P. Dugan, J. E. Owen, C. Slack, & W. Wagner (Eds.), *The handbook for student leadership development* (2nd ed., pp. 35–37). San Francisco, CA: Jossey-Bass.

Evans, N. J., Forney, D. S., Guido, F. M., Patton, L. D., & Renn, K. A. (2010). *Student development in college: Theory, research and practice.* San Francisco, CA: Jossey-Bass.

Ferdman, B. M., & Gallegos, P. I. (2001). Racial identity development and Latinos in the United States. In C. L. Wijeyesinghe & B. W. Jackson, III (Eds.), *New perspectives on racial identity development: A theoretical and practical anthology* (pp. 32–66). New York: New York University Press.

Gándara, P. (2015). Fulfilling America's future: Latinas in the U.S., 2015. *The White House Initiative on Educational Excellence for Hispanics.* Retrieved from http://sites.ed.gov/hispanic-initiative/files/2015/09/Fulfilling-Americas-Future-Latinas-in-the-U.S.-2015-Final-Report.pdf

Garcia-Navarro, L. (2015). Hispanic or Latino? A guide for the U.S. presidential campaign. *NPR.* Retrieved from http://www.npr.org/sections/parallels/2015/08/27/434584260/hispanic-or-latino-a-guide-for-the-u-s-presidential-campaign

hooks, b. (1994). *Teaching to transgress: Education as the practice of freedom.* New York, NY: Routledge.

Komives, S. R., Owen, J. E., Longerbeam, S. D., Mainella, F. C., & Osteen, L. (2005). Developing a leadership identity: A grounded theory. *Journal of College Student Development, 46*(6), 593–611.

McCain, K. R. (2016, November). *A narrative approach to leadership development: Applications for leadership education.* Paper presented at the meeting of the International Leadership Association, Atlanta, GA.

Onorato, S., & Musoba, G. D. (2015). La líder: Developing a leadership identity as a Hispanic woman at a Hispanic institution. *Journal of College Student Development, 56*(1), 15–31.

Priest, K. L., & Middleton, E. (2016). Exploring leader identity and development. In R. Reichard & S. Thompson (Eds.), *New directions for student leadership, No. 149: Leader developmental readiness: Pursuit of leadership excellence* (pp. 37–47). San Francisco, CA: Jossey-Bass.

Ramirez, T. L., & Blay, Z. (2016). Why people are using the term "Latinx." *Huffington Post.* Retrieved from http://www.huffingtonpost.com/entry/why-people-are-using-the-term-latinx_us_57753328e4b0cc0fa136a159

Rendón, L. (2009). *Sentipensante pedagogy.* Sterling, VA: Stylus.

Valdes, F. (1996). Foreword: Latina/o ethnicities, critical race theory and post-identity politics in postmodern legal culture: From practices to possibilities. *La Raza Law Journal, 9,* 1–31.

CHAPTER 10

LATINO MALE LEADERSHIP

A Social Justice Perspective

Juan R. Guardia and Cristobal Salinas Jr.

Casi todo fue una mentira
Se les olvidó que nos robaron nuestra tierra y libertad
Se les olvidó que he cruzado fronteras visibles e invisibles

Me dijeron que sin mí este país no existiría
Me dijeron que en las buenas y en las malas me tratarian con dignidad

Se les olvidó que me prometieron que jamás me dejarían
Se les olvidó que me prometieron acceso a una escuela

Se les olvidó que también trabajamos por este país
Que somos obreros, campesinos, profesionistas, deportistas, artistas, militares
Que dimos nuestra vida, nuestra juventud, nuestras ideas, nuestro trabajo
Para hacer este país mas grande

¿Y ahora pretenden quitarnos todo por lo que luchamos,
separarnos con muros de nuestra familia,
se niegan a educarnos, nos discriminan por nuestra raza o color?

Changing the Narrative, pages 145–157

Todo este dolor se puedo haber evitado
Si me hubieran hablado con la verdad
Pero se les olvidó que soy un líder
Y no me daré por vencido
Porque soy guerrero de mi comunidad[1]

Creating leadership educational programing for Latino male students requires action from educators who understand the student population's needs, wants, challenges, and goals. Having awareness of their interests, joys, successes, challenges, mistakes, and reflections can help create transformational leadership opportunities. Developing leadership opportunities for Latino male students by empowering them to continue developing their talents and skills as leaders reinforces the importance of leadership and coalition. In this chapter, the authors provide an overview of Latino male leadership by using the three-level model of oppression (Vaccaro, 2011), and then provide a context of how Latino male students continue to be disenfranchised at each level. Finally, the authors highlight promising practices for higher education educators.

Most higher education institutions continue to develop leadership education programming for particular student populations and organizations, (i.e., fraternity and sorority life, men of color, women, and engineering); however, all too often these leadership programs neglect some identities of the student participants. For example, as leadership programming is created for men of color, they often lack the cultural awareness of their student participants. As Latino men who work in divisions of student affairs in higher education institutions, we have frequently been asked to participate in programming for men of color undergraduates.

While these initiatives have great intentions for men of color, they still lack representation of cultural awareness, leadership, and representation of Latino male students overall. Harris III and Wood (2013) noted research of Latino student males is "...woefully lacking" (p. 181). Therefore, we argue more leadership educational programming and research on Latino males is needed, and "...there is a need to understand their unique leadership experiences" (Garcia, Huerta, Ramirez, & Patrón, 2017, p. 1). Furthermore, most research on Latino male leadership has focused on students at 4-year institutions, leaving a gap in understanding Latino male leadership at 2-year institutions.

Leadership is a term that has entered higher education and student affairs within the last two decades (Komives, Lucas, & McMahon, 2007). Research on leadership among college students continues to evolve our understanding of how to best create transformational learning experiences for students. We believe, through leadership education for Latino males, we must incorporate meaningful social justice conversations. These conversations challenge us to share knowledge, tools, resources, and practices to support our leadership and social justice educators.

LATINO VERSUS LATINX

We have specifically chosen to use the term Latino instead of Latinx to recognize and create inclusive spaces for Latino/x students. As this chapter focuses on Latino males, and Chapter 9 focuses on Latina female students, we recognize the significant need for research that aims to understand Latinx leadership, which is beyond the scope of our offerings here.

Salinas and Lozano (2016) identified the term Latino has traditionally included both male and female genders, and it has evolved within the literature as Latin, Latino/a, Latin@, and Latinx. Furthermore, they define the term Latinx as an:

> . . . inclusive term that recognizes the intersectionality of sexuality, language, immigration, ethnicity, culture, and phenotype. While there are various arguments for the use of *Latinx,* it has evolved as a new form of liberation for those individuals that do not identify within the gender binary of masculinity or femininity, and it is used to represent the various intersectionalities of gender as it is understood in different ways within different communities of people. (Salinas & Lozano, 2016, p. 18)

We recognize that to truly advance leadership and social justice education for Latino/a/x students, one must recognize and use the term Latinx ". . . to advocate for people that are living in the borderlands of gender" (Salinas & Lozano, 2016, p. 22). We use the terms Latino and Hispanic interchangeably in the Latino demographic section to recognize how various agencies collect and report data on Hispanic/Latino population.

LATINO DEMOGRAPHICS

The Latino population continues to grow steadily in the United States. According to the U.S. Census Bureau (2017), the Hispanic population currently resides at 57.5 million. This is a 2% increase in the Hispanic population from July 2016 to July 2017. Of that, California accounts for 27% (15.3 million), the largest of all U.S. states for Hispanics (U.S. Census Bureau, 2017). As the Latino population continues to grow, so do Latino male college students on campuses across the nation. Latino college students represent the largest enrolled minority group of students in the country (Fry & Lopez, 2012). The Pew Research Center reported 2.3 million Hispanic college students in 2014 (Krogstad, 2016) and 60% of Latino students attended Hispanic Serving Institutions (HSIs; Santiago, Taylor, & Calderon Galdeano, 2016).

For Hispanic students across the country between the ages of 25 and 29, only 15% had earned a bachelor's degree or higher (Krogstad, 2016). One reason for this low percentage can be attributed to the high percentage of Latino student enrolled at 2-year and community colleges at a greater rate than members of any other racial or ethnic group (Krogstad, 2016). Latino males continue to lag behind their female peers with respect to attending college and earning degrees (Sáenz & Ponjuan, 2009). It is imperative for policy makers and educators to focus on the dearth of degrees among Latino undergraduates as their contributions are sorely needed in the academy and the workforce. Resources on college and university campuses aimed at members of this community greatly benefit these men and aid in building an inclusive and socially just campus.

LATINO LEADERSHIP

Several higher education scholars have explored the importance of student leadership development and outcomes (Astin 1993; Dugan & Komives, 2010; Posner, 2004; Renn & Bilodeau, 2005; Thompson, 2006). Yet, few have focused on Latino male student leadership development and outcomes. For example, Garcia et al. (2017) interviewed 24 Latino male students to gain an understanding of their leadership development. They discovered joining a fraternity, involvement in ethnicity-based student organizations, participating in an internship, and attending racial/cultural awareness workshops contributed to their leadership development. This study reaffirmed other scholars' (Antonio, 2001; Guardia & Evans, 2008) findings regarding similar leadership opportunities for Latino males.

Beatty and Tillapaugh (2017) shrewdly criticized the disproportionate research focus on fraternity men, noting "...very little [attention] has been paid to the connection between [Latino] masculinity and leadership among boys and young men" (p. 50). Ultimately, when Garcia et. al (2017) focused specifically on Latino males, they "found that culturally relevant experiences are of particular importance to their leadership development" (p. 15). When leadership development is holistic, cultural, and utilizes a social justice lens, it allows Latino males more freedom to bring their authentic selves to spaces where they are free to experience their surroundings academically, culturally, socially, and personally.

Lozano's (2015) groundbreaking text, *Latina/o college student leadership: Emerging theory, promising practice,* was the first collective scholarly contribution focusing specifically on Latino student leadership. She conducted a study focused on Latino students' leadership development experiences at predominantly White institutions and found students "...tended to view leadership as holistic and action-oriented" (Lozano, 2015, p. 10). In addition, students' leadership journeys were characterized by four broad themes:

1. *Comunidad:* Finding and creating a community;
2. *La Lucha:* The struggle for change;
3. *Nuestra Fuerza:* Our strengths as Latina/os; and
4. *Urgencia y legado:* Sense of urgency and legacy (Lozano, 2015, p. 13).

Most importantly, Lozano's (2015) study highlighted the "...need for more cultural awareness regarding how Latina/o students view leadership..." (p. 28) and the role in which faculty and administrators can play an important role and contribution to their leadership experiences.

Beyond student organizational leadership development, classroom pedagogy also contributes to the growth of students' leadership capabilities. Cress and Duarte (2013) described how *pedagogia communitaria* (pedagogy of community) had a major influence of Latino student leadership development. Their work asserted "[c]onstructivist teaching strategies (e.g., group-decision making, social issues discussions) significantly facilitated Latino students' growth in civic leadership" (Cress & Duarte, 2013, p. 62). Such strategies aided and enhanced Latino students' ways of thinking and "...facilitated developmental and leadership gains associated with increased civic participation and global awareness" (Cress & Duarte, 2013, p. 65).

Gonzales (2015) also described how faculty members at HSIs apply funds of knowledge in the classroom to validate and authenticate Latino students' experiences. Funds of knowledge theory is "...the competence and knowledge embedded in the life experiences of underrepresented [communities]" (Rios-Aguilar, Kiyama, Gravitt, & Moll, 2011, p. 164). For many Latino male students, this approach would be the first time they view themselves as co-facilitators and contributors in their education process. Subsequently, "[p]roviding space for students to understand their life experiences as a form of valid knowledge is the first significant step forward reshaping the production and legitimization of knowledge within academia" (Gonzales, 2015, p. 128). When Latino students' experiences are validated and contribute to classroom learning, this authentication can be empowering; contributing to their social and personal identities, including leader identity development.

Bordas (2013) described how culturally based leadership has also influenced Latino leadership development. Latino cultural values such as familism (or *familismo*), being congenial (*simpatico*), showing respect (*respeto*), being honest (*honesto*), and *personalismo* (value of each person) are strong, contributing factors in Latino leadership development. Of importance, Bordas (2010) placed emphasis on Latino leadership as collective, and ultimately, people-centered leadership. As such, it is similar to servant leadership theory, where "[s]ervant leadership theory begins by viewing the leader first as the servant, a person who first wants to serve others" (Komives et al., 2007, p. 56). It is clear Bordas' (2010) Latino-relevant, people-centered leadership and servant leadership theory's primary focus are both on people and the community's need; they are placed in importance first and foremost and the leader's needs are secondary. Moreover, within the Latino community, the leaders' emphasis on their *comunidad y gente* [community and people] contributes to the *respeto* [respect] of the leader.

Understanding the Three Levels of Oppression for Latino Males

We believe leadership is about working together as a "…common purpose and a goal…" (Komives et al., 2007; Northouse, 2016), as well as argue "…common purpose…" is "…often referred to as assimilation, is in conflict with the strategies theories, and concepts of contemporary social justice efforts" (Landreman, 2013, p. xiv). Efforts of creating leadership opportunities for students "…have resulted in specific cultures' being ignored and excluded, negatively affecting [leadership] and educational attainment for many" (Landreman, 2013, p. xiv). Socially just leadership in higher education is representative of Latino/a/x people. This requires acknowledging and addressing equity opportunities for low income Latino/a/x students, Gay, Lesbian, Bisexual, Trans*, and Queer Latino/a/x students, Latino/a/x students with disabilities, and the intersections of other marginalized social identities.

Historically popular notions of leadership were developed from hierarchical perspectives. Some individuals might approach and engage in leadership conversations and practices with differential hierarchical assumptions. Hierarchical approaches usually consist of a singular institution, culture, or individual placing an emphasis on "power" at the top with subsequent levels of power below them. Hierarchical approaches have historically oppressed, marginalized, and rendered Latinos male students invisible (Noguera & Hurtado, 2012; Sáenz & Ponjuan, 2009; Sáenz, Ponjuan, & Figueroa, 2016) at the institutional, cultural, and individual levels (Vaccaro, 2011). In order to understand Latino male leadership development, socially just leadership instructors recognize and acknowledge how members of this student population continue to be overlooked and constantly experience oppression. Using the three-level model of oppression presented by Vaccaro (2011), we provide a context of how Latino male students have continued to be disenfranchised at the institutional, cultural, and individual levels.

Institutional oppression manifests in "... social institutions such as education, politics, healthcare, economy, media, religion, family, the military, and higher education" (Vaccaro, 2011, p. 30). Institutional oppression for Latino male students might manifest in educational opportunities, "... housing or employment discrimination, or a tradition of leadership that all whole dominant social group identities (e.g., White, educated, male)... This might also look like intentional and culturally relevant outreach to communities [Latinos] that typically lack access to the institution" (Salinas & guerrero, in press). For example, Latino males are overrepresented among the ranks of the incarcerated and underrepresented in postsecondary educational institutions (Noguera & Hurtado, 2012).

Cultural oppression manifests in "... societal norms, language, values, icons, and popular culture..." including jokes, music, and shared beliefs (Vaccaro, 2011, p. 30). Salinas and guerrero (in press) provide the example of White supremacy as a form of cultural oppression. This refers to beliefs "... that White individuals are superior, less violent, and better citizens than any other race... ," while Latino males, "... might be portrayed as criminals, rapists, and drug dealers" (Salinas & guerrero, in press). A current example of cultural oppression for Latino male students is the perception and reference to "bad *hombres*" [bad men] by political leaders. This contributes to the belief Latino males are violent criminals and bad people (Moreno, 2016).

Individual oppression manifests in personal beliefs, behaviors, and interactions, emerging "... through active or passive interpersonal interactions and stems from conscious or unconscious prejudice" (Vaccaro, 2011, p. 30). While Latino males recognize the merit of education (Noguera & Hurtado, 2012), teachers or peers might dismiss or devalue their educational goals.

When working in leadership development programs for Latino male students, socially just educators and practitioners deconstruct hierarchical leadership and empower Latino male students in the fluidity of leadership practices. Latino male leaders are found in student government, orientation, residence life, Greek life, and hold other leadership positions across various student organizations. However, all too often they are the only Latino and/or student of color in those roles. Through socially just leadership education, Latino male student leaders learn about their privilege as males, and oppression as members of a historically marginalized community—other social identities that coincide with both privilege and oppression. The goal should be to gain and demonstrate awareness of how their oppressed and privileged identities inform their socially just leadership on their campuses and in their communities.

PROMISING PRACTICES FOR EDUCATORS

Institutional Level

Most institutions of higher education specifically recruit Latino males based on their social identities. As such, Latino male leadership development requires explicit focus within the mission and outcomes of educational programs and curriculum for student development. As student- and academic-affairs educators empower and educate Latino male students by creating and implementing organizational structures and programs, and as they enter the dialogue of Latino male leadership through the lenses of intersection and identity, it is critical that they understand and have perspective about who their Latino males students are, and their point of entry for these Latino students (i.e., traditional students, nontraditional, first generations, social economic status, immigration status, linguistics). Institutions must recognize the prior frames of reference students use in systems of higher education. Institutions often convince Latino males obtaining a college degree will improve their life chances by learning new skills, but it is important for student- and academic-affairs educators to provide the necessary tools for Latino students to gain better self-understanding as well as how to develop personal and career goals.

Cultural Level

There are many "mirrors" of how Latino male students are perceived by society. These do not reflect the way Latino male students want to be perceived; it is the way they are perceived by others and how those perceptions limit their opportunities to succeed. When Latino males are seen as *bad hombres*, why would other individuals want to offer opportunities to advance? Latino males might already have preconceived notions of those offering opportunities, and to whom those opportunities are offered since most of those opportunities are not accessible to Latino students. This is important for student affairs and academic affairs educators to recognize, as they are the people at the institutions creating opportunities for students. When leadership educators do not explicitly respect and dignify members of the Latino community, colleges, universities and the agents they employ perpetuate cultural oppression.

Individual Level

Individual oppression is a consequence of not being valued, heard, or recognized. This includes supporting Latino male students as they gain understanding of their characteristics, skills, purpose, and how to negotiate spaces with intentionality. However, when educators and institutions say they recognize the value of advanced degrees, but they summarily dismiss Latino male students' values and educational goals, members of these populations of students might become demotivated and their confidence will plummet. In order to support and help Latino male students advance in leadership, socially just student affairs and academic affairs educators create supportive and understanding emotional spaces.

Overall, socially just student affairs and academic affairs educators consider inclusive and culturally-based leadership opportunities for Latino male students. As noted, these programs and services aid in the leadership development for Latino male students. At an institutional level, socially just student affairs and academic affairs educators advocate for them within their respective student affairs units and the overall division. With regard to culturally based organizations, socially just educators advocate for the inclusivity of ethnic student organizations, Latino fraternities, and other leadership development opportunities to provide Latino male students with opportunities for developmental growth during their collegiate years and preparation for the world of work. Socially just educators place emphasis on the importance of interdisciplinary approaches to leadership, adopt social justice practices, and accept new and experiential knowledge of Latino males in order to challenge ideologies that have victimized, oppressed, marginalized, and undervalued Latino male leadership.

Socially just academic administrators and faculty advocate for teaching styles and pedagogies that are culturally inclusive. As mentioned earlier, the funds of knowledge framework demonstrates how Latino students' lived experiences, when weaved into the curriculum, enhances and empowers them academically and personally. In addition, socially just academic affairs colleagues take time at an individual level to personally know more about their students, in particular Latino males, to understand how their culture and multiple identities personally affect their academic experiences. Finally, professional development about Latino male students' development should be mandatory for all student affairs and academic affairs educators. Through professional development, a culture of leadership development can be embedded within institutions, with the goal of development trickling down to the students.

Socially just leadership educators ask students to reflect on what they have learned, apply their learning into actions, and critically analyze social issues. We also encourage educators to "...first educate themselves about their feelings, beliefs, and attitudes centered around [Latino] marginalized populations and communities" (Salinas & Beatty, 2013, p. 28). Educators must be "...aware of how well-intended work can do harm if good intention and seemingly powerful exercises are assumed to be all it takes to be effective educators" (Landreman & MacDonald-Dennis, 2013, p. 15). Then, educators should create meaningful dialogue spaces for them, their students, and colleagues to discuss their feelings, beliefs, and attitudes towards Latino male students in order to create, support, and advance Latino male leadership development.

CONCLUSION

This chapter provided an overview of Latino male leadership and demonstrated the gaps in research on Latino/a/x leadership. Also, by using the three-level model of oppression (institutional, cultural, and individual; Vaccaro, 2011) it provided a context of how Latino male disenfranchisement is perpetuated in higher education and leadership studies. Moreover, we validated how Latino male students, and other students of color, "...often feel as their histories, experiences, cultures, and languages are devalued, misinterpreted, or omitted within formal education settings" (Delgado Bernal, 2002, p. 105). Therefore, we support socially just educators who continue to move forward by advancing and promoting Latino male leaders as the "...holders and creators of knowledge" (Delgado Bernal, 2002, p. 105).

West (2001) emphasized leadership is about freedom, democracy, and equality, deserving cultivation and support to advance communities. Furthermore, he stated,

> [T]he major challenge is to meet the need to generate new leadership. The paucity of courageous leaders... requires that we look beyond the same elites and voices that recycle the older frameworks. We need leaders—neither saints nor sparkling television personalities—who can situate themselves within a larger historical narrative of this country and our world, who can grasp the complex dynamics of our peoplehood and imagine a future grounded in the best of our past, yet who are attuned to the frightening obstacles that now perplex us. (West, 2001, pp. 12–13)

Therefore, we recommended educators engage in critical thinking and discuss their feelings, beliefs, and attitudes towards Latino male students in order to create, support, and advance socially just Latino male leadership development and education.

Almost everything was a lie
They forgot that they robbed our lands and freedom
They are forgotten that I have crossed visible and invisible borderlands
They told me that without me this country would not exist
They told me that in the good and in the bad they would treat me
with dignity

They forgot that they promised me they would never leave me
They forgot that they promised access to a school
They forgot that we also contributed to this country
That we are worker, farmers, professionals, athletes, artists,
army men/women
That we gave our lives, our youth, our ideas, our work
To make this country better
And now they want to take everything that we work and fight for,
By separating us from our families with a border wall,
They deny us an education, and they discriminate us because
of our skin color?
All this pain could have been avoided
If they had spoken to me with the truth
But since they forgot that I am a leader
I will not give up
Because I am a warrior grown by my community

NOTE

1. Inspired by Salinas (2015), the authors write this epigraph as a form of healing and capturing through poetry some aspects of the history of Latinos in the United States. And as a reminder of the power Latinos hold in leadership and society. It also recognizes the Latino/a/x community as often being overlooked and invisible. The last paragraph of this chapter provides a general translation of the epigraph.

REFERENCES

Antonio, A. L. (2001). The role of interracial interaction in the development of leadership skills and cultural knowledge and understanding. *Research in Higher Education, 42,* 593–617.

Astin, A. W. (1993). *What matters in college: Four critical years revisited.* San Francisco, CA: Jossey-Bass.

Beatty, C., & Tillapaugh, D. (2017). Masculinity, leadership, and liberatory pedagogy: Supporting men through leadership development and education. In D. Tillapaugh & P. Haber-Curran (Eds.), *New directions for student leadership, No. 154: Critical perspectives on gender and student leadership* (pp. 47–58). San Francisco, CA: Jossey-Bass.

Bordas, J. (2010). Inclusive leadership. In R. A. Couto (Ed.), *Political and civic leadership: A handbook* (pp. 794–803). Thousand Oaks, CA: SAGE.

Bordas, J. (2013). *The power of Latino leadership: Culture, inclusion, and contribution.* San Francisco, CA: Berrett-Koehler.

Cress, C. M., & Duarte, R. (2013). Pedagogía Comunitaria: Facilitating Latino student civic engagement leadership. *AUDEM: The International Journal of Higher Education and Democracy, 4*(1), 54–78.

Delgado Bernal, D. (2002). Critical race theory, Latino critical theory, and critical raced-gender epistemologies: Recognizing students of color as holders and creators of knowledge. *Qualitative Inquiry, 8*(21), 105–126.

Dugan, J. P., & Komives, S. R. (2010). Influences on college students' capacity for socially responsible leadership. *Journal of College Student Development, 51,* 525–549.

Fry, R., & Lopez, M. H. (2012). *Hispanic student enrollment reaches new highs in 2011.* Washington, DC: Pew Research Center. Retrieved from http://www.pew hispanic.org/2012/08/20/hispanic-student-enrollments-reach-new-highs -in-2011/

Garcia, G. A., Huerta, A. H., Ramirez, J. J., & Patrón, O. E. (2017). Contexts that matter to the leadership development of Latino male college students: A mixed methods perspective. *Journal of College Student Development, 58*(1), 1–18.

Gonzales, L. D. (2015). How faculty in Hispanic-serving institutions can reshape the production and legitimization of knowledge within academia. In A. M. Nunez, S. Hurtado, & E. Calderon Galdeano (Eds.), *Hispanic-serving institutions: Advancing research and transformative practice* (pp. 121–135). New York, NY: Routledge.

Guardia, J. R., & Evans, N. J. (2008). Factors influencing the ethnic identity development of Latino fraternity members at a Hispanic serving institution. *Journal of College Student Development, 49*(3), 163–181.

Harris, F., III, & Wood, J. L. (2013). Student success for men of color in community colleges: A review of published literature and research, 1998–2012. *Journal of Diversity in Higher Education, 6*(3), 174–185.

Komives, S. R., Lucas, N., & McMahon, T. R. (2007). *Exploring leadership: For college students who want to make a difference* (2nd ed.). San Francisco, CA: Jossey-Bass.

Krogstad, J. M. (2016). *5 facts about Latinos and education.* Retrieved from http://www .pewresearch.org/fact-tank/2016/07/28/5-facts-about-latinos-and-education/

Landreman, L. M. (Ed.). (2013). The *art of effective facilitation: Stories and reflections from social justice educators.* Sterling, VA: Stylus.

Landreman, L. M., & MacDonald-Dennis, C. (2013). The evolution of social justice education and facilitation. In L. Landreman (Ed.), *The art of effective facilitation: Stories and reflections from social justice educators* (pp. 3–22). Sterling, VA: Stylus.

Lozano, A. (2015). Re-imagining Latina/o student at a historically White institution. In A. Lozano (Ed.), *Latina/o college student leadership: Emerging theory, promising practice* (pp. 3–28). New York, NY: Lexington Books.

Moreno, C. (2016). Here's why Trump's "bad hombres" comment was so offensive. *Huffpost.* Retrieved from http://www.huffingtonpost.com/entry/heres-why -trumps-bad-hombres-comment-was-so-offensive_us_5808e121e4b0180 a36e9b995

Noguera, P., & Hurtado, H. (2012). Invisible no more: The status and experience of Latino males from multidisciplinary perspectives. In P. Noguera, H. Hurtado, & E. Fergus (Eds.), *Invisible no more* (pp. 1–15). New York, NY; Routledge.

Northouse, P. G. (2016). *Leadership: Theory and practice (7th ed.)*. Thousands Oaks, CA: SAGE.

Posner, B. Z. (2004). A leadership development instrument for students: Updated. *Journal of College Student Development, 45*, 443–456.

Renn, K. A., & Bilodeau, B. L. (2005). Leadership identity development among lesbian, gay, bisexual, and transgender student leaders. *NASPA Journal, 42*, 342–367.

Rios-Aguilar, C., Kiyama, J. M., Gravitt, M., & Moll, L. C. (2011). Funds of knowledge for the poor and forms of capital for the rich? A capital approach to examining funds of knowledge. *Theory and Research in Higher Education, 9*(2), 163–184.

Sáenz, V. M., & Ponjuan, L. (2009). The vanishing Latino male in higher education. *The Journal of Hispanic Higher Education, 8*(1), 54–89.

Sáenz, V. B., Ponjuan, L., & Figueroa, J. L. (Eds.). (2016). *Ensuring the success of Latino males in higher education: A national imperative*. Sterling, VA: Stylus.

Salinas, C. (2015). Latino/a leadership retreats. In A.S. Lozano (Ed.), *Latina/o college student leadership: Emerging theory, promising practices* (pp. 101–121). New York, NY; Lexington Books.

Salinas, C., & Beatty, C. C. (2013). Constructing our own definition of masculinity: An intersectionality approach. In Z. Foste (Ed.), *Looking forward a dialogue on college men and masculinities* (pp. 24–29). Washington, DC: College Student Educators International (ACPA); Standing Committee on Men and Masculinities.

Salinas, C., & guerrero, A. (In press). Tokenizing social justice. In P. Sasso & J. DeVitis (Eds.), *Colleges at the crossroads: Taking sides on contested issues*. New York, NY: Peter Lang.

Salinas, C., & Lozano, A. S. (2016). *Documenting and recontextualizing the evolution of the term latinx*. Paper presented at the National Conference on Race and Ethnicity (NCORE); Forth Worth, TX.

Santiago, D.A., Taylor, M., & Calderon Galdeano, E. (May 2016). *From capacity to success: HSIs, Title V, and Latino students*. Washington, DC: Excelencia in Education.

Thompson, M. D. (2006). Student leadership process development: An assessment of contributing college resources. *Journal of College Student Development, 47*, 343–350.

U.S. Census Bureau. (2017). *The nation's older population is still growing, census bureau reports*. Retrieved from https://www.census.gov/newsroom/press-releases/2017/cb17-100.html

Vaccaro, A. (2011). The road to gender equality in higher education: Women's standpoints, successes, and continued marginalization. *Wagadu: Journal of Transnational Women's and Gender Studies, 9*, 25–53.

West, C. (2001). *Race matters*. Boston, MA: Bacon Press.

CHAPTER 11

SOCIAL JUSTICE LEADERSHIP FOR FAITH AND PHILOSOPHICAL COMMUNITIES

Vivechkanand S. Chunoo and Gabrielle Garrard

Institutions of higher education have made great strides with respect to race, ethnicity, and gender diversity over the past few decades, as well as sexual orientation more recently. However, with the important exception of religiously-affiliated colleges, most postsecondary institutions have not adequately addressed issues of religious diversity. The time has come to ameliorate this oversight. We believe American colleges and universities can and should seek ways to intentionally prepare socially just leaders for an increasingly religiously diverse society. To these ends, we advocate Eboo Patel's (2016) conceptualization of interfaith leadership as a blueprint for social justice faith leadership. When leadership education programs take an interfaith leadership stance on issues of religious and philosophical social justice, they are better able to produce social justice leaders for faith and philosophical communities. This chapter provides theoretical, conceptual,

Changing the Narrative, pages 159–173
Copyright © 2018 by Information Age Publishing
All rights of reproduction in any form reserved.

and practical guidance for socially just faith and philosophically-based leadership education. We believe American higher education institutions generally, and leadership education programs in particular, have a role to play in preparing socially just faith leaders and we offer our ideas to inform those who agree.

FAITH AND PHILOSOPHICAL LEADERSHIP

We frame our recommendations in our best understandings of what is needed for success in a sincere effort to begin a meaningful discussion of how to prepare individuals for socially just leadership in faith and philosophical communities. We have distilled some of the keenest thinking about faith and philosophical leadership; models, theories, dynamics, examples, and responsibilities of students and their institutions to set the stage for our most practical suggestions for educators. The scholars honored in this section are by no means the only people thinking, writing, and living this work, but their perspectives have been foundational in our understanding of how we can all become better leadership educators working toward the development of religious, spiritual, faithful, and philosophically-sound leaders.

Inner Meaning and Leadership

One of the most relevant models to shaping our understanding of how we can become better leadership educators with regard to religion and spirituality, Kriger and Seng (2005) produced an integrative model of leadership based on individuals' meaning-making, vision-setting, and moralistic orientations in organizations. Drawing upon common tenets of Islam, Christianity, Judaism, Hinduism, and Buddhism, their contingency theory of leadership incorporated "...workplace spirituality..." or "...a framework of organizational values evidenced in the culture that promotes employees' experience of transcendence through the work process, facilitate their sense of belonging connected to others in a way that provides feelings of completeness and joy" (Giacalone & Juriewicz, as quoted in Kriger and Seng, 2005, p. 775). While workforce language may not reflect a leadership orientation, the ideas of transcendence, belonging, and joy are valuable to leadership education across settings.

Additionally, Kriger and Seng's (2005) model considered charisma in spiritual leadership as helpful in communicating a shared vision, taking risks and making sacrifices, inspiring confidence in others and managing perceptions and group dynamics. Helpfully, the authors distinguished leadership based on *having* or *doing* from that which is based on *being*. Having leadership positions or doing the work of leadership, they argued, are constructs familiar to those in organizations. However, "...the direct experience and understanding of 'being' has atrophied in the western world today due largely to an overemphasis on 'observables'" (Kriger & Seng, 2005, p. 788). While the outward products of leadership and leading (i.e., observables) continue to matter in an outcomes-driven world, a sustained focus on being a socially just leader along dimensions of spirituality is the heart of this composition.

Drawing upon the aforementioned influences, Kriger and Seng (2005) extended Yukl's (2002) multiple contingency model, including spiritual leadership from a multi-religion perspective. However helpful this model might be, its practicality is limited; including unnamed elements the authors themselves describe as problematic. Despite these limitations, their work in offering a multi-religion lens to view spiritual leadership uncovers many of the nuances and challenges in grappling with how to do this work. Undaunted, socially just educators consider the rich interplay of specific religions, as well as multi-religion perspectives when teaching toward faith- and philosophical-community leadership.

Taking the ideas of religious pluralism to colleges and universities in particular, Patel and Meyer (2009) discussed the role of interfaith leadership on campus. They framed interfaith leadership as social justice by claiming, "...this kind of leadership is about more than just maintaining a fragile sense of tolerance, but of actually creating a cultural shift, so that interfaith cooperation is not an anomaly but becomes a social norm" (Patel & Meyer, 2009, p. 2). We see the connection in the need for cultural shifts on campuses in the results of the IDEALS study, a 5-year longitudinal study on how religious pluralism shows up on college campuses (Rockenbach, 2017). It follows a cohort of students through their collegiate experience to understand how students define their worldview and how their worldview evolves over time (Rockenbach, 2017). The researchers defined worldview as "a guiding life philosophy, which may be based on a particular religious tradition, a nonreligious perspective, ideological views, aspects of one's cultural background and personal identity, or some combination of these" (Rockenbach, 2017, p. 149). The findings of this study demonstrated the extent to which interfaith leadership opportunities are needed in colleges and universities. Patel and Meyer (2009) provided recommendations of college leaders working toward this shift, including becoming fluent in stories from their own faith- and philosophical-traditions, organizing initiatives for common interfaith action, and transforming campus climates by helping students think about sustainable commitments to religious pluralism.

Each of those recommendations are important considerations in socially just leadership education for faith- and philosophical-communities. To highlight the value of these recommendations, and the contributions leadership educators can make toward the goal of sustainable multi-religion leadership, Patel and Meyer (2009) offered the Faiths Acting in Togetherness and Hope (F.A.I.T.H.) organization's work in combating Antisemitism at Stanford University. This illustration of how the knowing, doing, and being of leadership (Kriger & Seng, 2005) could interact with their own earlier recommendations (Patel & Meyer, 2011b) to produce short-term crisis management and long-term interfaith leadership. Taken together, the elements of this discussion helps frame the practical orientation of socially just leadership educators for faith—and philosophical—communities.

However, this work is not without its challenges. Religious diversity initiatives can be just as harmful as helpful when poorly performed, but Patel and Meyer (2011a) offered meaningful reminders of how students can play a role in building and sustaining postsecondary interfaith cooperation. Three specific challenges plague settings where religious diversity exists: ignorance, intolerance, and tension. Religious ignorance occurs when either individuals are not exposed to religious knowledge, or when they are exposed to misinformation about religions. When negative attitudes toward a religion, or its members, manifest into harmful or exclusionary behaviors, religious intolerance has occurred. Finally, religious tension is the result of codified religious intolerance, either through policy or practice, experienced at group- and community-levels. In these ways, Patel and Meyer (2011a) laid bare the oppressive thoughts, actions, and social dynamics posing risk to multi-religious leadership orientations. Luckily, they offer a solution in the form of interfaith cooperation.

Interfaith cooperation, as a counter to ignorance, intolerance, and tension, consists of, "...spreading interfaith literacy and promoting positive, meaningful encounters between people of diverse religious background with a focus on common action" (Patel & Meyer, 2011a, pp. 4–5). Interfaith literacy involves examining faith and philosophical traditions for imperatives toward collaboration, seeking knowledge of historical interfaith cooperation, and appreciation for knowledge of other traditions (Patel & Meyer, 2011a). Each of these are elements socially just leadership educators can incorporate into their pedagogy and practice. Additionally, they actively seek or create opportunities for meaningful encounters between members of different religious or spiritual groups, as these relationships challenge and erode ignorance and conflict.

Student leaders, as well as university administrators, have a role to play in socially just faith- and philosophical-leadership. Socially just student leaders are prepared to spread interreligious literacy and bring people together in ways that build social capital and cohesion. Socially just institutions of higher education engage with the reality of religious diversity on their campuses, embrace opportunities for interfaith leadership, and actively confront ignorance, intolerance, and tension through their curricular and cocurricular program, policies, traditional practices, and symbols. Among these recommendations leadership educators are uniquely positioned campus agents who can connect the resources of the institution to the experiences of their students in mutually beneficial and reciprocal ways. Understanding the challenges as presented by Patel and Meyer (2011a) protects these individuals from erroneously believing this work will be simple or easy and empowers toward the path ahead.

Cooperation as an Institutional Commitment

Much of the discussion of this chapter, as well as this entire book, focuses on leadership educators and their students. We would be remiss if we did not turn our attention toward institutional dynamics and dedicated some of our discussion to interfaith cooperation as an institution-wide concern. Patel and Meyer (2011b) offered a framework for embracing religious diversity on campus, involving an organization-wide vision, collaborations across every dimension of the campus, and keen focus on attainable campus- and student-outcomes, with implications for short- and long-term impact. Setting an institutional vision for interfaith cooperation entails establishing urgency, importance, and goals (Patel & Meyer, 2011b).

The ecological approach, as advocated by Patel and Meyer (2011b), requires shifting from a programmatic focus and toward, "... seeing each campus environment as a unique system of relationships and initiatives that will be implicated in any campus-wide initiative" (p. 3). Socially just outcomes include enhanced interfaith literacy—improvements in religious diversity knowledge, attitudes, and values, while institutional outcomes include warmer campus climate, greater resource allocation, and enhanced capacity-building experiences for faculty and staff (Patel & Meyer, 2011b). Socially just leadership educators support the vision, ecology, and outcomes necessary to transform their students and their campuses into those prepared for positive, sustainable leadership for faith- and philosophical-communities. While in many ways the scholarship around the institution's role in interfaith literacy is still developing, the demonstrated need for these socially just leadership educators has never been greater.

Despite being a sample of the scholarship available, we hope the topics reviewed in the preceding section are helpful to orient you in the broader landscape of literature resting at the intersection of faith and leadership. The clarity of these authors has helped us better understand the needs and challenges for social justice-oriented faith and philosophical leaders, and we hope it has done so for you as well. In the next section, we leverage this awareness as we build a case for a particular model of leadership education we believe informs educators who have, or are willing to adopt, a socially just perspective in their practice and pedagogy.

INTERFAITH LEADERSHIP AS A BLUEPRINT FOR SOCIAL JUSTICE

Patel's (2016) conceptualization of interfaith leadership serves as a blueprint for social justice faith and philosophical leadership. When leadership education programs take an interfaith leadership stance, they are better able to produce social justice leaders for faith and philosophical communities. This section provides more conceptual and practical guidance for socially just faith and philosophically-based leadership education. Starting with definitions of social justice faith leaders and leadership, we review the faith leadership knowledge base necessary for socially just leadership, as well as the social justice faith leadership skill set. This discussion sets the stage for practical recommendations regarding this work in action. Taken together, the model as described by Patel (2016) represents the clearest path toward building socially just leadership education experiences for faith- and philosophically-based leadership.

Social Justice Faith Leaders and Leadership

According to Patel (2016), interfaith leaders, "...engage the reality of diversity to achieve the positive vision of pluralism. Approaching the three parts of pluralism—respect for diverse identities, relationships between different communities, and a commitment to the common good..." (p. 79) furthers the social justice mission of leadership and leadership education. In this way, Patel's ideas about interfaith leaders have the potential to produce socially just faith and philosophical leaders as they work toward respect, collaboration, and cooperation. The work of these leaders, "...facilitates the flow of contributions by increasing understanding of diverse identities and thereby reducing the barriers erected by prejudice" (Patel, 2016, p. 78).

Tearing down the walls of oppression and marginalization arising from such prejudice is the work of all social justice advocates and social change leaders. Ultimately, by honoring and empowering differential faith, spiritual, and philosophical identity expressions, cultivating positive and sustainable relationships between communities, and raising the standards of the broader community in which we all live, socially just faith and philosophical leadership combats religious ignorance, challenges religious intolerance, eases religious tensions (Patel & Meyer, 2011a), strengthens social cohesion, and bridges social capital among members and groups in society. According to Patel (2016), "By 'bridging' the social capital between diverse religious communities and channeling it toward a positive civic purpose[s], interfaith leaders have the opportunity to make a profound impact on social problems ranging from poverty to disease" (Patel, 2016, p. 78). While interfaith leaders may seek these opportunities, socially just leaders create them by leveraging the power of vision, morals, and mission toward deep change.

Educators play a significant role in preparing leaders to bridge faith and philosophical gaps in society. Socially just leadership educators provide emerging faith- and philosophical-leaders with frameworks and language to effectively articulate their own identities while simultaneously building productive relationships with those of similar and different traditions. Patel's (2016) framework in preparing interfaith leaders is one place to start. As an element of the blueprint, Patel suggested religious iconography can be used as part of a "binding national narrative" (p. 79) to communicate the sacredness of diversity within society. Educating students, or having them educate each other, about various religious and philosophical texts, icons, rituals, artefacts, and symbols can open up dialogue on commonalities between various faith structures and create a *binding classroom narrative* to articulate the value of inclusion in leadership learning spaces. Additionally, since interfaith, and therefore socially just, leaders actively engage diversity toward pluralism (Patel, 2016), leadership educators should explicitly name pluralism as a learning objective in their syllabi, work towards understanding it when planning activities, and seek evidence of its existence in grading and evaluating student assignments. By formally incorporating leadership frameworks, co-learning about traditions, and codifying holistic and robust notions of faith and philosophy, socially just educators improve the leadership learning of those preparing to serve their communities.

Social Justice Faith Leadership Knowledge Base

Understanding the distinction between social justice leaders and leadership in the context of faith and philosophical communities, we turn our attention to the sets of knowledge socially just leaders should have to effectively lead their communities. We agree with Patel's (2016) assertion that effective leaders, "... have a knowledge base that includes an appreciative knowledge of other traditions, a theology of interfaith cooperation, and a history of interfaith cooperation" (p. 79). More specifically, knowledge that appreciates other traditions, honors their multidimensionality, and respects the contributions it and its followers have made to humanity is a meaningful area for socially just leadership educators to construct their intended learning activities. Furthermore, "[a] theology of interfaith cooperation means interpreting the key sources of a tradition in a way that puts forth a coherent narrative and deep logic that calls for positive relationships with people who orient around religion differently" (Patel, 2016, p. 80). We would extend this "theology" to include groups of people who organize around non-religious philosophies as well, including atheists, agnostics, and otherwise secular individuals.

We recognize those who identify deeply with a specific faith tradition or a religious orientation may begin to see socially just leadership as in opposition to the tenets of those belief systems. Socially just leadership educators help students process these tensions and broaden their perspectives to see socially just leadership as central to the value structure underlying most religious or philosophical orientations. Socially just leadership educators also view, "...mobilizing other people who view themselves as connected to particular traditions is [as] important..." (Patel, 2016, p. 81) as empowering those who do not view religion as centrally in their own lives, but nonetheless have strong moral, ethical, and philosophical beliefs.

The final relevant component of Patel's (2016) knowledge base is, "...knowing something of the history of positive interaction between people of different religions" (Patel, 2016, p. 81). It is especially important to resist portrayals of faith organizations as riddled with conflict. Socially just leadership educators ground their positioning of history in asset-based ways to leverage cooperation and collaboration in the classroom, as well as in larger campus life, so as to practice coalition- and caucus-building in their post-college leadership.

Social Justice Faith Leadership Skill Set

Vision and knowledge are necessary, but not entirely sufficient, for socially just leadership in faith and philosophical communities. Skills, such as crafting language around social identities and their intersections, building influential and inclusive stories, curating activities toward cooperative relationships, and facilitating positive and productive dialogues, help leaders articulate values and share knowledge as ways to spurn action. As important elements of socially just leadership, with implications for educators, we now offer each of these skills in more detail.

A vital social justice faith leader skill is related to having, or developing, a "radar screen" (Patel, 2016, p. 83) for religious diversity. This awareness develops from paying attention to the different and intersecting social identities leaders and followers hold which impact meaningful change. However, beyond mere detection of social identities and their attendant dynamics, socially just faith and philosophical leaders leverage language around issues of identity and forms of marginalization to motivate and empower others to act. The absence of such language, and subsequently the radar screen for diversity in belief structures, often leads to the types of conflict that undermine leaders of these communities. Socially just leadership educators who do not seek opportunities to develop and cultivate religious diversity radar screens among emerging leaders render them underprepared for the reality of spiritual and philosophical life.

Relatedly, socially just faith leaders foster a "... public narrative [by] ... being able to effectively relate positive [faith and] interfaith stories and dispel myths of negative [faith and] interfaith stories" (Patel, 2016, p. 80). This is done by learning how to relate an influential story, referred to as some as a "message," to others while simultaneously living the values of said story. One of the biggest challenges to a congruent public narrative is being aware of the stories leaders are competing against. According to Patel (2016), "[t]he most common competing narrative interfaith leaders face is that religious diversity inevitably becomes barriers and bludgeons" (p. 83); a challenge which is also faced by socially just leaders. Propagated through most forms of media, stories of interfaith conflict and accounts of religious strife dominate the discourse about how faith and philosophical diversity manifests in our lives. Uplifting influential and inclusive stories about socially just faith and philosophical communities and their members is one way leaders can leverage public narrative for the good of all.

Curating activities toward cooperative relationships is also the work of socially just faith leaders. Such activities, "... bring a wide range of people who orient around religion differently together in compelling projects that highlight shared values and create the space for powerful sharing, storytelling, and relationship building" (Patel, 2016, p. 84). By contrast, poorly constructed activities exclude people, incite divisiveness, emphasize divisions, orient conversations toward social fissures, or are simply boring. The best cooperative activities result in (re)affirming individuals' faith or philosophical orientations, connect tasks with belief structures, and inspire participants to connect their values, faith or philosophical orientations, and ways of being. Ultimately activities that build cooperation strengthen connections to one's own traditions and forge bonds between people.

The final skill we have chosen to highlight is facilitating dialogue. Dialogue is most effective when leaders leverage shared activities (like those described above), common language, shared values, trust, and goodwill (Patel, 2016). One of the keys to facilitating such dialogues stems from asking questions that can be answered from a wide range of perspectives, motivate storytelling, and inspire others to see the world from another's point of view. The best questions, we would argue, are those that thought-provokingly deepen individuals' relationships with their own faiths and philosophies while also drawing them into deeper and more meaningful contact with those around them. The art of facilitating dialogue is holding the space between, "...widely held and deeply shared values" (Patel, 2016, p. 84).

Figure 11.1 depicts the interconnections between the aforementioned skills, knowledge, and goals of socially just leadership for faith and philosophical communities. Restated briefly, socially just leadership for faith and philosophical communities entails increasing understanding and deconstructing barriers of prejudice between and among communities and their members. Socially just faith leaders engage diversity to achieve pluralism and egalitarianism among those who orient around religion and various philosophies differently. In order to do this, these leaders have appreciative knowledge, which feeds interfaith cooperating, process tensions and broaden perspectives within and between communities and their members, as well as know and bring to bear the history of interfaith cooperation to affect positive and sustainable social change. Furthermore, socially just interfaith leaders pay attention to the multiple and intersecting identities of those around them, foster meaningful dialogue between members with the intent of building productive public narratives, and curate activities and actions toward cooperative relationships. Socially just leadership educators working with aspiring faith and philosophical community leaders have a variety of approaches to leverage; we now turn our discussion toward recommendations regarding their work.

Figure 11.1   Knowledge base and skill set for pluralism and social justice.

PEDAGOGICAL APPROACHES TO LEADERSHIP LEARNING FOR FAITH AND PHILOSOPHICAL COMMUNITIES

After identifying the thinking behind interfaith leadership as socially just leadership for faith and philosophical communities, and the content educators can embrace toward those ends, attention must be paid to the mechanisms educators can leverage in their craft. While current scholarship points to a variety of strategies that can be brought to bear in leadership education (see Guthrie & Jenkins, 2018), we have chosen three approaches to discuss in greater detail: case study, service-learning and site visits, and classroom guests. Through these, students are equipped with theoretical tools and perspectives to meaningfully engage the reality of spiritual and secular life, be presented with opportunities to practice interfaith and cross-philosophy relationship building, and curate engagement within and beyond the leadership classroom.

Case Studies for Exploring Interfaith Cooperation

As the public narrative around religious belonging, identity, and diversity in the United State remains divisive, it is of little surprise that such tensions manifest in classrooms full of American college students. Case studies serve as an interactive pedagogy for engaging students in the practical challenges of socially just faith leadership. To these ends, Suomala (2013) offered case studies that centered students in decision making and problem solving. Resulting from an Interfaith Youth Core partnership, Suomala's (2013) case studies were designed to connect with other pedagogical tools appropriate for a variety of leadership learning contexts.

Suomala (2013) advocated for a two-staged, individual- and group-centered approach to using cases in the classroom. Each case consisted of two parts; the first of which was required individual reading before class, and the second of which was processed in small in-class groups. Additionally, discussion questions were offered, including those drawing students' attention to the issue or problem in the case, the context of the problem, perspectives or positions which were difficult for students to relate to or empathize with, opinions or solutions available to leaders, and the applicability of the case, its context, and possible solutions to their own campus or leadership positions. Furthermore, Suomala (2013) encouraged educators to reconvene learners from their small groups such that class-level discussion could take place to compare and contrast each groups' conversations, highlighting even further the diversity of perspectives, approaches, and solutions among leadership learners. The approach advocated by Suomala

(2013) mirrors that found in many leadership-, interfaith-, and social justice-learning spaces.

Service-Learning as Interfaith Engagement Pedagogy

In early 2011, then President Barack Obama challenged American colleges and universities to develop annual interfaith service projects to promote interfaith engagement and cooperation (Sapp, 2011). Sapp (2011) provided guidelines regarding how service-learning experiences could be constructed toward faith engagement, and we believe these recommendations can be adapted to frame interfaith engagement as well. First, "[a] shared humanity can be understood through concentric circles of belonging that connect all people to each other and contribute to a broad sense of kinship across the human family" (Sapp, 2011, p. 284). Second, interfaith service requires active engagement in both the acts of service and the critical reflection necessary to make meaning of said service. Finally, as part of the "language of faith" (Sapp, 2011, p. 286) interfaith service-learning gives students opportunities to become more proficient in appreciating how, "...humans best live out their faith and beliefs in the world around them" (Sapp, 2011, p. 287). In these ways, interfaith engagement through service-learning benefits the common good as well as draws together the basic humanity, meaning-making, and love at the heart of socially just leadership.

Service-learning projects are adaptable to a range of commitments, including single engagements with community partners, to semester- and year-long projects bringing together campus and community stakeholders. Socially just service-learning projects focus on working in partnership with community members, as opposed to "being served by" students. Additionally, identification of a genuine need resulting in substantive and mutually agreed upon change is vital. Guided questions and reflections before (preflection), during, and after the experience can motivate students to make meaning of their experiences. Finally, showcasing the interfaith service-learning experiences of students through symposia, conference presentations, and publications can help other leadership educators and students through their own socially just leadership education journeys.

Site Visits and Classroom Guests From Religiously Diverse Backgrounds

In order to increase empathy towards others, students should be exposed to a wide variety of worldviews. As socially just educators, we should aim to create spaces on campus that allow students to learn about different faith-based, spiritual, and non-faith structures from individuals who practice and believe in them. Court and Seymour (2015) emphasized the importance of six strategies that allow students to engage in interfaith education and dialogue: (a) learning for purposes of contrast, (b) learning about, (c) learning from, (d) learning with, (e) learning to deepen my own faith, and (f) learning for spiritual growth (pp. 521–522). In the context of socially just leadership education, we focus on the strategy of "learning from." Court and Seymour (2015) defined learning from as "lett[ing] representatives of a religious tradition teach" (p. 525). In our definition, we include other spiritual and non-faith structures. The practice of letting individuals speak from experience is important and allows individuals to define themselves and their worldviews in their own words.

The Interfaith Youth Core (IFYC) suggests two pedagogies for creating these kinds of spaces: site visits and classroom guests. For site visits, IFYC encourages a tour of various places of worship with a resident educator over attending a formalized service, because people may be unaware of sacred practices and rituals ("Experiential and Engaged Learning," 2017). Alternatively, educators can invite a designated leader within a certain tradition or a lay member practitioner to speak of their faith or philosophical understandings ("Experiential and Engaged Learning," 2017). Oftentimes, however, it may create more interesting dialogue if a lay member practitioner is invited because they may be able to critically speak about nuance in the official teachings in ways designated leaders are unable to ("Experiential and Engaged Learning," 2017). In learning from these individuals, students will have a better understanding of and empathy towards people who hold different beliefs and values, and in turn it will provide the students with important knowledge and skills, which will form their foundation of interfaith leadership.

CONCLUSION

American higher education often falls short of its potential in preparing socially just leaders for faith and philosophical communities. This chapter leveraged theoretical, conceptual, and practical guidance in the extant literature toward improvements in leadership education. We advocate emerging faith and philosophical leaders developing fluency in their own faith- and philosophical-traditions, organizing initiatives toward interfaith collaboration, and transforming society by making sustainable commitments to religious pluralism. This type of interfaith cooperation spreads interfaith literacy, promotes, meaningful encounters and prioritizes common action as remedies as a counter to ignorance, intolerance, marginalization, and oppression.

When leadership education programs adopt interfaith perspectives, they are more likely to produce social justice leaders who confront the complexities of diversity and work toward positive pluralism. Respect for diverse identities, productive relationships across communities, and commitments to the wellbeing of all are the goals of such leadership. Effective leadership is rooted in appreciative knowledge of other traditions, a theology of interfaith cooperation, and a historical legacy of interfaith cooperation. Crafting language around intersecting social identities, building influential and inclusive stories, curating cooperative activities and relationships, as well as fostering substantive dialogues are the skills leaders develop to connect values, knowledge, and action.

Case Studies, service-learning projects, site visits, and featured speakers are appropriate pedagogies for socially just education focused on faith and philosophical leadership. Case studies engage students in the practical challenges of leadership. Service-learning projects can represent a range of short- and long-term commitments, bringing together a wide variety of stakeholders. Site visits can vary from tour of places of worship to formalized services to raise awareness of diverse observances. Finally, educators can draw successful interfaith leaders into their courses to embody their ways of leading directly to students. We challenge all educators who prepare others for leadership to consider the faith and philosophical development of their students, for when we fail to engage the belief-based dimensions of leadership, we risk the mistreatment of individuals who need social justice now more than ever.

REFERENCES

Court, D., & Seymour, J. L. (2015). What might meaningful interfaith education look like? Exploring Politics, Principles, and Pedagogy. *Religious Education, 110*(5), 517–533.

Experiential and Engaged Learning in Interfaith and Interreligious Studies Courses. (2017). Retrieved January 5, 2018 from https://www.ifyc.org/resources/experiential-learning

Kriger, M., & Seng, Y. (2005). Leadership with inner meaning: A contingency theory of leadership based on the worldviews of five religions. *The Leadership Quarterly, 16*, 771–806.

Patel, E. (2016). Preparing interfaith leaders: Knowledge base and skill set for interfaith leaders. In K. L. Guthrie, T. Bertrand Jones, & L. Osteen (Eds.), *New directions for student leadership, No. 152: Developing culturally relevant leadership learning* (pp. 75–86). San Francisco, CA: Jossey-Bass.

Patel, E., & Meyer, C. (2009). Engaging religious diversity on campus: The role of interfaith leadership. *Journal of College & Character, X*(7), 1–8.

Patel, E., & Meyer, C. (2011a). The civic relevance of interfaith cooperation for colleges and universities. *Journal of College & Character, 12*(1), 1–9.

Patel, E., & Meyer, C. (2011b). Introduction to "Interfaith cooperation on campus": Interfaith cooperation as an institution-wide priority. *Journal of College and Character, 12*(2), 1–6.

Rockenbach, A. (2017). Building inclusive community by bridging worldview differences: A call to action from the interfaith diversity experiences and attitudes longitudinal survey (IDEALS). *Journal of College and Character, 18*(3), 145–154.

Sapp, C. L. (2011). Obama's interfaith service challenge: A call for a new theology of service in American higher education. *Dialog: A Journal of Theology, 50*(3), 280–288.

Suomala, K. R. (2013). *Case studies for exploring interfaith cooperation: Classroom tools.* Chicago, IL: Interfaith Youth Core.

Yukl, G. A. (2002). *Leadership in organizations* (5th ed.). Englewood Cliffs, NJ: Prentice-Hall.

CHAPTER 12

SOCIAL JUSTICE IMPLICATIONS OF ASSUMED LEADERSHIP SELF-EFFICACY IN FIRST-GENERATION STUDENTS

Erin Sylvester

Two unifying beliefs thread themselves throughout a variety of socially just leadership education philosophies, lenses, and pedagogies: (a) leadership can be taught/learned and (b) leadership, as a process, should be open to all who seek it. In order for students to build a capacity for leadership, however, they must first be self-aware and develop their own self-efficacy. The development of self-efficacy leads to exploration of their leader identities. Exploration of "self-as-leader" is a unique process for each student, with particular implications for first-generation students who "likely have less access to information about higher education, particularly in terms of tacit information about how one negotiates the college experience" (Lundberg, Schreiner, Hovaguimian, & Slavin Miller, 2007, p. 59). This puts them at a

Changing the Narrative, pages 175–191
Copyright © 2018 by Information Age Publishing
All rights of reproduction in any form reserved.

disadvantage when exploring who they are as individuals, engaging in campus programs or organizations, and having the confidence to seek positions of leadership among their peers. Traditional leadership education models assume self-efficacy as a starting point, but how can socially just educators also create space for students who first need to develop self-efficacy in order to craft their leader identity?

First-generation college students have different needs than students from families with college-going histories based on their systems of support, prior experiences, familiarity with higher education, and the pressures often associated with being the first family member to attend college in the United States. "Not only do first-generation students confront all the anxieties, dislocations, and difficulties of any college student, but their experiences often involve substantial cultural as well as social and academic transitions" (Pascarella, Pierson, Wolniak, & Terenzini, 2004, p. 250). As our world becomes more multicultural and diverse, and as colleges and universities work to provide more access to incoming students, we will see a rise of first-generation students on our campuses. "Previous research has shown that students' leadership interests and abilities are largely dependent on their entering characteristics" (Thompson, 2006, p. 344), which places particular focus on the unique needs of first-generation students.

There are students on our campuses who often come to college with the belief that a "leader" is someone else and not a title aligning with how they view themselves. First-generation students specifically can struggle to confidently navigate the experiences we know help to build leader identity. "In both precollege characteristics and their experiences during their first year in college, first-generation students differ in many educationally important ways from the students higher education has traditionally served," (Terenzini, Springer, Yeager, Pascarella, & Nora, 1996, p. 20), yet that does not mean institutions of higher learning should accept and maintain the status quo. We should attempt to find a balance between encouraging students to navigate dissonance, empowering them in their ability and leadership skills, while also supporting them through the risk and pain associated with leadership. The chapter explores the social justice implications of assuming students enter college with the same efficacy starting point. In order to ensure *all* of our students, especially first-generation students, believe they have the opportunity to develop their leadership skills, there are certain considerations that socially just leadership educators should take into account.

First-generation college students encounter difficulties continuing-generation students may not experience when navigating a college environment. We know, from high-quality scholarship in the field, "[f]irst-generation college students tend to be at a distinct disadvantage with respect to basic knowledge about postsecondary education (e.g., costs and application process), level of family income and support, educational degree expectations and plans, and academic preparation in high school" (Pascarella et al., 2004, p. 250). Because our experiences and individual backgrounds influence our capacity for leadership, we have a responsibility to implement theoretical frameworks to more effectively engage first-generation students in the practice of leadership, realizing that their view of leadership positions and the process of leadership may appear different from those of other groups of students. Many of these students may first be challenged to overcome socially constructed messages about the traditional view of a leader and the influences those messages may have on their own identity definitions. To continue to teach leadership for a socially just future, we must work toward every student feeling included.

Considerations for more equitable leadership teaching methods will be explored in this chapter to identify strategies for teaching leadership and building leadership capacity to aid first-generation college students in building self-efficacy and exploring leader identity. When leadership educators help all students to see their leadership potential, we create richer and more inclusive leadership classrooms. We also empower future generations of students to break cycles of oppression by making a more educated public, and more informed and aware groups of leaders within communities. Through the promotion of self-efficacy in all types of students from all backgrounds and lived experiences, we can ensure that diverse individuals and their unique perspectives are validated, affirmed, and spread through their leadership within communities.

FIRST-GENERATION STUDENTS

Students who are the first in their family to attend American higher education are typically referred to as "first generation." Their peers who have one or more family members (parents, grandparents, siblings) who have attended or completed college are referred to as "continuing generation" students to note their familial connection to higher education and that they are not the first in their family to attend some level of college or university (Redford & Mulvaney Hoyer, 2017). There is a body of literature about first-generation college students that explores their academic ability, transition to college and degree completion, yet "surprisingly little is known about their college experiences or their cognitive and psychosocial development during college" (Pascarella et al., 2004). First-generation students experience the typical anxieties of attending college and the additional concern of navigating a new environment in which their parents are not able to help guide them. Horn (1998) noted that "their fellow college students often seem to be members of a club of insiders to which they do not belong"

(p. 7) contributing to the fact that "almost one-fourth of first-generation students who enter four-year colleges in the United States do not return for a second year" (Cushman, 2007, p. 44). First-generation students may also experience difficulty when in positions to "reconcile the conflicting roles and demands of family membership and educational mobility" (Terenzini et al., 1996, p. 2) as they seek the benefits of higher education; namely advances in their social mobility and marketability, yet at the same time separates them from their families.

Research comparing first-generation students to their continuing-generation peers has produced evidence they are more likely to be "from low-income families, to be Hispanic, to have weaker cognitive skills (in reading, math, and critical thinking), to have lower degree of aspirations, and to have been less involved with peers and teachers in high school" (Terenzini et al., 1996, p. 16). College campuses seem to be overwhelmingly insular, connected, and exclusionary to students who already doubt their ability to participate fully or feel as though they are part of the "out" group. First-generation students may feel overwhelmed in the classroom, and excluded outside the classroom, which leaves little opportunity to find a sense of belonging.

Additional research supports the notion "first-generation status has a positive effect on student learning, but a negative effect on involvement," (Lundberg et al., 2007, p. 57) affirming there are still barriers preventing first-generation students from fully engaging in the campus community. This could be a symptom of financial restrictions, holding multiple jobs, living off-campus or a variety of other variables, but is likely also connected to feeling invited or included. When first-generation students actively engage in cocurricular experiences with their peers, they show stronger positive outcomes than comparable continuing-generation students (Pascarella et al., 2004). By getting involved on campus and forming relationships with other students, first-generation students can gain cultural capital (Lundberg et al., 2007) which can help to compensate for some of their fears, doubts, and confusions.

SELF-EFFICACY

Efficacy is rooted in an internal belief in one's ability to accomplish a given task or challenge. This belief can be influenced by others through validation, gained internally through a growth-based mindset, and impact how an individual feels in relation to others and a community as a whole. Efficacy can impact how students feel, think, motivate themselves and behave, therefore; an essential component of first-generation students' development (Bandura, 1993). The following section outlines the role of cultural capital in the development of efficacy for first generation students, the impact of validation and growth mindset, and how each can influence the development of self-efficacy in first-generation students.

In many leadership classrooms or cocurricular experiences, leadership educators assume some self-efficacy is present among their students. There is a certain amount of self-efficacy required to enroll in a formal leadership course or to seek a leadership role in an organization. However, among our first-generation students, we may not readily recognize their inner voice asking, "Can I do this? Am I a leader?" Leadership models suggest "high self-efficacy will lead individuals to set challenging goals, persist in the face of obstacles, work harder on tasks, direct cognitive and behavioral resources toward goal relevant actions, and actively search for effective task strategies" (McCormick, 2001, p. 26). Not only a necessary precursor to leadership identity development, but also for meeting the demands of adult life, self-efficacy is a key component of individual growth.

For many first-generation students, the notion of leader may be seen as a single person of positional authority, or as is common in minoritized communities, leader has historically been portrayed as "servant" or "activist" for the greater community. Dugan, Kodama, Correira, and Associates (2013) shared that one's leadership capacity can either be empowered or constrained. This depends on the messages from our social context which create assumptions about what leaders should look like and how they should act. These messages can negatively affect students from traditionally marginalized populations. These assumptions are social justice obstacles for leadership educators and student affairs professionals (Bertrand Jones, Guthrie, & Osteen, 2016).

Smart, Ethington, Riggs, & Thompson (2002) mentioned "the importance that students attach to their leadership development prior to entering college has a great influence on their participation in leadership related activities, and subsequently, their behavioral leadership preference development" (Thompson, 2006, p. 344). As educators, we must account for how the initial characteristics and identities of first-generation students can interact with leadership teaching both from curricular and cocurricular contexts. We should be mindful that not every student has developed self-efficacy and therefore may not have a strong foundation on which to build leader identity.

For many first-generation students, their most salient identity will likely be one that feels most marginalized on a college campus. Despite the ways in which a student may identify in other more privileged areas, their strongest social identity may bring self-doubt in their ability to be successful on a college campus (Komives, Owen, Longerbeam, Mainella, & Osteen, 2005). Personal identities contribute to the ability to develop a self-efficacy in the college environment—a crucial step in developing a leadership identity. Self-doubt of skills, characteristics, and ability can act as barriers to developing the belief that they *can* and *should* engage in leadership. The "trait of self-confidence (self-efficacy) impacts leadership performance through the mediating mechanism of leadership self-efficacy—a person's confidence in his or her ability to successfully lead" (McCormick, 2001, p. 24). Socially just leadership educators build students' self-efficacy through validation of their skills, performance, and belonging on campus.

Cultural Capital

Cultural capital can be conceptualized as the "the extent to which one is comfortable and familiar with the norms and culture of an institution," which in the context of higher education can translate into an ability to confidently navigate systems, processes, relationships, and involvement that lead to academic and personal success (Lundberg et al., 2007, p. 59). With a perceived deficit in cultural capital, first-generation students may experience self-doubt in their abilities or their rightful belonging in a college campus or its surrounding community. This self-doubt is closely and negatively linked to self-efficacy. The initial belief for students that they have the capabilities to belong and succeed in a university setting serves as a precursor to developing leadership self-efficacy; belief that one can lead.

Validation and Mattering

According to Rendon Linares and Munoz's (2011) Theory of Validation, the sense of mattering (on the individual, group, or global level) helps build academic success and interpersonal growth. Scholars have argued, "[a]ctive intervention in the form of validation [is] needed to encourage nontraditional students to become more involved in campus life and enhance their self-esteem" (Patton, Renn, Guido, & Quaye, 2016, p. 39), which is closely connected to self-efficacy. Validating students who may have self-doubt closes the gap between those who are achieving leader self-efficacy and those who are still struggling with belonging and confidence. Rendon's findings indicated. "students who [are] validated developed confidence in their ability to learn, experienced enhanced feelings of self-worth, and believed they had something to offer" to others and the greater community (Patton et al., 2016, p. 41). It is from this initial belief; a small spark of efficacy, that a flame can grow within an individual student helping them feel more confident in their engagement in and outside the classroom as a leader. Subsequently, "[v]alidation is necessary for every student but is particularly critical for students who may doubt their ability to succeed" (Patton et al., 2016, p. 41).

Fixed Versus Growth Mindset

Carol Dweck described growth mindset as an approach to validating and motivating students to learn by focusing on their ability to change over time, rather than seemingly static personal characteristics. According to Dweck (2007), "[s]ome students believe that their intellectual ability is a fixed trait" (p. 37). with only a certain amount that cannot be increased or decreased. Other students, those with a growth mindset, "...believe that their intellectual ability is something that can be developed through effort and education" which becomes their primary focus (Dweck, 2007, p. 34). Students who possess or are motivated by a growth mindset "...are more likely to respond to initial obstacles by remaining involved, trying new strategies and using all the resources at their disposal for learning," which will help first-generation students specifically to grow their self-efficacy (Dweck, 2010). Recursively, students who have high self-efficacy envision scenarios where they will be successful, which facilitates positive support and guidance. Meanwhile, those who doubt their efficacy instead become overwhelmed by visualizations of failure and poor performance (Bandura, 1993). Therefore, growth mindsets can contribute to a greater sense of self-efficacy and a strong sense of efficacy can lead to a growth mindset. Consequently, "[p]eople with high efficacy approach difficult tasks as challenges to be mastered rather than as threats to be avoided" (Bandura, 1993, p. 144) similarly to how people with a growth mindset approach problems or challenges.

LEADER IDENTITY DEVELOPMENT

The path towards leadership self-efficacy involves a foundation of self-efficacy and the development of a leader identity. For many students this is a process heavily influenced by their environment, peer interactions, and experiences in positional leadership roles. College students encounter many of these contributing factors during their experiences in campus programs or organizations, but some of the foundational messages around leadership are established long before a student ever enters a college campus. High quality scholarship on entering college students indicate "[b]oth the perceived leadership abilities of students as freshmen and the emphasis they place on the development of leadership abilities as freshman have significant and positive direct, indirect, and total influences on perceptions of their leadership competencies 4 years later" (Smart et al., 2002, p. 126). How "leader" is defined in the minds of each individual student is a definition that may previously exist as either consistent or inconsistent with their view of self and can influence their decisions to participate in building leader identity or not.

Leadership efficacy is "...one's internal belief in the likelihood that they will be successful when engaging in leadership" (Dugan et al., 2013, p. 6). Some undergraduates developed leadership self-efficacy through civic organizations, sports teams, or involvement in high school. However, first-generation students may not have had the luxury of being able to participate in extracurricular activities or possessed the self-efficacy required to engage in early leadership roles to begin the development of leadership self-efficacy. "For someone to be successful in a leadership role, he or she must have a healthy sense of personal effectiveness as a leader. This implies that enhancing leadership self-efficacy should be an important objective..." for those teaching leadership and for those empowering and encouraging first-generation students toward leadership experiences (McCormick, 2001, p. 31).

There is a paradoxical relationship between leadership self-efficacy and leadership experiences in which they can be so directly related that one may question which must come first (see Figure 12.1). "Leadership self-efficacy is a necessary though not sufficient factor contributing to leadership effectiveness" (McCormick, 2001, p. 30), yet, establishing the belief that one is capable and competent in leading may come from being a non-positional leader within a group or from experiences where an individual takes on a direct leadership role. The spark needed to start this cyclical relationship is simple—once students have "acknowledged that they were leaders or [have] leadership potential, they began to incorporate that identity into their sense of self" making them more likely to engage in future leadership experience and to seek more formal knowledge and leadership training (Komives et al., 2005, p. 600).

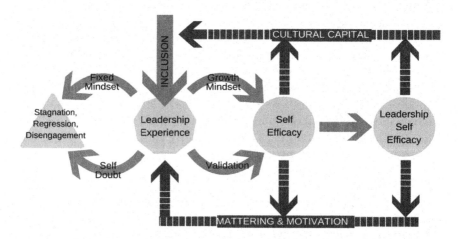

Figure 12.1 Influence of mindset on developing leadership self efficacy.

SOCIAL JUSTICE CONSIDERATIONS FOR BUILDING LEADER CAPACITY

As we develop leadership capacity in students, it is important to remember the individual narratives each student brings into leadership situations. The unique stories, life situations, and lived experiences of students differ greatly; we therefore cannot assume the same, or even similar starting points. Pascarella et al. (2004) found "being a first-generation student had a small negative total effect on end-of-second-year learning for self-understanding" when compared to their peers who had one or more parent who had obtained a college education (p. 267). From a social justice lens, we should first encourage all students to reflect on their life experiences, explore who they are as an individual, and then guide them toward ways in which that individual can also be a leader in communities within and beyond the college campus. Our diverse and ever evolving world calls for leaders from all backgrounds, experiences, and characteristics. As we prepare students for leadership in a global society, we must ensure we are empowering all students, especially those who may not feel included or invited, to engage in leadership.

Teaching With Efficacy in Mind

In many leadership classrooms, and the informal interactions we have with students practicing leadership, we implicitly make certain assumptions about students' self-efficacy. We presume that to have "made it" successfully in the college environment, to be engaged in community with their peers, and to be in a leadership role, through position or influence, that students believe in their ability to practice leadership. But for some students this may be an unfair assumption—either due to a moment of doubt, a crisis that prevents them from their normal functions, or the prior messaging (or lack thereof) around leadership ability, their belief that they can be a successful leader is hindered.

When we appreciate the different experiences that first-generation students have in and outside the classroom, and choose to view those experiences from an asset-based rather than a deficit-based point of view, faculty and leadership educators can validate the experiences of first-generation students and help them to overcome barriers to self-efficacy. When students enter the classroom or leadership environment with feelings of doubt or question their belonging, "public expression [often associated with leadership training] can be especially daunting. Leadership Educators recognize this possibility and restructure active learning opportunities so students can safely collaborate with others in ways that minimize personal risk" (Lundberg et al., 2007, p. 74).

Helping students find courage and self-empowerment for their first leadership experience is vital because of the cyclical nature created in the yielded benefit of leadership experiences. The more students experience leadership roles, the greater their leadership self-efficacy, which then promotes participation in more experiences. "Greater work responsibilities and living off-campus probably contributed substantially to the tendency of first-generation college students to also have significantly lower levels of extracurricular involvement, athletic participation, and volunteer work" which are hallmark areas through which student affairs professionals typically deliver leadership education and training (Pascarella et al., 2004, p. 265). These activities, which we know first-generation students are less likely to participate in, help to build self-confidence and self-efficacy that are critical for building a capacity for leadership skills.

Teaching Towards Inclusion

From a social justice perspective, it is the duty of leadership educators and student affairs professionals to develop inclusive trainings, experiences, activities, and programs we provide for all students, regardless of their entry point. Socially just leadership educators keep inclusion in mind when considering the environments, activities, and prerequisites associated with leadership experiences. For some students, inclusion can be attained with a simple invitation to participate. Other students, specifically first-generation students, need assistance breaking down the initial belief of "I am not a leader" that is often associated with the early stages of leader identity. They also deconstruct and reframe historical messaging within communities of color, cultural groups, and low-income communities who paint leaders as servants or activists rather than using the term leader (Guthrie, Bertrand Jones, Osteen, & Hu, 2013).

Oppressive social forces have shaped how first-generation students view leaders and leadership. We can redefine and affirm how individuals can be leaders, and express leadership, in some contexts more than others. Komives et al. (2005) encourages us to differentiate the "...concept of leadership; acknowledging that leadership could come from those in non-positional roles (i.e., members) and increasingly as a process among people in the group..." (p. 605) to shift internal and external narratives toward seeing themselves as leaders.

Research on leadership development found a strong influence of adult role modeling on the leader identity building of students as they help to promote an initial involvement in organizations or encourage a leadership role (Komives, et al., 2005). Adults, such as parents, student affairs professionals, faculty, or staff, have the ability to invite students to experience leadership by creating a welcoming and inclusive environments around such opportunities. By feeling invited, validated, and appreciated, first-generation students give themselves permission to participate in leadership activities and leadership learning like their continuing-generation peers. When campus agents, especially faculty members and mentors, reach out to first-generation students, they have the ability to provide confidence extending beyond academic ability and create validation and motivation in students (Cushman, 2007).

Additionally, by teaching toward greater inclusion and creating welcoming and inviting spaces for first-generation students, we provide places for social capital building. Postsecondary scholarship on such factors indicates, "[t]he social capital gained through extracurricular and peer involvement during college may be a particularly useful way for first-generation students to acquire the additional cultural capital that helps them succeed academically and benefit cognitively" (Pascarella et al., 2004, p. 278). Socially just educators carefully consider how the cost of leadership coursework or leadership training programs narrows, rather than widens the inclusion gap for students. For example, "[f]inancial need may limit first-generation students' involvement in campus experiences, as they invest more time off campus to support themselves and their families" (Cushman, 2007). See Chapter 5 for more discussion on this topic.

Messages embedded into campus culture also contribute to how first-generation students navigate the classroom and leadership experiences. Campus culture is communicated in ways extending beyond the words of a mission statement or the traditions that occur each year. The values, symbols, activities, and actions of a university can communicate what is important, and who is welcome to participate in the university itself (Higgins, McAllaster, Certo, & Gilbert, 2006). The behavior of administrators, the traditions and rites of passage for students, the names of buildings, the programs that receive funding, and even the language we use sends messages to first-generation students, about who matters in an institutional community (Higgins et al., 2006) even though first-generation students may not fully understand how to decode them. Socially just leadership educators carefully consider what messages are being communicated to first-generation and continuing-generation students about "who leadership is intended for" and "who belongs in positional leadership roles" within campus organizations. Whether intentional or not, the culture of a university campus and within a classroom can communicate messages about who is welcome and included at the proverbial leadership table.

This is further supported by Schlossberg's Transition Theory (Patton et al., 2016), which demonstrates how collegiate environments exert influence, impacting a students' success. Schlossberg's theory suggests the self (individual), support systems, strategies (like coping mechanisms) and the situation (environment) influence students' transitions through developmental challenges. Socially just leadership educators actively seek ways to validate the lived experiences and personal characters of the self (the individual) and support students in navigating challenges in their social environment.

Contributing to an Environment of Empowerment

Human development theories, like Bronfenbrenner's Ecological Model (Patton et. al., 2016), contend environmental influences are strong contributors to an individual's behavior and development of their self-view (see Chapter 14). The contextual environments individuals experience influence their holistic development; those as intimate as the family structure, to those as wide as the world events and history. Proximate influences of the family, school, friends, and religious communities are most salient, however; messages from political systems, economic structures and other indirect environments can have an influence on the messages and social influences that impact a students' view of themselves. If these messages are supportive, empowering and uplifting they can give students an advantage in self-efficacy and leader identity growth. However, if students have received messages of distrust, disregard, worthlessness, and disempowerment, those messages can negatively impact their self-view. Socially just leadership educators balance encouraging students as they navigate dissonance, empowering their leadership abilities and skills, and supporting them through the sacrifices of leadership.

To intentionally empower first-generation students as capable and worthy to be included in leadership experiences, conversations, and classrooms, we must first validate their individual characteristics and experiences as first-generation students. Validation can help in building belief-in-self and strengthening self-confidence. This validation of self and lived experiences is needed for first-generation students to accept their experiences and characteristics as necessary and beneficial contributions to the university community. Only after accepting and validating the experiences of first-generation students can we move them to a place of self-capableness, self-efficacy, and ample potential for leadership opportunity (Rendon Linares & Munoz, 2011).

Validation theory "... embraces students' personal voices and experiences, which are as important as traditional, objective ways of knowing" (Rendon Linares & Munoz, 2011, p. 14). Validation should be distinguished from praise—when praising a trait about a student, like their intelligence, it "gives them a short burst of pride, followed by a long string of negative consequences" (Dweck, 2007, p. 36). Instead, validating the "effort tended to put [students] in a growth mindset (you're developing these skills because you're working hard" (Dweck, 2007, pp. 36–37).

Dweck's (2010) research has shown that in praising/validating students for "...the process they have engaged in—the effort they applied, the strategies they used, the choices they made, the persistence they displayed, and so on—yields more long-term benefits than telling them that they are 'smart' when they succeed" (p. 2). First-generation students need validation as a platform to achieve a vantage point from which to engage in leadership activities since, "[t]he most vulnerable students [including first-generation students] will likely benefit from external validation that can serve as the means to move students toward gaining internal strength resulting in increased confidence and agency in shaping their own lives" (Rendon Linares & Munoz, 2011, p. 17). Through validation, leadership educators can help affirm positive interactions and leadership experiences from which students can begin to build leadership self-efficacy.

Validation in Practice

Socially just leadership educators create environments, situations, and experiences to promote empowerment for first-generation students. Specifically,

> Rendon (1992) stresses the importance of more subtle forms of support, what she calls validating experiences—encounters with administrators, faculty, and other students who send important signals to first-generation students that they are competent learners, that they can succeed, that they have a rightful place in the academic community, and that their background and past experiences are sources of knowledge and pride, not something to be devalued. (Terenzini et al., 1996, p. 17)

Leadership educators help students to overcome self-doubt or lack of belonging by validating their lived experiences, honoring their cultural backgrounds, and encouraging engagement and interaction with others. Students' leadership development results from, "...complex interaction[s] of attributes they bring to college as freshmen...the priorities of their campuses in terms of providing an environment that emphasizes student development, and their involvement in leadership activities during their undergraduate experience" (Smart et al., 2002, p. 128). As socially just educators, we cannot (and wouldn't want to) change or influence who they are when they arrive, but we can influence the messages they receive about their self-efficacy, their invitation to leadership, and their ability to feel validated in their leadership experiences.

Creating validating spaces in leadership classrooms and leadership experiences requires leadership educators and student affairs professions to "actively reach out to students to offer assistance, encouragement, and support and provide opportunities for students to validate each other through encouraging comments that validate the work of peers" (Rendon Linares & Munoz, 2011, p. 17). When working with first-generation students, the more educators can do to encourage operating from a growth mindset, the more these students can identify that their leadership ability is not a fixed trait, but a muscle to be built based on experiences and learning. The more interaction first-generation students have with their continuing-generation peers, the greater increase in their social capital and ability to navigate the college environment and leadership environments within it. "Pascarella et al. suggest that while first-generation students may enter college with less cultural capital, academic experiences in college may contribute to cultural capital in ways that benefit first-generation students more than continuing-generation students who already possess that cultural capital" (Lundberg et al., 2007, p. 73). Helping first-generation students feel validated and approach challenges from a growth-mindset can help to increase leadership self-efficacy, which can lead to an increase in social capital on a college campus and in leadership environments with their peers.

CONCLUSION

The following recommendations can promote self-efficacy and leadership capacity in first-generation students and represent a variety of possibilities for socially just and inclusive leadership learning spaces:

- Do not assume high self-efficacy among students, especially first-generation students.
- Affirm first-generation student's lived experiences as unique and valid in their contribution to a classroom, the university community, and in positional leadership roles.
- Create classroom environments where all students respect each other as equals and are open to the experiences and ideas of others to decrease the influence of social capital.
- Openly discuss self-efficacy as a concept and connect to a cycle of building leadership self-efficacy through reflection on continued leadership experiences.
- Mentor and encourage first-generation students to seek leadership experiences and validate their ability to contribute to and matter in the greater university community.
- Challenge, hold accountable, and motivate first-generation students in leadership and academic experiences to discourage the development of a fixed mindset or self-doubt.

Socially just leadership educators open the door of leader identity for students who otherwise may not view themselves as leaders, with implications for other doors for students to open later in their leadership journeys. Validation theory suggests validating the skills and experiences of first-generation students creates opportunities for "faculty and staff to work with students to promote equitable outcomes, to eliminate racist and sexist views about students and to promote inclusive classrooms" for leadership learning (Rendon Linares & Munoz, 2011, p. 25).

It is important for socially just leadership educators to keep in mind that for many first-generation students, the college experience, and tangentially the leadership experience, is not only a value-added goal. Many first-generation students see themselves as breaking, as opposed to furthering, family traditions in their educational pursuits. To be fully immersed in the leadership experiences and engagement of campus can include greater risk, pain, and loss for first-generation students than their continuing-generation peers may experience because it further widens the growing schism between themselves and their family members. In their reflections on the college transitions,

> [first-generation] students revealed what a challenge it has been to remain true to themselves in an environment where they differ from the norm. Keeping that balance means changing, but it also means remembering their roots. They learn what both the old and new settings call for, and they continually move in and out of different cultures. (Cushman, 2007, p. 47)

The more opportunities leadership educators provide for first-generation students to explore and celebrate their identity and experiences, the more self-efficacy building occurs, which leads to enhanced capacity for leadership self-efficacy. Shertzer and Schuh claimed leadership educators help shift campus culture "...from a 'leading by the chosen few' perspective (hierarchical) to 'leadership by all' perspective (systemic) [which] may better facilitate leadership empowerment and success amid first-generation students" (as quoted in Thompson, 2006, p. 349). We must consider how we prepare students for lifelong leadership. Surely our preparation will lead to their ability to be globally minded leaders of diverse and inclusive communities in which everyone is invited to leadership, as opposed to a world where leadership is reserved for only the chosen few. The future is one of uncertainty in which students will need to be prepared to lead through dissonance, across difference, and toward inclusion and positive change.

REFERENCES

Bandura, A. (1993). Perceived self-efficacy in cognitive development and functioning. *Educational Psychologist, 28*(3), 117–148.

Bertrand Jones, T., Guthrie, K. L., & Osteen, L. (2016). Critical domains of culturally relevant leadership learning: A call to transform leadership programs. In K. L. Guthrie, T. Bertrand Jones, & L. Osteen (Eds.), *New directions for student leadership, No. 152: Developing culturally relevant leadership learning* (pp. 9–21). San Francisco, CA: Jossey-Bass.

Cushman, K. (2007). Facing the culture shock of college. *The Prepared Graduate, 64*(7), 44–47.

Dugan, J. P., Kodama, C., Correira, B., & Associates. (2013). *Multi-Institutional Study of Leadership insight report: Leadership program delivery.* College Park, MD: National Clearinghouse for Leadership Programs.

Dweck, C. S. (2007). The perils and promises of praise. *Educational Leadership, 65*(2), 34–39.

Dweck, C. S. (2010). Even geniuses work hard. *Educational Leadership, 68*(1), 16–20.

Guthrie, K. L., Bertrand Jones, T., Osteen, L. K., & Hu, S. (2013). *Cultivating leader identity and capacity in students from diverse backgrounds: ASHE Higher Education Report, 39*(4). Hoboken, NJ: Wiley.

Higgins, J. M., McAllaster, C., Certo, S. C., & Gilbert, J. P. (2006). Using cultural artifacts to change and perpetuate strategy. *Journal of Change Management, 6*(4), 397–415.

Horn, L. (1998). *Stopouts or stayouts? Undergraduates who leave college in their first year.* Washington, DC: Department of Education.

Komives, S. R., Owen, J. E., Longerbeam, S. D., Mainella, F. C., & Osteen, L. (2005). Developing a leadership identity: A grounded theory. *Journal of College Student Development, 46*(6), 593–611.

Lundberg, C. A., Schreiner, L. A., Hovaguimian, K., & Slavin Miller, S. (2007). First-generation status and student race/ethnicity as distance predictors of student involvement and learning. *NASPA Journal, 44*(1), 57–83.

McCormick, M. J. (2001). Self-efficacy and leadership effectiveness: Applying social cognitive theory to leadership. *The Journal of Leadership Studies, 8*(1), 22–33.

Patton, L. D., Renn, R. A., Guido, F. M., & Quaye, S. J. (2016). *Student development in college: Theory, research, and practice* (3rd ed.). San Francisco, CA: Jossey-Bass.

Pascarella, E. T., Pierson, C. T., Wolniak, G. C., & Terenzini, P. T. (2004). First generation college students: Additional evidence on college experiences and outcomes. *The Journal of Higher Education, 75*(3), 249–284.

Redford, J., & Mulvaney Hoyer, K. (2017). First-generation and continuing-generation college students: A comparison of high school and postsecondary experiences. *U.S. Department of Education Stats in Brief, September 2017.* Retrieved from https://nces.ed.gov/pubs2018/2018009.pdf

Rendon Linares, L. I., & Munoz, S. (2011). Revisiting validation theory: Theoretical foundations, applications, and extensions. *Enrollment Management Journal, 5*(2), 12–33.

Smart, J. C., Ethington, C. A., Riggs, R. O., & Thompson, M. D. (2002). Influences of institutional expenditure patterns on the development of students' leadership competencies. *Research in Higher Education, 43*(1), 115–132.

Terenzini, P., Springer, L., Yeager, P. M., Pascarella, E. T., & Nora, A. (1996). First-generation college students: Characteristics, experiences, and cognitive development. *Research in Higher Education, 37*(1), 1–22.

Thompson, M. D. (2006). Student leadership process development: An assessment of contributing college resources. *Journal of College Student Development, 47*(3), 343–350.

CHAPTER 13

FOSTER CARE YOUTH ALUMNI TO COLLEGIATE LEADERS

How Non-Traditional Family Structures Impact Leadership Development

Jennifer Farinella

Relationships are at the core of engaging in leadership. According to Rost (1993), a multidirectional relationship among leaders and followers is an essential element for leadership to occur. The ability to develop a student's leader identity and subsequent leadership capacity can be contingent on their contextual knowledge of relationships, which are shaped by known beliefs about personal familial relations. Through this text, nontraditional family structures will be examined with particular attention to foster care youth alumni; and the opportunities afforded to engage in leadership development programs. Approximately 20% of former foster youth enroll in college, and this percentage continues to decrease among those students who attain a degree or certificate (Wolanin, 2005). This exploration is necessary

Changing the Narrative, pages 193–209
Copyright © 2018 by Information Age Publishing

because socially just leadership strives to provide greater inclusivity and opportunity for students of all backgrounds. Larson and Murtadha (2002) referenced the work of Freire's *Pedagogy of the Oppressed* as it is argued "the banking approach" is often utilized in educational settings (p. 146). This method caters to individuals of privilege with the delivery of education on the presupposition of a knowledge bank possessed by each student. Former foster care youth, along with other students from nontraditional family structures, have the potential to be viewed as members of a marginalized population who may not gain equitable exposure to build a "bank" of knowledge.

DEFINING THE TRADITIONAL FAMILY STRUCTURE

The traditional family structure appears to receive universal acceptance as a societal norm defining the quintessential familial relationship. In this view, most commonly two heterosexual parents characterize a family, promoting stability through a husband serving as the dominant breadwinner, and the wife tending to childcare needs and maintaining the household. Quite simply, the traditional family as expressed by Ball (2012), "is the 'natural reproductive unit' of mom, pop and children all living under one roof" (as cited in Stephens, 2013, p. 27). Ironically, Lamb (1999) noted this societal norm was not established until the industrial era, although traditionally maternal roles have always tended to favor care of children. In an ever-changing society, this norm is drastically shifting as diverse familial and community support configurations change shape. However, even as additional diversity is introduced to family structure ideals, it should be noted individuals from traditional structures often experience a certain level of privilege from this normalized status.

EXAMINING NONTRADITIONAL FAMILY STRUCTURES

"Fewer than half (46%) of U.S. kids younger than 18 years of age are living in a home with two married heterosexual parents in their first marriage" (Livingston, 2014, para. 1). The idea of a traditional family structure continues to be a benchmark; however, the once societal norm is in continual decline. Research in 2005 demonstrated, "... 67% of children lived with two parents, 23% lived with single mothers, 5 % lived with single fathers, and 5% lived with neither parent" (U.S. Census Bureau 2010, Table 69 as cited in Stephens, 2013, p. 28). Given these data, it is important to critique generalizations about unique family structures and their relationship to success. Society is experiencing a shift in the "normal" family structure, thus acknowledgement from college personnel is needed to accommodate for the increasing breadth of diversity.

Parental Influence

Individuals of nontraditional configurations gain support and form a knowledge base for developing relationships from their established familial context. A child's ability to engage in their respective family system can stimulate or hinder confidence in interactions with others outside of their immediate unit (Terry-Leonard, 1999). Individuals readily mimic the behavior modeled throughout their development from individuals of authority. Thus parental figure(s) serve as a paramount source for children to learn methods to interact, and can either instill a voice of confidence to approach engagement or stimulate an innate fear.

Single Parenthood

Traditionally, single parent homes experience greater emotional, financial, and physical demands; "One third of the live births in the United States today are to unmarried mothers, although most single-parent families are created by divorce" (Lamb, 1999, p. 9). Children can often experience a transfer of the responsibilities faced by single parents, as these parents are also less likely to have a consistent support system. Lamb (1999) noted, "McLanahan and Teitler show that children who grow up in single-parent families are disadvantaged psychologically, educationally, and economically" (p. 10).

Merged Families

Approximately 75% of blended families include a step-father, which increases the likelihood of withdrawal behaviors, aggression, and depression in their children (Altamirano & Chandler, 2013). The introduction of another parental figure during a child's development can be difficult in the adjustment period; however, Altamirano and Chandler (2013) discussed the potential of establishing familial customs among members of the newly formed unit to combat these negative feelings and establish a bond.

Lack of Parental Influence

While nontraditional family structures gain greater representation in society, there is still great concern for students in educational and occupational systems with little to no support. Foster care youth alumni often experience a lack of consistent support or influence from parental, or otherwise established authority figures. The upbringing of these individuals is often defined by perpetual turbulence when attempting to establish a support system and consistency throughout their development. Pecora (2012) reported on placement statistics of children within a foster care setting throughout the 2009 federal fiscal year. Over 40% of youth resided in three or more placements; 38% of youth live in a group home or shelter, and the same percentage is preparing to transition to independent living.

The Code of Federal Regulations categorizes foster care youth as children receiving substitute care of minimally 24 hours outside of their home (Child Welfare Information Gateway, 2016). These foster care environments include, "...nonrelative foster family homes, relative foster homes (whether payments are being made or not), group homes, emergency shelters, residential facilities, and preadoptive homes" (Child Welfare Information Gateway, 2016, p. 2). In 2014, reports estimated approximately 415,129 children were in foster care. There were 264,467 children entering foster care during this year, and 238,230 who exited care (Child Welfare Information Gateway, 2016). From those children exiting care in 2014, approximately 51% were, "...reunited with their parents or primary caretaker" (Child Welfare Information Gateway, 2016, p. 2). Children entering foster care for even the shortest periods possible are still affected by instability inherent to the system.

DEVELOPMENT OF STUDENTS FROM NONTRADITIONAL FAMILY STRUCTURES

Students from a nontraditional family structures face greater challenges in meeting basic needs compared to their peers. In accordance with Maslow's (1943) *Hierarchy of Needs*, these students may often be lacking basic needs creating further barriers in development.

Distinct Challenges

Prior to entering a collegiate environment, a student's challenges and triumphs throughout childhood lay the foundation for their maturation. "The family role will define the type of behavior a member will exhibit as well as the process used to deal with the environment" (Terry-Leonard, 1999, pp. 7–8). Most notably, students from nontraditional family structures could lack models of family functioning. Traumatic experiences affect approximately 90% of children in care, and almost 50% will experience diverse types of traumatic events (Fratto, 2016). According to results from the adverse childhood experience (ACE) study, which examines the correlation between adult health concerns as influenced by stressors from childhood, the maltreatment experienced by these youths bears a direct relationship with the development of oppositional reactions later in life (Fratto, 2016).

Turbulent childhood conditions most frequently manifest in a foster care youth's inability to gain access to consistent education and health resources; "Most children who enter foster care have already been exposed to conditions that undermine their chances for healthy development" (Bass, Behrman, & Shields, 2004, p. 10). Although, children in care are traditionally provided access to health insurance, a gap in services often occurs due to lack of stable living arrangements. These students are not able to meet basic health needs, which undermines the foundation of a physiological need as defined in Maslow's (1943) hierarchy. Taormina and Gao (2013) noted, "a 'need' can be characterized by, and defined as, a lack of something that is essential to an organism's (a person's) existence or well-being" (p. 156). Individuals' development and movement through the levels outlined by Maslow (1943), requires a respective meeting of each basic need to fulfill the highest need of self-actualization. Maslow (1943) noted self-actualization "refers to the desire for self-fulfillment, namely, to the tendency for... [one] ... to become actualized in what... [one] ... is potentially" (p. 382).

Support Discrepancies From Traditional Family Structures

The relative inability for foster care youth to have basic physiological needs met may hinder them in progressing toward self-actualization, which could have consequences for leader identity and capacity development. Much of one's self-actualization is developed as a result of affirmations and constructive reinforcement from familial and community members. Maslow (1943) suggested individuals, "who have been made secure and strong in the earliest years, tend to remain secure and strong thereafter in the face of whatever threatens" (p. 388).

Often members of these nontraditional units exhibit a greater level of resilience in the face of adversity, such as coping with parental divorce (Lamb, 1999). Additionally, children of nontraditional structures frequently establish greater independence, on basis of need. "One of the fundamental characteristics of resilience is that it allows individuals to take difficult experiences in their lives and use them as opportunities to learn" (Hernez-Broome & Hughes, 2004, p. 29). If educators are able to channel this resiliency in generating students' leader identity, it could greatly assist the students' development.

Smyte et al. (2012) examined the relationship between reactive attachment disorder and institutional maltreatment. The two forms of reactive attachment included, "emotionally withdrawn (inhibited type) and indiscriminately social (disinhibited type)" (Smyte et al., 2012, p. 508). Their findings indicated children placed in institutional care more often than not exhibited attachment disorders, with important implications for their interpersonal development. Findings such as these have important consequences when considering former foster youth's motivation and capacity for leadership rooted in relationships.

Students' Self-Esteem and Identity

Research suggests positive relationships between parental nurturance and self-esteem development (Terry-Leonard, 1999). The self-esteem of a foster care child may be impacted by traumatic experiences, especially during adolescent developmental years. In accordance with attachment theories, "... an unwanted child will develop internal working models of their parents as unwanting and themselves as unwantable" (Luke & Coyne, 2008, p. 403).

Initial attachment beliefs form during early relationships between children and caregivers. These perceptions shape "... expectations about the self, others and the world, or 'working models'" (Otway & Carnelley, 2013, p. 218) for future relationships. Engaged interactions with responsive caregivers often result in positive views of self and attachment, while unengaged caregivers can promote negative self-perceptions and lack of appropriate reliance on others (Otway & Carnelley, 2013).

Long-term system care produced negatively influenced identity development among adolescents (Kools, 1997). Perceptions of how individuals believe they are viewed or affirmed/disaffirmed by others often contribute to their identity development. The perpetuation of stereotypes further fuels devaluation of foster care youth. Kools (1997) noted the manifestation of devaluation often comes in the form of "depersonalization and stigmatization" (p. 266). As foster youth often experience inconsistency in care through rotational caregivers, their interactions with others become impersonal. Furthermore, stigmatization often materializes as anticipation of negative behaviors by individuals of foster care youth, and is interpreted as a particular mentality: "I am who others think I am and I will behave accordingly" (Kools, 1997, p. 267). Frequently foster care youth will act out and conform to an identity perpetuated by stereotypes, or further build a negative self-image, and ultimately an identity, around society's stigmas. As a result of this internal stigmatization, research in the field finds "[n]early 20 percent of young prison inmates and 28 percent of homeless individuals spent some time in foster care as a youth" (Martha Burt et al., 1999 as cited in Doyle, 2007, p. 1583). Clearly, the treatment of individuals in and beyond the foster care system is a social justice issue.

EDUCATIONAL PURSUIT AND BARRIERS

Dworsky and Perez (2010) noted the challenges presented to foster care youth when pursuing higher education did not originate from a lack of aspirations, but could be attributed to barriers of access and resources. Foremost, navigating the college application process can be daunting without guidance. Additionally, these students often experience significant shifts in physical placement, which results in inconsistent education. Foster care youth are also often not aware of financial aid options. Furthermore, challenges are presented to foster care youth when overcoming "mental and behavioral health problems" (Dworsky & Perez, 2010, p. 256). These challenges often persist through adulthood, especially when they do not receive consistent treatment. Lastly, the authors noted campus personnel may not be educated on the unique needs of these students or how to best assist them during college (Dworsky & Perez, 2010).

It remains incredibly rare for foster care youth alumni to progress to the collegiate level; adding undergraduate leadership development creates even greater complexity. Foster care youth alumni who pursue higher education matriculate at significantly lower rates than others, with graduates constituting only 1 to 11% comparative to their otherwise comparable peers, who demonstrate a 30% graduation rate (Snyder, Dillon, & Hoffman, 2008 as cited in Dworsky & Perez, 2010, p. 255).

ENGAGING FOSTER CARE YOUTH IN LEADERSHIP DEVELOPMENT

Overwhelmingly, leadership programs do not cater specifically to foster care youth alumni and foster care youth independent living preparation programs do not focus on leadership development. However, we need leadership development programs to address and incorporate the needs of foster care youth alumni. Often assumptions are made about student potential, capacity, and their ability to engage in leadership development, either from a leader or follower perspective. Foster care youth alumni bring a diverse set of skills as well as skepticisms to the table when engaging on a college campus. Leadership development programs and foster care support systems need to collaborate to assist students in the formation of leader identity.

Self-Perception in the Collegiate Environment

Foster care youth alumni often retain negative self-perceptions or struggle to establish self-efficacy due to social stigmas. Enhanced self-efficacy allows individuals to believe they can be effective in achieving intended outcomes (Bandura, 1995). Messages from society implicitly and explicitly contribute to personal perceptions of self-esteem; "When the child in foster care internalizes the negative views that others have of him or her, this devalued status is internalized into the self-concept" (Kools, 1997, p. 267). A child may sense abandonment when entering foster care. Campus personnel who work with these students counter feelings of abandonment, which could hinder students' success. Self-efficacy is often enhanced in college by engagement in leadership activities, and growing confidence in the developed identity and capacity as a leader (Guthrie, Bertrand Jones, Osteen, & Hu, 2013). The foremost difficulty in engaging former foster youth is ensuring they feel comfortable participating, along with balancing the new rigors brought by collegiate academic studies and the challenges of independent living.

Connection With Peers

While college promotes transition and growth for all students as they embark on a new season of life, it could be an exceptionally more challenging transition for those students from nontraditional families. Two defining aspects of transition to the higher education environment are (a) learning to cope with greater independence and (b) merging into a community of diversity. These are accomplished through connections with peers, mentors, and other members of the collegiate community. Collegians with a background as foster youth could experience considerable more and different challenges when establishing themselves in the overarching institutional environment as a result of their internalized barriers to attachments and trusting relationships. Otway and Carnelley (2013) discussed how secure individuals more readily achieve self-actualization, which accordingly allows them to better manage stress and challenges in college. Former foster youth most likely experience these stressors and challenges differently, as they may not have developed coping mechanisms associated with self-actualization.

Leadership development, as defined by Komives, Lucas, and McMahon (2013), is built on relationships: "Any leadership setting can be viewed as a community of people working together for shared purposes. Relational leadership is best practiced by thinking about any kind of group or organization as a community" (Komives et al., 2013, p. 283). When leadership development is predicated on relationships, former foster care youth encounter hurdles due to disconnects with peers on a basis of trust. Unrau, Seita, and Putney (2008) highlighted how, "[t]his mistrust is adaptive and intended to protect them against further disappointments and pain" (p. 1263). Subsequently, reframing trust in leadership is vital for college foster care youth.

Former foster care youth grapple with attachment and thus relationship establishment can be tenuous if it happens at all. Unrau et al. (2008) captured testimonies from former foster care youth, and one quoted saying,

"I never attached...I learned not to trust anybody but myself. You know I was extremely detached from any caretaker that I ever had purposefully 'cause that was my survival technique" (p. 1261). Individuals experiencing encounters with the foster care system are bound to feel a sense of abandonment regardless of the time expanse. Bernath and Feschbach (1995) commented on the development of trust in childhood noting, "trusting that caregivers will provide reliable support and protection, that peers will be honest, cooperative and benevolent, and that one's self will be stable, controllable, and safe, enables the child to risk and enjoy life's experiences with objects, activities, and relationships" (p. 1).

Stability is often initiated through familial interactions and norms established in the respective family unit. Foster youth often experience turbulence with not only the immediate family or primary caregivers, but as a by-product, do not receive consistent relations with teachers, health providers, or other community personnel who further the development process of trust. Trust is viewed as a fundamental value, but the development of this ability is established by a positive caregiver relationship (Bernath & Feschbach, 1995).

In absence of consistent, positive caregiver/child relationship, deconstructive trust begins to develop in young minds as a guiding belief. The feelings of trust or mistrust cultivated through one's childhood maintain truth as an individual leaves the foster care system. When engaging in decision-making, an individual formulates their response on the basis of previous experiences with others, which builds a constructive or destructive view of safety and reliance on others (Unrau et al., 2008). It is more likely students from a supportive traditional structure will have a more constructive view of trust and themselves due to positive, reciprocal interactions experienced throughout childhood (Bernath & Feschbach, 1995).

CAMPUS SUPPORT PROGRAMS
FOR FOSTER CARE YOUTH ALUMNI

Recently, advocates, policies, and programs have increased support for students from the foster care system. These agendas are implemented at national, state, and institutional levels to broaden access to opportunities for members of this population. Issues of access must be considered before practitioners can engage these students in exploring the concept of leadership.

Current Programs

Across the nation, there is a greater presence of programs ranging from generating early awareness to helping students better understand the process of gaining admission to experiencing success in college. Many programs attempt to focus on the K–12 system and early intervention, but more recently there has been a greater proliferation of programs supporting collegiate students throughout their journey.

State- and Federal-Supported Initiatives

Florida is seen as pioneering support for foster care youth toward a college education. In the latter part of the 20th century, Florida was among the first to offer sustained programs to promote greater access. Most notably, tuition and fee exemption afforded to foster youth who aged out of the system or adoption occurred after May of 1997. Through this legislation, Florida Statute §240.235(6)(a) (1988), provided an opportunity to attain an undergraduate education free of tuition and fees. This statute extends to the 28 public state institutions (Florida's Children First, 2014). While it is a financial benefit, it does not compensate for the hardships experienced by these individuals. The Florida Board of Governors granted institutional autonomy in regards to implementing the policies, as no exact guidance on uniformed application is provided (Florida's Children First, 2014). Florida's Children First (2014) reports that as of 2014, approximately 15% of the nearly 23,000 students eligible utilized this tuition waiver. The belief as to why a larger majority of students do not utilize this benefit is credited to lack of knowledge, discrepancies in eligibility requirements, and the intensity of paperwork to apply among other barriers to higher education (Florida's Children First, 2014).

Institutional Initiatives

Florida State University supports the Unconquered Scholars Program to further assist in overcoming the barriers associated with the waiver benefit and overall transition to the institution for students from the foster care system along with other disadvantaged backgrounds. This program was established through the institution's Center for Academic Retention and Enrichment to provide specific support for "students who have experienced homelessness, foster care, relative care, or ward of the state status" (Garcia, 2016, p. 5). Through this program, other institutional resources and support services are leveraged to create a cost-effective program specific to this particular population.

RE-ORIENTING LEADERSHIP DEVELOPMENT PROGRAMS TO REACH FOSTER CARE YOUTH

For foster care youth to receive the most benefit from leadership education, programs should be reconfigured to acknowledge and address their specific constellation of needs. Specifically, "[a] socially just education requires educational leaders to...defend and extend principles of human dignity, community, and realization of democratic processes" (Blackmore, 2002, p. 218). It is essential to first assist with the realization aspect when engaging students of a foster care system background, or those individuals from a nontraditional family structures. Many of these students may not possess what are commonly considered basic tools to not only engage in leadership processes as a follower, but develop leader identity as well.

Impacts on the Individual Student, Peers, and Institution

It is essential to ensure leadership development is not only accessible, but framed appropriately for students of nontraditional families, particularly to former foster youth. Conversations stimulating leader identity and subsequent leadership development take into account the need for growth among all students, yet there will inherently be additional challenges presented to students from nontraditional families. Engaging students in leadership activities provides opportunities for students to build on their self-esteem and subsequently their self-efficacy, along with the establishment of relationships. Programs promoting the logistical transition to higher education in regards to financial, academic, and campus navigation are formative in setting a foundation to better adapt to the educational environment. There is a growing trend of programs across campuses to primarily assist with meeting students' basic needs to support the transition to the collegiate environment. Engagement in leadership development can also assist in enhancing self-perceptions and interactions with peers.

In active leadership, it is most beneficial to bring together diverse individuals in leader and follower relationships. Students from the foster care system bring unique stories to their collegiate journey, and contribute traditionally excluded diverse perspectives. These voices are rare as approximately 10% of former foster youth maintain enrollment at an institution of higher education (Kirk, Lewis, Nilsen, & Covlin, 2011). In relation to the overall student population, these students continue to be a minority and will face continual barriers to be considered in conversation. The relational leadership model proposed by Komives et al. (2013) promotes engagement among diverse individuals and further places the focus of leadership on people. In order to promote socially just leadership development, no population can be excluded. Additionally, former foster youth often encompass even greater diversity in a student's identity, which may transcend multiple marginalized populations.

Many former foster youths are expected to experience challenges with assimilation to an institution akin to first generation students, even if by definition they are not. A challenge posed to student support staff is avoiding deficit-based interaction with these students when engaging in leadership development. Former foster youth are predisposed to additional barriers, which inhibit overall success, yet there needs to be a distinct approach in how support is given. Macias (2013) suggested for, "...practitioners and researchers alike, it is critical... to fully understand the challenges that first-generation students face. However, a perpetual focus on deficits and gaps has caused us to expect deficiency" (p. 18). Macias (2013) urged staff members to re-orient their focus when interacting with first-generation and other students predisposed to barriers. The author offers personal accounts as a student who experiences educators who focused on his deficits, which were detrimental in overcoming collegiate challenges.

PRACTICAL APPLICATIONS

Socially just educators work specifically with former foster care youth and assist in helping the students overcome prevalent barriers, in addition to structuring environments to promote development of self-efficacy. They carefully examine resources, people, and institutional structures for opportunities to assist. Also, socially just educators recognize and activate opportunities to customize and deliver more inclusive environments, which could greatly differ among institutions; it is important to start creating change in one's immediate purview.

Resources

A culture shift must take place to better serve students of nontraditional families, particularly foster youth alumni. Shifting widely-accepted norms in higher education, or even at one institution, can be difficult. We are working to reimagine serving students in appropriate ways even before the conception of this text. The first action that practitioners can take for practical implementation would be to examine the available resources that exist in their current environment. This includes any opportunity for cross programming, better leveraging of current initiatives or simply altering our approaches and responses.

When engaging with students of this population, it is important to first examine the structural environment. As supported by high-quality research in the field, these students often struggle interacting with people in power or a hierarchical setting. The first question to ask: how can I change the power dynamic to establish a consistent and level environment? It is not wrong to acknowledge different levels of authority; however, it is imperative to communicate and model that a leader/follower dynamic is not on the basis of power. Socially just educators should create an environment for these students that allows them to voice their concerns and establish themselves within an organization. When practitioners understand mistrust is a mechanism for protection, we can recreate environments to provide opportunities to safely explore positive relationships. The key component is to acknowledge this process will take patience; however, that each professional has the opportunity to impact students with their personal resources. This is done through a supportive frame of reference, and avoiding a deficit approach.

People

People can be difficult to influence, and while very few, if any, individuals in higher education settings would purposefully exclude students of nontraditional families, it can easily happen by omission. Often we do not regularly consider these distinct needs when inventorying the overall needs of students. We need to take into account the perspectives of staff, but also peer students. Many individuals of the foster care system have not been exposed to leader/follower dynamics as a result of the nontraditional family structure; their peers of traditional structures often see this exhibited with parents and/or siblings.

Trust can be an issue for any individual, but as noted previously, foster care youth alumni often begin developing feelings of mistrust early in life. These negative feelings toward trust ruminate in students' minds, as members of this population do not regularly experience trusting relationships. These feelings can be combated by working judiciously with all students. It will be just as necessary to educate students and staff from traditional family structures on the distinct challenges faced by their unlike peers, and how these differences may manifest in interactions. This could be done through interactive presentations/trainings and they will serve to generate awareness of the potential barriers and concerns experienced by their peers. I believe that this cannot be a solution-focused training that directs students of traditional family structures on how to respond, as there is not one correct way; rather, I believe it should provide them with a better understanding of their peers' challenges and how to also be supportive.

As these kinds of programs are developed, socially just leadership educators intentionally spend independent and group time with students of nontraditional family structures. The biggest hurdle beyond overarching barriers (health, monetary, and self-perception concerns) would be working to establish trust. This process could take a variety of forms; I believe it will necessary to first model trust and then work to engage individuals one-on-one and ultimately integrate trust into a group environment. There is not enough research on how long this process could take to reverse feelings of mistrust and cultivate a positive perception of trust.

Institutional Structures

Postsecondary institutions, despite being hubs of innovation, are still bureaucratic structures with hierarchical organizations. Professionals often share systemic challenges of implementing novel ideas or programs not because of poor quality, but rather, due to internal resistances and lag. The hope for practitioners would be that their groundwork would launch institutional change by adapting resources and reframing perceptions. This change could come in the form of establishing staff distinctly dedicated to support these students, much like that of the aforementioned Unconquered Scholars Program; or providing training campus-wide to prepare staff to best assist students of nontraditional structures. While there are programs that establish logistical and emotional support as students engage in transition, there needs to be a call for these programs to also equip students and staff to readily engage in common campus leadership opportunities. It is important to acknowledge the need to include these students into campus-wide leadership rather than limiting to opportunities with population-focused programming.

Institutional structures are influenced by state and federal policy, so it is important to note the legislature distinct to one's state. For instance, Florida provides a statute that eliminates the concern of tuition costs for many of these students. If some barriers can be alleviated from a student, then it will be easier for them to focus on leadership development and engagement initiatives. It is imperative that institutions acknowledge policies, which positively contribute to access and leverage them to best serve these students. As noted earlier, the tuition waiver in the state of Florida is not as widely utilized due mostly to lack of information. Institutions will need to start their outreach prior to college application to best assist in this transition by pairing with the K–12 system. The goal is to remove as many barriers as possible, with the least obstruction.

While working with members of this population it is important to not lose sight of academic needs. A foremost concern for all students, but in particular members of this population is balancing academics while overcoming significant personal barriers. Traditionally, these students are predisposed to mental health challenges, greater insecurities, and lack of support (Dworsky & Perez, 2010; Garcia, 2016). It is imperative to balance academic achievement and leadership development. Ultimately, working with these distinct students require staff members to unite their efforts to make a strong community of support services and stability. While working with this population, it is important to do so through a positive lens and not to perpetuate the deficits by labeling them throughout their development.

CONCLUSION

The goal for broadening socially just leadership education is to not only account for students of the foster care system and peers from other nontraditional family structures in this process, but to be truly inclusive. The hurdles these students must overcome are rooted in mistrust and instability, but are often countered with a level of resiliency to combat the instances of abandonment. It is imperative to continue to support these students not only in their academic pursuits, but also complimenting their successes with engagement in leadership development. Professionals must be cautioned not to approach this population from a deficit perspective when engaging in developing leader identity and capacity. It will be imperative to engage in specific support measures for these students by foremost building their self-confidence and self-esteem. Additionally, many of these students may have challenges with establishing trust with their peers—trust is established from experience. Thus, it will be imperative to provide an environment accounting for a level of mistrust and exploring techniques to break down this barrier. A potential avenue to assist in this process could be done so with reliance on the relational leadership model by Komives et al. (2013). While there is a myriad of applicable models, the relationship model could serve as a strong foundation.

The ultimate goal of socially just leadership is to actively engage all individuals equitably. Former foster youth experience additional challenges entering higher education, but this should not undercut opportunities to establish a leader identity and engage in leadership processes. In order to equitably engage with peers from traditional family structures, intensive investments need to be made in building individual identity. Revolutionary leadership programs on campuses pave the way in supporting members of this population. In order to change campus culture, similarly oriented initiatives need to be ingrained in campuses across the nation to broaden access for these students and support their academic pursuits. Additionally, socially just leadership educators weave components of leadership development to provide a holistic educations, while also establishing wider foundation of community support and resources to transform foster care youth alumni into successful collegiate leaders.

REFERENCES

Altamirano, N., & Chandler, D. (2013, December 10). Is a nontraditional family structure completely doomed for failure? (How you can make sure your child thrives despite the odds). Retrieved from https://my.vanderbilt.edu/developmentalpsychologyblog/2013/12/is-a-nontraditional-family-structure-completely-doomed-for-failure-how-you-can-make-sure-your-child-thrives-despite-the-odds/

Bandura, A. (1995). *Self-efficacy in changing societies.* Cambridge, England: Cambridge University Press.

Bass, S., Behrman, R. E., & Shields, M. K. (2004). Children, families and foster care: Analysis and recommendations. *Children, Families and Foster Care, 14*(1), 5–29.

Bernath, M. S., & Feschbach, N. D. (1995). Children's trust: Theory, assessment, development, and research directions. *Applied and Preventive Psychology, 4*(1), 1–19.

Blackmore, J. (2002). Leadership for socially just schooling: More substance and less style in high-risk, low-trust times? *Journal of School Leadership, 12,* 198–222.

Child Welfare Information Gateway. (2016). Foster care statistics 2014. Washington, DC: U.S. Department of Health and Human Services, Children's Bureau. Retrieved from https://www.childwelfare.gov/pubPDFs/foster.pdf

Doyle, J. J. (2007). Child protection and child outcomes: Measuring the effects of foster care. *The American Economic Review, 97*(5), 1583–1611.

Dworsky, A., & Perez, A. (2010). Helping former foster youth graduate from college through campus support programs. *Children and Youth Services Review, 34,* 255–263.

Florida's Children First. (2014). *Fostering higher education success: Tuition and fee exemption for Florida's foster youth.* Retrieved from http://www.floridaschildrenfirst.org/wp-content/uploads/2014/01/Tuition-Exemption-White-Paper-Floridas-Children-First.pdf

Fratto, C. M. (2016). Trauma-informed care for youth in foster care. *Archives of Psychiatric Nursing, 30*(3), 436–446.

Garcia, S. (2016). Un-housed and unsupported: Homeless and foster youth in higher education. *Congressional Hispanic Caucus Institute White Paper.* Retrieved from https://chci.org/Garcia_Sara.pdf

Guthrie, K. L., Bertrand Jones, T., Osteen, L. K., & Hu, S. (2013). *Cultivating leader identity and capacity in students from diverse backgrounds: ASHE Higher Education Report, 39*(4). Hoboken, NJ: Wiley.

Hernez-Broome, G., & Hughes, R. L. (2004). Leadership development: Past, present, and future. *Human Resource Planning, 27*(1), 24–32. Retrieved from http://home.mycybernet.net/~taylors/Publish/leadership%20development.pdf

Kirk, C. M., Lewis, R. K., Nilsen, C., & Covlin, D.Q. (2011). Foster care and college: The educational aspirations and expectations of youth in the foster care system. *Youth & Society, 45*(3), 307–323.

Komives, S. R., Lucas, N., & McMahon, T. R. (2013). *Exploring leadership: For college students who want to make a difference.* San Francisco, CA: Jossey-Bass.

Kools, S. M. (1997). Adolescent identity development in foster care. *National Council on Family Relations, 46*(3), 263–271.

Lamb, M. E. (1999). *Parenting and child development in nontraditional families.* Mahwah, NJ: Psychology Press.

Larson, C. L., & Murtadha, K. (2002). Leadership for social justice. *Yearbook of the National Society for the Study of Education, 101*(1), 134–161.

Livingston, G. (2014, December 24). *Fewer than half of U.S. kids today live in a "traditional" family.* Retrieved from http://www.pewresearch.org/fact-tank/2014/12/22/less-than-half-of-u-s-kids-today-live-in-a-traditional-family/

Luke, N., & Coyne, S. M. (2008). Fostering self-esteem: Exploring adult recollections on the influence of foster parents. *Child & Family Social Work, 13,* 402–410.

Macias, L. V. (2013). Choosing success: A paradigm for empowering first-generation college students. *About Campus, 18*(5), 17–21.

Maslow, A. H. (1943). A theory of human motivation. *Psychological Review, 50*(4), 370–396.

Otway, L. J., & Carnelley, K. B. (2013). Exploring the associations between adult attachment security and self-actualization and self-transcendence. *Self and Identity, 12*(2), 217–230.

Pecora, P. (2012). Maximizing educational achievement of youth in foster care and alumni: Factors associated with success. *Children and Youth Services Review, 34,* 1121–1129.

Rost, J. C. (1993). *Leadership for the twenty-first century.* New York, NY: Praeger.

Smyte, A. T., Zeanah, C. H., Gleason, M. M., Drury, S. S., Fox, N. A., Nelson, C. A., Guthrie, D. (2012). A randomized controlled trial comparing foster care and institutional care for children with signs of reactive attachment disorder. *American Journal of Psychiatry, 169*(5), 508–514.

Stephens, M. E. (2013). The non-traditional family: An introduction. *The Review of Black Political Economy, 40*(1), 27–29.

Taormina, R. J., & Gao, J. H. (2013). Maslow and the motivation hierarchy: Measuring satisfaction of the needs. *The American Journal of Psychology, 126*(2), 155–177.

Terry-Leonard, B. L. (1999). *The relationship of self-esteem, perceived parental nurturance, and family functioning across three family structures in a sample of non-traditional undergraduate students.* (Doctoral dissertation). Retrieved from ProQuest Dissertations Publishing (9928749).

Unrau, Y. A., Seita, J. R., & Putney, K. S. (2008). Former foster youth remember multiple placement moves: A journey of loss and hope. *Children and Youth Services Review, 30,* 1256–1266.

Wolanin, T. R. (2005). *Higher education opportunities for foster youth: A primer for policymakers.* Washington, DC: Institute for Higher Education Policy.

PART II

SOCIALLY JUST LEADERSHIP EDUCATION PROCESSES AND ENVIRONMENTS

CHAPTER 14

CREATING BRAVE SPACES IN LEADERSHIP EDUCATION

Rose Rezaei

Socially just leadership educators are uniquely positioned in higher education to provide constructive developmental environments for students to
learn leadership. Developmental environments are based on the pedagogy
that emphasizes learning is constructed by students making meaning of
their experiences (Baxter Magolda, 2001; Baxter Magolda & King, 2004).
These experiences take place in a variety of settings situated in several environments within a larger system (Guthrie & Jenkins, 2018). Knowing individuals reciprocally influence their environments, socially just leadership
educators have the ability to create contexts where leadership education
occurs; therefore, influencing the conditions under which individuals develop. Socially just leadership educators can do this through the promotion
of *brave spaces*.

The brave spaces framework was introduced by Arao and Clemens (2013)
to acknowledge the need for "courage rather than the illusion of safety"
(p. 114) in spaces where diversity and social justice learning occurs. Arao
and Clemens (2013) formulated this framework in response to the idea of
safe spaces (Holley & Steiner, 2005); conditions where participants engage

Changing the Narrative, pages 213–228
Copyright © 2018 by Information Age Publishing
213

in activities with little risk or fear, as reasonable expectations for students engaged in diversity and social justice work (Arao & Clemens, 2013). Arao and Clemens (2013) argued the language of safety encourages "the entrenchment in privilege..." and "...contributes to the replication of dominance and subordination, rather than a dismantling thereof" (p. 140). Brave spaces frameworks were designed to push students to "the edges of their comfort zones to maximize learning" (p. 143). To apply their *brave spaces* framework in a social justice education, Arao and Clemens (2013) suggested reframing how facilitators and participants establish ground rules for dialogue by being critical about how ground rules "help or hinders students in full and truthful engagement" (p. 143). Brave spaces imply that risk is always taken when engaging in conversations around diversity and social justice and confronting risk aids those who engage in these spaces by encouraging their authentic participation (Arao & Clemens, 2013).

The context in which individuals partake in leadership learning can influence their development (Owen, 2011; Rainey & Kolb, 1995). These contexts can be physical spaces like classrooms, programmatic venues, workplace environments, or service-learning agencies. Contexts can also include psychosocial elements such as sense of belonging, feeling accepted and empowered, or having the ability to contribute. Furthermore, context can also be examined through relational dynamics among peers or between students and instructors. Heifetz (1994) discussed how physical or psychological holding environments could be created so individuals can learn. Hall (2004) expanded the idea of holding environments by stating these environments must allow individuals to feel vulnerable and safe in order to engage in identity development. These holding environments occur in various environmental systems, which influence, and are influenced by, individuals interacting within these systems. For the purposes of this chapter, I want to explore how leadership educators can promote social justice leadership education by applying the brave spaces framework within leader identity development (LID).

LEADERSHIP EDUCATION IN HIGHER EDUCATION

The approach to leadership education in higher education has changed over time. Historically, preparing college students as future leaders has been seen as a goal of college education (Chunoo & Osteen, 2016; Dugan & Komives, 2011). Until the early 1990s, educators promoted leadership education through an industrial view of leadership that was leader-centric, management-oriented, and individual achievement-focused (Dugan & Komives, 2011; Rost, 1991). Today, advocates for postindustrial leadership approaches call for socially responsible, developmental, and process-oriented leadership education (Dugan & Komives, 2011). This postindustrial view has been accepted in various professional organizations in higher education. The Council for the Advancement of Standards (CAS) in Higher Education (2015) updated their standards for student leadership programs to reflect this postindustrial view of leadership. What does it mean to be socially responsible in leadership education? In order for this to be explored, leadership educators need foundational knowledge on social justice and how the brave spaces framework can be used to contribute to social justice leadership education.

Social Justice Framework

Recent critiques of leadership theory call for a reexamination of the context in which these theories emerged (Dugan, 2017). Several industrial leadership models marginalize members of many communities including students of color, women, individuals with varying abilities, and those from lower socioeconomic backgrounds (Dugan & Komives, 2011). As a result, students with marginalized identities may equate *leader* or *leadership* to positional abuse of power, oppression, and control. Postindustrial leadership theories have tried to address some of these issues by shifting the view of leadership to be more relational and interdependent. While this shift was intended to make leadership more inclusive, much of the work still emphasized a majority White, upper-class, male perspective (Dugan & Komives, 2011). Socially just leadership educators explore the sociohistorical implications of leadership theory and leadership education from a social justice lens. In *Teaching for Diversity and Social Justice*, Adams (2016) described social justice as both a goal and a process:

> The goal is full and equitable participation of people from all social identity groups in a society that is mutually shaped to meet their needs. The process for attaining the goal of social justice should also be democratic and participatory, respectful of human diversity and group differences, and inclusive and affirming of human agency and capacity for working collaboratively with others to create change. (p. 28)

Leadership educators can utilize social justice education that supports "individuals to develop the critical analytical tools necessary to understand the structural features of oppression and their own socialization within oppressive systems" (Adams, 2016, p. 31). Leadership educators can use social justice frameworks in designing learning environments by incorporating a brave spaces framework so individuals are able to explore their socialization, how it impacts their identity development, and how they view and relate to others.

Programmatic Environments Within Leadership Education

Haber (2011) noted a recent shift in how professional communities categorize formal leadership programs. The shift moves away from categorizing programs in terms of size and scope (comprehensive), and toward describing them in terms of interconnectedness (integrative). The goal of integrative programs is to create environments where individuals weave together various individual experiences, contexts, and knowledge to deepen their understanding of how these parts are interconnected (Haber, 2011). These connections enhance students' critical thinking skills, intellectual judgment skills, and holistic development (Lucas, 2009). Leadership educators can apply an integrative approach to leadership education through formal leadership programs. Formal leadership programs are comprised of various individual experiences of leadership activities (Haber, 2011). These activities can take place in two formal programmatic environments—curricular or cocurricular.

Curricular Environments

Curricular programs are often connected to an academic/credit-bearing course or experience (Haber, 2011). There are several factors that affect course design. Leadership educators can determine the scope of leadership the course will cover (i.e., introductory, intermediate, or advanced). Leadership educators can also focus on specific topics (i.e., civic engagement, ethics in leadership, global leadership, or leadership theory). Additionally, leadership educators decide the intended audience for the course. For example, the course could be for a specific population, like students of color, women, LGBTQ+ students; for general populations, like first year students or graduate students; or for positional populations like resident assistants or peer mentors (Mainella & Martinez Love, 2011). Curricular programs can also have experiential component like credit-bearing internships that have learning outcomes associated with leadership development. Depending on the institution, curricular programs can be offered as a leadership minor, major, certification, or as a standalone leadership course situated within an academic discipline.

Cocurricular Environments

Many students engage in cocurricular programs in college. Astin and Astin (2000) noted "these activities almost always provide an opportunity to exercise leadership and to develop leadership skills" (p. 18). Socially just leadership educators capitalize on cocurricular programs by offering "non-credit bearing experiences that address leadership training, education, and development outside of the traditional classroom environment" (Haber,

2011, p. 246). These cocurricular programs can take a variety of formats including one-time programs (workshops, conferences, retreats, lectures) or sequential programs (workshop series, multi-year programs, cocurricular leadership certificate programs, etc.; Smist, 2011). Chapter 16 discusses socially just leadership education in cocurricular contexts more in-depth.

Brave Spaces Within Leadership Education Contexts

Formal leadership programs take place in a variety of settings and frequently intersect with other developmental environments; it is important for leadership educators to examine how individuals develop within their surroundings. The brave spaces framework can be incorporated through formal leadership programs in several ways. In curricular arenas, educators can integrate critical pedagogies to expand the consciousness of their students. Brown (2004) discussed critical theories as grounded in the lived experiences of people, structures, and cultures. They examine the historical and cultural context in which data was collected and call into question the inherent biases of research findings. Examples of critical theories include critical race theory (Bell, 1995) and intersectionality theory (Crenshaw, 1991). Critical theories help students rethink their socialized systematic worldview, uncovering how social identities are valued.

Leadership educators can disrupt power dynamics often encountered in traditional Western teacher–student relationships by acknowledging learning as a shared responsibility where all parties have the ability to create knowledge. The setting where leadership education is delivered can also be examined. If learning takes place in a classroom, the physical orientation of objects in the room (chairs, desks, lecterns, etc.) can dictate how individuals are expected to interact. For example, chairs in a circle may communicate that every person has the invitation to participate in the activity. A traditional lecture-style classroom may indicate a separation is expected between peers and the educator. This may prove to be a barrier to participation.

In cocurricular experiences, educators can encourage student facilitators to use a brave spaces framework by partnering with participants to explore the meaning of a brave space and use the exercise of setting ground rules as a valuable part of social justice learning (Arao & Clemens, 2013). For example, one ground rule Arao and Clemens (2013) suggested is to promote *controversy with civility* to support the idea that conflict is a natural part of discussion in diverse groups. This approach encourages participants to engage conflict with an ethic of care and allows for continued engagement towards common solutions. While leadership educators have the ability to be intentional about the context in which leadership education occurs, they must acknowledge the existence of other systems, which influence individuals and their development. The consideration of other systems can be explored through a human ecology lens.

Ecology of Human Development

Developmental psychologist Urie Bronfenbrenner (1981, 1994) explored the ecology of human development through five ecological systems. Human ecology considers the relationships between an individual and their environments. Leadership educators can use human ecology to examine how various environments influence individuals' leadership learning. Bronfenbrenner (1981, 1994) developed an ecological systems theory to explore five systems of various proximal environments and how each system effects human development. The individual is at the center of the systems and there is a dynamic influential relationship between the individual and the environment. The five systems (microsystem, mesosystem, ecosystem, macrosystem, and chronosystem) are interconnected and range from the most individual level to larger society.

Microsystem

The microsystem focuses on the individual's immediate environment including social roles, interpersonal relationships, and structures of immediate influence (Bronfenbrenner, 1994). For students engaged in the leadership process, this can take many forms including interactions with peers, educators, mentors, and administrators. It can also include interactions in leadership classes, workshops, or leadership engagement opportunities.

Mesosystem

The mesosystem is comprised of the linkages between processes taking place in two or more settings containing the developing person (Bronfenbrenner, 1994). This can also be thought of as relationships between microsystems. For example, one could examine the relationship between a student's multiple social identities and how this influences leadership efficacy. Educators can also examine multiple ways students learn leadership, for example, through a class or position in an organization. Are they complementary? Are they incongruent? Do they reinforce industrial or post-industrial paradigms of leadership?

Exosystem

The exosystem comprises of the linkages and processes taking place between two or more settings where at least one setting does not contain the developing person but events that occur in the linked setting indirectly impact the developing person (Bronfenbrenner, 1994). For example, leadership educators could examine how an institution prioritizes leadership opportunities for students. A way to examine this is to review trends in institutional funding for curricular and cocurricular programs.

Macrosystem

The macrosystem consists of broad-scale patterns of characteristics within a culture or subculture (Bronfenbrenner, 1994). These can include political systems, cultural ideologies, governing systems, social conditions, public policies, and economic patterns. For example, how does witnessing the first Black man be elected president of the United States impact the popular view of leadership? What effect does this have on students of color who have only seen White individuals in leadership roles?

Chronosystem

The chronosystem accounts for the overarching impact of time in terms of when events occur over an individual's lifespan and the sociohistorical circumstances within which these events occur (Bronfenbrenner, 1994). For example, the age at which an individual participates in a leadership program could shape their development; a student who is in their 40s and has children may face different challenges, and wield unique strengths, when compared to a more traditionally-aged college student. Another example could involve reviewing how students differentially participate in leadership learning under the current policy environments, including such legislature related to the Deferred Action for Childhood Arrivals program.

Socially just leadership educators are aware of human ecological development because identity development does not occur in isolation. For example, a student of color may feel tokenized when they are the only individual called on by the instructor to explain topics from a "diverse" perspective. Leadership educators can utilize the brave spaces framework in discussions by allowing individuals to contribute information freely and not target individuals because of their identities. That same student may feel isolated when they realize they are one of only a few students of color enrolled in the leadership certificate program and that they are often the only student of color in attendance at programs. To explore this, leadership educators can examine what factors contribute to students feeling welcomed or not welcomed to engage in the leadership certificate program and related activities. Utilizing a brave spaces framework, leadership educators have the ability to influence various systems in which students engage.

LEADERSHIP IDENTITY DEVELOPMENT

Identity is multidimensional; Hall (2004) observed "a healthy and authentic identity is one in which the components of subidentities are integrated" (p. 157). Leadership educators can use a brave space framework to help students examine how these identities interact. This can be accomplished through activities where students are encouraged to explore their various sub-identites and identify which are privilege and which are oppressed. Students can also explore how they were socialized in each identity and what norms were internalized as a result of socialization. This can be a powerful tool for leadership educators to use when discussing how identity can impact how a student views their leadership capacity and self-efficacy.

Day (2001) noted LID is individual and focuses on personal growth and understanding of self. Leader identity focuses on developing individual knowledge, skills, and abilities. Day and Harrison (2007) noted an individual is more likely to seek out experiences to develop the most salient leader identity. It further motives them to develop their leadership skills. This is why it is important for leadership educators to be intentional about the mechanisms in which these new capabilities are developed.

A recent shift in leadership theory centers how individuals develop identity as leaders. Komives, Owen, Longerbeam, Mainella, and Osteen (2005) developed the LID theory to understand the process individuals go through in the creation of leader identity. In 2006, the LID theory was expanded to the LID model in response to gaps in literature discussing how students develop self-efficacy to engage in the leadership process over time (Komives et al., 2005; Komives, Owen, Longerbeam, Mainella, & Osteen, 2006). The LID model was grounded in research concerning diverse student leaders (Komives et al., 2006). The LID model identified six developmental stages that students transition through to gain a deeper sense of leader identity. These stages include awareness, exploration/engagement, leader identified, leadership differentiated, generativity, and integration/synthesis. Environmental components move students along the stages (developing self, group influence, changing view of self with others, broadening view of leadership, and developmental influences) and transitions at the end of each stage represent shifts in thinking.

SOCIAL JUSTICE WORK THROUGH BRAVE SPACES AND LEADERSHIP IDENTITY DEVELOPMENT

The development of leader identity does not happen in isolation. Torres, Jones, and Renn (2009) explained identity is socially constructed, therefore; societal changes, including those on a campus environment, influence how one views self and others. Expanding on the work of Sanford (1966), Owen (2012) emphasized leadership educators must "... design intentional environments that provide the optimum level of support and challenge to spur development" (p. 18). To maximize these efforts, leadership educators apply the brave spaces framework at various stages in the LID model and within varied systems of human ecology. By applying the brave spaces framework in leadership education, leadership educators engage in social justice work.

Creating Brave Spaces in the LID Model

The LID model assists students across the lifespan of their LID. Socially just leadership educators are purposeful when creating environments where this development occurs by integrating knowledge, skills, and experiences in meaningful ways (Owen, 2012). Applying the brave spaces framework and social justice practices at various stages in the LID model, socially just leadership educators positively impact leader identity.

Stage 1: Awareness

Individuals at the Stage 1 view leadership as something separate from self. Adults can be seen as authority figures and leaders. Relationships between adults and students are important because adults teach norms, build confidence, and possibly model their involvement in leadership. Individuals in this stage have little recognition of a sense of self and are dependent on others. A transition from Stage 1 to Stage 2 happens when individuals recognize their potential to be involved in leadership.

At this level, individuals look within their microsystems to find adults who provide recognition and support. In a college setting, leadership educators can serve as these influencers by consciously engaging in developmental relationships with students. In these relationships, educators can role model vulnerability by sharing the process of their identity development and how their identities show up in the spaces they share with students. Leadership educators should be aware of how their own privileged and oppressed identities impact their ability to be vulnerable and recognize their students may have more to risk by engaging in these relationships.

At this stage students may not even see themselves as having leader potential so leadership educators can be influential in building a student's confidence as leaders. This can be accomplished by asking students to reflect about how they view leadership, who they think engages in the leadership process, and if they see themselves engaging in leadership. These reflections can be done on their own, in a group setting with peers, or in a one-on-one setting with the educator. Leadership educators can use a cultural autobiography assignment as an educational tool to encourage students to examine their self-awareness in regards to their cultural backgrounds (Brown, 2004). This assignment can motivate students' development of a critical consciousness and encourage exploration of the lenses through which their experiences are filtered. This assignment can be enhanced by asking students to explore what it means to be a leader or to engage in the process of leadership through their cultural filters. The process can reveal any potential risk or negative associations with leadership, which is useful knowledge for leadership educators to gauge foundational values or assumptions of leadership.

Stage 2: Exploration/Engagement.

Individuals in Stage 2 seek engagement with peers in group settings. An example of this could be joining organizations with similar interests as the individual. While individuals are engaging in these group settings, they are developing skills and building self-confidence. Individuals may begin to take on potential leadership responsibilities. While adults are still key influences in this stage, older peers begin to emerge as role models. Transitions from Stage 2 to Stage 3 begins when individuals recognize they have leadership potential and want to seek out new roles that demand increased skills needed for leadership.

At Stage 2, leadership educators leverage the power of peer influence. Trust is an important part of creating brave spaces. Leadership educators can examine the influence various social identities have on an individual and their interpersonal relationships. This can be examined through the mesosystems; the linkages between microsystems. Leadership educators can use cross-cultural interviews as an educational tool to expand an individual understanding of various worldviews (Owen, 2012). In cross-cultural interviews students listen to the narratives of those who have had different life experience and reflect on their process of learning, unlearning, and relearning what they know about various identities in order to build inclusive relationships. Leadership educators can also incorporate trust building exercises into group development activities. These activities can include conversations about vulnerability and teamwork.

Another way to build trust and support students entering the leadership process is through peer mentoring. Peer mentoring relationships can be through a formal program or through natural relationship building. Leadership educators can have conversations with members about the influence mentorship can have on someone's development and encourage group bonding. At this stage, leadership educators expose students to leadership and increase their skill set through increasing responsibilities in projects. For example, a student could volunteer to organize the sign-in table at a program and give input in how the sign-in process could be most effective. This opportunity may allow a student to build their confidence in their ability as a leader.

Stage 3: Leader Identified

Individuals in this stage believe leadership is primarily positional. They believe leaders are role models and solely responsible for accomplishing the goals of the group. There are two phases of this stage: emerging and immersion. In the emerging phase, individuals develop new skills and look to more experienced peers for ways to accomplish goals. As they progress through immersion, individuals become more comfortable with leadership and explore various ways of leading. In this stage, students relate to diverse peers while developing interpersonal skills. Leader identity in this stage is connected to one's role in the group: leader or follower. The transition from Stage 3 to Stage 4 involves understanding leadership as a process and how people must be interdependent to get tasks accomplished.

Leadership educators can apply various forms of the brave spaces framework at this stage and explore how relationships in an individual's microsystem can impact their development. To further develop interpersonal relationships between diverse groups, leadership educators can encourage sociocultural conversations between peers. This is important because individuals belong to multiple identity groups, which influence their development. Leadership educators can foster intergroup dialogue as an educational tool to examine these contextual influences. The goal of intergroup dialogue is to give groups the opportunity to seek understanding of various worldviews and discern how working across difference can create positive change. A social justice lens can be applied to intergroup dialogue by discussing how systems of oppression, power, and privilege influence one's worldview.

Leadership educators can encourage students to examine how their privileged and oppressed identities influence how they show up in the space and how this may impact their level of participation in the discussion. Ground rules are often established at the start of a discussion to encourage participants to create a space where they are able to be vulnerable and therefore able to participate. Arao and Clemens (2013) suggested reframing *don't take things personally*, a common safe space ground rule, by encouraging participants to *own your own intentions and your impact*. This shift in brave space language allows participants to realize that intent and impact are not always congruent and harm can occur to affected populations in the dialogue. This shift also allows participants to examine how certain privileged identities may minimize the risk associated with disclosure of identity, experiences, or opinions.

Leadership educators can also utilize critical reflection as an educational tool at this stage. Jacoby (2014) described critical reflection as "... the process of analyzing, reconsidering, and questioning one's experiences within a broad context of issues and content knowledge" (p. 26). Critical reflection reinforces principles of social justice by challenging students to investigate the context and conditions that influence their own perspectives and allows students to make connections within their experiences to create meaning and new ways of being. This can be explored through the chronosystem by examining how role, time, and sociohistorical circumstances influence the construction of knowledge. This can take place on an individual or group level. Individual reflection could be accomplished through exercises like journaling or meditation. Group processing can be accomplished through small group sharing, facilitated dialogue, or artistic creation. Dialogue journaling can be used as an educational tool to incorporate reflection on both an individual and group level (Brown, 2004). Dialogue journaling allows group members to comment on an individual's authored thoughts, experiences, or reflections. These comments can pose critical questions that may result in conflict. The brave spaces framework views conflict as a natural outcome of diverse groups and encourages continued dialogue to spur growth (Arao & Clemens, 2013).

Stage 4: Leadership Differentiated

Individuals in this stage see leadership as a process and disentangle positionality. The emerging and immersion phases are present in this stage. In the emerging phase, individuals begin to recognize leadership can come from anywhere in the group. In the immersion phase, individuals begin to become more concerned with building community and being an effective group member. An individual's identity as a leader begins to internalize. Self-awareness and working with diverse groups are more present and a new commitment to interdependence emerges. Coalition-building between groups with similar goals gains personal prominence. A transition between Stage 4 and 5 occurs when individuals want to serve a larger purpose or a transcendent goal. In this transition, individuals begin to mentor younger or less experienced peers in the leadership development process.

At Stage 4, individuals start to build coalitions with groups that have similar goals. Individuals may not have membership in each individual group but is impacted by how the groups come together to influence positive change. One programmatic way this can be actualized is through a conference. For example, many organizations can come together to present at a multicultural leadership conference. Attendees benefit from learning from various community members who may hold different identities. This conference can also provide an environment where groups connect to address various social issues in their campus community. Attendees can examine these social issues and what conditions in the exosystem and macrosystem of human ecology impact these issues. For example, attendees could examine how a bias-related incident towards one marginalized group on campus impacts the sense of belonging and safety among the other marginalized groups. This reinforces the idea that communities are interconnected and changes in one community could impact another community in the same environment.

Socially just leadership educators can also encourage students to incorporate the brave spaces framework into their spaces. For example, educators can model how setting ground rules for a discussion can create a space where individual viewpoints can feel heard, validated, and challenged in a way that is developmental. Leadership educators can also discuss what it means to internalize leader as a sub-identity and how that sub-identity intersects with other sub-identities.

Stage 5: Generativity

Individuals in Stage 5 are able to look beyond themselves and toward the welfare of others. They are concerned with the sustainability of their group so they seek to develop newer members through mentoring. Individuals in this stage have largely solidified their leader identity and are now able to reflect on their own LID. As a result, some seek to embed their leadership actions into long-term personal goals. Transition from Stage 5 to Stage 6 is marked by the ability to deeply reflect on their development and individuals seek to make meaning of their LID.

Leadership educators can examine how individuals in Stage 5 are influenced by and influence the overarching cultural system. In this stage, individuals realize the value of their participation in the leadership process and want to ensure the process is viable for others. Individuals can reflect on their leadership journey and identify who and what contributed to their development. Socially just leadership educators facilitate opportunities to sustain and invest in other individuals who want to engage in the leadership process. Through a social justice lens, individuals can critically reflect on their experiences and identify potential barriers they have faced or others may face in terms of engaging the leadership process. These barriers could exist on an individual, interpersonal, or systematic level. Activist action plans can be an educational tool leadership educators use to address some of these barriers (Brown, 2004). Activist action plans allow individuals to identify potential sources of conflict and create practical strategies for addressing them. This approach can be done on an individual level or on a group level.

At this stage, leadership educators are able to have meaningful conversations with individuals about their own development and how others influenced their development. They also have the opportunity to discuss how an individual's process of LID has influenced others aspect of meaning making. For example, engaging in the leadership process may have revealed to an individual that their responsibility to build others in their community can transcend beyond the leadership process and into other environments.

Stage 6: Integration/Synthesis

Stage 6 is centered on internalizing self-development and LID as lifelong processes. Individuals determine when their actions are congruent with their beliefs. Individuals in Stage 6 are able to apply their crystallized lenses into new context and new environments. This allows them to determine where to direct their efforts. They are also able to recognize the interdependence of groups in a system.

Leadership educators at this stage continue to orient their leadership education efforts through a human ecological systems lens. Capstone projects allow individuals to reflect on their developmental journey and how their experiences and relationships shaped their worldview of leadership. Students can also create plans for how they can continue to actively engage LID. Leadership educators can have conversations with students about how their synthesized identity as a leader can impact systems of power and oppression. Activist action plans can be utilized at this stage to engage students in the processes of deconstruction of societal norms based on dominant groups and reconstruct norms to address social change.

CONCLUSION

Weaving social justice into leadership education creates a foundation for social change, one that creates space for students to think, reflect, debate, and expand their worldview. The ability to influence the context in which students develop their identity as a leader, however, is a large responsibly. Acknowledging that individuals influence and are influenced by their environments, leadership educators have the choice to be intentional and critical about the context in which this development occurs. This requires a deep rethinking about the content, delivery, and assessment of leadership education.

Socially just leadership educators can utilize the brave spaces framework to support the creation of vulnerable environments where students are able to expand their self-awareness, identity development, and make meaning of their identity as a leader. These vulnerable environments involve taking risks for both the student and leadership educator involved in the leadership process. Taking risks may lead to positive outcomes like an increased sense of self or belonging. Since individuals apply their own labels and meaning to their identity, brave spaces framework encourages critical reflection on the development of identity. Students who engage in LID have the opportunity to create a positive association with being a leader.

REFERENCES

Adams, M. (2016). Pedagogical frameworks for stoical justice education. In M. Adams, L. A. Bell, & P. Griffin (Eds.), *Teaching for diversity and social justice* (3rd ed., pp. 15–33). New York, NY: Routledge.

Aroa, B., & Clemens, K. (2013). From safe spaces to brave spaces: A new way to frame dialogue around diversity and social justice. In L. M. Landreman (Ed.), *The art of effective facilitation: Reflections from social justice educators* (pp. 135–150). Sterling, VA: Stylus.

Astin, A. W., & Astin, H. S. (2000). *Leadership reconsidered: Engaging in higher education in social change.* Battle Creek, MI: W. K. Kellogg Foundation.

Baxter Magolda, M. B. (2001). *Making their own way: Narratives for transforming higher education to promote self-development.* Sterling, VA: Stylus.

Baxter Magolda, M. B., & King, P. M. (2004). *Learning partnerships: Theory and models of practice to educate for self-authorship.* Sterling, VA: Stylus.

Bell, D. (1995). Who's afraid of critical race theory? *University of Illinois Law Review 1995, 4,* 893–910.

Bronfenbrenner, U. (1981). *The ecology of human development: Experiments by nature and design.* Cambridge, MA: Harvard University Press. Retrieved from https://khoerulanwarbk.files.wordpress.com/2015/08/urie_bronfenbrenner_the_ecology_of_human_developbokos-z1.pdf

Bronfenbrenner, U. (1994). Ecological models of human development. In M. Guavian & M. Cole (Eds.), *Readings on the development of children* (2nd ed., pp. 37–43). New York, NY: Freeman.

Brown, K. B. (2004). Leadership for social justice and equity: Weaving a transformative framework and pedagogy. *Educational Administration Quarterly, 40*(1), 77–108.

Chunoo, V., & Osteen, L. K. (2016). Our purpose, mission, and context: The call for educating future leaders. In K. L. Guthrie & L. Osteen (Eds.), *New directions for higher education, No. 174: Reclaiming higher education's purpose in leadership development* (pp. 9–20). San Francisco, CA: Jossey-Bass.

Council for the Advancement of Standards in Higher Education. (2015). CAS Standards for leadership programs. In *CAS professional standards for higher education* (9th ed.). Washington, DC.

Crenshaw, K. (1991). Mapping the margins: Intersectionality, identity politics, and violence against women of color. *Stanford Law Review, 43*(6), 1241–1299.

Day, D. V. (2001). Leadership development: A review in context. *Leadership Quarterly, 11,* 581–613.

Day, D. V., & Harrison, M. M. (2007). A multilevel, identity-based approach to leadership development. *Human Resource Management Review, 17*(4), 360–373. Retrieved from https://www.sciencedirect.com/science/article/abs/pii/S105348220700054X

Dugan, J. P. (2017). *Leadership theory: Cultivating critical perspectives.* San Francisco, CA: Jossey-Bass.

Dugan, J. P., & Komives, S. R. (2011). Leadership theories. In S. R. Komives, J. P. Dugan, J. E. Owen, C. Slack, & W. Wagner (Eds.), *The handbook for student leadership development* (2nd ed., pp. 35–57). San Francisco, CA: Jossey-Bass.

Guthrie, K. L., & Jenkins, D. M. (2018). *The role of leadership educators: Transforming learning.* Charlotte, NC: Information Age.

Haber, P. (2011). Formal leadership program models. In S. R. Komives, J. P. Dugan, J. E. Owen, C. Slack, & W. Wagner (Eds.), *The handbook for student leadership development* (2nd ed., pp. 231–257). San Francisco, CA: Jossey-Bass.

Hall, D. T. (2004). Self-awareness, identity, and leader development. In D. V. Day, S. J. Zaccaro, & S. M. Halpin (Eds.), *Leader development for transforming organizations: Growing leaders for tomorrow* (pp. 153–176). Mahwah, NJ: Psychology Press.

Heifetz, R. A. (1994). *Leadership without easy answers.* Cambridge, MA: Harvard University Press.

Holley, L. C., & Steiner, S. (2005). Safe space: Student perspectives on classroom environment. *Journal of Social Work Education, 41*(1), 49–64.

Jacoby, B. (2014). *Service-learning essentials: Questions, answers, and lessons learned.* San Francisco, CA: Jossey-Bass.

Komives, S. R., Owen, J. E., Longerbeam, S. D., Mainella, F. C., & Osteen, L. (2005). Developing a leadership identity: A grounded theory. *Journal of College Student Development, 46,* 593–611.

Komives, S. R., Owen, J. E., Longerbeam, S. D., Mainella, F. C., & Osteen, L. (2006). A leadership identity development model: Applications from a grounded theory. *Journal of College Student Development, 47,* 401–418.

Lucas, N. (2009). The influence of integrative and interdisciplinary learning, In B. Jacoby (Ed.), *Civic engagement in higher education* (pp. 99–116). San Francisco, CA: Jossey-Bass.

Mainella, F., & Martinez Love, M. (2011). Curricular programs. In S. R. Komives, J. P. Dugan, J. E. Owen, C. Slack, & W. Wagner (Eds.), *The handbook for student leadership development* (2nd ed., pp. 259–286). San Francisco, CA: Jossey-Bass.

Owen, J. E. (2011). Considerations of student learning in leadership. In S. R. Komives, J. P. Dugan, J. E. Owen, C. Slack, & W. Wagner (Eds.), *The handbook for student leadership development* (2nd ed., pp. 109–133). San Francisco, CA: Jossey-Bass.

Owen, J. E. (2012). Using student development theories as conceptual frameworks in leadership education. In K. L. Guthrie & L. Osteen (Eds.), *New directions for student services, No. 140: Developing students' leadership capacity* (pp. 17–35). San Franscisco, CA: Jossey-Bass.

Rainey, M. A., & Kolb, D. A. (1995). Using experiential learning theory and learning styles in diversity education. In R. R. Sims & S. J. Sims (Eds.), *The importance of learning styles: Understanding the implications for learning, course design, and education.* Westport, CT: Greenwood Press.

Rost, J. C. (1991). *Leadership for the twenty-first century.* Westport, CT: Praeger.

Sanford, N. (1966). *Self and society.* New York, NY: Atherton Press.

Smist, J. A. (2011). Co-curricular programs. In S. R. Komives, J. P. Dugan, J. E. Owen, C. Slack, & W. Wagner (Eds.), *The handbook for student leadership development* (2nd ed., pp. 287–306). San Francisco, CA: Jossey-Bass.

Torres, V., Jones, S. R., & Renn, K. A. (2009). Identity development theories in student affairs: Origins, current status, and new approaches. *Journal of College Student Development, 50*(6), 577–596.

CHAPTER 15

THE ROLE OF LIBERATORY PEDAGOGY IN SOCIALLY JUST LEADERSHIP EDUCATION

Cameron C. Beatty and Amber Manning-Ouellette

Leadership as a field of study has many complexities built around social constructs, evolving need, and predominant scholars' voices guiding the direction of the discipline. The lineage of leadership studies knowledge indicates how we understand the current field and its constant evolution through the decades. It is clear that predominant voices steer the conversations around leadership, contributing to the needs and movements of each era; yet we question if and how the field of leadership education represents the lived experiences of all students and the current injustices facing society? This chapter will revisit those voices through a brief history to understand predominant theories that shape our knowledge of leadership.

Dugan (2017) acknowledged the use of critical theory and perspectives is "a direct response to scholarly calls for greater attention to issues of justice in leadership theory" (p. xvi). This chapter will add to the discourse and continue the call for a shift to more socially just leadership curriculum by leadership educators engaging in liberatory pedagogy. Finally, we highlight practical applications for developing socially just leaders through curriculum and classroom engagement by using critical case studies and questions for consideration.

This chapter contributes to the literature focused on moving toward a more socially just leadership praxis by offering a pedagogical approach; one that considers the complexity of leadership educators' identities and the learning spaces they operate within. Thoughtfully employing a liberatory pedagogy invites leadership educators to leverage critical and intersectional/systemic lenses. These lenses leverage personal experiences toward the interrogation and reconstruction of educational content, approaches, structures, and contexts. This chapter focuses on leadership theories, curriculum, and practice, and it may be useful for educators whose professional success and personal liberation are threatened by curricula rooted in Whiteness or oppressive learning environments.

HISTORY OF LEADERSHIP AS A FIELD OF STUDY

In 1978, James McGregor Burns called for a systematic approach to understanding leadership, insisting on the formal development of programs to transform trait leadership and understand leadership as a process (Burns, 1978). From this call, the identification of leadership as a body of knowledge, behaviors, and skills was born (Bryman, Collinson, Grint, Jackson, & Uhl-Bien, 2011; Harvey & Riggio, 2011; Stogdill & Bass, 1982). This conversation emerged through studies of individual traits and behaviors, managerial approaches, and positionality, while later voices framed leadership around shared commitment to change (Northouse, 2010; Rost, 1991).

Leadership studies moved toward scholarship and programs at postsecondary institutions over the past 35 years as well. With the need to produce skilled and competent individuals, leadership programs emerged in teaching theory and behavioral-based content (National Clearinghouse for Leadership Programs, n.d.; Riggio, 2011). Leadership education programs evolved in higher education alongside the study of leadership, with organizations and scholars adding to the dialogue. One of the first organizations to support the early leadership conversation was the American College Student Personnel Association (ACPA). Further, predominant scholars opened capacity around the study of student leadership (Astin & Astin, 2000; Komives, Owen, Longerbeam, Mainella, & Osteen, 2005; Komives, Wagner, & Associates, 2017; Kouzes & Posner, 2017). With gates open for student leadership development, leadership studies programs began to emerge in programmatic and academic formats.

Rise of Leadership Studies Programs

The 1970s saw the creation of the Center for Creative Leadership (CCL) and formation of the National Clearinghouse for Leadership Programs (NCLP) shortly followed in the late 1980s. Attention to these organizations, coupled with the leadership scholarship of Rost (1991), led to enhanced traction of leadership education in the United States. Further, movement toward formalizing academic programs increased during the 1980s and 1990s. Komives et al. (2011) indicated some of the early established leadership studies programs were instituted through private donor support at the University of Richmond and at Marietta College. Additionally, the first leadership studies doctoral program was established in 1979 at the University of San Diego (University of San Diego, n.d.).

As the leadership studies movement grew, formalized courses arose in several universities, including one of the first documented taught by Ronald Heifitz at Harvard University in 1983. Finally, the emergence of certificate and minor programs continued to solidify at universities such as Kansas State University and Fort Hayes University in the mid-1990s (Komives, 2011). By 2015, the International Leadership Association (ILA, 2015) identified more than 2,000 leadership programs in their database. Further, the NCLP inventoried over 18 universities that offered graduate degrees and 84 universities that offered undergraduate degrees in leadership studies.

Leadership scholars have created a common understanding of the goals and purpose of leadership education in higher education while also questioning historical theories which dominate narratives of who can be a leader and how leadership manifests (Dugan, 2017; Guthrie, Bertrand Jones, Osteen, & Hu, 2013; Komives et al., 2017). This questioning of leadership studies as a field has allowed for a critical examination of which voices are highlighted in leadership education curriculum and address whose voices are marginalized (Dugan, 2017).

Purpose of Leadership Studies Programs in Higher Education

Throughout history, there has been a great debate around the purpose of higher education on several fronts. The nature and knowledge of leadership is ever evolving, along with its role within higher education. In this section, we focus on the neoliberal views of higher education, addressing how leadership studies programs answer these viewpoints.

Over the past 15 years, higher education scholars argued the impact of neoliberalism on higher education (Aronowitz, 2000; Giroux, 2005; Kezar, 2004; Sanders, 2010). Kezar (2004) described postsecondary education through neoliberal ideology as focused on individual and economic gains.

Further, Sanders (2010) argued, "...what is new to the neoliberal university is the scope and extent of these profit-driven, corporate ends, as well as how many students, faculty, administrators, and policy makers explicitly support and embrace these capitalistic goals and priorities" (p. 55). In other words, higher education constituents continue to perpetuate the ideology of neoliberalism in university messaging and communication around the importance of particular majors that feed individual and economic gains. This forces professionals and families to advise students to choose majors and disciplines that will help students attain higher paying careers. The pressure to choose a major guaranteeing a high salaried career is inescapable as well as the conversation about involvement and specifically, leadership.

Scholars agree the development of future leaders is part of the purpose of higher education (Astin & Astin, 2000; Burkhardt & Zimmerman-Oster, 1999; Chunoo & Osteen, 2016; Council for the Advancement of Standards in Higher Education, 1999). Moreover, higher education's purpose involves the development of civically engaged individuals (Altbach, Gumport, & Berdahl, 2011; Bok, 2013). Leadership studies supports the market interest of higher education because of academic and programmatic focus on skill development, civic engagement, and the drive to hire individuals with leadership experience. Leadership training and education are valuable to employers and individuals as they traverse their career path and assume positions in the workforce (Kouzes & Posner, 2017). Recent survey results from the National Association of College and Employers (NACE) found that when deciding between two candidates who are equally qualified for a position, employers over the past 5 years have valued the candidates' majors and leadership experience above other factors (NACE, 2017). The development of future societal and workforce leaders is a key outcome for higher education.

Leadership programs leverage a wide array of academic frameworks to enhance students learning across disciplines. Moreover, leadership studies programs surpass neoliberal views of higher education through communitarian approaches; developing students as social change agents. Programs employ approaches such as the social change model of leadership development (Higher Education Research Institute, 1996), and adaptive leadership theory to develop curricula around systemic change (Heifetz, Grashow, & Linsky, 2009; Komives et al., 2017).

LEADERSHIP STUDIES THROUGH A CRITICAL LENS: DISRUPTING THE CENTERING OF WHITENESS

When social change and disrupting inequity are critical parts of teaching leadership, socially just educators question traditional programs designed under socially unjust leadership theories (Beatty & Tillapaugh, 2017;

Dugan & Komives, 2011). Socially just leadership faculty address these practices and teach critical consciousness of leadership, incorporating socially diverse learning environments, and model how to deconstruct Whiteness (Dugan & Komives, 2010; Guthrie et al., 2013; Mahoney, 2016).

Historically, leadership theories have omitted marginalized student identities, owing their emergence to research on White people as normative (Hage, 2012). Watt (2016) argued traditional leadership programs assume and operate from teaching cultural differences, yet this perspective reinforces a system of dominance and positions nondominant groups as "others." Further, Brunsma, Brown, and Placier (2012) highlighted how many predominantly White institutions perpetuate "White spaces" by constructing experiences and realities around Whiteness, limiting White students' exposure and engagement of other identities on campus and in the world. Mahoney (2016) also indicated introductory leadership courses do not include the voices of people of color in the curriculum. As faculty introduce and teach leadership concepts, the normalization of White supremacy is rampant in leadership philosophies and course design.

In recent years, leadership researchers have developed a critical stance on leadership theories, through examining the historically leader-centric approaches grounded in White supremacy (Chin, 2010; Dugan, 2017; Dugan, Jacoby, Gasiorski, Jones, & Choe Kim, 2007; Guthrie, Bertrand Jones, & Osteen, 2016). Established leadership theories emerged through a paradigm holding certain assumptions about realities of leadership (Dugan, 2017; Kezar, Carducci, & Contreras-McGavin, 2006). Given these assumptions, leadership theories are developed out of social construction. Dugan (2017) explained, "...social constructions often take-for-granted beliefs they function as powerful framers of reality for people and can be difficult to change" (p. 7). Subsequently, leadership theory and narratives perpetuate dominant group ideologies and ignore individual voices and experiences that do not reflect power positions, therefore upholding Whiteness (Chin, 2010; Dugan, 2017; Guthrie et al., 2016; Mahoney, 2016). The social construction of leadership maintains the dissemination of socially unjust ideologies to students enrolled in leadership programs unless faculty members are conscious and move toward critical perspectives of teaching leadership. Institutions should examine their leadership education programs, predominant theoretical frameworks driving programmatic design, and adopt more critical perspectives. Moreover, the succeeding section examines teaching socially just leadership and moving through resistance from students.

Understanding and Engaging in Liberatory Pedagogy

The goal of liberatory pedagogy is to provide a lens through which educators are more capable of examining, interacting with, and critiquing the politics of education (Sayles-Hannon, 2007). Liberatory pedagogy, which has roots in critical pedagogy (Freire, 1970; Giroux, 2006), refers to "educational theories and practices intended to raise learners' critical consciousness concerning oppressive social conditions" (Sayles-Hannon, 2007, p. 34). In critical pedagogy, students and educators reflect on structures of power and use the classroom as a place for the exchange of knowledge, in contrast to the "banking" style of teaching (Freire, 1998, p. 33). Freire's critical pedagogy continues to ask questions about the relationships between theory/practice and reflection/action as we consider power in our social institutions.

Liberatory pedagogy challenges educators, students, and administrators to recognize, engage, and critically examine undemocratic practices and institutions that maintain inequality and oppress identities (Sayles-Hannon, 2007). This method promotes the development of educational practices that encourage educators and students to critically examine and identify relationships of power, ideology, and culture; and then how this critical investigation can then inform praxis. In order to examine the diverse histories and perceptions of race, class, gender, ethnicity, sexuality, and nationality, it is imperative for students' and educators' voices to be heard. By engaging both the students' and faculty members' voices in classroom discussions, educators unchain themselves from traditional relationship restraints with students. By centering multiple voices and deconstructing the power dynamics in the classroom, new relationships are forged through engaging dialogue that moves towards liberation (Sayles-Hannon, 2007).

Engaging dialogue amongst educators and students has the potential to initiate processes of humanization. For Freire, "humanization is the goal of liberation; it has not yet been achieved, nor can it be achieved so long as the oppressors oppress the oppressed" (Weiler, 1991, p. 452). We believe liberatory pedagogy helps negotiate the terms of authority within the classroom, and throughout the ongoing development of student leadership capacity. Liberatory pedagogy seeks to empower and encourage students to formulate reflective communities in and outside of the classroom, confronting issues of social justice. As leadership educators facilitating the learning process in leadership studies programs, we feel strongly that this is an important step in our work to not only interrupt leadership theories rooted in Whiteness or from a White perspective, but also the racism and injustice that can be experienced inside the classroom. For developing and implementing a liberatory pedagogy in the field of leadership education we call for specific attention to curriculum development, pedagogical approaches, and learning assessment.

Considerations For Application

Perspectives from liberatory pedagogy are most effective when applied in multiple and varied ways; beyond informing educators instructional decisions. A comprehensive application of liberatory pedagogy helps to map and disrupt the presence and performance of power in the classroom and in society. Educators working to cultivate critical consciousness must curate liberatory learning spaces. A liberatory praxis calls for educators to think critically about their course content, teaching strategies, and course structure.

> When we try to change the classroom so that there is a sense of mutual responsibility for learning, students get scared that you are now not the captain working with them, that you are after all just another crew member and not a reliable one at that. To educate for freedom, then, we have to challenge and change the way that everyone thinks about pedagogical process. (hooks, 1994)

Socially just leadership educators critically review their approaches to learning in the classroom. Liberatory praxes challenge us as educators to critique our teaching approaches and ask questions: (a) Is my approach to the classroom as a facilitator of learning inclusive of all social identities?; (b) Do I have a process of understanding and checking my own unconscious bias in the classroom?; and (c) What scholarly voices are represented and highlighted in the curriculum and whose voices are marginalized or erased all together from the curriculum? These questions are vital for the critical self-reflection and self-awareness work needed to develop a liberatory praxis.

Liberatory approaches to leadership education encourage interventions empowering students to interrogate their own lives and exercise agency regarding the meanings they construct rather than being passive spectators in the learning interaction (Lakey, 2010; Love, 2013). Socially just leadership educators facilitate critiques of leadership models and theories as well as campus programs and activities embedded in dominant hegemony and Whiteness (Beatty & Tillapaugh, 2017). When programs and models promote a dominant narrative of leadership, they also reinforce constricted notions of masculine and feminine approaches to leadership practice which need to be modified to be more inclusive for all students (Beatty & Tillapaugh, 2017). The same needs to be said for race, ethnicity, ability, religious backgrounds, gender, and sexuality. By critically examining and calling out dominant approaches to leadership, all students are able to practice this skill in the classroom and should be challenged to apply this in their practice.

Teaching in a Divided America

Teaching in college classrooms has always been challenging; involving issues from classroom management, engaging critical thinking, connecting theoretical content to applied knowledge, and addressing resistance. The necessity of engaging in discussions around privilege and leadership in a divided world is vital if faculty want to move toward freedom from oppressive leadership practices (Watt, 2016). This work is critical in preparing future leaders to foster more inclusive and equitable spaces, but the toll on faculty is great. The work load doubles when teaching social justice—not only do faculty members engage in the critical consciousness of students—they engage in the examination of their own positionality as leadership faculty. hooks (1994) described this difficult work as meaning "that teachers must be actively committed to a process of self-actualization that promotes their own well-being if they are to teach in a manner that empower students" (p. 15). Leadership faculty must examine their positions of power and privilege, reflect on these roles, and move toward activism in the classroom.

The elevation of this responsibility during a time of opposition is a large call, but imperative, if faculty members seek liberation from oppressive systems of leadership. Considering and thinking through the resistance faculty might experience from students who have never been challenged in the classroom to consider power, privilege, and oppression is an important strategy to employ because these situations will happen. The better prepared faculty are to address resistance, the stronger the outcomes of liberation will be for all students. We provide a case study for you to consider your own process of navigating resistance in the classroom and questions to consider as you build your own liberatory praxis.

Case Study—Navigating Resistance

Jaclyn is a sophomore at a 4-year public university in the Midwest. She grew up on a rural cattle farm that her great-grandparents started and has been passed down for generations. The town Jaclyn grew up in has a population of 1,500 people and her high school graduating class had 50 people, all identifying as White. Jaclyn aspires to run the family farm one day and is majoring in animal science in the College of Agricultural Sciences and minoring in leadership studies. The university was a big step because it enrolls over 30,000 students from diverse backgrounds; much different than her rural town. She was nervous attending the university but enjoys its diversity and meeting new people.

For the Fall semester, Jaclyn enrolled in a university diversity course entitled LEAD 310: Leadership in a Diverse World. Her goal for taking the course and working on a leadership certificate is to develop her leadership capacity and identity in order to one-day successfully manage her family's farm. She anticipates the course will discuss diversity and how to be a better leader and feels comfortable because many of her peers are in the course with her. The course enrolls 30 students—the majority White and two students of color—and is taught in a traditional course face-to-face format.

During the course, Jaclyn reads several chapters and articles on social identities, models of cultural sensitivity, and White privilege (Johnson, 2006; McIntosh, 1988). She becomes irritated with the concept of White privilege because her family has always worked very hard on their farm and for all of their opportunities. She is offended that someone would say that she was *given* advantages because of her skin color. Jaclyn does not agree and resists reading the chapters, avoiding the course material, and stonewalling during in-class conversations.

During one class, the faculty member opened a discussion about privileged identities and leadership roles. The faculty member prompted the students to analyze their privilege through a "matrix of oppression" activity. Jaclyn reluctantly participated in filling out the matrix document. When discussion opened up to the class, Jaclyn was called upon to reflect on her experience with the activity. Her response included,

> well, I don't see color as an identifier of privilege, all people have the same struggles and it's those that choose to work hard that receive benefits and have success. Everyone is given the same opportunities to prove themselves in leadership. If you can't see someone for more than their race when leading, then you're the problem. It's like, gender and race shouldn't matter, like the scholarships that are designed for minority students. The color of your skin should not matter regarding attending a university or the money you are given for cost of attendance. That is a form of discrimination against people that are not minorities too. I was not able to receive a scholarship to attend this university because I am not a minority, this simply isn't fair.

Jaclyn was pleased with her response because many of her peers agreed and added their personal experiences around their hard work to get into college and pay for their personal vehicles and college expenses. The conversation became heated when a few students of color in the class challenged Jaclyn and her peers on the topic.

Questions for Consideration:

- How might the faculty member address the comments, honoring the introductory-level of the students' knowledge in the course? What would a liberatory pedagogical response include?

- What role should the faculty member take in challenging the identity politics and rurality of the majority of students?
- How might the faculty member deconstruct the students' oppressive comments while teaching to a point of critical thought?
- How does the faculty member support the students of color who might be impacted or offended by Jaclyn's comments?

Case Study—Intersecting Identities

Maria decided she would spend the early part of her summer on a Global Leadership study abroad program in Copenhagen, Denmark. Maria was nervous about the trip because she frequently required use of a wheelchair for transport. Before she went on the trip, Maria asked the faculty leaders if she would be able to navigate the city given her accessibility needs. The faculty leaders consulted and noted that there would be challenges due to the architecture of an older city and cobbled streets but overall, there would be support for her on the trip.

Maria, 17 other students, and two faculty members traveled for 1 month to Copenhagen as part of a Global Leadership study abroad. While abroad, students were enrolled in two courses: Global Leadership and Gender and Leadership as part of the leadership studies program. Maria is a communication studies major with a certificate in leadership studies with a goal of going into public relations.

After 1 week on the trip, Maria was noticeably tired, sad, and struggling with issues of group dynamics. Maria came to one of the faculty members with an issue, "I don't know if you know but I found out that on the first day that we were traveling through the airport, one of the other students said, 'I don't know why Maria came, she is going to be such an inconvenience.' The other students told me the other day and I feel like I am a burden here. It makes me feel like I don't deserve to be here." Maria wept as she explained that other students had told her because they were angry the other student had made the comment and wanted her to know. "It's a student I am rooming with so things are awful now." The faculty director and Maria discussed the course of actions to take to work through the situation. Fortunately, the courses for the trip addressed intersecting identities, specifically, ableism in leadership, which would open up broader discussions about privilege.

As the trip continued, the student that made the comment to Maria intentionally polarized herself from the rest of the students on the trip, not addressing her comment and the implications it had. This continued to impact group dynamics and participation in critical discussions of intersectional women's leadership. Students did not acknowledge the tension in the group and avoided confrontation.

Questions for Consideration:

- What was the role of the leadership faculty director as an advocate for socially just leadership approaches?
- What would teaching through controversy look like in this situation?
- How does the faculty member hold students accountable and work to build a more equitable experience for Maria?

When considering this case study and these questions we hope that you start to think through the process of developing your own liberatory pedagogy and praxis. What does working towards liberation in your own circle of influence look like for you? In the next section we offer some strategies for you to consider when teaching through resistance in the classroom.

STRATEGIES FOR TEACHING THROUGH RESISTANCE

In socially just leadership, faculty "name the elephant in the room" and work through resistance. The faculty in both case studies developed class-room spaces to identify issues and encourage students to analyze Whiteness and ableism, respectively. While students begrudgingly discussed Whiteness and ableism, they did so in safe ways; skirting the experience on the trip with Maria and discussing race generally with Jaclyn. Maria described her experiences on the trip but the other students avoided confronting specific individuals. The tension in the group dynamic continued until the end of the trip, affecting individual experiences, leaving Maria to feel ostracized by the other students. Jaclyn felt since she worked so hard White privilege was offensive to her and she was not afforded opportunities due to her race.

- *Extensive self-reflection with self and peers.* Faculty must engage in personal analysis of privilege and the intersections of background, experiences, and current roles. This is accomplished by journaling, reading current work that includes scholars of historically marginalized backgrounds, and analyzing personal experiences. Further, faculty should engage in critical conversations around diversity and social identities of students in their institutions, examining the limited cultural experiences of students.
- *Embracing vulnerability and mistakes.* Faculty must engage in difficult conversations that project bodies and voices into vulnerable situations. These vulnerable spaces must include colleagues and students. Noting that faculty will make mistakes in the classroom when discussing challenging topics is one way to align with vulnerability and embrace it. Acknowledging that faculty might not know the

"correct" answer is an initial dialogue that is important. Identifying uncomfortable or controversial dialogue and making meaning of it, models vulnerability and identifies humility.

- *Focus energy on the students that are on the fence.* Students at the cusp of critical consciousness are not always identifiable; however, focusing energy on those who are minimally engaged helps breathe movement into a sea of resistance. This does not mean that faculty should avoid resisting students. It does mean that while reflecting on difficult discussions from the course, focusing on the malleable students invites more creative thinking, positivity, and drive for faculty to continue to teach through controversy.

- *"Call in" all students.* We need educators to "call in" or challenge students who are performing oppressive forms of leadership or ascribing to only dominant narratives or theories on what it means to be a leader and ask these students why they are choosing to engage in these ways that often marginalize others. By "calling in" students through liberatory pedagogy, radical change in the power relationships that show up in leadership can be acknowledged and named in order for students to develop personal strategies to address oppressive forms of leadership practice (Beatty & Tillapaugh, 2017).

CONCLUSION

Love (2013) argued "a liberatory consciousness enables humans to live their lives in oppressive systems and institutions with awareness and intentionality, rather than on the basis of the socialization to which they have been subjected" (p. 601). Important empirical outcomes demonstrate students engaged in social justice and diversity work have greater efficacy for socially responsible leadership (Dugan & Komives, 2010). In the field of leadership studies, developing critically reflective students who strive for social change will result in socially just societal leaders that are continuing to move towards liberation in addressing all social inequities. Liberatory pedagogy calls for leadership educators to unlearn the oppression they themselves are products of, and in some ways, are socialized to reproduce. When leadership educators ascribe to working towards liberation in the classroom, there is an attendant expectation for them to help change their institutions, departments, programs, and other structures to promote campus climates that are liberatory in nature and egalitarian in practice. As leadership educators, modeling the process of resisting and responding to racism, sexism, ableism, homophobia and other injustices in the classroom is vital to creating and sustaining a liberatory pedagogy. Student leaders then follow this model of resisting and responding in their own practice of leadership.

REFERENCES

Altbach, P. G., Gumport, P. J., & Berdahl, R. O. (2011). *American higher education in the twenty-first century: Social, political, and economic challenges.* Baltimore, MD: The Johns Hopkins University Press.

Aronowitz, S. (2000). *The knowledge factory: Dismantling the corporate university and creating true higher learning.* Boston, MA: Beacon Press.

Astin, A. W., & Astin, H. S. (2000). *Leadership reconsidered: Engaging higher education in social change.* Battle Creek, MI: W. K. Kellogg Foundation.

Beatty, C.C., & Tillapaugh, D. (2017). Masculinity, leadership, and liberatory pedagogy: Supporting men through leadership development and education. In P. Haber-Curran & D. Tillapaugh (Eds.), *New directions for student leadership series, No. 154: Critical perspectives on gender and student leadership* (pp. 47–58). San Francisco, CA: Jossey-Bass.

Bok, D. (2013). *Higher education in America.* Princeton, NJ: Princeton University Press.

Bryman, A., Collinson, D., Grint, K., Jackson, B., & Uhl-Bien, M. (2011). *The SAGE handbook of leadership.* Thousand Oaks, CA: SAGE.

Brunsma, D. L., Brown, E. S., & Placier, P. (2012). Teaching race at historically White colleges and universities: Identifying and dismantling the walls of Whiteness. *Critical Sociology, 39,* 717–738.

Burkhardt, J. C., & Zimmerman-Oster, K. (1999). How does the richest, most widely educated nation prepare leaders for its future? *Proteus, 16*(2), 9–12.

Burns, J. M. (1978). *Leadership.* New York, NY: Harper & Row.

Chin, J. L. (2010). Introduction to the special issue on diversity and leadership. *American Psychologist, 65,* 150–156.

Chunoo, V., & Osteen, L. K. (2016). Our purpose, mission, and context: The call for educating future leaders. In K. L. Guthrie & L. Osteen (Eds.), *New directions for higher education, No. 174: Reclaiming higher education's purpose in leadership development* (pp. 9–20). San Francisco, CA: Jossey-Bass.

Council for the Advancement of Standards in Higher Education. (1999). CAS standards for leadership programs. Washington, DC: Author.

Dugan, J. P. (2017). *Leadership theory: Cultivating critical perspectives.* San Francisco, CA: Jossey-Bass.

Dugan, J. P., & Komives, S. R. (2010). Influences on college students' capacity for socially responsible leadership. *Journal of College Student Development, 51,* 525–549.

Dugan, J. P., & Komives, S. R. (2011). Leadership Theories. In S. R. Komives, J. P. Dugan, J. E. Owen, C. Slack, & W. Wagner (Eds.), *The handbook for student leadership development* (pp. 35–57). San Francisco, CA: Jossey-Bass.

Dugan, J. P., Jacoby, B., Gasiorski, A., Jones, J. R., & Choe Kim, J. (2007). Examining race and leadership: Emerging themes. *Concepts & Connections, 15,* 13–16.

Freire, P. (1970). *Pedagogy of the oppressed.* New York, NY: Continuum.

Freire, P. (1998). Pedagogy of freedom: Ethics, democracy, and civic courage. Lanham, MD: Rowman & Littleman.

Giroux, H. (2005). The terror of neoliberalism: Cultural politics and the promise of democracy. Boulder, CO: Paradigm.

Giroux, H. A. (2006). *The Giroux reader.* Boulder, CO: Paradigm.

Guthrie, K. L., Bertrand Jones, T., & Osteen, L. (Eds.). (2016). *New directions for student leadership,* No. 152: *Developing culturally relevant leadership learning.* San Francisco, CA: Jossey-Bass.

Guthrie, K. L., Bertrand Jones, T., Osteen, L., & Hu, S. (2013). Cultivating leadership identity and capacity in students from diverse backgrounds. *ASHE Higher Education Report, 39*(4). San Francisco, CA: Jossey-Bass.

Hage, G. (2012). *White nation: Fantasies of White supremacy in a multicultural society.* New York, NY: Routledge.

Harvey, M., & Riggio, R. E. (2011). *Leadership studies: The dialogue of disciplines.* Cheltenham, England: Edward Elgar.

Heifetz, R., Grashow, A., & Linsky, M. (2009). *The practice of adaptive leadership: Tools and tactics for changing your organization and the world.* Cambridge, MA: Harvard Business Press.

Higher Education Research Institute. (1996). *A social change model of leadership development guidebook* (Version III). Los Angeles: University of California, Los Angeles.

hooks, b. (1994). *Teaching to Transgress.* New York, NY: Routledge.

International Leadership Association [ILA]. (2015). *Leadership program directory.* Retrieved from http://www.ila-net.org/Resources/LPD/index.htm

Johnson, A. G. (2006). *Power, privilege, and difference* (2nd ed.). New York, NY: McGraw-Hill.

Kezar, A. (2004). Obtaining integrity? Reviewing and examining the charter between higher education and society. *The Review of Higher Education, 27*(4), 429–459.

Kezar, A. J., Carducci, R., & Contreras-McGavin, M. (2006). Rethinking the "L" word in higher education: The revolution in research on leadership. *ASHE Higher Education Report, 31*(6). San Francisco, CA: Jossey-Bass.

Komives, S. R. (2011). Advancing leadership education. In S. R. Komives, J. P. Dugan, J. E. Owen, C. Slack, W. Wagner, & Associates (Eds.), *The handbook for student leadership development* (2nd ed., pp 1–34). San Francisco, CA: Jossey-Bass.

Komives, S. R., Dugan, J. P., Owen, J. E., Slack, C., Wagner, W., & Associates. (2011). *The handbook for student leadership development* (2nd ed.). San Francisco, CA: Jossey-Bass.

Komives, S. R., Owen, J. E., Longerbeam, S. D., Mainella, F. C., & Osteen, L. (2005). Developing a leadership identity: A grounded theory. *Journal of College Student Development, 46*, 593–611.

Komives, S. R., Wagner, W., & Associates. (2017). *Leadership for a better world: Understanding the social change model of leadership development.* A publication of the National Clearinghouse for Leadership Programs. San Francisco, CA: Jossey-Bass.

Kouzes, J., & Posner, B. (2017). *The leadership challenge: Five practices for becoming an exemplary leader (6th ed.).* San Francisco, CA: Jossey-Bass.

Lakey, G. (2010). *Facilitating group learning: Strategies for success with adult learners.* Hoboken, NJ: Wiley.

Love, B. (2013). Developing a liberatory consciousness. In M. Adams, W. J. Blumenfeld, C. Castaneda, H. Hackman, M. Peters, & X. Zuniga (Eds.), *Readings for diversity and social justice* (3rd ed., pp. 601–606). New York, NY: Routledge.

Mahoney, A. D. (2016). Culturally responsive integrative learning environments: A critical displacement approach. In K. L. Guthrie, T. Bertrand Jones, & L. Osteen (Eds.), *New directions for student leadership, No. 152: Developing culturally relevant leadership learning* (pp. 47–59). San Francisco, CA: Jossey-Bass.

McIntosh, P. (1988). White privilege: Unpacking the invisible knapsack. *Independent School, 49*(2), 31–53.

National Clearinghouse for Leadership Programs. (n.d.). *Curricular programs.* Retrieved from https://nclp.umd.edu/resources/CurricularPrograms.aspx

National Association of Colleges and Employers. (2017, August). *Major the key factor between otherwise equal candidates.* Retrieved from https://www.naceweb .org/talent-acquisition/internships/major-the-key-factor-between-otherwise -equal-candidates/

Northouse, P. G. (2010). *Leadership: Theory and practice.* Thousand Oaks, CA: SAGE.

Riggio, R. E. (2011). Is leadership studies a discipline? In M. Harvey & R. E. Riggio (Eds.), *Leadership studies: The dialogue of disciplines* (pp. 9–19). Cheltenham, England: Edward Elgar.

Rost, J. C. (1991). *Leadership for the twenty-first century.* Westport, CT: Praeger.

Sanders, D. B. (2010). Neoliberal ideology and public higher education in the United States. *Journal for Critical Education Policy Studies, 8*(1), 41–77.

Sayles-Hannon, S. J. (2007). Feminist and liberatory pedagogies: Journey toward synthesis. *The International Journal of Diversity in Organizations, Communities and Nations, 7*(2), 33–42.

Stogdill, R. M., & Bass, B. M. (1982). *Stogdill's handbook of leadership: A survey of theory and research, revised and expanded.* New York, NY: The Free Press.

University of San Diego. (n.d.). *History and facts.* Retrieved from https://www.sandi-ego.edu/soles/about-soles/history-and-facts.php

Watt, S. K. (2016). The practice of freedom: Leading through controversy. In K. L. Guthrie, T. Bertrand Jones, & L. Osteen (Eds.), *New directions for student leadership, No. 152: Developing culturally relevant leadership learning* (pp. 35–46). San Francisco, CA: Jossey-Bass.

Weiler, K. (1991). Freire and a feminist pedagogy of difference. *Harvard Educational Review, 61,* 449–474.

CHAPTER 16

CREATING COCURRICULAR SOCIALLY JUST LEADERSHIP LEARNING ENVIRONMENTS

Kathy L. Guthrie and Jane Rodriguez

Higher education is constantly called upon to prepare future leaders. Chunoo and Osteen (2016) argued higher education must reclaim the distinctive role of leadership development in students. In fact, leadership learning has become central to educators in American postsecondary institutions (Dugan, 2006; Thompson, 2006). Mission statements for colleges and universities have increasingly focused on creating future leaders, which often requires realigning the purpose, mission, and context of postsecondary education with student leadership learning (Chunoo & Osteen, 2016). Although collegiate educators and advisors are frequently positioned to provide leadership learning opportunities for students, they are often unsure how to carry it out. These leadership learning opportunities occur in both curricular and cocurricular environments.

Through all of the learning opportunities we are called upon to create, we are developing leaders: ethical leaders in various industries, community leaders who create social change, and global leaders who will work

Changing the Narrative, pages 245–258

across nations for the common good. However, serious questions around how the learning opportunities we develop reflect the diverse populace of our nation and world abound. These questions include: Do we focus leadership learning opportunities on collaborative learning practices which place social justice at the forefront? Do we identify opportunities in cocurricular spaces for deep socially just leadership learning? This chapter focuses on leadership learning in cocurricular spaces, and places educators in the role of conduit rather than distributor. We discuss how creating culturally relevant leadership learning (CRLL) environments is critical for socially just leadership education and provide strategies for socially just leadership educators and advisors in creating such contexts.

LEADERSHIP LEARNING AND EDUCATION

Merriam and Caffarella (1999) described learning as "a process by which behavior changes as a result of experiences" (p. 250). Leadership itself is a process of learning where individuals make meaning from their experiences, seek to discover leader identities within themselves, and work collaboratively in communities of practice with others (Antonacopoulou & Bento, 2004). Higher education has historically been a place of curricular and cocurricular learning. However, these experiences are sometimes developed by giving priority to teaching and instructional strategies over placing focus on learning processes. Postsecondary education should focus on learning; when learning is at the heart of education, student- and learning-centered approaches emerge (Barr & Tagg, 1995). This learner-centric focus places educators in the role of conduit of knowledge rather than distributor. Being a conduit in this sense requires personal responsibility for development, attention to collaborative learning practices, and the construction of inclusive learning communities (Guthrie & Jenkins, 2018).

We define leadership learning as changes in knowledge, skills, attitudes, behavior, and values resulting from educational experiences; both cocurricular and curricular in nature, associated with the activity of leadership (Guthrie & Jenkins, 2018). Leadership development and leader identity development are vital to leadership learning. Guthrie, Bertrand Jones, Osteen, and Hu (2013) provided distinctions between the two: "Leader development focuses on individual students' capacity and identity, with or without formal authority, to engage in the leadership process... [and]... leadership development is a collective focus on a group's relationships and process" (p. 15). With this in mind, leadership learning can be understood as a dynamic process where individuals influence, and are influenced by, interactions, experiences, and reflection. The definition of leadership learning we have presented creates opportunities for more creative and intentional approaches to designing, implementing, and assessing educational opportunities, with specific implications in cocurricular contexts.

Groundbreaking scholarship regarding educators' approaches to leadership learning was represented by Roberts and Ullom's (1989) model of training, education, and development; the TED model. Guthrie and Osteen (2012) expanded the TED model by adding engagement as essential to learning leadership. Further augmenting these works, Guthrie and Jenkins (2018) proposed a leadership learning framework that educators and advisors can use both conceptually and in practice to create programs that focus on the learner and the learning that can occur. The six aspects of leadership learning include knowledge, development, training, observation, engagement, and metacognition, all within the context of leadership (Guthrie & Jenkins, 2018).

As seen in Figure 16.1, by using the metaphor of a steering wheel, the leadership learning framework proposed by Guthrie and Jenkins (2018) provides educators a clear depiction to understand the multiple ways students can learn leadership. It also provides a mechanism for students to take control and steer their own learning. Some students might not have ever experienced a sense of empowerment in their personal learning; socially just leadership educators take into account experiences of all students, including students of color in supporting and empowering their own leadership learning journeys.

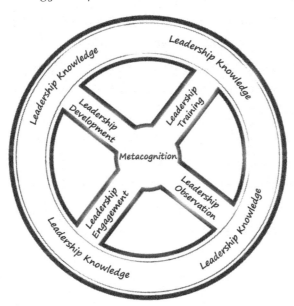

Figure 16.1 Leadership learning framework. Reprinted from Guthrie & Jenkins, 2018.

The six aspects of leadership learning—knowledge, development, training, observation, engagement, and metacognition—are separately and collectively powerful in the leadership learning journey. Leadership knowledge encompasses the entire wheel, as the knowledge of theories and concepts are foundational for all leadership learning. Knowledge is adjoined to all of the other aspects of leadership learning because knowledge acquisition generally occurs in all programs; from using traditional leadership language and concepts to the creation of new models and approaches. Working in from the rim of leadership knowledge are the four aspects of development, training, observation, and engagement, which all contribute to metacognition.

As previously mentioned, the leadership knowledge aspect of the leadership learning framework mainly entails the acquisition of knowledge about the process of leadership. Leadership development refers to intrapersonal aspects of leadership learning. This is where learning focuses on the individual, including, but not limited to personal needs and values, identity, motivation and readiness to lead, and multiple other dimensions of self (Guthrie & Jenkins, 2018). Leadership training focuses on the skill- and competency-based behavioral aspects of learning. Frequently, cocurricular leadership programs are built around aspects of leadership training (Guthrie & Jenkins, 2018). Leadership observation, which is constructivist in nature, refers to the social, cultural, and perceived aspects of leadership learning. Through observation, learners make meaning about interactions of effective and ineffective leaders and followers related to social and cultural contexts. Leadership engagement refers to the interactional, relational, experiential, and interpersonal aspects of leadership learning where the learner is an active participant. The aspects of knowledge, development, training, observation, and engagement all lead into metacognition. Metacognition is central to leadership learning because without critical reflection of the learning experience, learners cannot make meaning from the multitude of learning experiences or begin to apply what was learned.

Connecting the leadership learning framework to context is important in creating environments where socially just leadership education can occur. Learning is a personal journey, involving developmental readiness (Reichard & Walker, 2016), leadership capacity, motivation, efficacy, and enactment (Dugan, 2017), as well as identity (Jones, 2016). Each of these are vital to intentionally creating leadership learning opportunities that are culturally relevant for all participants. To these ends, we draw from the CRLL model (Bertrand Jones, Guthrie, & Osteen, 2016).

CULTURALLY RELEVANT LEADERSHIP LEARNING

The CRLL model (Bertrand Jones et al., 2016) incorporates leader identity, capacity, and efficacy in conjunction with the contextual dimensions of campus climate as well as the broader environmental social climate. CRLL challenges previous paradigms of leadership education, prompting innovative ways of engaging diverse students in leadership learning. This model directs leadership educators to use leadership learning to confront the complexities of social inequality. CRLL recognizes the power inherent in leadership, drawing attention to use of language, as well as how institutional culture and climate influences students' identity, capacity, and efficacy.

Identity, capacity, and efficacy are vital components of CRLL regarding how one understands themselves. Identity is socially constructed but grounded in historical, political and cultural forces (Jones & Abes, 2013). Capacity is students' knowledge, abilities, and skills related to the processes of leadership (Dugan, 2017). Efficacy is the internal belief of success when engaging leadership (Bandura, 1977). Identity, capacity, and efficacy are intertwined and motivate students to engage in the leadership process (Reichard & Walker, 2016).

Guthrie, Bertrand Jones, and Osteen (2017) used the metaphor of a house when operationalizing CRLL. In Figure 16.2, identity, capacity, and efficacy act as doorways into engagement. Learners enter into a space of creating positive change through the understanding of identity, capacity, and efficacy. The architectural structure of the house is the organizational climate. Understanding of the organizational climate builds off the work of Hurtado, Milem, Clayton-Pedersen, and Allen (1999) and Milem, Chang, and Antonio (2005). The five domains that create the architectural structure of the house are (a) historical legacy of inclusion/exclusion, (b)

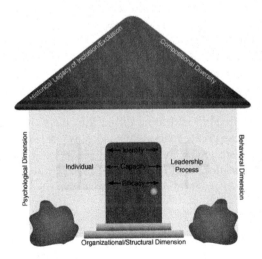

Figure 16.2   The culturally relevant leadership learning model. Reprinted from Guthrie, Bertrand Jones, & Osteen, 2017.

compositional diversity, (c) psychological climate, (d) behavioral climate, and (e) organizational/structural aspects. In reflecting on how we build a house, structural components are vital; a solid floor, walls, and roof provide a solid, or not so solid, foundation. These domains of CRLL push educators to consider the importance of individuals' experience of broader organizational climate, and how one engages in the leadership learning context. CRLL provides a framework in which educators can operationalize to transform leadership programs and organizations; building houses where everyone is included.

Advisors and educators acknowledge the tools students bring which come in the shape of their own knowledge, skills, and lived experiences (Ladson-Billings, 1995). Socially just leadership educators use these individual gifts to empower and encourage leader identity, capacity, and efficacy. It is the role of educators and advisors to invest in the development of all students and validate their knowledge and lived experiences as strengths rather than weaknesses. Through this process, they can "...acknowledge the ways leadership identity intersects with other dimensions of identity such as race, culture, sexual orientation, gender, religion, and social class" (Owen, 2012, p. 29). While we continue to understand the intersections of identity with leader identity, it is important to embrace the power of socially just leadership education.

STRATEGIES FOR SOCIALLY JUST LEADERSHIP EDUCATORS AND ADVISORS

As we create and foster environments where socially just leadership learning and development occurs, we offer strategies for educators and advisors to build upon. In institutions where formal academic leadership education does not exist, it is the role of student organization advisors to develop student leaders in cocurricular settings. Since this is a responsibility that falls between both roles as advisors are "...the primary support for students in their leadership emergence" (Rosch & Collins, 2017, p. 13), our recommendations honor ways both leadership educators within the classroom and advisors beyond the classroom can create spaces where socially just leadership can occur. As we provide these strategies, we encourage readers to reflect on practices at their current institutions and determine if these strategies are already in place, opportunities to enact them, or develop action plans to support them.

Setting the Foundation

A robust foundation of leadership learning for students is one of the most important concepts to develop. As discussed earlier, this includes six aspects of leadership learning including knowledge, development, training, observation, engagement, and metacognition (Guthrie & Jenkins, 2018). In areas where in-class leadership education does not exist, it is the role of the advisor to provide a foundation of information that is congruent with all student leaders. This allows for a shared knowledge and language resulting in all students having an understanding of leadership. Within the classroom, leadership educators are able to provide this foundation of knowledge, and emphasize that this education can also happen beyond the classroom. It is imperative for all leadership educators to work together to ensure that this shared knowledge is consistent among all platforms, whether or not in-class leadership education exists.

Additionally, leadership educators and advisors are encouraged to analyze leadership learning through a socially-just lens. How does leadership emerge among students from diverse backgrounds? How can we can take these perspectives into consideration when planning, implementing, and assessing leadership education? Through education, we can encourage students to consider how the lived experiences, perspectives, and truths of those with differing identities allow for a greater understanding of leadership. These are the first steps in ensuring that socially just leadership learning is occurring. As education is an ongoing process, educators and advisors can transition into leadership training, which focuses on developing specific skills that can be practiced inside and outside of the classroom. Outside of the classroom, leadership training is focused on specific moments of time such as retreats or role training often associated with positional roles that allow students to gain an understanding of their responsibilities as a leader. Inside the classroom, this training can shift to gaining skills on how to facilitate conversations, building relationships with peers, or developing an awareness to socially just issues. Both of these training techniques can take place in any environment.

Leadership development requires facilitation from educators and advisors to reinforce how knowledge gained from educational experiences, and skills obtained from training, are strengthened through reflection. These reflections encourage students as they reach new levels of self-awareness and move toward increased self-efficacy. Reflection is an essential component of leadership learning which, "...can result in greater self-awareness and self-knowledge that then contributes to more effective choices in terms of actions, behaviors, and emotional self-regulation over time (Avolio & Hannah, 2008, p. 338). Additionally, reflection allows for increases in developmental readiness; "...how prepared an individual is to benefit and learn from a developmental experience" (Day, Harrison, & Halpin, 2009, p. 16). The introspection attendant to reflection prompts student leaders to develop meaning around their experiences. Furthermore, during reflective exercises, students gain clarity on their own identities, and their identity as a leader, and are in turn better equipped to create inclusive environments.

Leadership engagement is the last component of leadership learning and connects theory to practice. While knowledge acquisition and skill development is in progress, students can apply their leadership learning in innovative ways. Engagement can translate into the roles students play in an organization or program, or can manifest through final projects encompassing all of their leadership learning. It may appear in form of activism initiatives or service projects intended to challenge inequity and promote socially just environments. As leadership educators and advisors establish themselves as conduits of socially just leadership learning, it is important to recognize the intersections of varied identities with leader identity.

Once the foundation is established, it is important to consider how this leadership learning is occurring in a socially just environment. One approach to creating such environments is to promote and advocate for the representation of differing identities in every capacity. This representation can appear in the form of leadership educators, professors, administrative roles, teaching assistants, advisors, and other higher educational professional positions. The importance of having a diverse staff is often underestimated. From students' perspectives, seeing individuals with similar identities as them in leadership positions, increases their self-efficacy and reduces imposter syndrome. Imposter syndrome has been described as:

> ...feeling like a fake, or [holding] the belief that one does not deserve his or her success or professional position...attributing success to luck, that is, to other external reasons and not one's internal abilities; and discounting their success, or the tendency to downplay to disregard achievement of success. (Dancy & Brown, 2011, p. 615)

Imposter syndrome can affect any student, but is commonly seen in first-generation students or members of marginalized populations (Sherman, 2013). The representation of individuals with multiple diverse identities in these roles allow for the sharing of salient experiences, which may result in these professionals advocating for a diverse student leader population. For students, being able to relate to an educator, advisor, or a mentor in multiple ways can greatly impact their learning, development, and persistence at institutions of higher learning.

Representation of Marginalized Populations

While representations of diverse backgrounds among the people students communicate with regularly is critical, this diversity must translate into the makeup of student leaders and student organizations. Socially just leadership educators advocate for students from marginalized populations to see themselves as leaders, act in accordance with that self-perception, and secure positional leadership roles. In order to accomplish this, it is important to review the language and imagery used in student-facing materials; from websites to leadership position applications and marketing items, just to name a few. Careful consideration of messaging is essential to socially just leadership education in curricular and cocurricular initiatives.

For example, in leadership position applications, what language is used to encourage all students to apply? Is there anything that can hinder a student from a marginalized population to apply? Take a look at where these applications are being promoted and who the targeted audience might be. If these applications are not being promoted in spaces where marginalized populations are present, then it is probable that not many students from these populations will apply for these positions. Additionally, analyze any images shown on a website, flyer, or even social media. Are these images demonstrating the creation of inclusive spaces? Do you see students from different backgrounds in these images? This lack of presence can be a factor that discourages students from participating in certain offices or organizations. It is vital to intentionally seek out members of these student populations and encourage them to obtain roles and participate in opportunities to help the office create and sustain socially just spaces.

Use of Language

Socially just leadership educators are mindful of their own language. Creating inclusive and socially just spaces starts with leadership educators and how they wield their language to remain true to their mission. Language has a deep impact on how a space is created and how others perceive that space. It is important to take into consideration how language is always evolving and work toward staying abreast of those changes. Taking it upon themselves to stay consistently informed and willing to adapt, socially just leadership educators are role models to their students on how to strive for inclusive environments. Something as simple as attaching one's personal pronouns to email signatures, or offering similar descriptors whenever one is introduced publicly, are simple but impactful examples of productively using language to foster socially just environments. As leadership educators, "... being aware of developmental differences by race, gender, sexual orientation, and other identity categories helps... facilitate the development of leaders in student organizations" (Kezar, Avilez, Drivalas, & Wheaton, 2017, p. 47). Socially just leadership educators intend to be conscious of what is said to students in every environment; whether at events, meetings or even one on one interactions to demonstrate how important it is to be respectful in spaces where leadership learning happens.

Additionally, socially just leadership educators listen to the language used by students and leverage that information to decipher how they perceive themselves. Are they constantly putting themselves down or empowering themselves? What is their internal dialogue? Are their behaviors self-sabotaging? Or are they constantly finding ways to grow? (Sherman, 2013). Cultivating spaces for students to discuss thoughts and feelings with someone they trust is important. We can encourage students to seek help through other venues, but having an understanding of how to help student leaders through imposter syndrome is an important tool.

Combating this phenomenon opens the door for students from marginalized population to enter environments where socially just leadership learning can take place with less fear of failure. Through leadership opportunities, students can develop stronger senses of self and gain confidence in their abilities. As students get involved, they "...experience threefold levels of growth—as their skills improve, their leadership self-efficacy grows as well, given the real-world impact they see...their motivation to lead increases as well" (Rosch & Collins, 2017, p. 17). When we introduce marginalized students to these environments, the impact can be everlasting and encourages other similar students to confidently be a part of this community as well.

Creating Socially Just Spaces

The spaces students occupy can directly influence how they view leadership, who they interact with, and what they learn. Spaces can be anything from a classroom to a student organization meeting, to events hosted by student organizations or the institution itself. In these settings, "...students can learn from their peers, incorporate new perspectives, and practice new behaviors" (Rosch & Collins, 2017, p. 10) in addition to sharing and reflecting personal stories and experiences. Areas in which most leadership learning occurs involves challenging experiences, being able to learn from other people, or through the use of formal leadership programs. The majority of these learning opportunities are accessible through student clubs or organizations and "...serve as environments where students learn how to lead, either through the experiences that they encounter or through their interactions with others in these situations" (Sessa et al., 2017, p. 24). Student organizations are impactful environments that promote growth and development within all of their members.

Students in these environments are able to interact with students that may have differing identities, resulting in diverse perspectives. Experiencing this change, "...leaders begin to internalize how their perspective is not the only valid one and how their particular demographic profile and experiences shape their outlook and way of doing things" (Sessa et al., 2017, p. 25). Giving students the opportunity to learn from others and be challenged in their own perspective is an effective way to experience dissonance leading to growth and advocacy for socially just environments. Accordingly, office culture and climate should also be considered.

Inclusive environments need to be taken into consideration not only within office climate, but within institutions as well. By being intentional and understanding the identities and needs of student leaders and student organizations, "...institutions can foster the intersectionality of identities that students bring to different leadership opportunities" (Kezar et al., 2017, p. 49). If there is an absence of inclusive environments, socially just offices and their institutions consider and implement assessment of how campus climate impacts student development, including the presence or absence of leadership opportunities. Allowing spaces for students of all identities to engage in these opportunities, have conversations surrounding social justice, or feel welcome can greatly increase the presence of these student populations (Kezar et al., 2017).

Diversity of Programming

In order to better achieve socially just leadership learning environments, we must look at the events that are being planned both by the students and for the students. Once all of these factors such as representation of staff, diverse student leaders, and the role language takes is taken into consideration, we must analyze whether or not the programs or initiatives that are being created are representative of the student body. Assessing the breadth of identities present at events is an indicator of whether or not programs or initiatives are connecting with multiple student populations. Socially just leadership educators carefully review the events that are hosted by their student organizations and institutions. Are they events that would appeal to different identities? An effective way to plan programs that will get the attention of students with different identities would be to cosponsor or collaborate with different campus partners and other student organizations. For example, if your organization would like to plan an event for Hispanic Heritage Month, consider collaborating with identity-based student organizations (e.g., Hispanic/Latinx Student Union). Connecting with these organizations cannot only help students within those organizations to develop themselves as leaders, but allows all student leaders to interact with others that have perspectives different from their own.

Through programs and initiatives, educators and advisors fill gaps where socially just leadership opportunities do not usually occur. Fostering such environments leads to increased engagement among students. Collaborating across organizations aids all involved, "...because identity-based organizations may not always be well connected to traditional leadership development offices, it may take extra effort for leadership educators to engage with them" (Kodama & Laylo, 2017, p. 78). Supporting these organizations invites students in these identity-based organizations to feel welcome and included on campus. Additionally, this prevents repetitive programming and could lead to the sharing of funds and resources to promote the growth of each organization. Collaborations are an effective way to reach out to students that would have been otherwise unaware of the types of organizations on campus. The best way to successfully integrate and produce diverse programming is to connect with an array of organizations that bring different experiences and perspectives to the table.

CONCLUSION

Educators and advisors have responsibility in creating socially just leadership learning environments in cocurricular spaces. By serving as conduits of creating these spaces, socially just leadership education will become the standard. As discussed in this chapter, the leadership learning framework (Guthrie & Jenkins, 2018) and the CRLL model (Bertrand Jones et al., 2016) are helpful in building socially just leadership learning opportunities beyond the classroom. Being intentional about representation of marginalized populations, being conscious of language and imagery used, and being deliberate about how space is created for all learners are avenues for creating socially just leadership education in cocurricular spaces. As educators and advisors we cannot do this work alone. We need to build coalitions and caucuses of colleagues who also do this work. Only together can we change the narrative toward socially just cocurricular leadership education.

REFERENCES

Antonacopoulou, E. P., & Bento, R. F. (2004). Methods of "learning leadership": Taught and experiential. In J. Storey (Ed.), *Leadership in organizations: Current issues and key trends* (pp. 81–102). London, England: Routledge.

Avolio, B. J., & Hannah, S. T. (2008). Developmental readiness: Accelerating leadership development. *Consulting Psychology Journal: Practice and Research, 60*(4), 331–347.

Bandura, A. (1977). *Social learning theory.* Englewood Cliffs, NJ: Prentice Hall.

Barr, R. B., & Tagg, J. (1995). From teaching to learning—A new paradigm for undergraduate education. *Change: The Magazine of Higher Learning, 27*(6), 12–26.

Bertrand Jones, T., Guthrie, K. L., & Osteen, L. K. (2016). Critical domains of culturally relevant leadership learning: A call to transform leadership programs. In K. L. Guthrie, T. Bertrand Jones, & L. Osteen (Eds.), *New directions for student leadership, No. 152: Developing culturally relevant leadership learning* (pp. 9–22). San Francisco, CA: Jossey-Bass.

Chunoo, V., & Osteen, L. K. (2016). Our purpose, mission, and context: The call for educating future leaders. In K. L. Guthrie & L. Osteen (Eds.), *New directions for higher education, No. 174: Reclaiming higher education's purpose in leadership development* (pp. 9–20). San Francisco, CA: Jossey-Bass.

Dancy, T. I., & Brown, M. I. (2011). The mentoring and induction of educators of color: Addressing the impostor syndrome in academe. *Journal of School Leadership, 4*, 607–634.

Day, D. V., Harrison, M. M., & Halpin, S. M. (2009). *An integrative theory of leadership development: Connecting adult development, identity, and expertise.* New York, NY: Psychology Press.

Dugan, J. P. (2006). Involvement and leadership: A descriptive analysis of socially responsible leadership. *Journal of College Student Development, 47*(3), 335–343.

Dugan, J. P. (2017). *Leadership theory: Cultivating critical perspectives.* San Francisco, CA: Jossey-Bass.

Guthrie, K. L., Bertrand Jones, T., & Osteen, L. (2017). The teaching, learning, and being of leadership: Exploring context and practice of the culturally relevant leadership learning model. *Journal of Leadership Studies, 11*(3), 61–67.

Guthrie, K. L., Bertrand Jones, T., Osteen, L. K., & Hu, S. (2013). *Cultivating leader identity and capacity in students from diverse backgrounds: ASHE Higher Education Report, 39*(4). Hoboken, NJ: Wiley.

Guthrie, K. L., & Jenkins, D. M. (2018). *The role of leadership educators: Transforming learning.* Charlotte, NC: Information Age.

Guthrie, K. L., & Osteen, L. (Eds.). (2012). *Developing students' leadership capacity.* (New Directions for Student Services, Number 140). Hoboken, NJ: Wiley.

Hurtado, S., Milem, J., Clayton-Pedersen, A., & Allen, W. (1999). *Enacting diverse learning environments: Improving the climate for racial/ethnic diversity in higher education. ASHE Higher Education Report, 26*(8).

Jones, S. R. (2016). Authenticity in leadership: Intersectionality of identities. In K. L. Guthrie, T. Bertrand Jones, & L. Osteen (Eds.), *New directions for student leadership, No. 152: Developing culturally relevant leadership learning* (pp. 23–34). San Francisco, CA: Jossey-Bass.

Jones, S. R., & Abes, E. S. (2013). *Identity development of college students: Advancing frameworks for multiple dimensions of identity.* San Francisco, CA: Wiley.

Kezar, A., Avilez, A. A., Drivalas, Y., & Wheaton, M. M. (2017). Building social change oriented leadership capacity among student organizations: Developing students and campuses simultaneously. In D. M. Rosch (Ed.), *New directions for student leadership, No. 155: The role of student organizations in developing leadership* (pp. 45–58). San Francisco, CA: Jossey-Bass.

Kodama, C. M., & Laylo, R. (2017). The unique context of identity-based student organizations in developing leadership. In D. M. Rosch (Ed.), *New directions for student leadership, No. 155: The role of student organizations in developing leadership* (pp.71–82). San Francisco, CA: Jossey-Bass.

Ladson-Billings, G. (1995). Toward a theory of culturally relevant pedagogy. *American Educational Research Journal, 32*(3), 465–491.

Merriam, S. B., & Caffarella, R. S. (1999). *Learning in adulthood: A comprehensive guide.* San Francisco, CA: Jossey-Bass.

Milem, J. F., Chang, M. J., & Antonio, A. L. (2005). *Making diversity work on campus: A research-based perspective.* Washington, DC: Association American Colleges and Universities.

Owen, J. E. (2012). Using student development theories as conceptual frameworks in leadership education. In K. L. Guthrie & L. Osteen (Eds.), *New directions for student services, No. 140: Developing students' leadership capacity* (pp. 17–35). San Francisco, CA: Jossey-Bass.

Reichard, R. J., & Walker, D. O. (2016). In pursuit: Mastering leadership through leader developmental readiness. In R. J. Reichard & S. E. Thompson (Eds.), *New directions for student leadership, No. 149: Leader developmental readiness: Pursuit of leadership excellence* (pp. 15–25). San Francisco, CA: Jossey Bass.

Roberts, D., & Ullom, C. (1989). Student leadership program model. *NASPA Journal, 27*(1), 67–74.

Rosch, D. M., & Collins, J. (2017). The significance of student organizations to leadership development. In D. M. Rosch (Ed.), *New directions for student leadership, No. 155: The role of student organizations in developing leadership* (pp. 9–20). San Francisco, CA: Jossey-Bass.

Sessa, V. I., Alonso, N., Farago, P., Schettino, G., Tacchi, K., & Bragger, J. D. (2017). Student organizations as avenues for leader learning and development. In D. M. Rosch (Ed.), *New directions for student leadership, No. 155: The role of student organizations in developing leadership* (pp. 21–32). San Francisco, CA: Jossey-Bass.

Sherman, R. O. (2013). Imposter syndrome: When you feel like you're faking it. *American Nurse Today, 8*(5), 57–58.

Thompson, M. D. (2006). Student leadership process development: An assessment of contributing college resources. *Journal of College Student Development, 47*(3), 343–350.

CHAPTER 17

INFUSING LEADERSHIP EDUCATION IN ADVISING IDENTITY-BASED ORGANIZATIONS

Danielle Morgan Acosta

Leadership education continues to be a pivotal component of the undergraduate experience. It supports the development of students who are leaders: prepared and willing to engage in creating positive change in our local and global communities. Leadership education is a vital component of developing active citizens and successful alumni. Recently, much of leadership education has focused on learning taking place outside of formalized organizational positions, highlighting leadership as a process of working together towards change, regardless of title. This distinction has been pivotal in engaging more students in leadership learning processes. The expansion of opportunities for students to participate in leadership education and development through more inclusive ways, such as leadership studies programs, has been a hallmark of many campuses (Guthrie, Bertrand Jones, Osteen, & Hu, 2013). However, leadership educators sometimes may work

Changing the Narrative, pages 259–275

in silos of their programs and services, while many student organizations and advisors continue to operate from a management and task-oriented framework. It is necessary for student organization advisors to work in conjunction with other leadership educators, and as leadership educators themselves, through organizational advising processes.

This chapter seeks to highlight the importance of organizational advisors knowing and applying a leadership education framework to their work with student organizations and offer concrete examples grounded in leadership to achieve that goal. Identity-based student organizations and their advisors are examined in detail, as such organizations on college campuses engage diverse student populations and have missions focused on advocating for real change and social justice. Often identity-based student organizations are comprised of students unwilling to take on the title of leader, yet also eager to have a political voice, advocate for their peers, explore their identity, or share experiences with those that are similar to them (Ozaki & Johnston, 2008). Supporting these students in the leadership process and helping them develop their leader identities furthers many institutions' missions in creating a more socially just world. It is within these organizations advisors can influence and support students' leader identity development through education. Situating advisors within these experiences and calling for a shift in how advising is framed is a critical next step for higher education professionals.

LEADERSHIP DEVELOPMENT IN HIGHER EDUCATION

The concept of leadership has been defined and debated in a variety of academic contexts. A postindustrial approach to leadership can be defined as an interactive process of leaders and followers coming together in an influence relationship to solve problems or create positive change (Guthrie et al., 2013; Rost, 1993). With or without formal titles or positions of authority, and absent an election or selection team, students can come together to create change. Leadership hinges on relationships and a collaboration of individuals working together for a common purpose, the interactions of those individuals, and the experiences that take place as they come together (Komives, Lucas, & McMahon, 2013). Leadership education can occur inside and outside the classroom, focusing on theoretical understandings of leadership, groups, communities, personal identity development, and change.

Expanding the conversation regarding *who* participates in leadership and *how* are critical components to understanding leadership education (Bertrand Jones, Guthrie, & Osteen, 2016). Engagement in leadership processes and reflection of students as leaders is vital to leader identity development. Student organizations may be focused on positional leaders who help manage organizations, support structure, and create accountability, but they are also ripe for engaging relationship building and challenging the process. Leaders are not born, but made. Similarly, while not limited to organizations and positional roles, these structures provide opportunities for learning and reflection, where students gain leadership skills, knowledge, and capacity.

As participants in leadership education, students learn to recognize and identify themselves as a leader. Komives, Owen, Longerbeam, Mainella, and Osteen's (2005) leadership identity development (LID) model described stages students move through as they develop leader identities. Each stage describes how students view themselves as they broaden their views on leadership, develop meaningful involvement, and learn from influence relationships with influential others. The model highlighted moments, often within groups such as student organizations, where students engaged leadership as part of their journey. As students develop their leader identity, they further engage in the processes of leadership (Guthrie et al., 2013).

Leader identity can be supported and engaged by leadership educators and advisors alike through celebrations or rituals, relationships and mentoring, engaging in new challenges, and taking time to reflect and self-assess (Bertrand Jones et al., 2016). Identity development can also inform students' capacity, or "the knowledge, skills, and attitudes" to lead (Dugan, Kodama, Correia, & Associates, 2013, p. 6). The Multi-Institutional Study of Leadership, a multi-year research project that has engaged over 300,000 students worldwide, found experiences such as leadership positions and membership in student and off-campus organizations, sociocultural conversations with other students, mentoring relationships, and community service are critical in building leader capacity in students (Multi-Institutional Study of Leadership, 2017).

Leadership can be learned by all students; although often, students must believe they have the ability and capacity to engage leadership prior to doing so. Leadership self-efficacy can be developed through interactive experiences, role modeling, supportive peers and mentors, emotional cues, and positional leadership roles (Bandura, 1997; Bertrand Jones et al., 2016; Dugan et al., 2013). Acknowledging motivation, ability, and support to engage in leadership is critical in helping students develop efficacy, capacity, and leader identity (Reichard & Walker, 2016; Rosch & Villanueva, 2016). Understanding and cultivating leadership developmental readiness within the context of the campus climate and community is necessary.

Culturally relevant leadership educators are keenly aware of the institutional history of inclusion or exclusion, compositional diversity of the campus, psychological and behavioral climates, and structural aspects of campus (Bertrand Jones et al., 2016; Milem, Chang, & Antonio, 2005; Reichard & Walker, 2016). Often, identity-based organizations exist in response to historical injustices or hostile campus climates, and are best understood through lived experiences of their current and previous memberships. The purposes of these student organizations can be leveraged towards social justice and help students learn to lead.

INVOLVEMENT AND IDENTITY-BASED STUDENT ORGANIZATIONS

Involvement in on-campus student organizations has long been regarded as an important aspect of the collegiate experience (Astin, 1984, 1993; Pascarella & Terenzini, 2005). Organizations play an important role in participation and engagement outside the classroom, and aid in supporting a sense of belonging for students. Research has shown individual participants in student organizations increased skills and learned behaviors related to the intended outcomes of a college education, such as networking and practical competency skills, increased affective and cognitive learning through problem-solving, and self-confidence (Dunkel & Schuh, 1998; Pascarella & Terenzini, 2005). Such involvement has become a central component of student affairs work, with formalized registration processes for student organizations and opportunities for students to engage within a variety of different types of groups (Dunkel & Schuh, 1998).

The involvement opportunities students from marginalized backgrounds seek, and have access to, are often social identity-based student organizations, particularly at predominantly White institutions. It is within such groups they can initially engage in exploring leadership in different ways than they have before. As college campuses become more diverse, identity-based student organizations play not only a critical role in students' identity development tied to race, ethnicity, sexual orientation, or gender but their leader identity development as well. Having a clearer understanding of the role identity-based student organizations play on campuses, and for students involved in them, helps connect concepts of leadership education and advising of these important change-agent organizations on college campuses.

Frequently, identity-based organizations are rooted in complex activist, collective, or service framework as well as operate as counter-spaces for students from historically marginalized identities; particularly at predominantly White institutions (Bordas, 2013; Solorzano, Ceja, & Yosso, 2000). These organizations offer opportunities for students to come together with those from similar life experiences to create community, building upon their cultural histories and shared experiences. Students in these organizations may develop strong connections with alumni, learn about historical figures in their campus community with the same identity, and carve out spaces that make them feel like they belong. Identity-based organizations not only solidify space for individuals who share these identities within the campus framework, but may be the home or family for students searching for community or a sense of belonging within the collegiate environment (Arminio et al., 2000; Komives et al., 2005).

For students, salient identities are often tied to their minority status, and shape the organizations in which they participate (Jones, 1997). Engaging collectively with peers who share social identities often leads organizations to have a core purpose of community and advocacy that may look different from other student organizations. Students engaged in identity-based organizations may feel a strong weight or responsibility to the group. They are often invested in their organizations' creating safer campus spaces for their peers and advocating for changes that will affect their community positively. While marginalized students engage in a variety of organizational opportunities throughout their collegiate career, they often seek participation in identity-based organizations for their involvement as they relate to a student's psychosocial identity with regards to race, ethnicity, sexual organization, gender, or veteran status (Guiffrida, 2003; Harper & Quaye, 2007; Renn & Ozaki, 2010).

Studies have examined students' participation in identity-based organizations, explaining gains in their own individual identity development. Guiffrida (2003) found African American student organizations aided students in social integration, established peer connections, as well as fostered a culture of giving back to the community at a predominantly White institution. Similarly, Inkelas' (2004) work showed a positive impact of students' commitment to their own racial or ethnic community due to participation in identity-based organizations. Guardia and Evans' (2008) study of Latino men in an identity-based fraternity found involvement increased students' sense of their Latino identity, and opportunities to interact with similar others as a way to strengthen their connection to culture, the institution, and each other. In examining Black male participation at six predominantly White institutions, Harper and Quaye (2007) learned identity-based organizations provided opportunities for student identity development and expression. Involved students mentioned the importance of uplifting their community, fighting stereotypes, breaking down barriers, working to have their voices heard, paving the way for others, while also engaging with majority students and developing cross-cultural communication skills.

Museus (2008) found identity-based student organizations aided in the development of individual skills for Black and Asian students at predominantly White institutions. He also found organizations supported cultural adjustment to college for marginalized students by creating spaces of cultural familiarity, cultural validation, and opportunities for advocacy and cultural expression. Identity-based organizations aided students in finding connections across campus and giving them a sense of belonging, which could be translated to supporting adjustment to collegiate life, social involvement, and academic persistence. By facilitating adjustment and community for students of color, these organizations were critical in the collegiate experience and success of student participants (Museus, 2008).

Identity-based student organizations pursue social justice and allow students to develop within their marginalized identities and leader identity (Museus, 2008; Onorato & Musoba, 2015; Renn & Ozaki, 2010). When applying the LID model to students involved in LGBT organizations, Renn and Bilodeau (2005) found students developed their leader identity while expanding their identities as LGBT persons. The multifaceted growth and development of students provided opportunities for learning about their personal identities and developing their leader identity. Such organizations may also lend themselves to concepts of leadership from the collectivist, activist, and service framework in which they were created and through which they continue to function (Bordas, 2013). The sense of responsibility students feel to their identity-communities provides a critical opportunity to connect their collegiate experience, personal identity, and LID (Arminio et al., 2000; Renn & Bilodeau, 2005).

Identity-based organizations seem to have deeper purposes than the often-studied importance of involvement and engagement for students. By their nature and their participants, they serve a critical purpose for marginalized communities on and off campus; helping students to find a voice and community, particularly at predominately White institutions (Museus, 2008; Ortiz, 2004; Ozaki & Johnston, 2008). Rooted in social justice, identity-based organizations have already been found to be epicenters for identity development and student learning. Ultimately, there are numerous benefits to being involved on campus and being active in identity-based student organizations. Critical too, are the advisors who work or volunteer to support these student experiences, and in turn, support student learning and development. By training advisors to infuse fundamental components of leadership education into their advising processes, more learning and development can take place. Advisors can cultivate student leaders within their identity-based student organizations and help fill a void in leadership education.

STUDENT ORGANIZATIONAL ADVISING
IN AMERICAN HIGHER EDUCATION

Identity-based student organizations are often advised by student affairs administrators working in multicultural affairs, student activities, or student governance offices and roles. However, at some institutions, faculty members or other college staff who share an identity with the group may serve as advisors to organizations, either formally or informally (Dunkel & Schuh,

1998). While much research has been dedicated to students' participation in student organizations, little formalized training exists for most advising roles. In an extensive study of student affairs administrators, DeSawal (2007) found most learn how to advise by relying upon their personal experiences as a student and professional, utilizing trial and error strategies throughout their careers. Many institutions have handbooks or manuals outlining policies, but they often take a practical or institutionally-specific managerial approach, and may not necessarily engage in the process of advising or leadership.

The same can also been seen in the majority of advising resources available more broadly. The preeminent advising manual, Dunkel and Schuh's (1998) *Advising Student Groups and Organizations*, first published in the 1990s and updated in 2014, focuses on practical necessities of advising; particularly in the ever-changing policy landscape of higher education. The book is a skill-based resource for advisors regarding functions, group dynamics, balancing student and institutional interest, financial management, and legal issues. *Advising Student Groups and Organizations* engages advisors' roles in student organizations and addresses how to support students and needs of the institution simultaneously. This transactional approach provides practical advice and examples to professionals working with student organizations.

By focusing on functions of advisors, *Advising Student Groups and Organizations* does not fully engage experiential learning and identity development that takes place in student organizations. Leader identity and leadership development is briefly mentioned with regards to organizations based on Hersey and Blanchard's (1988) and Kouzes and Posner's (1987) work regarding leaders and followers, influence, and effective organizations, but identity is not mentioned in the original manual (Dunkel & Schuh, 1998). Examples of helping students identify expectations of each other and motivations to participate are good tools for advisors to use. Yet, further education, dialogue and training regarding advising and infusing leadership and leader development can further move organizations to mobilizing together for social change.

Dunkel and Spencer's (2006) *Advice for Advisers* is situated in residence hall government advising, particularly within the National Association of College and University Residence Halls (NACURH). While still a beneficial tool in the "nuts-and-bolts matters of advising" (Dunkel & Spencer, 2006, p. xi) and more focused on advisor development and interactions with group members, the book serves a practical purpose, utilizing case studies and sample documents to aid advisors. Focused on residential environments, and written by seasoned organizational advisors, the training manual provides actionable skills and knowledge of expectations and some information on group dynamics and advising styles. It is mostly situated for entry-level professionals who would advise a hall government or engage in their first advising experience.

Both resources, perhaps the most widely used resources in the field, provide information to aid advisors and help them function within organizations. However, there is little expansion or discussion of leadership, leader identity, or identity-development through organizations; either in general or the specific role of the advisor in supporting these processes. Leadership, when mentioned, is loosely defined. Although there are brief discussions of the importance of diversity and role of advisors within those organizations, social justice is not mentioned. Practical skills and information provided in these resources regarding responsibility, training, effectiveness, financial management, and organizational models are beneficial, but leave a gap in the resources available to student organization advisors to help aid and create more meaningful engagement and development for students (Dunkel & Schuh, 1998; Dunkel & Spencer, 2006).

Identity-Based Organization Advising

Advising resources for identity-based organizational advisors are even more limited than the tools previously reviewed. Most additional resources focus on cultural nuances and encourage advisors to be more knowledgeable about how students identify, the developmental models associated with the group, and the cultural values important to those students (Delgado-Romero & Hernandez, 2002). Ozaki and Johnston (2008) call for professionals to support multiracial identity-based student organizations in ten ways, focusing on vision and goals, advocating for their students, supporting students as they navigate politics, creating opportunities for dialogue. Writing from personal experiences of advising a Latino student organization, Delgado-Romero and Hernandez (2002) challenged advisors of identity-based organizations to foster leadership among their students and to understand their critical role in engaging racism and oppression on campus. Identity-based student organization advisors are already being called upon to move beyond management and exude cultural competence to help students manage and maneuver systems that weren't designed for their success in the first place. Equally important, and yet seemingly missing, is the call for leader development and leadership education.

Professional Competency

The most recent student affairs professional association competencies may not necessarily join concepts of advising, leadership, and social justice in salient ways for identity-based student organization advisors. The revised ACPA/NASPA Professional Competencies (2015) refocused advising student organizations under the "advising and supporting competency." The name change expands administrators' roles while also engaging students in the process. In labeling administrators as facilitators of learning, advisors are called to actively listen, engage students, challenge and support students, be knowledgeable of legal and technological issues, intuitively examine group dynamics, and support goal setting within the organization. Separately, the Leadership competency calls student affairs administrators to shape leadership learning through education, training, development and engagement. The social justice and inclusion competency encourages administrators to incorporate social justice and inclusion through all areas of their practice (ACPA/NASPA Professional Competencies, 2015). This may include defining social justice and leadership, reflecting on personal experiences, and engaging in the dismantling of oppressive systems and practices on campus.

Organizational advisors must engage themselves and their students in leadership education and social justice. Combining advising, leadership, and social justice allows for culturally relevant leadership learning, understanding, and practice to be possible (Bertrand Jones et al., 2016). Ending systematic oppression should be a goal for all student affairs administrators and student organizations; identity-based organizations and their advisors perhaps most naturally lend themselves to such a goal based on their natures and histories.

Advisors must be trained and educated not only on technical and legal skills, or the cultural tensions and climate of a campus, but as leadership educators. The additional insight, knowledge, and experiences called upon for identity-based student organization advising is already felt and acknowledged, and leadership learning can be readily added to this role. With all of the information regarding benefits of student organizations in general, and identity-based organizations in particular, it is a disservice that more active and engaging training and learning opportunities do not exist for advisors. Conversations regarding the roles advisors serve, such as mentor, supervisor, teacher, leader, and follower (Dunkel & Schuh, 1998) organically lend themselves to being developed through a leadership lens.

Advisors—and leadership educators broadly—are missing an essential opportunity to infuse leadership education into experiential learning and identity development within social identity-based student organizations. Students engage with organizations as their full selves, and their identities, leader identity, and understanding of leadership and change can be developed through the experiences they have in these organizations. Weaving identity and leader development into identity-based student organizations has beneficial outcomes and can be accomplished with a clear focus of advisors as active facilitators of the learning process.

CALL FOR ACTION

Student participation in positional leadership is one component of their leader development. Nonetheless, it serves as a critical step in the process. When advisors are skilled and knowledgeable in leadership development, education principles, and the identity development of leaders, they are better able to train, motivate, support, and engage students in the interactive processes of leadership. Roles of advisors are continually changing based on the needs of students and their organizations. A perpetually critical element of advising student organizations is organizational management; however, of similar importance is developing students, understanding their role in leadership processes, and identity as a leader. Advisors can work to infuse not only basic training into their work with student organizations, but a better understanding of leader education, training, development, and engagement in their practice (Guthrie & Osteen, 2012). This section outlines some fundamental ways advisors, particularly those of identity-based student organizations, can be leadership educators.

Advisor Individual Leadership Learning and Training

Advisors must first engage themselves in learning about leadership. They should be able to articulate their definition of leadership, and understand the history of the term, as well as examples that exist within and outside of structural organizations and positional roles. Awareness of the LID model, leadership developmental readiness, relational leadership model, and work such as the multi-institutional study of leadership allows advisors to be equipped to engage students in developing their leader capacity, efficacy, and identity, while continuing to support student efforts within their identity-based organization to create change on campus (Komives et al., 2005; Komives et al., 2013; Rost, 1993; Thompson & Reichard, 2016; Dugan et al., 2013).

Personal work and investment in leadership concepts, when infused with identity-based and cultural knowledge, produces advisors who are able to better support learning and involvement of students engaged on campus. An understanding of culturally relevant leadership learning and more diverse approaches to leadership allows for additional tools to shape the learning experiences for all students engaged in the process (Bertrand Jones et al., 2016; Bordas, 2012). Advisors who serve as leadership educators believe leadership can be learned, and that they facilitate opportunities for students to engage and learn about it (Owen, 2012). In order to do so, they must practice and engage in leadership themselves; constantly learning, being, and doing as practitioners and as leaders (Komives et al., 2013).

Infusing Leadership Education in the Executive Board

Equipped with leadership knowledge, advisors can infuse leadership learning into many activities within identity-based organizations. Defining a leadership paradigm with students focused on people in relationship to others can occur on a daily basis, during executive board meetings, and as the group develops a common vision. A discussion of the history of leadership with involved students can facilitate the processes of engagement in leadership in novel ways. When advisors believe leadership can and should be taught, each conversation continues to build upon the last; challenging students' thinking and acting within the realm of their positions to move closer toward creating change with others. There will be times when management—not leadership—is at the forefront of organizational actions. Striking a healthy balance allows advisors to guide conversations about important parts of leadership and management processes, helping students critically think and learn through each event and decision. The benefit of advisors facilitating leadership education within organizations is those conversations can occur in more meaningful ways, specifically those tied to the individual's identity development.

Many advisors already embark on trainings or retreats with their student organizations. However, just as advisor training can move beyond transactional tasks and liability, so can organization retreats and trainings. For identity-based organizations, trainings must not only explain roles and responsibilities of each position, but also embrace the history and social context of the identity-based group, both nationally and on a particular campus. Acknowledging the political climate, and giving voice to the collective experience of students, is critical in establishing agency, trust, and a common purpose. Beyond roles and expectations of individuals in positions and traditional bonding exercises, advisors-as-leadership-educators can engage students around issues in leadership (e.g., goals and vision setting), and how to connect with others. By intentionally organizing retreats infused with leadership education outcomes, personal reflection, and assessment, many activities can take on multiple purposes and lay the groundwork for LID and engagement in the leadership process.

An example of how advisors may begin to incorporate leadership education into the advising of identity-based student organizations can be seen at Florida State University. Approximately 80 positional leaders from the Asian American student union, Black student union, Hispanic Latino student union, Pride student union, Women student union, and Veteran student union come together for a conference-style training experience called the "All Agency Advance," in which introductory position-driven skills and leadership principles are infused together for an afternoon of learning and relationship building. All participating students have a position on the executive board or serve in a positional role on a committee within their respective organizations. Students receive a variety of management-oriented training materials, such as policies regarding funding and budgets, event planning, advertising, and travel.

They are also provided multiple opportunities for self-reflection and personal growth. Often, student leaders come together for a meal with an accompanying overview of their organization's history and current context. These types of sessions may include time for self-reflection on each members' purpose in the organization and personal vision for their involvement. Coupled with time to review the tasks associated with their specific roles, and various relevant institutional policies, these meetings help student leaders develop a sense of camaraderie pivotal to their future success. The day ends with reflection of their learning, independently and as a large group, and with an affirmation celebration recognizing positive contributions for the campus community. Each component of the retreat is grounded in leadership learning: laying out, and then building upon leadership concepts, motivating and supporting leader self-efficacy, and creating community bonding experiences that encourage collaboration and establish a common vision for change.

Highlighting the activist and collectivist nature of organizations, and their students, the All Agency Advance provides a springboard for conversations to be continued throughout the academic year and at individual organizations' retreats. Those smaller, organization-specific days or weekends focus on additional leadership skills and better understanding of self and how one interacts with others through a series of developmental exercises. They also engage students in critically thinking and planning how to tackle issues facing their communities, with the understanding their peer organizations are working towards similar goals. This comradery allows for the facilitation of conversation across difference, and acknowledgement of partnerships that can be made at the crossroads of identity intersectionality. Engaging identity-based organizations with each other allows for defining a common purpose, sociocultural conversations regarding identity, and a better understanding of the complex issues facing others.

Leadership education through advising is an ongoing process. Development, or reflection, and incorporation of leadership values, skills, and knowledge can be infused by advisors in executive board and one-on-one meetings at minimum (Bertrand Jones et al., 2016). Advisors can play an important role in group growth by supporting the creation of safe and brave environments for students to engage in difficult conversations, building trusting relationships, and challenging each other through civil discourse. Utilizing the bonding that may have taken place at a retreat, or is continuing to develop in meetings and successful task completion, an advisor can nudge group members to grow in how they engage in leadership processes.

Individual Student Leadership Learning

At the individual level, one-on-one meetings with advisors provide the best opportunities for leadership education and LID. The one-on-one advising relationship can often evolve into a mentor relationship as student leaders are in need of those who can support, encourage, and challenge them through the leadership process (Komives et al., 2013). Ensuring time is set aside regularly for these meetings, and focusing not only on tasks the student must complete, but engaging in overarching dialogue about leadership, goal-setting, growth, and learning, are key components to folding leadership education into advising. One-on-one communication can provide insight to advisors about other components of a students' life, and help them connect learning to students' personal passions and motivations along the way.

Advisors can engage students in a "letters to self" activity at the beginning of a term, with a halfway point, or end mark to refer back and discuss achievements that have developed. Check-ins at the end of the semester or year can be beneficial with regards to developing students' self-awareness. One-on-ones are advisors' opportunity to provide critical feedback, and encourage student self-assessment and reflection of their actions, learning, and development through their leadership journey (Guthrie et al., 2013). They can also be critical learning and meaning-making moments for students as they process decisions made by the organization, interacting with those different from them, and how to work within a group to affect change.

Advisors can also utilize one-on-one meetings to develop a better understanding of a student's self-concept as a leader. Learning students' passions, purposes, and motivations to participate in the organization, as well as how they perceive themselves as a leader and with regard to their salient identities, provides a strong starting point to engage in learning and developmental conversations with a student. Individual one-on-one meetings also provide a framework to help students develop the ability to lead, not only by focusing on tasks they need to complete in order to be successful for an activity, but by also engaging them in thinking through complex issues, encouraging structured risk taking, and challenging leadership principles (Reichard & Walker, 2016). Doing so also allows for opportunities to praise learning and development, to offer feedback and opportunities for growth, and to help students situate leadership learning within their intersecting social identities.

Cultivating Leaders in Organizations

Often, advisors' duties seem to keep them interacting only with students who retain positional leadership roles. Advisors who serve as leadership educators know the work taking place in executive board meetings and one-on-ones must permeate throughout the entire organization as well. Attendance at large scale events, interacting with and providing positive feedback, and thoughtful conversations with general student membership is a critical component of cultivating involved students into leaders as well. Reaching out to campus partners, and areas of campus that attract different students to participate in the organization, is also a way to invite students into leadership. Finding ways to help students connect and feel a sense of belonging in a group can expand their understanding of leadership, and thus help learning begin. This may include nominating an active student to participate in a leadership course or a committee role, reaching out to them at regular events, or encouraging their participation when they are seen across campus. Supporting students who are actively involved in identity-based organizations, learning more about their passions and motivations, and challenging them to work in collaboration with others are other ways to facilitate leadership and LID.

Throughout the organizational experience, advisors support students' leadership engagement. That is, advisors work to facilitate the application of leadership values, skills, and knowledge routinely (Bertrand Jones et al., 2016). Grounding organizations and student leaders in their larger purpose allows both leadership and management to coexist in organizational conversations. Engaging in this process expands the experiential learning already taking place within the identity-based student organization to include leadership education. Advisors who also serve as socially just leadership educators help students create more meaningful opportunities through their involvement in positional roles within identity-based student organizations, and support identity development of not only their salient identities, but their leader identity as well.

CONCLUSION

Now, more than ever, issues of social justice and leadership can be seen as one and the same. Infusing social justice into leadership learning is necessary for long-term success and inclusion. Leadership education takes place across forums and experiences; inside and outside of classrooms. Indeed, leadership is learned, and identity-based student organizations provide an excellent structure and backdrop to engage in learning and LID, as they are organizations founded on principles of social change and social justice. Such organizations are an entry point for students to engage in leadership processes and begin to self-identify as a leader. Advisors of these organizations are key influencers; yet many have not been prepared to serve in their role with these intentions. Asked to focus on management and development, advisors are leadership educators through relationships with students and organizations.

Appropriate training and leadership learning should be expectations held by organizational advisors. Advisors practice leadership with diverse students and utilize the organizational structure to challenge students' thinking and understanding of leadership. Adding leadership education to advising provides a critical expansion of leadership education, reaching another student population that may not connect with leadership in other ways on campus. Many advisors engage students in experiences that help students practice leadership and develop as leaders. Others still can learn about leadership for themselves and infuse that knowledge into opportunities for students to learn within their organizations. With so many opportunities within student organizations to foster learning and infuse leadership education, higher education under-serves students by not intentionally framing advising in the leadership education paradigm. Identity-based student organizations are only the beginning of transforming advising roles to truly implement cocurricular leadership learning into the student experience.

REFERENCES

ACPA/NASPA Professional Competency Areas for Student Affairs Educators. (2015). Retrieved from https://www.naspa.org/images/uploads/main/ACPA_NASPA _Professional_Competencies_FINAL.pdf

Arminio, J. L., Carter, S., Jones, S. E., Kruger, K., Lucas, N., Washington, J., . . . Scott, A. (2000). Leadership experiences of students of color. *NASPA Journal, 37*(3), 496–510.

Astin, A. W. (1984). Student involvement: A developmental theory for higher education. *Journal of College Student Personnel, 25*(4), 297–308.

Astin, A. (1993). *What matters in college? Four critical years revisited.* San Francisco, CA: Jossey-Bass.

Bandura, A. (1997). *Self-efficacy: The exercise of control.* New York, NY: Freeman.

Bertrand Jones, T., Guthrie, K. L., & Osteen, L. K. (2016). Critical domains of culturally relevant leadership learning: A call to transform leadership programs. In K. L. Guthrie, T. Bertrand Jones, & L. Osteen (Eds.), *New directions for student leadership, No. 152: Developing culturally relevant leadership learning* (pp. 9–22). San Francisco, CA: Jossey-Bass.

Bordas, J. (2012). *Salsa, soul and spirit: Leadership for a multicultural age.* San Francisco, CA: Berrett-Koehler.

Bordas, J. (2013). *The power of Latino leadership: Culture, inclusion and contribution.* San Francisco, CA: Berrett-Koehler.

Delgado-Romero, E. A., & Hernandez, C. A. (2002). Hispanic students through student organizations: Competencies for faculty advisors. *Journal of Hispanic Higher Education, 2,* 144–157.

DeSawal, D. M. (2007). *Understanding how student organization advisors approach advising* (Doctoral dissertation). Retrieved from ProQuest Dissertations and Theses database. http://hdl.handle.net/2022/7744

Dugan, J. P., Kodama, C., Correia, B., & Associates. (2013). *Multi-institution study of leadership insight report: Leadership program delivery.* College Park, MD: National Clearinghouse for Leadership Programs.

Dunkel, N. W., & Schuh, J. H. (1998). *Advising student groups and organizations.* San Francisco, CA: Jossey-Bass.

Dunkel, N. W., & Spencer, C. L. (2006). *Advice for advisers: Empowering your residence hall association.* Columbus, OH: Association of College and University Housing Officers–International.

Guardia, J. R., & Evans, N. J. (2008). Factors influencing the ethnic identity development of Latino fraternity members at a Hispanic Serving Institution. *Journal of College Student Development, 49*(3), 163–181.

Guiffrida, D. A. (2003). African American student organizations as agents of social integration. *Journal of College Student Development, 44*(3), 304–319.

Guthrie, K. L., & Osteen, L. (Eds.). (2012). Developing students' leadership capacity. *New Directions for Student Services, No. 140.* San Francisco, CA: Jossey-Bass.

Guthrie, K. L., Bertrand Jones, T., Osteen, L., & Hu, S. (2013). Cultivating leader identity and capacity in students from diverse backgrounds. *ASHE Higher Education Report, 39*(4).

Hersey, P., & Blanchard, K. H. (1988). *Management of organizational behaviors.* Englewood Cliffs, NJ: Prentice Hall.

Harper, S., & Quaye, S. J. (2007). Student organizations as venues for black identity expression and development among African American male student leaders. *Journal of College Student Development, 48*(2), 127–144.

Inkelas, K. K. (2004). Does participation in ethnic co-curricular activities facilitate a sense of ethnic awareness and understanding? A study of Asian Pacific American undergraduates. *Journal of College Student Development, 45*(3), 285–302.

Jones, S. R. (1997). Voices of identity and difference: A qualitative exploration of the multiple dimensions of identity development in women college students. *Journal of College Student Development, 38,* 376–386.

Komives, S. R., Lucas, N., & McMahon, T. R. (2013). *Exploring leadership: For college students who want to make a difference* (3rd ed.). San Francisco, CA: Jossey-Bass.

Komives, S. R., Owen, J. E., Longerbeam, S. D., Mainella, F. C., & Osteen, L. (2005). Developing a leadership identity: A grounded theory. *Journal of College Student Development, 46*(6), 563–611.

Kouzes, J. M., & Posner, B. Z. (1987). *The Leadership Challenge.* San Francisco, CA: Jossey-Bass.

Milem, J. F., Chang, M. J., & Antonio, A. L. (2005). *Making diversity work on campus: A research-based perspective.* Washington, DC: American Association of Colleges and Universities.

Multi-Institutional Study of Leadership. (2017). *About.* Retrieved from https://www.leadershipstudy.net/about/

Museus, S. D. (2008). The role of ethnic student organizations in fostering African American and Asian American students' cultural adjustment and membership at predominantly White institutions. *Journal of College Student Development, 49*(6), 568–586.

Onorato, S., & Musoba, G. D. (2015). Developing a leadership identity as a Hispanic woman at a Hispanic-serving institution. *Journal of College Student Development, 56*(1), 15–31.

Ortiz, A. M. (2004). Promoting the success of Latino students: A call to action. In A. M. Ortiz (Ed.), *New directions for student services, No. 105: Promoting the success of Latino students: A call to action* (pp. 89–97). San Francisco, CA: Jossey-Bass.

Owen, J. E. (2012). Using student development theories as conceptual frameworks in leadership education. In K. L. Guthrie & L. Osteen (Eds.), *New directions for student services, No. 140: Developing students' leadership capacity* (pp. 17–35). San Francisco, CA: Jossey-Bass.

Ozaki, C. C., & Johnston, M. (2008). The space in between: Issues for multiracial student organizations and advising. In K. A. Renn & P. Shang (Eds.), *New directions for student services, No. 123: Biracial and multiracial students* (pp. 53–61). San Francisco, CA: Jossey-Bass.

Pascarella, E. T., & Terenzini, P. T. (2005). *How college affects students: A third decade of research.* San Francisco, CA: Jossey-Bass.

Reichard, R. J., & Walker, D. O. (2016). In pursuit: Mastering leadership through leader developmental readiness. In R. J. Reichard & S. E. Thompson (Eds.), *New directions for student leadership, No. 149: Leader developmental readiness: Pursuit of leadership excellence* (pp. 15–25). San Francisco, CA: Jossey-Bass.

Renn, K. A., & Bilodeau, B. L. (2005). Leadership identity development among lesbian, gay, bisexual, and transgender student leaders. *NASPA Journal, 42*(3), 342–367.

Renn, K. A., & Ozaki, C. C. (2010). Psychosocial and leadership identities among leaders of identity-based campus organizations. *Journal of Diversity in Higher Education, 3*(1), 14–26.

Rosch, D. M., & Villanueva, J. C. (2016). Motivation to develop as a leader. In R. J. Reichard & S. E. Thompson (Eds.), *New directions for student leadership, No. 149: Leader developmental readiness: Pursuit of leadership excellence* (pp. 49–59). San Francisco, CA: Jossey-Bass.

Rost, J. C. (1993). *Leadership for the twenty-first century.* New York, NY: Praeger.

Solorzano, D., Ceja, M., & Yosso, T. (2000). Critical race theory, racial microaggressions and campus racial climate: The experiences of African American college students. *The Journal of Negro Education, 69*(1/2), 60–73.

Thompson, S. E., & Reichard, R. J. (2016). Context matters: Support for leader developmental readiness. In R. J. Reichard & S. E. Thompson (Eds.), *New directions for student leadership, No. 149: Leader developmental readiness: Pursuit of leadership excellence* (pp. 97–104). San Francisco, CA: Jossey-Bass.

CHAPTER 18

INCREASING EMOTIONAL INTELLIGENCE TO ENHANCE SOCIALLY JUST LEADERSHIP EDUCATION

Robyn O. Brock

What motivates an individual to be a part of a leadership process? Why do some leaders intuitively understand the emotions of those in the room while others are oblivious? How can educators in higher education empower students to become emotionally intelligent leaders? How can educators create purposeful opportunities for students to understand their motivations to lead and how their emotions can affect them? In turn, how can emotionally intelligent leaders create spaces and opportunities for students to use these skills to create a more socially just campus and community? This chapter will explore the theoretical framework of motivation to lead, the concept of EI, and how these two constructs can be combined to create opportunities for leadership education grounded in social justice. Relevant literature and research will increase understanding of and connection between the two topics. The closing section will provide practical applications

Changing the Narrative, pages 277–290
Copyright © 2018 by Information Age Publishing
All rights of reproduction in any form reserved.

for practitioners in higher education and leadership education focused on spaces and programs, as well as the need for facilitator training.

MOTIVATION TO LEAD

Motivation to lead (MTL) is a theoretical framework created by Chan and Drasgow (2001), comparing the relationship between individual differences and various leader behaviors. The authors described MTL as:

> ... an individual-differences construct that affects a leader's or leader-to-be's decisions to assume leadership training, roles, and responsibilities that affect his or her intensity of effort at leading and persistence as a leader. (p. 482)

This definition grounds the MTL framework's examination of relationships within a multidimensional approach of a leader including personality, leadership self-efficacy, and values. The authors postulated when meaningful relationships exist between these three dimensions, secondary MTL constructs may emerge which support connections among the factors.

A key assumption Chan and Drasgow (2001) identified relates noncognitive abilities, such as personality and values, to leader behaviors through MTL, which also affect the individual's participation in leadership roles and activities. The framework examines the role of trait (distal) and state (proximal) antecedents. Distal antecedents fall into three categories: (a) general cognitive ability; (b) the Big-Five personality traits of extraversion, agreeableness, conscientiousness, openness to experience, and emotional stability; and (c) values based on horizontal and vertical perspectives on collectivism and individualism. Proximal antecedents include past leadership experience and leadership self-efficacy.

This framework, examined through three studies, supports five main findings: (a) MTL can be measured by three related factors including affective-identity MTL, non-calculative MTL, and social-normative MTL; (b) cognitive ability is not related to MTL whereas the other antecedents included are; (c) each MTL factor is generally consistent throughout the sample; (d) direct and indirect paths exist from distal antecedents to MTL; and (e) MTL may be used as a predictor of leadership potential. The message in high-quality research utilizing this framework details how personality and values play key roles in motivation and leader behaviors. Socially just leadership educators share the concepts of social justice through leadership education to help shape emerging leaders' motivations and behaviors. The practical implication from this, according to the authors, is to incorporate leadership training at an early age in school to help increase self-efficacy and self-awareness for greater future benefits.

Rosch and Villanueva (2016) offered another perspective in their work focusing on the role of motivation in readying leaders to be successful and how motivation can be used for a larger developmental impact. Their four focus areas were defining motivation, examining precursors and outcomes of motivation to develop leadership, identifying key challenges, and offering strategies for success in increasing motivation to develop student leadership. Motivation was defined as the individual drive to achieve a goal. The need for such MTL should be supported to increase potential student leader capacity. Rosch and Villanueva (2016) included several other theories to further link motivation to leader development.

Hong, Catano, and Liao (2011) examined leader emergence, MTL, and EI. The authors postulated MTL can be divided into three distinctions: (a) affective-identity MTL, which is an individual's natural tendencies to lead or leadership talent; (b) social-normative MTL, leading out of duty, responsibility, and social norms, or leadership responsibility; and (c) non-calculative MTL which is associated with levels of altruism, or leadership selflessness. The authors evaluated connections between the MTL, leader emergence, and EI. The results, "...suggest[ed] that MTL can be considered a proximal predictor of leader emergence" (Hong et al., 2011 p. 335).

Understanding one's MTL can be difficult given the variety of personalities, experiences, and values each individual may hold. It can be difficult for anyone to fully understand their own motivations, much less someone else's. However, understanding motivations to lead is relevant in classrooms across the educational spectrum. How educators can facilitate and create opportunities for students to increase and understand their MTL is important in helping students establish and reinforce their self-awareness and leadership self-efficacy. MTL theories fully acknowledge the need to include multidimensional constructs including personality and values. Experiences, identities, and context are all a part of the multidimensional person. This sense of self-awareness can lead to greater awareness of others' identities; key components of creating leaders who are aware of social justice concepts.

EMOTIONAL INTELLIGENCE

MTL constructs encourage early development of self-awareness and leadership self-efficacy; both of which involve an awareness and understanding of emotions. Socially just leadership education includes self-awareness and managing emotions. This is known as emotional intelligence (EI), which emerged in the 1990s in a variety of fields. EI has also been called emotional quotient, social intelligence, and identified as a part of positive psychology (Bar-On, 2001). This section will broadly review the three constructs of EI to create a foundation to integrate EI, MTL, and leadership learning.

Salovey and Mayer (1990) presented concepts of EI focusing on people's attention to solving problems in emotion-related areas. They included four branches of EI: (a) managing emotions to attain a goal; (b) understanding emotions, emotional language, and the signals conveyed by emotions; (c) using emotions to facilitate thinking; and (d) perceiving emotions accurately in oneself and others. These four branches are neither hierarchical nor mutually exclusive. Mayer, Caruso, and Salovey (2016) updated and clarified their conceptualization of EI by adapting the seven principles of EI, including:

1. EI is a mental ability.
2. EI is best measured as an ability.
3. Intelligent problem solving does not correspond neatly to intelligent behavior.
4. A test's content—the problem solving area involved—must be clearly specified as a precondition for the measurement of human mental abilities.
5. Valid tests have well-defined subject matter that draws out relevant human mental abilities.
6. EI is a broad intelligence.
7. EI is a member of the class of broad intelligences focused on hot information processing.

To summarize the seven principles, EI is a mental ability that can be measured through problem solving directly related to emotions and responses. These principles further clarify EI as a part of broad form intelligence, which themselves are hierarchical in nature with classes and subclasses. The last principle addresses the concepts of cool and hot intelligences; "[c]ool intelligences are those that deal with relatively impersonal knowledge . . . people use hot intelligences to manage what matters most to a person such as senses of social acceptance, identity coherence, and emotional well-being" (Mayer et al., 2016, p. 292). Hot intelligence is readily linked to the research on MTL: both include a focus on values. If someone values identity coherence, it could be inferred that there is self-awareness of the layers of identity. By understanding the multiple facets of individual identity, someone may be more aware of the identities others hold. This could be a demonstration of both EI and an awareness of identities of others. The authors offer the Mayer, Salovey, and Caruso Emotional Intelligence Test (MSCEIT) for further investigation.

The authors updated the four branches of EI to include reasoning and provided examples for each branch (Mayer et al., 2016). The update implied the first level is perceiving emotions; the second level is facilitating thought using emotion. The last two levels are understanding emotions with the culmination being managing emotions. The 25-year history of research on EI lends credibility and reliability that EI can predict important outcomes. Moreover, EI may be an integral part of both personal and social intelligence (Mayer et al., 2016). Personal and social intelligence can be identified as skills needed to identify social inequities.

Goleman (1999) also explored EI, identifying five components specifically in the context of work as self-awareness, self-regulation, motivation, empathy, and social skill. Goleman (1999) described self-awareness as, "…a person's understanding of his or her values and goals…and an ability to assess oneself realistically" (p. 8). Self-regulation was described as being in control of one's feelings and impulses. Goleman (1999) postulated self-regulation may enhance integrity due to increased thoughtfulness and decreased impulsivity. Motivation was presented as the ability and desire to achieve (Goleman, 1999).

Goleman (1999) identified two final components of EI as empathy and social skill; each of which focuses on relationship management. Empathy was described as thoughtfully considering feelings of others in the decision making process (p. 15). Social skill is, "…friendliness with a purpose" (p. 17) and is a culmination of the other four components. Goleman asserted EI can be learned and increases with age. This mirrors the MTL framework demonstrating that past experiences can impact leadership self-efficacy and motivation.

The third model, the Bar-On model of emotional-social intelligence (Bar-On, 2001), provided yet another definition of emotional–social intelligence as a "…cross-section of interrelated emotional and social competencies, skills, and facilitators that determine how effectively we understand and express ourselves, understand others, and relate with them, and cope with daily demands" (p. 3). The assessment associated with the Bar-On model is the Emotional Quotient inventory (EQ-i); a 133-question assessment allowing individuals to score themselves into 5 categories and 15 subcategories. These categories reflect two previous approaches to EI in that intrapersonal, interpersonal, stress management, adaptability, and general mood are the five categories identified. Bar-On continued to update the EQ-i in six major stages over 17 years. Similar results were found in the research: older individuals scored higher in EQ-i than younger individuals indicating that EI may be learned.

Table 18.1 compares and contrasts the key components of EI based on the three models previously described. Using Mayer et al. (2016) themes, Goleman (1999) and Bar-On's (2001) models were adopted to demonstrate the overlapping definitions related to EI. Overlap exists most consistently in the managing emotions and perceiving emotions frames, aligning multiple areas from all three theories.

TABLE 18.1   Comparison of Emotional Intelligence (EI) Themes by Theorist

Mayer, Salovey, & Caruso 4 Components	Goleman 5 Components	Bar-On 5 Components
Managing emotions	Self-awareness, self-regulation	General mood, adaptability, stress management
Understanding emotions in language and signals	Self-awareness, empathy	Interpersonal, intrapersonal
Using emotions to facilitate thinking	Motivation	Stress management
Perceiving emotions accurately in self and others	Self-awareness, social skills	Interpersonal, intrapersonal

MOTIVATION TO LEAD AND EMOTIONAL INTELLIGENCE

Hong et al. (2011) explored the relationship between MTL and EI as a part of leader emergence. They first defined MTL based on the Chan and Drasgow (2001) research with the three constructs of MTL as affective-identity, social normative, and non-calculative. Hong et al. (2011) wrote EI can be identified with an ability-based definition to include perceive, appraise, and express emotions, to access and/or generate feelings, to understand emotion and emotional knowledge, and to regulate emotions to promote growth. Motivation was defined in their study as an individual's direction, intensity, and duration of effort. The nuances of these definitions reflect the current literature while also providing a lens through which the authors drew connections.

Hong et al. (2011) conducted two studies of undergraduate and master's degree students in small group interactions based on the need to solve the Survivor on the Moon game created by the National Aeronautics and Space Administration (NASA). This simulation had individuals rank a provided list of survival items. After the individuals ranked their items, the group had to come to a consensus on a final list. The process of organizing the items allowed researchers to study group interactions. The key findings for both studies indicated MTL can be considered a proximal predictor of leader emergence. In comparing EI leadership, both studies suggested people who were able to manage their emotions were more likely to be rated higher in, affective-identity (natural tendency) and social normative. Managing emotions is a part of multiple developmental frameworks; it is also a key component for leadership learners. These skills include empathy and understanding, as well as a willingness to think through emotions before making assumptions. From a social justice perspective, leaders who are able to demonstrate empathy and not make assumptions have gained a strong skill set. This is another indicator that EI is needed as a part of leader development and social justice education.

Hong et al. (2011) cited multiple sources in their article corroborating, "EI increases one's overall confidence, goal-orientation (Offermann, Bailey, Vasilopoulos Seal, & Sass, 2004), motivation, job satisfaction (Wong & Law, 2002), and work performance" (Barling, Slater, & Kelloway, 2000, p. 323). The authors offered a variety of future research directions, including longitudinal studies about the differential effects of EI, the longitudinal relationships between EI and MTL, and EI's role in groups and among different people. There may also be implications of different linkages between EI and leadership outcomes, specifically using gender as a predictor. Including members of different age groups may also change some of the findings. The authors closed with practical implications for team dynamics, MTL related to social norms in a group, and the awareness that using emotions to facilitate thought processes is most important when selecting motivated leaders. It is clear that MTL is an important construct for leader emergence; the context, location, and experiences and ages of the participants matter.

EMOTIONALLY INTELLIGENT LEADERS

As the terms *leader* and *leadership* have been continually redefined and adapted to fit different needs across a variety of areas, it is important to recognize how recent literature includes identity and culture as major components shaping leader identity. Much of the modern scholarship on leadership theories includes identity, ethics, and social responsibility as integral parts of leadership. In order to further clarify the meaning of leadership learning, it is important to distinguish the difference between leader and leadership. In the monograph, *Cultivating Leader Identity and Capacity in Students from Diverse Backgrounds*, Guthrie, Bertrand Jones, Osteen and Hu (2013) focused an entire section on language to define leader and leadership. They defined leader and leadership in a straightforward manner, stating, "leaders are the individuals, with or without positions of authority, working together to tackle tough problems; leadership is the interaction, the process occurring among and between them" (p. 14). Guthrie et al. (2013) offered further insight by distinguishing leader development as person-, as opposed to process- or environment-centric. It is clear through MTL and EI that there is a strong connection to leader identity grounded in values, ethics, and self-efficacy.

Allen, Shankman, and Miguel (2012) connected concepts of EI and leadership to create a framework for emotionally intelligent leadership (EIL). Allen et al. (2012) reviewed the three main approaches of EI to create a mixed model, combining the constructs of EI and leadership. The three primary factors of EIL were context, self, and others; these three factors branch out into 21 capacities of EIL. These capacities are also reflective of the aforementioned EI theories including emotional self-perception, environmental awareness, empathy, and flexibility.

One key component of the EIL model is the focus on context as a part of leadership. Context was defined as "...being aware of the environment in which leaders and followers work" (Allen et al., 2012, p. 184). It included two capacities: environmental awareness and groups savvy. Self as defined as, "being aware of yourself in terms of your abilities and emotions" (Allen et al., 2012, p. 184). Self has nine capacities including: emotional self-perception, honest self-understanding, healthy self-esteem, emotional self-control, authenticity, flexibility, achievement, optimism, and initiative. The third factor—others—was described as, "...being aware of your relationship with others and the role they play in the leadership process" (Allen et al., 2012, p. 185). Others has 10 capacities: empathy, citizenship, inspiration, influence, coaching, change agency, conflict management, developing relationships, teamwork, and capitalizing on differences. Each of these capacities has been empirically validated by research in their respective fields.

Allen et al. (2012) provided an explicit working definition of EIL and outlined the assumptions made in the EIL theory. These assumptions included: leadership is about relationships and context, deliberate choices are important, and EIL can be developed. Once again, the work of these scholars reminds us leadership skills and EI can be taught. There are several resources for the development of EIL, including Shankman and Allen's (2010) book *Emotionally Intelligent Leadership*, as well as an updated workbook (Shankman, Allen, & Haber-Curran, 2015) for students, which includes an EIL inventory for students and the corresponding facilitation guide.

Given the EIL framework, emotionally intelligent leaders are able to understand their environment, emotions, and relationships. While these three aspects vary and change—sometimes by the minute—emotionally intelligent leaders continue to grow and develop. In turn, they learn to manage their emotions as a part of their identity development. This allows for multidimensional personalities, including leadership self-efficacy and values that are discussed in the MTL framework, to flourish. In the ever-changing world of higher education, students face challenges to their identities, environments, emotions, and relationships all the time. When students understand their complex identities, manage their emotions, and understand their motivations to develop as leaders, there is the potential for greater understanding of others and the challenges they face. It is also important for leader and leadership development to be grounded in social justice. This is a critical component for emotionally intelligent leaders.

TOWARD SOCIALLY JUST EMOTIONALLY INTELLIGENT LEADERSHIP

Connecting motivation, EI, and leadership development seems logical, especially in a higher education setting. The opportunities for personal growth and development are endless; the need for social justice understanding is tremendous. Figure 18.1 provides an overview of the theories presented in this chapter. The theories focus on individual leader development; one that requires a strong understanding and awareness of the individual's own personal values, motivation, and leadership self-efficacy. MTL and EI focus on the individual; EIL adds the layer of context as well. These connect to socially just leadership education by demonstrating the need to increase capacity for self-awareness and empathy for others. As socially just leadership education is incorporated into the higher education environment, consideration should be given to the college context, informal and formal settings, and intentional leadership learning opportunities. The practical applications of these connections can be seen through spaces, programs, education, and training.

Creating Spaces and Programs That Work

If MTL is impacted by personality, values, and past leadership experiences, and MTL is a dynamic construct that can be changed through social-learning processes and experiences, then socially just educators create

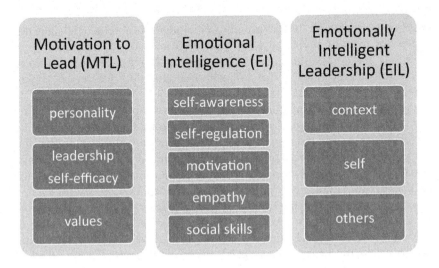

Figure 18.1 Theory overview.

opportunities for change while increasing identity awareness for students. Each person carries a variety of visible and invisible identities; each of which is a vital part of the individual. It is a delicate balance to create programs for all students while also honoring identities. How campus communities, student leaders, staff, and faculty work together to create these spaces and opportunities greatly impacts the student experience.

We know leaders face uncertainty and challenging environments that can rapidly change (Hong et al., 2011). Socially just institutions of higher education create spaces to honor freedom of speech and expression, ensuring students are able to express themselves and experience cognitive dissonance. Students must be able to explore all aspects of their identities in spaces that are safe and welcoming. We all have a variety of identities that may include race, gender, ethnicity, culture, age, relationship status, and veteran status, among others. Space can be a building, an office, a room, a house, or any part of or type of facility that supports student growth and development. There should be icons and symbols that students choose to represent their identity-based organization. These may also be incorporated into the campus architecture as a celebration of our identities and differences. These spaces may be used formally and informally to create a culture of inclusion within the campus community. These spaces help students establish a sense of belonging based on their own identities.

As a part of increasing EI and leadership learning opportunities, socially just educators purposefully help all students recognize the need for welcoming spaces. For example, if a student uses a wheelchair, and is in a historic campus building, there is a possibility the student may not be able to access all areas of the building. Cobblestone walkways may appear attractive, but would be limiting for a visually impaired person. Students may receive messages students with disabilities are not welcome in those spaces. Socially just educators examine intentional and unintentional messages their campus' buildings, images, symbols, and icons send to students, faculty, staff, and community. Being aware of this and acknowledging our differences are key parts of EIL and creating a socially just society.

Campus programming can be both formal and informal. Many institutions offer welcome weeks, entertainment options such as a concert, involvement fairs, and risk reduction focused programs during the first few weeks of classes in the fall. Often, there are cultural and heritage celebrations hosted by students and/or staff that happen weekly or monthly such as Black History month or Women's History month. Campus events such as Homecoming and sporting events increase the sense of community. These programs help students develop their identities while creating a sense of belonging. Socially just leadership educators are aware of these needs and work collaboratively to produce comprehensive programs.

Focused areas within the student population also offer unique opportunities through retreats, educational sessions, and social events. Student leader retreats within specific areas like student government associations, student activities programming boards, and other student organizations' leadership are common. Some institutions are able to offer formal courses as a part of student leadership development; others provide consistent space and time with staff to allow for similar opportunities for leadership education.

For the managers of campus events, it is important to consider space, timing, and content from the EIL perspective. Emotionally intelligent administrators are strategic about who serves on the planning committees, who facilitates programs, and how programs are evaluated for effectiveness. Helping students and professionals examine programs through a variety of perspectives ensures administrators and students are creating programs with maximum impact. Intentionality of programming is critical so that all individuals feel welcome to attend and/or be a part of the events, even if they choose not to participate. Experiences shape individuals; higher education must provide wide-ranging opportunities that attract a variety of individuals. This is a part of creating a socially just environment that is open to everyone.

Informal, or passive, programming represents additional opportunities for campuses to engage students. One example might be having giant checkers in a common space or an oversized sand box with shovels and buckets set up outside the residence hall. Designated spaces for sharing opinions such as large movable chalkboards with open-ended prompts can be the catalyst for sharing opinions, ideas, and learning from peers. These types of passive programs allow for students to interact as they choose and hopefully build community. Banners, chalking on sidewalks, yard signs, and other marketing materials can also be included in intentional passive programming. Resident assistants may be experts at this as they change bulletin boards routinely. Social media outlets can be used as another aspect of passive programming.

Rosch and Villanueva (2016) offered two key challenges in cultivating motivation of leadership development from the programmatic perspective. The first challenge is understanding the different motivations to lead from a variety of participants. The second challenge is acknowledging how leadership development happens in a broader context with many external and internal influences. The authors underscored the need to create programs to address wide-ranging needs and desires of a diverse population while also being responsive to individual needs. Beliefs and emotions paired with the contexts in which leadership development occurs are also strong considerations for leadership program designers.

Leadership Education and Training

Education and training are the last two areas of practical applications to consider. Socially just higher education institutions create, implement, and evaluate leadership education experiences to enhance self-efficacy and self-awareness of the participants and facilitators. After this is successfully done at least once, repetition with appropriate evaluation and revision reinforces ongoing effectiveness and implementation of needed changes. Socially just leadership educators create learning experiences that allow students to develop their identities. When students understand who they are, they are better equipped to help their peers understand who they are. This exploration of identity is key to creating socially just leadership education.

Peer mentors or peer leaders often have a strong influence on other students. Ender and Newton (2000) and Newton and Ender (2010) created and updated *Students Helping Students: A Guide for Peer Educators on College Campuses* as a practical guide for student mentors and educators to explore their own identities and develop skills to be more impactful peer educators. This guide allows for peer educators to explore their own identities, thoughts, and beliefs through guided activities and reflection questions. When students understand their identities, they can be more effective in both the participant and facilitator roles. Through the concepts of EIL and MTL, students should be able to establish a stronger understanding of who they are while also ideally experiencing growth in these areas.

Socially just facilitators, trainers, and educators have a strong understanding of their own identities to help facilitate the development of student leaders' identities. One way to accomplish this is to train the trainers by having them go through the same exercises or a modified version of the program their students will complete. Not only will this aid in the facilitation of the activity, it also helps frame the material for the facilitators as participants. Furthermore, this allows for the facilitators to identify strong emotional reactions and limitations they may have as a part of the exercises. By understanding and managing their own emotions, space is created for wide-ranging student experiences, often with the potential for critical thinking, self-reflection or assessment, and cognitive dissonance. Emotionally intelligent facilitators understand their own identities and manage their own emotions. This can be done through a processing activity with the group of facilitators or through individual conversations. There are times when personal reflection may be the best way to process for individuals. Thorough understanding of identities combined with EIL skills allow for dynamic facilitation and growth. When planning leadership programs, with tenets of EI at the forefront, training the trainer is a necessity.

MOVING TOWARD A COMPLEX FUTURE

The world will continue to gain complexity and the identities our students share may become more difficult to understand. Students must be challenged to understand their MTLs, the identities they hold, and the connections between the two. In turn, students should be able to explore how to be emotionally intelligent leaders and how to actively engage in social issues to promote equity. Successful higher education professionals understand how to create spaces to allow for leadership learning and development on their campuses. Spaces, programs, and events must be designated for a variety of student identities to ensure that students have the opportunities and experiences to increase EI, understand their MTLs, and, in turn, become emotionally intelligent leaders. When done effectively, these types of experiences can shape identities and increase awareness of social inequities. The resounding cry is the need for a social justice focus in leadership education.

As the United States of America is facing a strong polarizing political climate, the need for socially just leadership education is increasing exponentially. Educators must take the time to understand their own emotions and identities—and manage them in a healthy way. There is an obligation to help students do the same thing regardless of personal beliefs about the issues. As educators, it is more important than ever before to create purposeful opportunities to explore individual and collective identities in a way that supports leadership development. It is through EIL that we can affect the most change.

REFERENCES

Allen, S. J., Shankman, M. L., & Miguel, R. F. (2012). Emotionally intelligent leadership: An integrative, process-oriented theory of student leadership. *Journal of Leadership Education, 11*(1), 177–203.

Barling, J., Slater, F., & Kelloway, K. (2000). Transformational leadership and emotional intelligence: An exploratory study. *Leadership & Organization Development Journal, 21*(3), 157–161.

Bar-On, R. (2001). Emotional intelligence and self-actualization: Emotional intelligence in everyday life. In J. Ciarrochi, J. P. Forgas, & J. D. Mayer (Eds.), *Emotional intelligence in everyday life: A scientific inquiry* (pp. 82–97). New York, NY: Psychology Press.

Chan, K. Y., & Drasgow, F. (2001). Toward a theory of individual differences and leadership: Understanding the motivation to lead. *Journal of Applied Psychology, 86*(3), 481–498.

Ender, S. C., & Newton, F. B. (2000). *Students helping students: A guide for peer educators on college campuses.* San Francisco, CA: Jossey-Bass.

Goleman, D. (1999). *Working with emotional intelligence.* New York, NY: Bloomsbury.

Guthrie, K. L., Bertrand Jones, T., Osteen, L. K., & Hu, S. (2013). *Cultivating leader identity and capacity in students from diverse backgrounds: ASHE Higher Education Report, 39*(4).

Hong, Y., Catano, V. M., & Liao, H. (2011). Leader emergence: The role of emotional intelligence and motivation to lead. *Leadership & Organization Development Journal, 32*(4), 320–343.

Mayer, J. D., Caruso, D. R., & Salovey, P. (2016). The ability model of emotional intelligence: Principles and updates. *Emotion Review, 8*(4), 290–300.

Newton, F. B., & Ender, S. C. (2010). *Students helping students: A guide for peer educators on college campuses.* Hoboken, NJ: Wiley.

Offermann, L. R., Bailey, J. R., Vasilopoulos, N. L., Seal, C., & Sass, M. (2004). The relative contribution of emotional competence and cognitive ability to individual and team performance. *Human performance, 17*(2), 219–243.

Rosch, D. M., & Villanueva, J. C. (2016). Motivation to develop as a leader. In R. J. Reichard & S. E. Thompson (Eds.), *New directions for student leadership, No. 149: Leader developmental readiness: Pursuit of leadership excellence* (pp. 49–59). San Francisco, CA: Jossey-Bass.

Shankman, M. L. & Allen, S. J. (2010). *Emotionally intelligent leadership for students.* Hoboken, NJ: Wiley.

Shankman, M. L., Allen, S. J., & Haber-Curran, P. (2015). *Emotionally intelligent leadership: A guide for students (2nd ed.).* San Francisco, CA: Jossey-Bass.

Salovey, P., & Mayer, J. D. (1990). Emotional intelligence. *Imagination, Cognition and Personality, 9*(3), 185–211.

Wong, C. S., & Law, K. S. (2002). The effects of leader and follower emotional intelligence on performance and attitude: An exploratory study. *The Leadership Quarterly, 13*(3), 243–274.

CHAPTER 19

SERVICE-LEARNING AS A PEDAGOGY FOR SOCIALLY JUST LEADERSHIP EDUCATION

Jillian Volpe White

In a world of increasingly complex challenges, the need for citizens who understand the process of creating change with communities is greater than ever. Students can develop the necessary skills for change through experiences that invite disequilibrium and engage them in thinking deeply about multifaceted social issues. Service-learning is a powerful pedagogical tool for leadership education and social justice. Through engaging with communities, students acquire knowledge, skills, and values for social change and sustained community participation. When well-executed, service-learning can be an effective tool to enhance reciprocal campus and community partnerships. However, when implemented poorly, service-learning can reinforce stereotypes and harm communities. This chapter highlights service-learning as experiential leadership education; discusses intersections of service-learning, leadership education, and social justice; acknowledges

Changing the Narrative, pages 291–304
Copyright © 2018 by Information Age Publishing
All rights of reproduction in any form reserved.

barriers that inhibit effective service-learning; and concludes with action-able ideas for educators seeking to enhance a social justice leadership education praxis.

LEADERSHIP EDUCATION AND SERVICE-LEARNING AS COMPLEMENTARY PEDAGOGIES

Leadership and service have long histories in higher education, though the way they have manifested in student learning and development has evolved over time. This does not imply the previous ways of thinking have been supplanted; rather, new frameworks reconsider previous assumptions and illuminate possibilities for conceptualizing leadership and service. Leadership development has been a goal of higher education since its founding, but in the last few decades, leadership education has shifted from a focus on people in positions of power and authority to a postindustrial model focused on leadership as a relational process through which people intending real change work collaboratively (Guthrie & Osteen, 2016; Rost, 1993).

Institutions of higher education were also founded to advance the public good. In the 1990's, service-learning gained prominence as a pedagogical tool for engaging students in public good work and promoting student learning (Jacoby & Associates, 1996). Over the last several decades, administrators and practitioners have worked to institutionalize civic and community engagement. Simultaneously, the field of service-learning has refocused on community needs and assets (Hamerlinck & Plaut, 2014). The shift in leadership education and service-learning to focuses on collaboration and community, respectively, creates opportunities for students to engage in experiential learning with communities that are aimed towards social justice.

Service-Learning

Service-learning is "a form of experiential education in which students engage in activities that address human and community needs, together with structured opportunities for reflection designed to achieve desired learning outcomes" (Jacoby, 2015, p. 2). Some definitions of service-learning emphasize an academic or course-based component (Furco, 1996). Other definitions allow for structured student learning and engagement through cocurricular experiences (Eyler & Giles, 1999; Jacoby, 2015). Service-learning can include direct service, indirect service, or community-based research. Mitchell (2008) distinguished between two approaches to service-learning, "a traditional approach that emphasizes service without attention to systems of inequality, and a critical approach that is unapologetic in its aim to dismantle structures of injustice" (p. 50). For Jacoby (2015), the hyphen between the words "service" and "learning" symbolized reflection. Reflection is a cornerstone of service-learning; students do not learn from experience alone but from processing and making meaning of experiences.

Leadership Education

Leadership learning is "a collaborative, interdisciplinary, and campus-wide endeavor that involves a wide range of students, faculty, staff, and community partners," which includes four components: "education, training, development, and engagement" (Chunoo & Osteen, 2016, p. 9). Guthrie and Thompson (2010) described three essential elements of leadership education as "formal education in theories and principles of leadership, practical experience, and reflection on experiences in light of formal education" (p. 50). Leadership education facilitates the development of knowledge, skills, and abilities, which enhances students' capacity to build relationships and create change in communities. Guthrie and Bertrand Jones (2012) acknowledged the importance of experiential learning and reflection in leadership education and noted leadership experiences "are ripe for helping students move from mere engagement to making meaning of and learning from their leadership experience" (p. 53).

Service-learning is one tool for leadership education. One year-long leadership course at Kansas State University used "...project-based social change advocacy and education, rather than direct service" so students "learned about the issue, considered the values involved in leading advocacy and education on the issue, and reflected on their leadership contributions to team and public activities in the process" (Hartman, 2016, p. 76). University of Maryland offers experiential leadership courses including Leadership and Education where students serve as classroom mentors for 4 to 6 hours per week. Leadership in Groups and Communities, a core course in the Florida State University Undergraduate Certificate in Leadership Studies, requires students to serve 30 hours as part of a team at a local nonprofit agency. Through service-learning, students apply classroom knowledge, address identified community needs, and reflect on experiences in order to better understand leadership theories and concepts.

Merging Service and Leadership

The organizational structure of service-learning and leadership programs varies by institution. How a campus situates this work is contextualized and depends upon resources, history, tradition, and philosophical orientation. On some campuses, service-learning and community engagement are housed in the same office; on others, they may be separated, reporting to different divisions. Of the 423 institutions that responded to the 2014 Campus Compact annual member survey, the placement of the service-learning/community engagement office in the institution varied: 40% reported to academic affairs, 37% reported to student affairs, 8% reported to both, and 6% reported directly to the president's office (Campus Compact, 2014). Leadership education is similarly situated in standalone centers, student activities, academic units, or a combination of departments. Jenkins and Owen (2016) combined multiple national datasets on leadership educators and found the majority of the respondents were divided amongst full-time faculty, full-time staff, and people in combined faculty/staff roles.

For the past 2 decades, higher education institutions have added programs, merged departments, and reorganized units; many of these organizational changes have combined service and leadership into one office or campus unit. Some examples include the Florida State University Center for Leadership and Social Change, Rollins College Center for Leadership and Community Engagement, University of Georgia Center for Leadership and Service, and Southern Methodist University Community Engagement and Leadership Center. However, little research focuses on these organizational shifts and the impact on student learning, community outcomes, or leadership education. Few organizational websites include history or documentation of changes to indicate when and why service and leadership were unified. Even if both service and leadership are housed in the same office, without a more in-depth examination of program and learning outcomes, it is difficult to determine the degree to which service-learning and leadership are integrated within coursework and programming. The merging of these concepts, philosophically and practically, provides opportunities to build capacity. The degree to which faculty, staff, and students are empowered and enabled to facilitate social justice leadership education is influenced by context including history, mission, and politics; however, having a link between service-learning and leadership education creates a foundation for richer community engaged learning experiences that include social justice education.

Intersections of Leadership, Service-Learning, and Social Justice

Service-learning and leadership education share complementary goals and objectives. These elements are reflected in the intersections between leadership education and service-learning highlighted by Wagner and Pigza

(2016a) which I elaborate on in the context of social justice. Additionally, Burns (1978) distinguished between transforming leadership, which focuses on developing all participants in the leadership process, and transactional leadership, which is based on an exchange without regard to developing followers. From the beginning, service-learning has been grounded in partnerships (Jacoby & Associates, 1996); however in recent years, scholars have highlighted the need to develop partnerships that are truly reciprocal and do not privilege the needs of the student or institution over the agency (Stoecker & Tryon, 2009). Heifetz and Linsky (1994) highlighted an adaptive approach to challenges which required "changing attitudes, values, and behaviors" in order to address complex challenges (p. 13). Service-learning students are often faced with complex social issues; confronted with these challenges, students must examine their beliefs and modes of thinking in order to move beyond quick fixes towards recalibrating their perspective.

The social change model of leadership development (SCM) described collaboration between individuals, groups, and communities concerned with affecting change (Higher Education Research Institute, 1996). Grounded in community, the SCM highlights service as a vehicle college students learn about and enact leadership. In order to create change, the SCM distinguishes between charity and social change, the latter of which addresses the root causes of social issues and requires collaboration among stakeholders (Wagner, 2009). The relational model of leadership (Komives, Lucas, & McMahon, 2013) is made up of five complex concepts—purposeful, inclusive, empowering, ethical, and process-oriented. With each concept, students develop knowledge, skills, and attitudes for working successfully with others.

These four areas where leadership and service-learning are connected—transforming leadership, adaptive leadership, leadership for social change, and relational leadership—also intersect with social justice. Mitchell (2008) identified three elements that distinguished traditional service-learning from critical service-learning: "a social change orientation, working to redistribute power, and developing authentic relationships" (p. 62). The elements of critical service-learning, which move learners toward justice, overlap with approaches to leadership that focus on building community, addressing the root causes of social issues, discovering adaptive solutions for complex challenges, and developing empowering relationships. Butin (2007) described the intersection of service-learning and social justice education as "justice-learning" and noted how this approach created possibilities for exploring belief systems and focusing "as much on the process of undercutting dualistic ways of thinking as on the product of deliberative and sustainable transformational change" (p. 180). Leadership frameworks that emphasize developing relationships, exploring ways of being, solving complex problems, and creating change can facilitate learning and action for social justice.

CRITICISMS OF SERVICE-LEARNING

Despite the benefits of service-learning, the pedagogy is not without criticism. While not an exhaustive discussion, this section confronts some of the realities of service-learning, which faculty and staff must consider to meaningfully engage in service-learning for social justice leadership education.

Incongruence of Campus and Community Needs

Most scholarship on service-learning focuses on students and faculty with relatively little scholarship on the benefits to community partners. Drawing from one study of 64 community organizations, Martin, SeBlonka, and Tryon (2009) identified challenges of short-term service-learning, which include "investment of time by the agency in training short-term service-learning students; incompatibility of short-term service-learning with direct service; issues of timing and project management; and community and campus calendar issues" (p. 58). If a goal of service-learning for social justice leadership education is students' understanding of the root causes of social issues, an abbreviated encounter at an agency may be insufficient to grasp the depth and complexity of the issues addressed. Mitchell (2008) summarized this sentiment best: "Social justice will never be achieved in a single semester nor systems dismantled in the two- to four-hour weekly commitment..." (p. 54). Additionally, for students interested in working with people, interacting with vulnerable populations requires training, and it may not be a good use of agency resources to train students who will not return consistently. One might wonder, with so many challenges, why do community partners take on short-term service-learners? The reasons agencies cited included educating students, recruiting long-term supporters, building capacity, and developing relationships with higher education institutions (Bell & Carlson, 2009).

Failure to Develop Reciprocal Partnerships or Recognize Power Dynamics

While reciprocity, with a balance between student learning and community outcomes, is a goal of service-learning, priorities often skew toward students and institutions. Following the first round of the Carnegie Center for the Advancement of Teaching Elective Community Engagement Classification, an analysis of the applications identified challenges for the field of engagement including "recognizing and documenting the authentic involvement of community partners in outreach and engagement efforts" (Sandmann, Thornton, & Jaeger, 2009, pp. 99–100). In the 2014 Campus Compact annual member survey, "while almost 100% of institutions report mutually beneficial community partnerships, only 33% have defined the characteristics of high quality partnerships, and 31% have a process in place for determining that partnerships are of high quality" (Campus Compact, 2014, p. 7).

Stoecker (2016) raised questions about the commitment of higher education to the change process and the efficacy of service-learning to address issues of community concern. He argued the underlying assumptions of service-learning, which he referred to as "institutionalized service learning," put it in danger of maintaining "exclusion, exploitation, and oppression" by helping people adjust to oppressive structures and existing social systems rather than challenging those systems (p. 6). Stoecker (2016) presented a model of "liberating service learning" where the primary focus was change and enhancing the capacity of people to produce knowledge. In liberating service-learning, the focus shifted from honoring student preferences and passions to placing community change at the center and requiring faculty and staff, who have more longevity and context, to be in relationship with communities. Agencies often hold little clout at the institution unless there are intentional processes to engage them in conversation, and even then it can be difficult to create opportunities for equal exchange.

Ignoring the Significance of Identity

Service-learning is praised for its ability to expose students to people with whom they may not typically interact, whether that is someone from a different race, class, socioeconomic status, religion, nationality, age, gender identity, sexual orientation, ability, or another social identity. Service-learning courses most often enroll students who are female, White, middle-class, and traditionally aged; these students are primarily serving "mostly poor individuals and mostly people of color" (Mitchell, Donahue, & Young-Law, 2012, p. 612). In a discourse analysis of the personal narratives of faculty nominated for a national service-learning award, 35 out of 109 respondents (32%) said service-learning was a strategy to expose students to diversity (O'Meara & Niehaus, 2009). While interactions across difference can be a benefit to service-learning, "encouraging student/community member interactions presents an emotional risk for all involved, with a particular risk for community members to be essentialized or stereotyped" (Wagner

& Pigza, 2016b, p. 12). While service-learning can present opportunities for interaction, these may not always be positive or educative for students or community members.

Using a compilation of observations of many service-learning faculty, Mitchell et al. (2012) illustrated challenges with service-learning as a pedagogy of Whiteness including instructors making assumptions about the experiences of students, using deficit-based language, and waiting until the end of the semester to talk about race, to name a few. The authors noted service-learning projects based on a pedagogy of Whiteness "have minimal impact on the community and result in mis-educative experiences for students, such as unchallenged racism for White students and isolating experiences for students of color, and missed opportunities for educators to make their own instruction more transformative" (Mitchell et al., 2012, p. 613). Disregarding the significance of identity or assuming exposure to a diverse group of people is sufficient to encourage learning can be harmful for students and communities.

STRATEGIES FOR SOCIALLY JUST SERVICE-LEARNING IN LEADERSHIP EDUCATION

Having identified the intersections between service-learning, leadership education, and social justice, as well as the challenges that may prevent service-learning from being an effective pedagogy for social justice leadership education, I will focus on approaches to preparing students, faculty, and community partners for meaningful engagement.

Preparing Students

Empowering students to serve effectively and learn about the root causes of social issues requires preparation and education. This includes understanding the context of where they are serving, learning the skills required to complete tasks, and considering how identity influences perceptions. Acquainting students with the community, the agency, and the tasks requires time. When students return to an agency consistently, they may be able to work more independently, which is another reason sustained engagement is beneficial for students and communities.

Break Away, the national nonprofit organization for alternative breaks, promotes eight components of quality alternative break trips, three of which emphasize how students prepare for service: education, orientation, and training. Education focuses on the social issue in the specific community; orientation highlights the history and context for the community, organization, and project; and training provides students with skills to complete the project (Break Away, 2018). A justice oriented approach to service requires students to understand social issues and community context, confront misperceptions and biases about communities, build partnerships with agencies, use inclusive language, and be prepared to contribute so as not to drain resources or create a burden for the community agency (Sumka, Porter, & Piacitelli, 2015).

Preservice preparation includes having a representative from the agency speak in class, watching documentary films, reading news articles, or learning skills required for the service tasks, such as how to facilitate a mentoring curriculum. Instructors should challenge students to uncover assumptions or biases they may hold regarding the community or social issue addressed by the service. An introductory leadership course at the University of Arizona where students served with underrepresented groups required a three-part approach to education including a 10–12 page research paper analyzing structures and systems, a proposal for a visit or interaction with a member of the community, and a reflection on the community interaction (Seemiller, 2006). In a year-long, first-year honors course at Kansas State University, students spent a semester learning about orphanage tourism and connecting their learning to leadership concepts before planning outreach events and developing deliverables requested by the community partner (Hartman, 2016). Before students engaged in service, they considered context and listened to members of the community. While nonprofit agencies provide training, faculty and staff are also responsible for preparing students, which may require their own reflection and preparation.

Preparing Faculty

The role of faculty in shaping service-learning experiences varies by institution and can include instructors who cede logistical responsibility to a central office or those who are personally invested with the agency and serve alongside students. Implementing effective service-learning that engages students in social justice leadership development goes beyond modifying the syllabus and identifying a community partner; two significant aspects of preparation are developing reciprocal partnerships and doing the self-work required to draw out meaningful reflections from students. Hartman (2016) suggested that to avoid harming communities or reinforcing stereotypes, faculty had "a profound ethical responsibility" to ensure community partners approved and supported service-learning practices (p. 80). A social justice leadership and community framework is built on relationships that encourage honest feedback, which could include a survey, an end of semester debrief meeting, or a more formal evaluation.

Mitchell et al. (2012) called attention to problems with service-learning that reinforced cultural norms for White students and isolated students of color. To counter this pedagogy of Whiteness, they outlined practices for faculty preparing to teach a service-learning course including "how to check one's assumptions and take a more reflective stance on service-learning, how to frame service learning and create structures promoting more thoughtfulness on issues of race, and how to teach about and lead discussions on race" (Mitchell et al., 2012, p. 624). Their vignette could serve as a teaching tool for faculty, both those new to engaged learning and those who have been in the field, to explore how service is framed and how to develop an environment that enhances learning for all students. To embrace their civic selves and invite dialogue into the classroom, educators need time for their own development including difficult conversations about leadership, community, identity, and social justice.

Preparing Community Partners

While students prepare to learn and serve effectively and faculty members develop partnerships and engage in reflection with students, community partners should also prepare for service-learners. Social justice leadership education invites community members to sit at the table as full partners in engaged work. Many campuses have processes in place for incorporating community perspectives and input. In the 2016 Campus Compact annual member survey, 94% of the 396 respondents had community partners come to classes as speakers, 83% sought partner feedback in the development and maintenance of engagement programs, and 68% of partners provided onsite reflection in community settings (Campus Compact, 2016). Inviting partners to campus and traveling to community agencies to meet creates possibilities for engaging dialogue.

In order to prepare for students, community partners should set clear expectations and be prepared to act as co-educators, acknowledging this requires time and energy on their part. "Anyone can serve" is a pervasive sentiment but Wagner and Pigza (2016b) pointed out "while this may be well intentioned, it is a false promise that does not recognize the need for learning first" and may even result in damage to the community when students are not properly trained (p. 12). Some community partners may also participate in reflection. Looking at a language exchange program that partnered university students with immigrants, d'Arlach, Sanchez, and Feuer (2009) found adding a "30- to 60-minute reflection during which social issues are discussed as a group, allowing for co-creation of knowledge" to the end of language exchange sessions opened up opportunities for learning and helped their clients realize they had something valuable to contribute to the partnership (p. 14). Students, faculty, and community partners can all benefit from collective reflection on service-learning, leadership education, and social justice.

Reflection

Reflection is an integral part of service-learning, leadership education, and social justice. To truly engage in justice learning, experiential leadership courses should incorporate critical reflection which "demands that experiences and issues be examined in light of social and political forces, link explicitly to further social action, and reveal hegemonic ideology—that is, the influence of unquestioned dominant cultures and philosophies" (Owen, 2016, p. 39). Critical reflection is based in the work of Freire (1970) whose concept of praxis, reflection and action for transformation, implored people to understand power, privilege, and oppression through a systems framework. Butin (2007) argued justice-learning and experiential strategies filled a gap in education, prompting discussion and debate in order to move beyond dualistic thinking towards transformational change. Critical reflection goes beyond individual experiences and engages students in thinking about structures and systems. Reflection enables students, faculty, staff, and community partners to engage authentically, provide feedback, and translate experiences into future actions for long-term social justice outcomes.

CONCLUSION

Service-learning, leadership education, and social justice work can exist separately, however, the intersection creates powerful opportunities for student learning and community change. Service-learning for social justice leadership education invites students, faculty, staff, and community members to be in relationship with one another and address issues of collective concern. These pedagogies implore educators, learners, and community members to dive deep and explore root causes, systems of inequality, and possibilities for change in a way that none could do as effectively on their own. It is incumbent upon scholars and practitioners to raise questions about our practice and look for opportunities to bring together pedagogical tools that reinforce one another and strengthen our capacity to educate students, enhance leadership development, engage with the community, and create positive change.

REFERENCES

Bell, S. M., & Carlson, R. (2009). Motivations of community organizations for service learning. In R. Stoecker & E. A. Tryon (Eds.), *The unheard voices: Community organizations and service learning* (pp. 19–37). Philadelphia, PA: Temple University Press.

Break Away. (2018). *Learn more about break away.* Retrieved from http://alternative breaks.org/about/.

Burns, J. M. (1978). *Leadership.* New York, NY: Harper & Row.

Butin, D. W. (2007). Justice-learning: Service-learning as justice-oriented education. *Equity & Excellence in Education, 40,* 177–183.

Campus Compact. (2014). *Three decades of institutionalizing change. 2014 annual member survey.* Retrieved from http://kdp0l43vw6z2dlw631ififc5.wpengine .netdna-cdn.com/wp-content/uploads/2015/05/2014-CC-Member-Survey.pdf

Campus Compact. (2016). *Revitalizing our democracy: Building on our assets. 2016 annual member survey executive summary.* Retrieved from https://compact.org/ initiatives/membership-survey/2016-annual-survey/

Chunoo, V., & Osteen, L. (2016). Purpose, mission, and context: The call for educating future leaders. In K. L. Guthrie, & L. Osteen (Eds.), *New directions for higher education, No. 174: Reclaiming higher education's purpose in leadership development* (pp. 9–20). San Francisco, CA: Jossey-Bass.

d'Arlach, L., Sanchez, B., & Feuer, R. (2009). Voices from the community: A case for reciprocity in service-learning. *Michigan Journal of Community Service Learning, 16*(1), 5–16.

Eyler, J., & Giles, D. E. (1999). *Where's the learning in service-learning?* San Francisco, CA: Jossey-Bass.

Freire, P. (1970). *Pedagogy of the oppressed.* New York, NY: The Continuum International.

Furco, A. (1996). *Service-learning: A balanced approach to experiential education.* Expanding boundaries: Serving and learning. Washington DC: Corporation for National Service.

Guthrie, K. L., & Bertrand Jones, T. (2012). Teaching and learning: Using experiential learning and reflection for leadership education. In K. L. Guthrie & L. Osteen (Eds.), *New directions for student services, No. 140: Developing students' leadership capacity* (pp. 53–64). San Francisco, CA: Jossey-Bass.

Guthrie, K. L., & Osteen, L. (2016). Editors' Notes. In K. L. Guthrie & L. Osteen (Eds.), *New directions for higher education, No. 174: Reclaiming higher education's purpose in leadership development* (pp. 5–8). San Francisco, CA: Jossey-Bass.

Guthrie, K. L., & Thompson, S. (2010). Creating meaningful environments for leadership education. *Journal of Leadership Education, 9*(2), 50–57.

Hamerlinck, J., & Plaut, J. (2014). *Asset-based community engagement in higher education.* Minneapolis: Minnesota Campus Compact.

Hartman, E. (2016). Decentering self in leadership: Putting community at the center in leadership studies. In W. Wagner & J. M. Pigza (Eds.), *New directions for student leadership, No. 150: Leadership development through service-learning* (pp. 73–83). San Francisco, CA: Jossey-Bass.

Heifetz, R. A., & Linsky, M. (1994). *Leadership without easy answers.* Cambridge, MA: Harvard University Press.

Higher Education Research Institute. (1996). *A social change model of leadership development: A guidebook.* Los Angeles, CA: Author.

Jacoby, B., & Associates. (1996). *Service-learning in higher education: Concepts and practices.* San Francisco, CA: Jossey-Bass.

Jacoby, B. (2015). *Service-learning essentials: Questions, answers, and lessons learned.* San Francisco, CA: Jossey-Bass

Jenkins, D. M., & Owen, J. E. (2016). Who teachers leadership? A comparative analysis of faculty and student affairs leadership educators and implications for leadership learning. *Journal of Leadership Education, 15*(2), 98–113.

Komives, S. R., Lucas, N., & McMahon, T. R. (2013). *Exploring leadership: For college students who want to make a difference* (3rd ed.). San Francisco, CA: Jossey-Bass.

Martin, A., SeBlonka, K., & Tryon, E. (2009). The challenge of short-term service learning. In R. Stoecker & E. A. Tryon (Eds.), *The unheard voices: Community organizations and service learning* (pp. 57–72). Philadelphia, PA: Temple University Press.

Mitchell, T. D. (2008). Traditional vs. critical service-learning: Engaging the literature to differentiate two models. *Michigan Journal of Community Service Learning, 14*(2), 50–65.

Mitchell, T. D., Donahue, D. M., & Young-Law C. (2012). Service learning as a pedagogy of Whiteness. *Equity & Excellence in Education, 45*(4), 612–629.

O'Meara, K., & Niehaus, E. (2009). Service-learning is… How faculty explain their practice. *Michigan Journal of Community Service Learning, 16*(1), 17–32.

Owen, J. E. (2016). Fostering critical reflection: Moving from a service to a social justice paradigm. In W. Wagner & J. M. Pigza (Eds.), *New directions for student leadership, No. 150: Leadership development through service-learning* (pp. 37–48). San Francisco, CA: Jossey-Bass.

Rost, J. C. (1993). *Leadership for the twenty-first century.* New York, NY: Praeger.

Sandmann, L. R., Thornton, C. H., & Jaeger, A. J. (2009). The first wave of community-engaged institutions. In L. R. Sandmann, C. H. Thornton, & A. J. Jaeger (Eds.), *New directions for higher education, No. 147: Institutionalizing community engagement in higher education: The First wave of Carnegie classified institutions* (pp. 99–104). San Francisco, CA: Jossey-Bass.

Seemiller, C. (2006). Impacting social change through service learning in an introductory leadership course. *Journal of Leadership Education, 5*(2), 41–49.

Stoecker, R. (2016). *Liberating service learning and the rest of higher education civic engagement.* Philadelphia, PA: Temple University Press.

Stoecker, R., & Tryon, E. A. (2009). *The unheard voices: Community organizations and service learning.* Philadelphia, PA: Temple University Press

Sumka, S., Porter, M. C., & Piacitelli, J. (2015). *Working side by side: Creating alternative breaks as catalysts for global learning, student leadership, and social change.* Sterling, VA: Stylus.

Wagner, W. (2009). What is social change? In S. R. Komives, W. Wagner, & Associates (Eds.), *Leadership for a better world: Understanding the social change model of leadership development* (pp. 7–41). San Francisco, CA: Jossey-Bass.

Wagner, W., & Pigza, J. M. (2016a). Editors' notes. In W. Wagner & J. M. Pigza (Eds.), *New directions for student leadership, No. 150: Leadership development through service-learning* (pp. 5–8). San Francisco, CA: Jossey-Bass.

Wagner, W., & Pigza, J. M. (2016b). Fostering critical reflection: Moving from a service to a social justice paradigm. In W. Wagner & J. M. Pigza (Eds.), *New directions for student leadership, No. 150: Leadership development through service-learning* (pp. 11–22). San Francisco, CA: Jossey-Bass.

CHAPTER 20

COALESCING COMMUNITIES

The Call for Critical Leadership Pedagogy in Leadership Education

Erica Wiborg

Leadership scholarship was rooted in industrial models until Rost (1991) called to redevelop leadership for the 21st century. As Rost (1991) began to question and develop a new understanding of leadership, he called for a shift toward the post-industrial ways of thinking about leadership. Post-industrial leadership was more collaborative, less competitive and more focused on power with others, rather than power over others (Rost, 1991) than industrial models. It requires a more collaborative and collective process for leadership, which should be informed by inclusion, accessibility, and respecting differences (Bordas, 2016). In the spirit of power with others, the field of leadership is beginning to recognize the need to bridge social justice and leadership education to empower voices often marginalized (Pendakur & Furr, 2016). Leadership education needs to construct new ways of being in curricular and cocurricular experiences to "resonate with our growing mosaic society" (Bordas, 2016, p. 61).

For the purposes of this chapter, social justice is defined as both a process and a goal (Bell, 2013). As Bell (2013) stated, "the goal of social justice is full and equal participation of all groups in a society that is mutually shaped to meet their needs" (p. 21). This involves individuals working with others to create change through their agency as social actors (Bell, 2013). Bell (2013) identified developing this process for social justice is not easy, especially in a society steeped in oppression. Understanding the goal helps align the process with our individual actions to be social actors aware of systems of power, privilege and oppression within the leadership education realm also steeped in hierarchy. Coupling instruction and social justice in leadership education, a potential answer to addressing inequities and building learning environments around tolerance, acceptance, and voice, is critical pedagogy.

Critical pedagogy is defined as a theory and practice of learning that seeks to liberate the learner from the oppressive societal structures that impede learning (Freire, 1970; hooks, 1994). It is a participatory process where teacher and student both engage actively to claim knowledge (Freire, 1970; hooks, 1994). This process of moving between teacher and learner offers an opportunity for everyone in the environment to grow together, to unite but still bring our unique identities, and to coalesce as a community. This chapter will present a goal and a process for applying critical leadership pedagogy (CLP) in leadership education. Critical pedagogy literature will be reviewed, the goal of CLP will be presented, and a process for creating, as well as sustaining an environment founded on CLP will be discussed.

CRITICAL THEORIES AND PEDAGOGIES

Critical pedagogy emerged from attempts to apply the tenets of critical theory. Critical theory originated from a school of thought and a body of scholarship striving for social equality across a variety of dimensions. This section introduces critical theory and how pedagogy has emerged as a way of advancing this school of thought. In addition, critical pedagogy is suited well to integrate social justice concepts into the realm of leadership education. The term CLP will be introduced in this chapter to set the foundation for the chapter.

Critical Theory

In the 20th century, scholars from the Frankfurt School or the Institute for Social Research in Germany examined how society came to build knowledge (Sensoy & DiAngelo, 2012). Sensoy and DeAngelo (2012) stated, "Critical theory developed in part as a response to this presumed superiority and infallibility of scientific method, and raised questions about *whose* rationality and *whose* presumed objectivity underlies scientific methods" (p. 4). Critical theory rose in North America in the 1960s alongside social justice movements. This lens aligned with other research in academia in that education is the extension of society and "society is structured in ways that marginalize some to the benefit of others" (Sensoy & DiAngelo, 2012, p. 5).

Critical theory combines inequality and the presence of a "master theory," which assists with both individual and collective meaning making and worldviews. Critical theorists assert knowledge is socially constructed; "... knowledge is reflective of the values and interests of those who produce it" (Sensoy & DiAngelo, 2012, p. 7). There is a problem in education; it is a system founded on power, privilege, and oppression because of the people who produce it. Scholars like Giroux (1997), Giroux and McLaren (1994), McLaren (1989), Freire (1970), hooks (1994), and many others, have presented this problem and identified how we might liberate the learner through interrupting the larger systems of oppression through our teaching.

Critical Leadership Theory

As leadership education emerged in higher education, theories and the models of leadership were founded, created, and often maintained by White male leadership scholars (Dugan & Komives, 2011) much like those in charge of the institutions influencing most academic fields (i.e., business, education, etc.). Critical theory perspectives, and a focus toward critical leadership theory, requires assessing the content of leadership studies through lenses of power, privilege, and oppression. From the development of industrial models of leadership, the field of leadership was started and gave primary power to men, particularly White men and this context is important in understanding the origins, and current condition, of the field of leadership. Diverse leadership scholars are beginning to contribute more collaborative approaches, but as Mahoney (2016) stated, "... there are still sociohistorical canonical limitations to diverse perspectives and who is affirmed as capable of producing valuable leadership knowledge" (p. 52). The sociohistorical elements of the field matter deeply to how we construct and apply theory, as well as how leadership educators approach theory, practice, and pedagogy.

Critical Pedagogy

Critical approaches to pedagogy were initiated by those committed to progressive education (Darder, Baltodano, & Torres, 2009). There have also been multiple critiques of critical pedagogy, which the concept itself invites, rooted in feminist views. The primary educator who influenced this critique, hooks (1994), developed a Black feminist critical pedagogy lens, offering ways of conceptualizing components of the classroom environment.

As we attempt to apply critical pedagogy to leadership education, we must critique critical pedagogy to inform our pedagogical framework through an intersectional lens. hooks (1994) stated:

> ...the work of various thinkers on radical pedagogy has in recent years truly included a recognition of differences—those determined by class, race, sexual practice, nationality, and so on. Yet this movement forward does not seem to coincide with any significant increase in black or other nonwhite voices joining discussions about radical pedagogical practices. (pp. 9–10)

The multiple perspectives she brings to her work are from anticolonial, critical, and feminist lenses. hooks (1994) did not offer succinct steps, but at the heart of her work is the union of mind, body, and spirit in teaching and learning, as well as the need to be self-actualized as a teacher. She encouraged resisting fear of the messy and complex nature of education, lest we fail as we open our classrooms up to dissent and the reconstruction of truths (hooks, 1994). She urges educators to recognize and confront implicit biases in teaching and learning if we are to change our teaching styles to prevent their perpetuation (hooks, 1994).

Critical Leadership Pedagogy

Pendakur and Furr (2016) utilized CLP, and explored critical pedagogy in leadership programs from both a curricular and cocurricular lens but particularly for college students of color. They focused on sharing their experiences and encouraging leadership educators to use critical pedagogy for full inclusion of all students. Pendakur and Furr (2016) stated:

> Critical pedagogy can help us develop curricula that are relevant to the lived experiences of race and racism for many college students of color, as well as produce leader identities that are grounded in an empowered sense of self. Furthermore, critical pedagogy can be applied to existing, canonical leadership models, such as the social change model, to help in meaningfully including social identities, such as race or sexual orientation, which are at the heart of students' leadership learning. (p. 54)

Mahoney (2016) and Pendakur and Furr (2016) reflected and asserted we need to look at the content of leadership education, and the process of engaging all learners to deconstruct systems of power, privilege and oppression that exist in the classroom.

Pendakur and Furr (2016) asserted CLP aligns espoused values of diversity and inclusion in higher education with the reality of including students who have been historically excluded in leadership education. Developing culturally relevant leadership learning (CRLL) requires leadership educators to use critical pedagogy in the deconstruction of "walls of Whiteness" (Mahoney, 2016, p. 47) to reconfigure leadership content/theory and curriculum. Through critical frameworks, as well as the deconstruction and reconfiguration of leadership education, Mahoney (2016) stated, we cannot just "leave the development of multicultural and equitable approaches to happenstance" (p. 57). A paradigm shift in our learning environments must occur in leadership education. In the spirit of Bell's (2013) definition of social justice, the next section of this chapter will present a goal for CLP, as well as a process for creating and sustaining this goal.

GOAL OF CRITICAL LEADERSHIP PEDAGOGY

Through this chapter, I advocate for CLP in creating coalescing communities of culturally relevant leadership co-learners. This goal will be approached from three conceptualizations: coalescing community, culturally relevant leadership, and co-learners. Each piece of this goal offers a process for CLP, and when combined can offer a goal for integrating liberation from the oppressive systems that can impede learning. In the spirit of praxis—reflection and action—I challenge you to reflect on these components and in the margins of this chapter consider and write out how you might act on these definitions. Later, this chapter will offer a process for integrating and reaching this goal, however; your agency as an educator will have far more power in your own domain of education and what better place to brainstorm disrupting the master narrative that exists in education than in the margin.

hooks (1994) recommended confronting implicit biases in educational frameworks and approaches, as well as understanding how knowledge is constructed from own lived experiences. As the author, I think it is important for you to know where my perspective and lens is coming from prior to considering this approach for your own leadership learning environments. As a White woman who teaches leadership and social justice, I sit in an extremely privileged position, but I have come to understand teaching from the centering and starting point of identity. My goal is for my voice to be the backdrop and the focus to be on the process of learning. I have learned this from messing up through my own biases and assumptions until I began to study social justice in the context of leadership education. As I continue to shed my blinders, I have listened and reflected at the intersection of storytelling and research. This took action individually, but also in relationship with others through collective work.

Coalescing Community

"Coalesce" means to unite or come together (Harro, 2000). Often used in conjunction with the word coalition, coalescing celebrates having more power with each other than without. Influenced by Harro's (2000) cycle of liberation, coalescing includes coming together as we to respond to overt oppression and stepping outside of the perceived roles as change agents. Harro (2000) stated, "We are refusing to collude in oppression, and to participate in self-fulfilling prophesies. We are refusing to accept privileges, and we are acting as role models and allies for others" (p. 623). This transformation of community is founded on shared power, trust, and hope for change. Rather than being a safe space, the commitment is founded on community and a common good, connecting each student (hooks, 1994). In the leadership classroom, coalescing communities can be powerful environments for dissent because of the trust built and how it can inform learners to understand working with others is far more meaningful than working in isolation. This sentiment models the exact way socially just leadership can be taught.

Culturally Relevant Leadership

As institutions become increasingly diverse, culturally relevant leadership educators transform learning to be inclusive of diverse students (Guthrie, Bertrand Jones, Osteen, & Hu, 2013). The CRLL framework addresses both the opportunities and challenges of difference in leadership education (Bertrand Jones, Guthrie & Osteen, 2016). Bertrand Jones et al. (2016) stated, "Culturally relevant leadership learning acknowledges power in leadership, specifically the power of language and the power of the institutional culture/climate to influence students' identity, capacity, and efficacy to create social change" (p. 10). This means leadership education that address social inequality, inclusion, and equity through teaching. The realm of leadership education should seek to coalesce and unite around issues of power and privilege to influence everyone's leadership learning.

Co-Learners

Historically, classrooms have been built around rigid structures and roles—you are either the teacher or the student. Pushing back against this paradigm, CLP seeks to reconstruct our understanding of the fluidity of these roles within academic contexts. This requires educators to teach about the process of learning in the classroom with the hope of becoming co-learners as well as equal contributors of knowledge. This can be scary for some people engaged in the process and students can be confused when there is a mutual responsibility for learning (hooks, 1994). This process requires us to teach students "how to listen, how to hear one another" (hooks, 1994, p. 150). Leadership is a lifelong process of learning, every person in the classroom has something to learn and a responsibility to learn it, therefore being committed co-learners is a necessary part of the goal and process for CLP.

CREATING AND SUSTAINING A COALESCING COMMUNITY

The process for CLP includes various roles and relationships, which include learners, teachers, and context. As previously stated, the learner and teacher roles are fluid in CLP. As the instructor or leadership educator, we move in and out of the teacher role to create space for coalescing and co-learning, as well as deconstructing the power barriers. However, at the end of the semester, we do hold the power to determine final grades or successful completion of academic programs. There are ways to incorporate inclusive and equitable grading practices to engage the learner through the grading process, which will be discussed later. The context is included in the relationships because what happens in the campus, community, state, national, and global context influences our individual and intersecting identities impacting our experience as leadership co-learners. We are not separate from environmental influences and impacts.

As an example of the integration of all three in a leadership learning classroom engaged in CLP, I will provide a story in my own work exhibiting these relationships. I taught a leadership and change course at my institution, which is a required course for students participating in the undergraduate certificate in leadership studies, but I also had students who had not taken a leadership course before. From the onset of the class, I made it clear we will all be teachers and learners at different points throughout the semester and even within individual class periods. There is a required assignment where the students facilitate a lesson on the readings. This assignment allowed every person to use their voice in the class and to assume the formal role of teacher during a class period. During the semester, a racialized hazing event was reported, which was allegedly perpetrated by a predominantly White male Greek-letter organization. I shifted the formalized plan and opened the class with an article about the event. We dug into what this occurrence meant for creating change at our institution and we had people across all racial/ethnic backgrounds, some close to the event, some not, speak and share with each other. Students challenged and supported each other simultaneously. The context mattered. In fact, it illuminated the leadership concepts far beyond whatever formalized plan I had for class. We talked about our personal feelings from the event and how they motivated us to create change or understand a different perspective.

To further describe and breakdown the process of CLP, a frame for creating coalescing communities was developed as a model to describe the mutual influences (see Figure 20.1). The outside circle represents the larger roles or relationships with the classroom communities of teacher, learner, and context. The inside circles and arrows represent orbs of influences to the community. These influences are domains from the CRLL model by Bertrand Jones et al. (2016) and serve as consideration of the role of climate in leadership learning. As a form of displacement and centering issues of social justice, diversity, inclusion, with identity at the core, these orbs matter to students' engagement in leadership education (Bertrand Jones et al., 2016; Mahoney, 2016).

As stated by Bertrand Jones et al. (2016), the historical legacy of inclusion/exclusion from a leadership perspective includes how people of color and other marginalized groups have been left out of curriculum, as well as understanding who has historically participated in leadership learning (courses, programs, certificates, etc.) at your institution. Compositional diversity goes beyond just who is present in your class or program from marginalized student populations, but also requires paying attention to

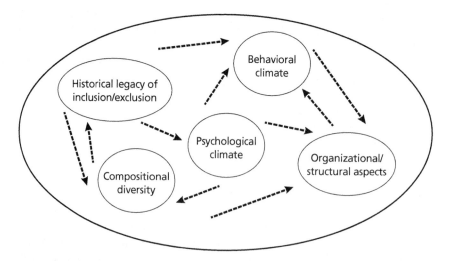

Figure 20.1 Coalescing community frame: Teacher–Learner–Context relationship

structural diversity and a commitment to increasing difference in the classroom. The psychological dimension "emphasizes individual views of group relations, perceptions of discrimination or conflict, attitudes about difference, and institutional responses to diversity" (Bertrand Jones et al., 2016, p. 17). This particular domain highlights how marginalized student populations have dissimilar experiences and therefore the learning environment must honor these differing experiences. The behavioral dimension is based on the interactions between the teachers and learners across difference. Finally, the organizational/structural dimension is based on the curriculum and policies of the classroom (syllabus, grading, hiring of instructors, etc.) or program. By centering these five domains in CLP, leadership educators can organize tangible practices for creating coalescing communities. The next section offers practical implications for the leadership education classroom and communities of co-learners we strive to sustain.

Practical Implications in Leadership Learning

At the start of this chapter, you were prompted to reflect on your own application of the CLP goal in creating a coalescing community of culturally relevant leadership co-learners. This section includes practical implications of integrating CLP into leadership learning environments. These suggestions below offer a starting point for considering integrating CLP into your personal practice to create coalescing communities; it comes from a point of positionality from myself as the author of this article and the individuals that have contributed to my lived experiences. These practical implications are a collection of voices from colleagues, peers, authors, researchers, and friends. They are lessons learned from phenomenal teachers and learners, I encourage you to star, highlight, and critique this section as you integrate your voice and experiences.

Historical Legacy of Inclusion/Exclusion

- *Center your leadership theories around activist strategies of women and people of color (Mahoney, 2016).* Select leadership theories that are more relational and collaborative, and that bring in the contextual influence and systematic influence that address sociohistorical effects (Mahoney, 2016). Utilizing Bordas' (2016) writing on leadership principles and values from communities of color, or centralizing activism and activist theories into the curriculum (Mahoney, 2016) would be suggestions that have been utilized in my personal practice.
- *Make it clear on the onset of your class or program that verbal contributions are required (hooks, 1994).* This ensures everyone has voice in the community. This can be setup during expectations for the class/

program. Prioritize doing this early to have clarity and begin practicing, as well as holding each other accountable. In my personal teaching practices, I have time early in the semester to give peer feedback on how they are contributing to the dialogue and advancing our learning as a collective class. Awkward at first, but students enjoy it and are more likely to continue to affirm or challenge each other in respectful ways.

- *Encourage student voice in deconstructing the concept of leadership in relation to social disparities through dialogue (Mahoney, 2016).* Ask pointed questions around how leadership is defined and narrated in our society. Through various leadership programs, I have seen structured dialogue work well that answers the question—leadership for whom? (Mahoney, 2016). Mahoney (2016) suggested asking the question, "What are the cultural, political, historical, and social investments in fostering this idea of leadership?" (p. 57).

- *Be open to different writing styles and encourage students to write in their native language then to translate, even if it is outside the Standard English requirements (hooks, 1994).* As students build their understanding and personal definition of leadership, encourage integrating culture into their articulation, which would include language. Affirming students in however they integrate their language into the leadership learning environment creates a space that does not erase the power of language in our own understanding and learning across difference.

- *Discuss the social identities and feature an "author" profile for each book selected in your core curriculum.* If students ask why identity is important to knowledge construction and reading materials, open the dialogue to seek value in understanding diverse perspectives. Consider including a picture and sharing their background, as well as their field of study, and other influences on the topic.

Compositional Diversity

- *Market your course registration to diverse groups of students.* Ensure you are sharing with groups of students who typically do not self-select into leadership learning programs or courses. Once you begin this process, word of mouth is a powerful vehicle for continuing engagement in culturally diverse communities.

- *Recruit diverse staff, faculty, and teaching assistants.* Leadership educators should select staff, faculty, and teaching assistants who are reflective of diverse voices. This means being aware of aligning demographics with institutional, local, state, national, and global demographics (Bertrand Jones et al., 2016).

- *Be aware of your own identities and social positionality in the classroom or in programs (race, class, gender, sexual orientation, ability, etc.) and how they influence your reactions (Sensoy & DiAngelo, 2012).* Figure out a practice for how you engage with reflection aimed at social justice and identity. As an example, I take extensive notes on what questions students are asking and utilize those notes to reflect on how I processed or responded. This active journaling not only assists with remembering who is contributing when to the learning community but also how my identities are contributing to the community.

Psychological Climate

- *Recognize and embrace experience, confessions, and testimonies as relevant knowledge constructions in the classroom and learning environment (hooks, 1994).* This allows students to process and apply theoretical information, particularly to challenge more dominant theories. In a program that utilized the social change model of leadership development (HERI, 1996), a student shared having issues with the concept of controversy with civility, one of the seven C's in the model. She felt civility was coded language to mean be peaceful and quiet. She questioned as a woman of color who defined civility and that some social change movements required actions beyond civility. It is imperative to affirm these narratives for students to see their knowledge construction is valuable and their identity as social change agents is relevant, as well as needed.
- *Call out energy, be aware of emotions, and bring up dissonance (hooks, 1994; Sensoy & DiAngelo, 2012).* This requires a flexibility in your agenda and a commitment for the coalescing community to be brave (Watt, 2016). Watt (2016) discussed how brave space allows for authentic and honest dialogue that leads to growth. By focusing on a brave space in leadership learning environments, co-learners can learn from the dissonance and discomfort to grow as a community.
- *Be prepared for students to say things like "I don't see color," "I accept people for who they are."* They are rooted in years of socialization from family members, media, and other institutions (Sensoy & DiAngelo, 2012; Mahoney, 2016). The community should unsettle these concepts and look at broader societal concepts.
- *Situate discussions on identity front and center to challenge notions of colorblindness (Mahoney, 2016).* When facilitating leadership curriculum, facilitate identity based reflection rather than self-assessments that are character or trait based. Consider incorporating identity wheels or activities that reflect on the learners' experiences growing up and throughout their life. Include sharing with each other in the community to coalesce and connect across differences.

Behavioral Climate

- *When students return from breaks, ask how the concepts they learned in class or in the leadership program impacted their experiences outside of class or program and with their families or friends (hooks, 1994).* After breaks where they may have been in a different environment, facilitate a pair-and-share activity including prompts on their observations, actions, or inactions. End the activity with a community-wide reflection on congruence and managing complexity between contexts. Recognize code-switching and contextual awareness as ways of managing environments. Affirm while engaging in dialogue about complexity of self in relation to context, and how we collaborate to create authentic spaces.

- *Intervene during instances of "tokenism" and from the onset share that no one is an expert or a "native informant" to experiences (hooks, 1994, p. 44).* It is important to include this in your expectations at the beginning of the program or class. If tokenism is perpetuated in the leadership learning environment, this puts an unfair burden on the student (hooks, 1994). Have narratives and stories available beyond the community through TED talks or social justice resources like Racial Equity Tools that include a wide range of voices, rather than relying on students with that marginalized identity.

- *Own up to the inherent power differences of student and instructor.* Challenge these constructs and perceptions early in the class setup (hooks, 1994). While the role of instructor is present, it is important to share that as instructors we do not know everything. Social justice and leadership education is a process of learning we will all be engaging in for a lifetime. Demystify the expectation of "expert on the topic" and commit to power being shared within the relationships to each other and the knowledge being presented in the class, not necessarily between the roles.

- *Encourage affirmations and feedback from their peers.* This will deconstruct needing affirmation from the instructor and redirect to each other's voices (hooks, 1994). The instructor can be a connector and facilitator of peer feedback. I often redirect questions back to the community if a question is asked directly to me. I may rephrase the question or dig deeper, but my hope is that they will listen to each other.

- *Share what you are learning from the students (hooks, 1994).* This allows for them to view you as a co-learner in the coalescing community. This requires vulnerability and open communication with your students. If you do not understand what a student is saying, ask, seek understanding.

- *Acknowledge instructors as well as students bring an array of unexamined assumptions and implicit biases to the classroom (Adams, 2007).* Confront them and give feedback on them. For example, asking questions to get at the root of a belief or perceived fact is important. Utilizing the following questions can create dialogue around assumptions and biases: How have you come to know that? Where did you learn that? How has that shown up in your personal life?

Organizational/Structural Aspects

- *As you build the syllabus, consider what policies you are including and how you are communicating the philosophy for the class.* These words matter and begin the process of the coalescing community. This is the place to include some of the above practical implications like requirement of utilizing voice or expectations around not tokenizing people or their experiences. The syllabus can serve as a contract for the class and can be revisited to assess where the co-learning environment is when it seems that the community is getting off track.

- *The source of power should be in the learning process, not the grading process.* This requires some flexibility in your grading. Try communicating you are an observer and students have the power as they control their engagement in the classroom. Have students assess their academic growth and you give real time feedback on what you have witnessed to couple their assessment (hooks, 1994). Resist students being passive consumers by providing ongoing feedback points throughout the course and clarifying goals, hopes, and expectations (hooks, 1994).

- *Use the physical environment strategically—move chairs and setup depending on the course content and setup.* Physical space matters to engagement and power dynamics. Standing up or sitting down communicates power as well. Sometimes the space is not flexible to move tables or chairs, so bring it up and ask what we can we do to offset the physical limitations.

- *Utilize reflection as tools for student-centered co-learning* (Adams, 2007). After activities, prompt students to consider their personal feelings or reactions to the content by writing them down. I have used this because it assists with raising awareness and consciousness prior to engaging in coalescing conversations. For example, in a first year leadership and identity-based program, I have students respond to the prompt, what needs to be present for collaborative leadership to be effective? They use post-it notes and individually write out their responses to the questions, one statement per post-it note. I then request that they get into groups and match commonalities without losing the uniqueness of their reflection. We then as a community build a collective understanding of the response to the term by having them report out to display on a large board. This process builds and we begin the program with a collective understanding of what the focus of our learning is.

This is certainly not an exhaustive list, but it does challenge us as leadership educators to examine our ways of knowing, being, and doing (Mahoney, 2016). It requires intentional planning and interactions between teacher, learner, and context. Osteen, Guthrie, and Bertrand Jones (2016) questioned, "…how do each of us in this process of learning, unlearning, relearning stay vulnerable, authentic, and self-aware?" (p. 104). As we integrate a new pedagogical framework into our teaching and learning environments, we must engage in critical, reflective self-work that hopefully leads to leadership educators who are more self-actualized and leaders who are ready to create change, even amongst the most complex or systematic challenges.

CONCLUSION

Critical pedagogy, most notably developed through the work of Paulo Freire (1970), promoted education that can and should liberate the learner. Significant research has been done through primary education, key scholars have focused on higher education, but little has been done to apply critical theory to leadership education (Zylstra, 2011). When we need leaders to create positive, sustainable change for our world, I cannot help but consider how our teaching and learning must be rooted in social justice. Hunt (1998) stated it beautifully: "When issues of social justice are at the heart of our classroom teaching, our students benefit from the rich history of people who didn't settle for the way things are" (p. xiii). Our teaching and learning environments in leadership education cannot settle either, and we need to figure out how to ground our instruction in CLP so it can be a practice of freedom, rather than another structure of oppression (hooks, 1994).

As we seek to empower diverse voices through our leadership education environments, we must commit to developing coalescing communities of culturally relevant leadership co-learners. This goal and process is neither simple, nor did I want to offer a checkbox for how to incorporate CLP into teaching. This is a messy process and this call is never easy as we strive to deconstruct barriers of power, privilege, and oppression. It is hard work, requiring incredible individual and collective engagement through critical thought. In a world needing engagement in relationship with others, I see CLP as a way to unite across difference while maintaining our individual and empowered voices through our learning. I leave you with a question— Where can you make changes to incorporate a paradigm shift in your teaching and learning now?

REFERENCES

Adams, M. (2007). Pedagogical frameworks for social justice education. In M. Adams, L. A. Bell, & P. Griffin (Eds.), *Teaching for diversity and social justice* (pp. 15–33). New York, NY: Routledge.

Bertrand Jones, T., Guthrie, K. L., & Osteen, L. (2016). Critical domains of culturally relevant leadership learning: A call to transform leadership programs. In K. L. Guthrie, T. Bertrand Jones, & L. Osteen (Eds.), *New directions for student leadership, No. 152: Developing culturally relevant leadership learning* (pp. 9–21). San Francisco, CA: Jossey-Bass.

Bell, L. A. (2013). Theoretical foundations. In M. Adams, W. J. Blumenfeld, C. Castaneda, H. W. Hackman, M. L. Peters, & X. Zuniga (Eds.), *Readings for diversity and social justice* (pp. 21–26). New York, NY: Routledge.

Bordas, J. (2016). Leadership lessons from communities of color: Stewardship and collective action. In K. L. Guthrie, T. Bertrand Jones, & L. Osteen (Eds.), *New directions for student leadership, No. 152: Developing culturally relevant leadership learning* (pp. 61–74). San Francisco, CA: Jossey-Bass.

Darder, A., Baltodano, M. P., & Torres, R. D. (2009). Critical pedagogy: An introduction. In A. Darder, M. P. Baltodano, & R. D. Torres (Eds.), *The critical pedagogy reader* (pp. 1–20). New York, NY: Routledge.

Dugan, J. P., & Komives, S. R. (2011). Leadership theories. In S. R. Komives, J. P. Dugan, J. E. Owen, C. Slack, & W. Wagner (Eds.), *The handbook for student leadership development* (2nd ed.; pp. 35–37). San Francisco, CA: Jossey-Bass.

Freire, P. (1970). *Pedagogy of the oppressed.* New York, NY: Continuum.

Giroux, H. (1997). *Pedagogy and the politics of hope: Theory, culture, and schooling.* Boulder, CO: Westview.

Giroux, H., & McLaren, P. (1994). *Between borders: Pedagogy and the politics of cultural studies.* New York, NY: Routledge.

Guthrie, K. L., Bertrand Jones, T., Osteen, L. K., & Hu, S. (2013). Cultivating leader identity and capacity in students from diverse backgrounds. *ASHE Higher Education Report, 39*(4).

Harro, B. (2000). The cycle of liberation. In M. Adams, W. Bluenfeld, R. Castenda, H. Hackman, M. Peters, & X. Zuniga (Eds.), *Readings for diversity and social justice* (pp. 618–625). New York, NY: Routledge.

Higher Education Research Institute (HERI). (1996). *A social change model of leadership development* (3rd ed.). Los Angeles: University of California Los Angeles, Higher Education Research Institute.

hooks, b. (1994). *Teaching to transgress: Education as a practice of freedom.* New York, NY: Routledge.

Hunt, J. E. (1998). Preface: Of stories, seeds, and the promises of social justice. In W. Ayers, J. A. Hunt, & T. Quinn (Eds.), *Teaching for social justice* (pp. xiii–xv). New York, NY: The New Press.

Mahoney, A. (2016). Culturally responsive integrative learning environments: A critical displacement approach. In K. L. Guthrie, T. Bertrand Jones, & L. Osteen (Eds.), *New directions for student leadership, No. 152: Developing culturally relevant leadership learning* (pp. 47–59). San Francisco, CA: Jossey-Bass.

McLaren, P. (1989). *Life in Schools: An introduction to critical pedagogy in the foundations of education.* New York, NY: Longman.

Osteen, L., Guthrie, K. L., & Bertrand Jones, T. (2016). Leading to transgress: Critical considerations for transforming leadership learning. In K. L. Guthrie, T. Bertrand Jones, & L. Osteen (Eds.), *New directions for student leadership, No. 152: Developing culturally relevant leadership learning* (pp. 95–106). San Francisco, CA: Jossey-Bass.

Pendakur, V., & Furr, S. C. (2016). Critical leadership pedagogy: Engaging power, identity, and culture in leadership education for college students of color. In K. L. Guthrie & L. Osteen (Eds.), *New directions for higher education, No. 174: Reclaiming higher education's purpose in leadership development* (pp. 45–55) San Francisco, CA: Jossey-Bass.

Rost, J. C. (1991). *Leadership for the twenty-first century.* Westport, CT: Praeger.

Sensoy, O., & DiAngelo, R. (2012). *Is everyone really equal? An introduction to key concepts in social justice education.* New York, NY: Teachers College.

Watt, S. K. (2016). The practice of freedom: Leading through controversy. In K. L. Guthrie, T. Bertrand Jones, & L. Osteen (Eds.), *New directions for student leadership, No. 152: Developing culturally relevant leadership learning* (pp. 35–46). San Francisco, CA: Jossey-Bass.

Zylstra, J. D. (2011). Why is the gap so wide between espousing a social justice agenda to promote learning and enacting it? In P. M. Magolda & M. B. Baxter Magolda (Eds.), *Contested issues in student affairs: Diverse perspectives and respectful dialogue* (pp. 375–386). Sterling, VA: Stylus.

CHAPTER 21

THE IMPERATIVE FOR ACTION

Beyond the Call for Socially Just Leadership Education

Vivechkanand S. Chunoo and Kathy L. Guthrie

A significant amount of literature, and even some chapters in this book, end on a call for action which attempts to motivate the reader toward creating change. Although we honor and value this deep tradition, the simple call to action is no longer enough. We believe the imperative for action with respect to socially just leadership education is about the moral and ethical obligation we all face; regardless of whether or not we choose to see it as such. In listening to narratives from diverse voices on their personal experiences regarding leadership development pushed us into action and see a need to not only open the conversation about socially just leadership education, but actively work towards changing the narrative.

A cursory review of any day's top news stories reveals a litany of injustices and societal imbalances. The problems faced by leaders have never been more nuanced or more deeply entrenched in the fabric of an unjust society. The only way forward requires a thorough disentangling of people, problems, and social structures. Our current leaders are complicit in this state

Changing the Narrative, pages 321–328
Copyright © 2018 by Information Age Publishing
All rights of reproduction in any form reserved.

of affairs; their relative inability (or unwillingness) to engage in egalitarian and shared leadership process hold back the coming tide of social justice.

However, those of us engaged in leadership education, and efforts toward social justice, are part of that wave. We see the progress of our students and the development of emerging leaders and ride those waves over the walls of oppression that have held us back from fully engaged leadership and democratic processes. Though, doing so effectively requires thoughtful and reflective approaches to theory, practice, and pedagogy. We must deconstruct the old ways of teaching social justice and leadership to reformulate socially just leadership education. Though the path ahead is uncharted and fraught with difficulty, we can no longer afford to reject the imperative for action before us.

CRITICAL CONSIDERATIONS FOR SOCIALLY JUST LEADERSHIP EDUCATION

Adopting a social justice orientation in leadership education requires educators to call into question what they teach, how they teach it, and toward which ends they teach. Dugan (2017) models this process by deconstructing the, "Story Most Often Told" (p. 59). This story, he argues, is perpetuated because of how rarely we interrogate assumptions associated with the interdisciplinary leadership cannon; the hegemony which has seeped into leadership theories and models; the commodification of leaders, followers, and leadership processes; or the flow of power between and among individuals engaged in leadership. This "willful blindness" makes us all complicit in, "...maintaining inequitable systems by failing to acknowledge or act..." (p. 66) in confronting how people from historically marginalized groups have been excluded from leadership. The authors included here have given us incredibly useful tools in deconstructing leadership education with implications for its socially just reformulation.

Leadership Education Deconstruction Tools

In Chapter 3, Miguel Angel Hernandez articulated a vision where participants in socially just leadership education are prepared to work toward positive and sustainable social change. By disentangling the notions of equity, diversity, multicultural, and social justice, he offered a path forward paved with more than just words. Walking that path, however, is the greater challenge. His transformation toward the inclusion model demonstrated how we can move from access to change through awareness and inclusion, and this kind of thinking is exactly what is needed in action-oriented social justice leadership education. The vocabulary provided in his writing provides a helpful bridge from our internal sense of social right and wrong to the actions of activism and advocacy needed to advance a social justice agenda in leadership education.

Marshall Anthony Jr. reminded us in Chapter 4 how deeply woven activism and advocacy are in the fabric of American colleges and universities. In doing so, he rekindles the fire that should be burning inside each of us, using concepts of activism heterogeneity, psychology, and behavior to push educators to the uncomfortable edges of righteous thinking and acting. Appreciating how each socially just leadership educator is situated in a particular context, with differential strengths to leverage and obstacles to overcome, means we can no longer accept structural or professional barriers; we may have very little business advocating on behalf of students if we cannot do so for ourselves and our field. The time has come to protect those of us in more dangerous conditions and to support those who are more advantageously positioned. Our students are watching and our leadership practices become their leadership learning.

Many more of our authors offered ways to formulate leadership education and social justice training toward greater alignment. These recommendations largely focus on reconsidering students' lived experiences and how these histories inform their leadership learning and that of others. They also constitute useful guidance in constructing egalitarian contexts for socially just leadership education to flourish. While any given educator may only be able to affect one, or the other, we encourage all instructors to think and act creatively to incorporate more of these recommendations then currently seem possible.

Leadership and Social Justice Reformation Recommendations

Sonja Ardoin's writing, in Chapter 5, on social class intersections with socially just leadership education challenges us to seek opportunities to build social and cultural capital in first generation, lower socioeconomic status, and historically underserved students. Her advice to use asset-based frameworks to reduce engagement barriers and more effectively market the value of leadership in general, and socially just leadership education in particular, represents significant shifts in how leadership has been traditionally taught. However, this shift is vital in changing the narrative around class in socially just leadership education.

Similarly, Erin Sylvester (Chapter 12) and Jennifer Farinella (Chapter 13) push socially just leadership educators to build caring communities for first-generation students, foster care youth, and those from a variety of family structures. Although we could not engage in writing about the impacts of other family systems, such as students with one or more incarcerated parent or guardian, intercultural households, same-sex parenting and guardianship, married students with or without children, or students with elder care responsibilities, we honor and value these dynamics and encourage educators to consider how they reinforce and challenge the family influences students bring with them. Keeping in mind the unique challenges and assets of students from diverse background and family configurations with respect to leadership and social justice can guide our actions in planning and performing the tasks of leadership education.

We specifically included chapters to help leadership educators complicate the conceptualization of leader to include intersections of race and gender, particularly for Black women, Black men, Latinas, Latinos, and Latinx individuals. We also recognize our omission of individuals of Asian, Native American, and multiracial backgrounds, as well as individuals across sexual orientations and those with visible and invisible disabilities (among others); although we may not have included those voices here, all socially just leadership educators consider how these individuals can alter the conversation around leadership, and actively invite them to disrupt the discourse with us.

The topics of religion and spirituality can be difficult to approach, especially on secular and public campuses. However, leadership is often a values-based enterprise. When we divorce students' beliefs from the values they hold, we fragment and fracture their ways of being, often to the detriment of their leader and leadership development. Even in places where faith and values are attended to simultaneously, atheist, agnostic, and other secular students are still marginalized. In Chapter 11, Vivechkanand S. Chunoo and Gabrielle Garrard offered a reframing of interfaith leadership as a way of preparing socially just leaders for faith and philosophical communities. By opening up the conversation around social justice and leadership toward faith and philosophy, we can more intentionally attend to students' beliefs and values, regardless of faith tradition, and help them become more fully integrated leaders.

Furthermore, socially just leadership educators scour their learning environments for opportunities to create the egalitarian conditions we strive toward in larger society. In their chapters, Rose Rezaei, Kathy L. Guthrie, and Jane Rodriguez impress upon leadership educators the balance between brave and safe spaces, in classrooms and across campus. Attending to how and where diversity is recognized and encouraged, and awareness around language, imagery, and symbols has important implications for how space is experienced by all learners. The implications of confronting marginalizing environmental factors inform the crafting of spaces where students' capacity, efficacy, and motivations to lead are enhanced and expanded. Socially just leadership educators have tremendous potential for shaping ultimately the climate and culture of their institutions, leveraging the controllable conditions where leadership learning takes place.

Finally, we recognize how difficult disentangling oppressive influences in leadership learning spaces can be without confronting the prejudices deeply embedded in leadership studies itself. Helpfully, Cameron C. Beatty, Amber Manning-Ouellette, and Erica Wiborg have provided recommendations for teaching leadership through critical lenses and liberatory pedagogy. Through liberatory pedagogy, socially just leadership educators embody the processes of resisting and responding to systemic oppression, as well as use critical perspectives to inform their teaching. Leadership learners, through resisting and responding in their own practice of leadership, embody the positive sustainable change necessary for a more socially just world. By naming and disrupting performative power in the classroom, leadership educators and learners can be freed from the confines of socialization, producing more just leaders and leadership.

THE PATH FORWARD

If integrating social justice and leadership education was as simple as we might make it seem, this book would not be necessary. It is because the path forward is so strewn with obstacles the field has not made more meaningful progress toward unification. In order to provide additional actionable direction to advance an integrated socially just approach to leadership education, we offer the following questions to guide leadership educators' thinking and action. These questions are organized into categories of: critical challenges, oriented toward developing a radar for socially just leadership education; critical hope, organized toward the deconstruction of institutional, ideological, and relational barriers; and critical creativity, intended to spurn the innovative thinking, as well as personal and professional agency to make meaningful, positive, and sustainable changes in leadership education toward social justice.

Critical Challenges

Many of the obstacles to socially just leadership education are so deeply embedded in institutional, departmental, and programmatic practices and culture, basic awareness of them can be challenging. In order to refresh the radar of social justice advocates and leadership educators, we offer the following:

- Where are the ideological walls which center majoritized identities and exclude learners from historically underrepresented communities (Beatty and Ouelette-Manning, Chapter 15)?
- How is language used to appropriately clarify distinctions between "diversity," "inclusion," "tolerance," and "multiculturalism" to not only be accurate but change the narrative around nationalism and ethnocentricity (Hernandez, Chapter 3)?
- How much student self-efficacy do our leadership programs, workshops, and courses assume (Sylvester, Chapter 12)?
- How do social class constructs invite and repel students from programs and initiatives? (Ardoin, Chapter 5)?
- How are students, faculty, and community partners prepared for service learning initiatives (Volpe White, Chapter 19)?
- How are gender dynamics framed with respect to their intersections with leadership education and social justice work (Haber-Curran and Tillapaugh, Chapter 6)?

The questions presented here can help establish a radar for issues of social justice in leadership education programs. The answers can take us to uncomfortable places in our institutions or in our own hearts. However, careful considerations of the issues we have highlighted form the basis of deep changes (Quinn, 1996); the kind of changes which require critical hope to deconstruct and critical creativity to reformulate.

Critical Hope

Most systems are resistant to change in active and passive ways. We honor the struggle of those who have long-standing efforts toward socially just leadership education, as well as those who may be earlier on their journey. We believe socially just leadership education requires critical hope in order to be transformative (Bozalek, Leibowitz, Carolissen, & Boler, 2013). Regardless of your position on the path, consider the following when attempting to address resistant people, systems, and structures:

- How can critical leadership pedagogy expose the weaker points of oppressive systems and highlight the contradictions that keep them in place (Beatty and Ouelette-Manning, Chapter 15)?
- What differential opportunities for socially just leadership learning exist in curricular and cocurricular contexts (Guthrie and Rodriguez, Chapter 16)?

- How can students' self-efficacy be more accurately assessed prior to, during, and after participation in leadership development initiatives (Brock, Chapter 18)?
- How do we build spaces safe enough for students to be brave in the future (Rezaei, Chapter 14)?
- How can constructs of social class be broken down so barriers to leadership education can be deconstructed (Ardoin, Chapter 5)?
- What structures, practices, and symbols reinforce divisions in the community of leadership learners, and why are they still used (Wiborg, Chapter 20)?

In engaging changes toward socially just leadership education, we also recognize the transitions which occur within individuals and among collectives. Bridges (2014) reminded us "it isn't the changes that do you in, it's the transitions" (p. 3), in his descriptions of the situational nature of change and the psychological dimensions of transitions. Socially just leadership educators grapple with psychological transitions by holding onto critical hope in order to drive meaningful changes in their programs and initiatives.

Critical Creativity

Finally, we respect the how reconstruction of leadership learning and social justice work consumes considerable resources; personal, professional, and institutional. These assets are best organized at the nexus of critical paradigms and innovation (McCormack & Titchen, 2006). In order to best marshal those energies, we ask:

- How can physical, financial, and human resources be acquired or organized to construct brave and safe spaces and places for leadership learning (Rezaei, Chapter 14; Guthrie and Rodriguez, Chapter 16)?
- How are we attending to important factors in the cultivation of Black female, Black male, and Latinx leaders (Meriwether, Chapter 7; Spencer, Chapter 8; Torres; Chapter 9; Guardia and Salinas, Chapter 10)?
- Which curricular and cocurricular spaces invite and honor diverse identities of leadership learners, and how can those that do not readily welcome those individuals be reshaped appropriately (Guthrie and Rodriguez, Chapter 16)?
- What role can activism and advocacy play in building self-efficacy in students from diverse backgrounds (Anthony Jr., Chapter 4; Sylvester, Chapter 12)?

- How do we create opportunities for students to be brave in leadership learning spaces? (Rezaei, Chapter 14)?
- How can interfaith perspectives help us rebuild socially just leadership education across faiths and philosophical orientations (Chunoo and Garrard, Chapter 11)?

Given higher education's consistently dwindling budgets and increasingly high demands, greater creativity is required at all levels and across a variety of areas to meet our goals and objectives. We advocate for the use of critical perspectives when developing creative and innovative ways of infusing leadership education with social justice work. Only through such approaches can we fully realize higher education's promise while upholding ideals of fairness, equitability, and empowerment.

Leadership programs that are socially just can no longer be treated as value-added experiences or educational opportunities at the periphery of the academy. Socially just leadership education *is* the value of the undergraduate experience and is core to the mission of higher education. Until social justice and leadership educators see their work as unified, and organize their efforts accordingly, the societal forces that perpetuate the existing social order will remain unchanged. The time has come for those of us who see this work as a moral and ethical imperative for students, for higher education, for our families, our friends, and ourselves to band together and change the narrative.

REFERENCES

Bozalek, V., Leibowitz, B., Carolissen, R., & Boler, M. (Eds.). (2013). *Discerning critical hope in educational practices.* New York, NY: Routledge.

Bridges, W. (2014). *Managing transitions.* Boston, MA: Nicholas Brealey.

Dugan, J. P. (2017). *Leadership theory: Cultivating critical perspectives.* San Francisco, CA: Jossey- Bass.

McCormack, B., & Titchen, A. (2006). Critical creativity: Melding, exploding, blending. *Educational Action Research, 14*(2), 239–266.

Quinn, R. E. (1996). *Deep change.* San Francisco, CA: Jossey-Bass.

ABOUT THE EDITORS

Dr. **Kathy L. Guthrie** is an associate professor of higher education in the Department of Educational Leadership and Policy Studies at Florida State University. In addition to teaching in the higher education program, Kathy also serves as the director of the Leadership Learning Research Center, whose mission is to inform and support scholars, educators, and practitioners regarding leadership teaching and learning through scholarship, curriculum development, and consultation. Kathy also coordinates the undergraduate certificate in leadership studies, which is a partnership between the FSU College of Education and the Center for Leadership and Social Change. Her research focuses on the learning outcomes and environment of leadership and civic education, online teaching and learning, and professional development for student affairs professionals.

Kathy serves on the advisory board for the new *Journal of Campus Activities Practice and Scholarship*, an editorial board member of the *Journal of College and Character*, and a regular reviewer for the *Journal of Leadership Education*. Currently, Dr. Guthrie is the associate editor of the *New Directions in Student Leadership* series and editor of the *Contemporary Perspectives on Leadership Learning* book series. Kathy is also active in several professional associations including ACPA, NASPA, and the International Leadership Association where she is the immediate past-chair for the Leadership Scholarship Member Interest Group.

Prior to becoming a faculty member, Kathy served as an administrator for 10 years in various functional areas within student affairs including campus activities, commuter services, community engagement, and leadership

Changing the Narrative, pages 329–330
Copyright © 2018 by Information Age Publishing
All rights of reproduction in any form reserved.

development. She has worked in higher education both administrative and faculty roles for almost 20 years and loves every minute of her chosen career path. Originally from Central Illinois, Kathy currently lives in Tampa, Florida with her incredible husband, and fun 5-year-old (collectively known as Team Guthrie). She loves Chicago pizza, Jimmy Buffett, baseball (Go Cubs!), and just being with Team Guthrie.

Dr. **V. Chunoo** is a graduate of the Higher Education PhD program at Florida State University. His work and research interests involve developing leader identity and capacity in first-generation college students, students of historically underrepresented racial and ethnic backgrounds, and students from lower socioeconomic communities. He completed a Bachelor of Science in Psychobiology and a Master of Science in Mental Health Counseling, both from the University of Miami. Also at UM, he was an academic advisor for 10 years, and concurrently the academic ombudsperson for 4 years. Currently, he retains a position as a research assistant for the Leadership Learning Research Center (LLRC).

V. is on the editorial board of the Journal of Student Leadership; a journal of student publications focused on issues of student leadership development in higher education. He has published articles in the *Journal of College Student Retention, Journal of Leadership Studies,* and *Journal of Student Affairs Research and Practice,* on such topics as cultural capital in high impact practices, cultural relevance in leadership learning, and self-authorship among student affairs professionals. During his time at FSU, he received the W. Hugh Stickler Memorial Dissertation grant to support his original research in cultural responsiveness in leadership education, as well as a National Association of Campus Activities Silver Scholar Award for a study on campus involvement and the development of socially responsible leadership values.

V. has presented scholarship at annual meetings of the Student Affairs Professionals in Higher Education (NASPA), Associational of College Student Educators International (ACPA), International Leadership Association (ILA), and the Jon C. Dalton Institute on College Student Values. Furthermore, he is a recipient of the Sherrill W. Ragans Leadership and Service Award, a Florida State University Legacy fellow, and a Hardee Center for Leadership and Ethics in Higher Education fellow.

ABOUT THE CONTRIBUTORS

Dr. Danielle Morgan Acosta is a student affairs practitioner with over a decade of professional experience educating and developing student leaders. She serves as the director of student affairs at Florida State University, working with the student government association and managing the advising and support of the identity-based student agencies and Allies & Safe Zones program. Danielle studies and practices leadership, student organization advising, and the development of justice-focused student and professional leaders.

Marshall Anthony Jr. is a doctoral student in the higher education program at Florida State University. He serves as graduate research assistant at the FSU Leadership Learning Research Center, as well as an instructor in the undergraduate certificate in leadership studies, which is a partnership between the FSU College of Education and the Center for Leadership and Social Change. His research explores student persistence, culturally relevant leadership learning, student activism, and traditionally underrepresented populations, specifically Black male, first-generation, and low-income students.

Dr. Sonja Ardoin is a learner, educator, facilitator, and author. A proud Cajun from a blue collar background, first gen to PhD, and scholar-practitioner, Sonja is currently serving as assistant professor of student affairs administration at Appalachian State University. She studies social class identity in higher education; college access and success for first generation college students and rural students; student and women's leadership; and career

Changing the Narrative, pages 331–336
Copyright © 2018 by Information Age Publishing
All rights of reproduction in any form reserved.

pathways in student affairs. Sonja also serves with organizations such as ACPA, NASPA, and LeaderShape.

Dr. Cameron C. Beatty is an assistant professor of higher education and student affairs at Salem State University. He earned his PhD in higher education and student affairs at Iowa State University in 2014 and taught in the leadership studies program there from 2013–2016. His research foci include the intersections of gender and race in leadership education, retention of students of color on historically White college campuses, and global leadership education for undergraduate students.

Robyn Brock is a doctoral student in higher education at Florida State University. She also works full time as the associate director of the Oglesby Union at FSU where she has the honor of working with a variety of amazing students and staff. Brock volunteers for the Coalition for Collegiate Women's Leadership as the associate executive director and member of the board of directors. Most importantly, she is a mom, wife, daughter, sister, and friend.

Dr. Vivechkanand S. Chunoo is a graduate of the Higher Education PhD program at Florida State University. His work and research interests involve developing leader identity and capacity in first-generation college students, students of historically underrepresented racial and ethnic backgrounds, and students from lower socioeconomic communities. At University of Miami, he was an academic advisor for 10 years and concurrently the academic ombudsperson for 4 years. Currently, he retains a position as a research assistant for the Leadership Learning Research Center at Florida State University—a curricular program overseen jointly by the FSU College of Education and the Center for Leadership and Social Change.

Jennifer Farinella completed her bachelor's degree in hospitality at the University of Central Florida, and her MEd in higher education and student affairs at the University of South Carolina. Jennifer currently works full time with the Florida State University College of Social Work as an academic program specialist, while also pursuing an EdD in the higher education program.

Gabrielle Garrard is a second-year master's student in the higher education program at Florida State University. She works as a graduate assistant for the Hardee Center for Leadership and Ethics in Higher Education in addition to serving as the graduate intern for the women's leadership institute and the women student union at Florida State. She is a graduate of Davidson College with a degree in political science.

Dr. Juan R. Guardia serves as assistant vice president for student affairs and dean of students at the University of Cincinnati. Previously, he was the assistant vice president for student affairs at Northeastern Illinois University, a Hispanic-serving institution, in Chicago and also worked at Florida State University, Iowa State University, and George Mason University. Juan has published and presented on ethnic identity development, Latina/o student leadership, cultural competency, and history of Latina/o fraternities and sororities.

Dr. Kathy L. Guthrie is an associate professor in the higher education program at Florida State University. She serves as director of the Leadership Learning Research Center and coordinator of the undergraduate certificate in leadership studies. She is serves as associate editor for the *New Directions in Student Leadership* series and a member of the *Journal of Campus Activities Practice and Scholarship* advisory board. Her research focuses on leadership learning outcomes, environment of leadership and civic education, and use of technology in leadership education.

Dr. Paige Haber-Curran is associate professor and program coordinator for the student affairs in higher education program at Texas State University. Paige has over 12 years of experience in the realm of college student leadership programs through coordinating cocurricular and curricular student leadership programs, teaching leadership courses, contributing scholarly work to the fields of Leadership Studies and student affairs, and consulting on topics of leadership. Her research focuses on college student leadership development, gender and leadership, and emotionally intelligent leadership.

Miguel Ángel Hernández serves as the associate director in the Center for Leadership and Social Change at Florida State University and is pursuing a doctorate degree in higher education. He currently teaches undergraduate and graduate courses focused on social justice, intergroup dialogue, and Black and Latinx education. Previously, Mr. Hernández served as the director for multicultural services and programs at the University of Georgia.

Dr. Amber Manning-Ouellette is a lecturer of Leadership Studies at Iowa State University. Dr. Manning-Ouellette teaches several courses in the leadership studies program including leadership strategies in a diverse society, women and leadership, and the leadership research capstone. She is also the director of the global leadership study abroad program which travels to Sweden and Nicaragua. Her research interests include women's voice in leadership, civic engagement of first-year students, and study abroad experiences of undergraduate students.

LaFarin R. Meriwether is a doctoral student in the higher education program at Florida State University. She received a bachelor's degree from the

University of Kentucky and her MBA from University of Cincinnati. LaFarin currently serves as the assistant director for learning and engagement in university housing at Florida State. LaFarin's research interests center around Black female identity development. Additionally, through her involvement with her professional housing organizations she is engaged in research focused on creating work environments that support and retain staff of color.

Rose Rezaei is an assistant director for the Center for Health Advocacy and Wellness at Florida State University. Her body of work encompasses power based personal violence prevention and sexual health education. As an instruction for peer health education, Rose works to create space for students to reflect on their lived experiences and develop skills to advocate for change. Rose received her MEd in Curriculum and Instruction: College Student Affairs from the University of South Florida.

Jane Rodriguez earned her bachelor's in hospitality management and event planning at Florida International University. In May 2018, she graduated with her master's in higher education from Florida State University (FSU). During her time at FSU, her assistantship was working with student organizations development and engagement in the student activities center. As a Latina, Jane strives to create socially just cocurricular environments that allow for the leadership development of all students.

Dr. Cristobal Salinas Jr. is an assistant professor in the Educational Leadership and Research Methodology Department at Florida Atlantic University. He coauthored the *Iowa's Community Colleges: A Collective History of Fifty Years of Accomplishment* book. Cristobal is the cofounder and managing editor for the *Journal Committed to Social Change on Race and Ethnicity*. His research promotes access and quality in higher education, and explores the social, political, and economic context of education opportunities for historically marginalized communities, with an emphasis on Latino/a communities of people.

Dorsey Spencer Jr. is an assistant director in the Oglesby Union at Florida State University. He has a bachelor's degree in sport management from Temple University, a master's degree in higher education from the University of Massachusetts Amherst, and is currently a doctoral student at Florida State University. He has had an array of experiences within higher education. Dorsey is also one of the instructors of the Black Male Leadership course at Florida State University and has taught other leadership courses as well.

Erin Sylvester is a part-time doctoral student in the higher education program at Florida State University where she works full time in the office of the vice president for student affairs coordinating events and professional development programs. She received a degree in philosophy and a certificate in leadership from Florida State, and completed a master's of education at the University of South Carolina. Her research interests include college access and affordability, first-generation college students, and higher education policy reform.

Trisha Teig is a doctoral candidate in higher education at Florida State University. Working in the Leadership Learning Research Center, her research and teaching focuses on leadership education, gender and leadership, and integrating social justice in leadership curriculum. Trisha developed her passion for leadership and social justice education while serving for 9 years as a student affairs professional. She seeks to explore leadership learning with her students and community to collectively tackle complex problems in our beautiful, challenging world.

Dr. Daniel Tillapaugh is assistant professor of counselor education and coordinator of the Counseling and College Student Personnel program at California Lutheran University. His research agenda is focused on intersectionality and the social contexts of higher education, particularly around issues of gender and sexuality as well as college student leadership development. He is a proud alumni of Ithaca College, University of Maryland, and the University of San Diego.

Maritza Torres is a doctoral student in the higher education program at Florida State University (FSU). While studying full-time at FSU, Maritza is a graduate assistant in the Leadership Learning Research Center which is a partnership of the FSU College of Education and the Center for Leadership and Social Change. She teaches in the undergraduate certificate in leadership studies program as well as serving as one of the advisors. Her research interests include leadership, Latinx leadership development, mentorship, and first generation students.

Dr. Jillian Volpe White serves as director of strategic planning and assessment in the office of the vice president for student affairs at Florida State University (FSU). She also serves as an adjunct instructor in the FSU Department of Educational Leadership and Policy Studies. Jillian has over 10 years of experience in community engagement and leadership development at the FSU Center for Leadership and Social Change and Florida Campus Compact. She received her doctorate, master's, and undergraduate degrees from Florida State University.

Erica Wiborg is a doctoral student in higher education from Florida State University with a primary research focus on critical race theory and critical pedagogy in leadership education and scholarship. Erica is a graduate assistant in the Leadership Learning Research Center where she conducts research and teaches in the undergraduate certificate in leadership studies. Previously, Erica worked full time as a program coordinator in the Center for Leadership and Social Change at Florida State University.

CPSIA information can be obtained
at www.ICGtesting.com
Printed in the USA
LVOW13s0416170718
583991LV00009B/89/P